POETRY FOCUS 2018

LEAVING CERTIFICATE POEMS & NOTES FOR ENGLISH HIGHER LEVEL

MARTIN KIERAN & FRANCES ROCKS

Gill Education
Hume Avenue
Park West
Dublin 12
www.gilleducation.ie

Gill Education is an imprint of M.H. Gill & Co.

© Martin Kieran & Frances Rocks 2016

ISBN: 978-0-7171-70401

All rights reserved. No part of this publication may be copied, reproduced or transmitted in any form or by any means without written permission of the publishers or else under the terms of any licence permitting limited copying issued by the Irish Copyright Licensing Agency.

Design: Tanya Ross, Elementinc.ie
Print origination: Carole Lynch
Cover design: Don O'Connor

At the time of going to press, all web addresses were active and contained information relevant to the topics in this book. Gill Education does not, however, accept responsibility for the content or views contained on these websites. Content, views and addresses may change beyond the publisher or author's control. Students should always be supervised when reviewing websites.

The authors and publisher have made every effort to trace all copyright holders, but if any have been inadvertently overlooked we would be pleased to make the necessary arrangement at the first opportunity.

For permission to reproduce photographs, the authors and publisher gratefully acknowledge the following:
© Alamy: 28, 33, 37, 42, 60, 110, 115, 145, 150, 155, 159, 165, 169, 177, 182, 202, 210, 215, 224, 232, 236, 314, 321, 345, 355, 358, 373, 392, 400, 443, 454; © Bridgeman Images: 47, 65, 276, 438, 474; © Collins Agency: 1, 459; © Corbis: 14; © Crawford Art Gallery, Cork: 378; © Francine Scialom Greenblatt: 85; © Getty Images: 5, 57, 74, 96, 129, 228, 245, 298, 303, 308, 336, 341, 363, 368, 382, 387, 405, 419, 425, 430, 434, 448, 464, 469; © Imagefile: 9, 23, 174, 198, 206, 219; © Irish Times: 134; © Mary Evans Picture Library: 327; © RTÉ Stills Library: 332, 415; © Shutterstock: 69, 78, 123, 248, 254, 260, 271, 280, 286; © Sportsfile: 103; © Topfoto: 18, 141, 186, 195, 295.

The paper used in this book is made from the wood pulp of managed forests. For every tree felled, at least one tree is planted, thereby renewing natural resources.

CONTENTS

Introduction v

EAVAN BOLAND 1
The War Horse 4
Child of Our Time* 9
The Famine Road 13
The Shadow Doll 18
White Hawthorn in the West of Ireland 22
Outside History 27
The Black Lace Fan My Mother Gave Me 32
This Moment* 37
The Pomegranate 41
Love* 46
Leaving Cert Sample Essay 51

PAUL DURCAN 57
Nessa 60
The Girl with the Keys to Pearse's Cottage .. 64
The Difficulty that is Marriage 69
Wife Who Smashed Television Gets Jail* 74
Parents* 78
'Windfall', 8 Parnell Hill, Cork 82
Six Nuns Die in Convent Inferno 92
Sport* 102
Father's Day, 21 June 1992 108
The Arnolfini Marriage 114
Rosie Joyce 120
The MacBride Dynasty 128
Three Short Poems 133
Leaving Cert Sample Essay 135

ROBERT FROST 141
The Tuft of Flowers* 144
Mending Wall* 149
After Apple-Picking 154
The Road Not Taken 159
Birches 164
Out, Out—* 169
Spring Pools 174
Acquainted with the Night 177
Design 182
Provide, Provide 186
Leaving Cert Sample Essay 190

GERARD MANLEY HOPKINS 195
God's Grandeur 198
Spring* 202
As Kingfishers Catch Fire, Dragonflies
  Draw Flame 206
The Windhover 210
Pied Beauty 215
Felix Randal 219
Inversnaid* 224
I Wake and Feel the Fell of Dark, not Day .. 228
No Worst, There is None 232
Thou Art Indeed Just, Lord, if I Contend 236
Leaving Cert Sample Essay 240

JOHN KEATS — 245

To One Who Has Been Long in City Pent	248
Ode to a Nightingale	252
On First Looking into Chapman's Homer*	260
Ode on a Grecian Urn	265
When I Have Fears That I May Cease to Be	271
La Belle Dame Sans Merci*	275
To Autumn	281
Bright Star, Would I Were Steadfast as Thou Art	286
Leaving Cert Sample Essay	290

PHILIP LARKIN — 295

Wedding-Wind	298
At Grass	302
Church Going	307
An Arundel Tomb	313
The Whitsun Weddings	319
MCMXIV	326
Ambulances*	331
The Trees	336
The Explosion*	340
Cut Grass	345
Leaving Cert Sample Essay	349

JOHN MONTAGUE — 355

Killing the Pig	358
The Trout	363
The Locket*	367
The Cage*	372
Windharp	378
All Legendary Obstacles	382
The Same Gesture	387
Like Dolmens Round My Childhood*	391
The Wild Dog Rose	398
A Welcoming Party	405
Leaving Cert Sample Essay	409

EILÉAN NÍ CHUILLEANÁIN — 415

Lucina Schynning in Silence of the Nicht	419
The Second Voyage	424
Deaths and Engines	430
Street*	434
Fireman's Lift	438
All for You	443
Following	448
Kilcash	453
Translation	459
The Bend in the Road	464
On Lacking the Killer Instinct	469
To Niall Woods and Xenya Ostrovskia, Married in Dublin on 9 September 2009*	474
Leaving Cert Sample Essay	479

Glossary of Common Literary Terms	485
Acknowledgements	487

*The poems marked with an asterisk are also prescribed for the Ordinary Level course.

Introduction

Poetry Focus is a modern poetry textbook for Leaving Certificate Higher Level English. It includes all the prescribed poems for the 2018 exam as well as succinct commentaries on each one. Well-organised and easily accessible study notes provide all the necessary information to allow students to explore the poems and to develop their own individual responses and enhance their skills in critical literacy. There is no single 'correct' approach to answering the poetry question. Candidates are free to respond in any appropriate way that shows good knowledge of and engagement with the prescribed poems.

- **Concise poet biographies** provide context for the poems.
- **Initial response** questions follow the text of each poem. These allow students to consider their first impressions before any in-depth study or analysis. These questions provide a good opportunity for written and/or oral exercises.
- **Study notes** highlight the main features of the poet's subject matter and style. These discussion notes will enhance the student's own critical appreciation through focused group work and/or written exercises. Analytical skills are developed in a coherent, practical way to give students confidence in articulating their own personal responses to the poems and poets.
- **Analysis is provided using graded sample paragraphs** which aid students in fluently structuring and developing valid points, using fresh and varied expression. These model paragraphs also illustrate effective use of relevant quotations and reference.
- **Class/Homework exercises** for each poem provide focused practice in writing personal responses to examination-style questions.
- **Summary points** provide a memorable snapshot of the key aspects to remember about each poet.
- **Full sample Leaving Certificate essays** are accompanied by marking-scheme guidelines and examiners' comments. These show the student exactly what is required to achieve a successful top grade in the Leaving Cert. The examiner's comments illustrate the use of the PCLM marking scheme and are an invaluable aid for the ambitious student.
- **Sample essay plans** on each poet's work illustrate how to interpret a question and recognise the particular nuances of key words in examination questions. Student evaluation of these essay plans increase confidence in developing and organising clear response to exam questions.
- **Sample Leaving Cert questions** on each poet are given at the end of their section.
- **A glossary of common literary terms** provides an easy reference when answering questions.

 The FREE eBook contains:

- **Investigate Further** sections which contain **useful weblinks** should you want to learn more.
- **Pop-up key quotes** to encourage students to select their own individual combination of references from a poem and to write brief commentaries on specific quotations.
- Additional sample graded paragraphs called '**Developing your personal response**'.

HOW IS THE PRESCRIBED POETRY QUESTION MARKED?

Marking is done (ex. 50 marks) by reference to the PCLM criteria for assessment.

- Clarity of purpose (P): 30% of the total (15 marks)
- Coherence of delivery (C): 30% of the total (15 marks)
- Efficiency of language use (L): 30% of the total (15 marks)
- Accuracy of mechanics (M): 10% of the total (5 marks)

Each answer will be in the form of a response to a specific task requiring candidates to:
- Display a clear and purposeful engagement with the set task (P)
- Sustain the response in an appropriate manner over the entire answer (C)
- Manage and control language appropriate to the task (L)
- Display levels of accuracy in spelling and grammar appropriate to the required/chosen register (M)

GENERAL

'Students at Higher Level will be required to study a representative selection from the work of eight poets: a representative selection would seek to reflect the range of a poet's themes and interests and exhibit his/her characteristic style and viewpoint. Normally the study of at least six poems by each poet would be expected.' (DES English Syllabus, 6.3)

The marking scheme guidelines from the State Examinations Commission state that in the case of each poet, the candidates have **freedom of choice** in relation to the poems studied. In addition, there is **not a finite list of any 'poet's themes and interests'**.

Note that in responding to the question set on any given poet, the candidates must refer to the poem(s) they have studied but are not required to refer to any specific **poem(s), nor are they expected to discuss or refer to all the poems they have chosen to study**.

In each of the questions in **Prescribed Poetry**, the underlying nature of the task is the invitation to the candidates to **engage with the poems themselves**.

EXAM ADVICE

- You are not expected to write about any **set number of poems** in the examination. You might decide to focus in detail on a small number of poems, or you could choose to write in a more general way on several poems.
- Most candidates write one or two well-developed **paragraphs** on each of the poems they have chosen for discussion. In other cases, a paragraph will focus on one specific aspect of the poet's work. When discussing recurring themes or features of style, appropriate cross-references to other poems may also be useful.
- Reflect on central **themes** and viewpoints in the poems you discuss. Comment also on the use of language and the poet's distinctive **style**. Examine imagery, tone, structure, rhythm and rhyme. Be careful not to simply list aspects of style, such as alliteration or repetition. There's little point in mentioning that a poet uses sound effects or metaphors without discussing the effectiveness of such characteristics.
- Focus on **the task** you have been given in the poetry question. Identify the key terms in the wording of the question and think of similar words for these terms. This will help you develop a relevant and coherent personal response in keeping with the PCLM marking scheme criteria.
- Always root your answers in the text of the poems. Support the points you make with **relevant reference and quotation**. Make sure your own expression is fresh and lively. Avoid awkward expressions, such as 'It says in the poem that...'. Look for alternatives: 'There is a sense of...', 'The tone seems to suggest...', 'It's evident that...', etc.
- Neat, **legible handwriting** will help to make a positive impression on examiners. Corrections should be made by simply drawing a line through the mistake. Scored-out words distract attention from the content of your work.
- Keep the emphasis on why particular poets **appeal to you**. Consider the continuing relevance or significance of a poet's work. Perhaps you have shared some of the feelings or experiences expressed in the poems. Avoid starting answers with prepared biographical sketches. Details of a poet's life are better used when discussing how the poems themselves were shaped by such experiences.
- Remember that the examination encourages **individual engagement** with the prescribed poems. Poetry can make us think and feel and imagine. It opens our minds to the wonderful possibilities of language and ideas. Your interaction with the poems is what matters most. Study notes and critical interpretations are all there to be challenged. Read the poems carefully and have confidence in expressing your own personal response.

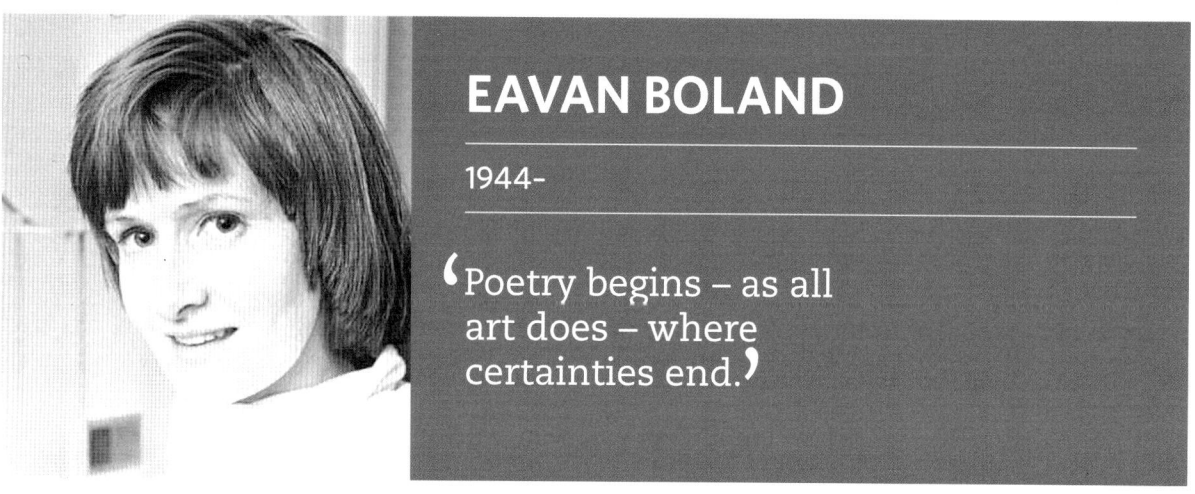

EAVAN BOLAND

1944-

'Poetry begins – as all art does – where certainties end.'

Eavan Boland has been one of the most prominent voices in Irish poetry and is the author of many highly acclaimed poetry collections. Born in Dublin but raised in London, she had early experiences with anti-Irish racism that gave her a strong sense of heritage and a keen awareness of her identity. She later returned to attend school and university in Dublin, where she published a pamphlet of poetry after her graduation. Boland received her BA from Trinity College in 1966. Since then she has held numerous teaching positions and has published poetry, books of criticism and articles. She married in 1969 and has two children. Her experiences as a wife and mother have influenced her to explore the beauty and significance of everyday living. Boland writes plainly and eloquently about her experiences as a woman, mother and exile.

She has taught at several colleges in Ireland and America where she has been a professor of English at Stanford University, California. In addition to traditional Irish themes, Eavan Boland explores a wide range of interests, including incisive commentaries on contemporary subjects and intensely personal poems about history, womanhood and relationships.

To find out more about Eavan Boland, or to hear readings of her poems, you could do a search of some of the useful websites available such as YouTube, bbc.co.uk and poetryarchive.org or access additional material on this page of your eBook.

Prescribed Poems — HIGHER LEVEL

❶ 'The War Horse'
A runaway horse in a quiet suburban estate is the starting point for Boland's explorations of attitudes to warfare and violence throughout Irish history. — 4

❷ 'Child of Our Time'*
Written in response to a newspaper photograph of a child killed in the 1974 Dublin bombings, the poem tries to draw some kind of meaning from the tragedy. — 9

❸ 'The Famine Road'
The poet dramatically recreates a tragic period in Irish history. Boland also links the Famine with another traumatic experience, the story of a woman diagnosed as infertile by her doctor. — 13

❹ 'The Shadow Doll'
Boland considers the changing nature of marriage since Victorian times. The silence and submission of women are signified by the porcelain doll in its airless glass dome. — 18

❺ 'White Hawthorn in the West of Ireland'
The poet's journey into the West brings her into contact with a wildly beautiful landscape where she can explore Irish superstitions and a strange, unspoken language. — 22

❻ 'Outside History'
Another poem addressing the experience of the marginalised ('outsiders') and reflecting Boland's own humanity as a female Irish poet. — 27

❼ 'The Black Lace Fan My Mother Gave Me'
This poem was inspired by the first gift given by Boland's father to her mother back in 1930s Paris. The souvenir is a symbol of young love and the mystery of changing relationships. — 32

❽ 'This Moment'*
In this short lyric, Boland unobtrusively captures the mystery and magic of the natural world and the beauty of loving relationships. **37**

❾ 'The Pomegranate'
Another personal poem in which Boland uses mythical references to examine the complexity of feelings experienced in mother–daughter relationships. **41**

❿ 'Love'*
This reflective poem is addressed to the poet's husband and considers the changing nature of romantic love. In developing her themes, Boland draws on Greek mythology. **46**

1 THE WAR HORSE

This dry night, nothing unusual
About the clip, clop, casual

Iron of his shoes as he stamps death
Like a mint on the innocent coinage of earth.

I lift the window, watch the ambling feather
Of hock and fetlock, loosed from its daily tether

In the tinker camp on the Enniskerry Road,
Pass, his breath hissing, his snuffling head

Down. He is gone. No great harm is done.
Only a leaf of our laurel hedge is torn –

Of distant interest like a maimed limb,
Only a rose which now will never climb

The stone of our house, expendable, a mere
Line of defence against him, a volunteer

You might say, only a crocus, its bulbous head
Blown from growth, one of the screamless dead.

But we, we are safe, our unformed fear
Of fierce commitment gone; why should we care

If a rose, a hedge, a crocus are uprooted
Like corpses, remote, crushed, mutilated?

He stumbles on like a rumour of war, huge
Threatening. Neighbours use the subterfuge

Of curtains. He stumbles down our short street
Thankfully passing us, I pause, wait,

Then to breathe relief lean on the sill
And for a second only my blood is still

With atavism. That rose he smashed frays
Ribboned across our hedge, recalling days

Of burned countryside, illicit braid:
A cause ruined before, a world betrayed.

'his breath hissing, his snuffling head'

Glossary

The War Horse: a powerful horse ridden in war by a knight or cavalry soldier.
4 *mint*: a place where money is made; a machine for making money.
4 *coinage*: collection of coins. Here it refers to imprints the horse makes on the suburban gardens.
5 *ambling*: walking at a leisurely pace.
6 *hock*: joint in the back of a horse's leg.
6 *fetlock*: tuft of hair that grows above and behind the hoof.
6 *tether*: rope for tying an animal.
8 *snuffling*: breathing noisily.
13 *expendable*: can be done without, can be sacrificed to achieve an object.
20 *mutilated*: prevented from having a limb.
22 *subterfuge*: trick used to avoid an argument or an awkward situation.
27 *atavism:* the recurrence of a trait present in distant ancestors.
27 *frays*: noisy quarrel or fight, or cloth that is ragged or strained.
29 *illicit braid*: illegal ribbon, a reference to an Irish secret society, the Ribbonmen, who wore a green ribbon in opposition to the Orangemen and carried out illegal acts such as burning.

INITIAL RESPONSE

1. Boland felt that 'the daily things I did ... were not fit material for poetry'. Discuss this statement in relation to 'The War Horse'.

2. Write your own personal response to the poem, highlighting the impact it made on you.

3. 'I wrote the poem slowly, adding each couplet with care.' Consider how the structure and style of the poem emphasise its message.

STUDY NOTES

'The War Horse' was written in 1972 by a newly married Eavan Boland after she had moved to the suburbs at the foothills of the Dublin Mountains. It was an icy winter, and the 'sounds of death from the televisions were heard almost nightly' as the news about the Northern Ireland Troubles was broadcast. In this poem, Boland questions ambivalent attitudes towards war.

This poem is based on a **real event**, **the appearance of a 'loosed' Traveller horse**, described in **lines 1–9**. Boland has said, 'It encompassed a real event. It entered a place in my heart and moved beyond it.' An aural description of the innocuous noise, 'nothing unusual', heralds the arrival of the horse. The horse, a menacing intruder that suggests the opposition between force and formality, wreaked havoc on the neat order of **suburban gardens**. The rigid control of the rhyming couplets mirrors the desire for order in the suburbs.

Onomatopoeia and the alliteration of the hard 'c' vividly describe the horse's walk, like something out of a young child's story: 'clip, clop, casual'. **The second couplet** counteracts this sense of ordinariness as it describes the damage the horse inflicts. The brutal verb 'stamps' jolts the reader as the garden, **'the innocent coinage of earth'**, is being destroyed. The simile of a mint, which puts an indelible mark on metal to make coins, is used to describe the destruction. The **consequences of war** are also permanent – people are wounded or killed ('stamps death').

The **poet is an observer**: 'I lift the window, watch'. A detailed description of the horse's leg, 'ambling feather/Of hock and fetlock', belies its capacity for violence. There then follows an explanation of where the horse came from, the 'tinker camp on the Enniskerry Road'. The **random nature of violence** is aptly contained in the verbs 'ambling', 'loosed' and also in the long run-on line 'loosed … Road'. The sounds the horse makes are vividly conveyed using onomatopoeia: 'hissing', 'snuffling'. The moment of danger passes: 'He is gone.' We can feel the palpable relief: 'No great harm is done.' Colloquial language reduces the event to a trivial disruption.

Lines 10–16 show that the poet has adopted a **sensible approach** as she surveys the **damage**, minimising it with an emphasis on the word 'only': 'Only a leaf is torn', 'Only a crocus', 'Only a rose'. These are all 'expendable'; they can be done without. The language becomes more unsettling as violent descriptions are used to show the mangled blooms: 'like a maimed limb … which now will never climb', 'Blown from growth'. All describe a world that will never be the same again, potential that will never be realised and life that is cut short. From Boland's perspective, 'the screamless dead' can no longer command attention.

And who cares anyway? It is of 'distant interest'. This **apathetic view** can be taken by people as they watch atrocities in other countries. The **language of war** is prominent: 'a mere/Line of defence', 'a volunteer', the head is 'Blown'. The poet's focus has now shifted away from the horse and is **concentrated on war, its consequences** and the vulnerability of victims.

In **lines 17–21**, Boland realises that 'we are safe'. War calls for commitment; people must choose to take sides, to fight. This is frightening: 'our unformed fear'. It is there but not expressed, nor given substance or form. Here in this domestic incident is war in miniature, the entry of an intruder who perpetrates damage. The poet asks why the community should care about something so insignificant as a damaged rose or a crushed crocus. She is challenging people who are blasé and examining their **insularity**: 'why should we care … corpses, remote, crushed, mutilated?' Are there consequences if people do not care?

Boland criticises her own community in **lines 22–30**, with the neighbours described as hiding behind curtains ('subterfuge'). This 'I don't want to know' attitude reflects the **ambivalence** about the Northern Troubles in the Irish Republic during the 1970s. The tension, 'I pause, wait', is followed by release: 'breathe relief'. At the conclusion, there are two insightful views. One is the suburban woman's; the other is an Irish person's awareness of connecting with past history. There is an ancestral memory, 'atavism', which associates the smashed rose with the destruction of the Irish. The ribbon trails back to the violence of English colonialism. Boland and her neighbours chose not to confront the horse, just like the Irish did not confront the invaders. The intruder (the horse, the British) destroyed something beautiful and precious (the rose, Irish culture). The mood here is one of loss and regret. Should both intruders have been challenged? How right is it to live so indifferently? The poem **ends on a bleak note,** a lament for **'a world betrayed'**.

ANALYSIS

'We are collectively involved in violence which occurs in our land.' Discuss how this poem reflects this statement. Illustrate your response with reference to the poem.

Sample Paragraph

Boland uses an ordinary, domestic incident, the arrival of a tinker's horse into a suburban garden, to explore the ambivalent attitude often prevalent to wars that seem distant. The colloquial phrase 'No great harm is done' and the neighbours who use 'the subterfuge/Of curtains' both illustrate this insular approach. Everything is all right so long as 'we' are safe. The consequences of war are listed as Boland itemises them: 'maimed limb', 'now will never climb', 'expendable', 'screamless dead'. The vulnerability of the innocent victims is laid bare. Can we afford to be so indifferent? The implicit statement is that we should care. She then conveys the ancestral memory of how Ireland was invaded by the British. The word 'Ribboned' recalls the Ribbonmen, a secret society that was active against the invaders for a while. We are left feeling that perhaps due to the majority of Irish people's indifference and through a lack of commitment, 'A cause' was lost. The poem ends with a lament, 'a world betrayed', with its long echoing 'ay' sound. I think Boland is upset at people's lack of commitment in a time of trouble.

Examiner's Comment

This response succinctly addresses the task through a discussion on the theme and style of the poem. It ranges from the local incident to war's inevitable consequences and people's indifference. Close engagement with the text is evident in the discussion of colloquial language and sound effects. Good use is made of the rhetorical question, 'Can we afford to be so indifferent?' This well-controlled answer merits the top grade.

CLASS/HOMEWORK EXERCISES

1. Is 'The War Horse' a private poem, or does it have a wider significance? Use reference to the text in your answer.
2. Eavan Boland creates an underlying sense of threat throughout 'The War Horse'. Discuss this view using close reference to the poem.

SUMMARY POINTS

- Themes include attitudes to conflict and violence throughout Irish history.
- Inclusive personal pronouns and rhetorical questions used to involve readers.
- Use of observational details, vibrant language, striking comparisons.
- Contrasting atmospheres and tones – reflective, accusatory.
- Memorable onomatopoeic effects – assonance, alliteration, internal rhyme.

CHILD OF OUR TIME
(FOR AENGUS)

Yesterday I knew no lullaby
But you have taught me overnight to order
This song, which takes from your final cry
Its tune, from your unreasoned end its reason,
Its rhythm from the discord of your murder   5
Its motive from the fact you cannot listen.

We who should have known how to instruct
With rhymes for your waking, rhythms for your sleep,
Names for the animals you took to bed,
Tales to distract, legends to protect,   10
Later an idiom for you to keep
And living, learn, must learn from you, dead,

To make our broken images rebuild
Themselves around your limbs, your broken
Image, find for your sake whose life our idle   15
Talk has cost, a new language. Child
Of our time, our times have robbed your cradle.
Sleep in a world your final sleep has woken.

'our times have robbed your cradle'

Glossary

5 **discord**: lack of harmony among people; harsh, confused sounds; conflict.

11 **idiom**: turn of phrase; words which when used together have a different meaning from when used singly.

INITIAL RESPONSE

1. Boland believes that the 'murder of the innocent' is one of the greatest obscenities. How is this explored in the poem? Write a paragraph in response.

2. Where are the two feelings, tenderness and outrage, evident in the poem? Use reference to the text in your response.

3. What is Boland implying about 'our times'? Is she satisfied or dissatisfied with what is happening? Refer closely to the text in your answer.

STUDY NOTES

'Child of Our Time' was written in 1974 at the height of the Troubles. It was prompted by a harrowing newspaper picture of a fireman tenderly carrying a dead child from the rubble of a bomb explosion in Dublin. It is dedicated to Aengus, the infant son of the poet's friend, who had suffered cot death. This lyric is a response to the sudden and unexpected death of all young children. It also puts an onus on adults to change their ways.

The title of this poem places the little child in a wider context than that of family and town – he is a child of 'our time'. He is our responsibility; he belongs to us. A child should be a **symbol of innocence**, growth, love, potential and the future, but this has been savagely and tragically cut short by 'our time'. Boland did not have children when she wrote this poem ('Yesterday I knew no lullaby'), but in the **first stanza** she describes how she has been taught to sing a lullaby which is different: 'you have taught me overnight to order/This song'.

The child's violent and tragic death demands a response, so she will form and order and 'reason' a poem from the child's 'unreasoned end'. It is a song made of harsh sounds, 'discord'. The tone moves from tender compassion ('lullaby') to indignation ('the fact you cannot listen'). There is no escaping the finality of death, yet the poet is a balanced, reasonable person trying to make **order out of disorder** in a poem that is carefully arranged in three stanzas.

The poem is also charged with **sadness and awareness**. The compassionate voice of the poet is heard in 'rhythms for your sleep,/Names for the animals you took to bed'. However, she is aware of the awfulness of the event: 'final cry', 'end', 'murder'. The language is formal, as befits such a solemn occasion: 'We who should have known', 'Child/Of our time'. This poem has elements of an elegy (a poem for the dead): it laments, praises and consoles. The poem's many half-rhymes mimic this discordant time: 'idle'/'cradle', 'order'/'murder'.

The collective 'We' in the second stanza is used to show the true context of the little child as a member of the human family. **It is 'We' who are responsible** for not making society safer so that childhood could consist of 'Tales to distract, legends to protect'. The repetitive sound of 'rhymes' and 'rhythms' imitates the rocking sound of a mother nursing her child. Boland's aim is clear: we must learn from our mistakes and reconstruct a better world out of 'our broken images'.

In the **third stanza**, the poet is insistent that **society takes on this responsibility**, that we 'find ... a new language'. We have to engage in dialogue, not 'idle/Talk', so that we can deliver a safer world for our children. Ironically, it is the little child, who 'our time' has 'robbed' from his cradle, who will form the scaffold around which we can build a new and better society: 'rebuild/Themselves around your limbs'. The final line of the poem is a **prayer and a hope**: 'Sleep in a world your final sleep has woken.' It is a wish that the little child be at rest now and that the world may be woken to its senses by his death.

ANALYSIS

'Eavan Boland is a "sensitive poet" who is "rarely thrown off balance by anger"'. Discuss this view of the poet in relation to the poem 'Child of Our Time'. Support your answer with reference to the text.

Sample Paragraph

'Child of Our Time' is an example of Boland's control in the face of what must be the most horrific event that humanity can witness: the brutal and senseless murder of an innocent child. The poem is carefully ordered into three stanzas that act as balanced paragraphs in an argument. The first stanza emphasises the meaningless atrocity of 'your unreasoned end'. The second stanza places responsibility where it belongs, on the adult society that should have known how to provide a safe environment for the young: 'We who should have known'. The third stanza urges the adults to do something now, to 'find for your sake whose life our idle/Talk has cost, a new language'. The language is formal and controlled, as befits an elegy. When I listen to Ravel's 'Pavane for a Dead Infant', I hear the same stately rhythm. There are just four sentences in this lyric. The child has taught the poet a lullaby with his death. The adults must learn from this tragedy – they have to learn to talk. May the child awake the world to a new time on account of his tragic death. The balance is impressive, as the poet makes order out of disorder rather than letting her anger explode. The poem lacks sentimentality or even spiritual consolation. Instead, the quiet, insistent voice states that 'we' 'must learn'. Sometimes a soft voice delivers a more powerful message. Boland sensitively deals with a tragic event with an absence of anger and with an insistence that, as a result, lessons must be learned. The poet has learned well from the dead child 'to order/This song'.

Examiner's Comment

Boland's careful management of ideas is explored in this answer to advance the view that she explores the tragic event in a controlled, sensitive way. Attention is paid to the form of the poem: 'The poem is carefully ordered into three stanzas that act as balanced paragraphs in an argument'. The comment relating to music also shows good personal engagement. Clear expression and effective use of accurate quotation enhances this highly successful top grade response.

CLASS/HOMEWORK EXERCISES

1. There is a 'difficult sort of comfort' in literature. Discuss this statement in relation to the 'Child of Our Time'. Support the points you make with reference to the text.

2. In 'Child of Our Time', Boland explores the universal experience of tragic violence. To what extent do you agree with this view? Support the points you make with reference to both the themes and language use in the poem?

SUMMARY POINTS

- Addresses issues surrounding the tragic death of a child.
- Striking images of innocence, poignant mood, repetition.
- Universal significance of random violence and tragedy.
- Solemn, didactic tone emphasised by extended uninterrupted lines.

3 THE FAMINE ROAD

'Idle as trout in light Colonel Jones,
these Irish, give them no coins at all; their bones
need toil, their characters no less.' Trevelyan's
seal blooded the deal table. The Relief
Committee deliberated: 'Might it be safe,　　　　　　5
Colonel, to give them roads, roads to force
from nowhere, going nowhere of course?'

*'one out of every ten and then
another third of those again
women – in a case like yours.'*　　　　　　10

Sick, directionless they worked; fork, stick
were iron years away; after all could
they not blood their knuckles on rock, suck
April hailstones for water and for food?
Why for that, cunning as housewives, each eyed –　　　　　　15
as if at a corner butcher – the other's buttock.

*'anything may have caused it, spores,
a childhood accident; one sees
day after day these mysteries.'*

Dusk: they will work tomorrow without him.　　　　　　20
They know it and walk clear. He has become
a typhoid pariah, his blood tainted, although
he shares it with some there. No more than snow
attends its own flakes where they settle
and melt, will they pray by his death rattle.　　　　　　25

*'You never will, never you know
but take it well woman, grow
your garden, keep house, good-bye.'*

'It has gone better than we expected, Lord
Trevelyan, sedition, idleness, cured　　　　　　30
in one; from parish to parish, field to field;
the wretches work till they are quite worn,
then fester by their work; we march the corn
to the ships in peace; this Tuesday I saw bones
out of my carriage window. Your servant Jones.'　　　　　　35

*'Barren, never to know the load
of his child in you, what is your body
now if not a famine road?'*

14 POETRY FOCUS

'the wretches work till they are quite worn'

Glossary

During the Irish Famine of 1845–48, the British authorities organised various relief schemes. The hungry were given a small wage to buy food for participating in road building and other community projects. Many of the new roads were constructed in remote areas and served little purpose other than controlling the starving population.

1 *Colonel Jones*: army officer and Chairman of the Board of Works.
3 *Trevelyan*: Charles Trevelyan, a senior civil servant in overall charge of famine relief.
4 *Relief Committee*: groups usually consisting of landlords, the clergy and influential people were set up to distribute food.
5 *deliberated*: considered, discussed.
17 *spores*: germs.
22 *typhoid pariah*: someone shunned because of this deadly blood disease.
25 *death rattle*: last sound of the dying.
30 *sedition*: subversion, treachery.
33 *corn/to the ships*: throughout the famine years, corn was exported from Ireland.

INITIAL RESPONSE

1. Describe the tone of voice in the opening stanza, using close reference to the text.

2. The poet links the abuse of famine victims with the mistreatment of women in modern society. Is this convincing? Explain your answer.

3. In your view, how chillingly pessimistic are the last three lines of the poem? Give reasons for your answer.

STUDY NOTES

The poem raises interesting questions about marginalised people, a favourite theme in Boland's work. Here she makes a connection between a famine road in the 1840s and an infertile woman in modern times. Boland presents the poem as a series of dramatic moments featuring a variety of characters.

Stanza one begins with the voice of Colonel Jones, a British official, reading from a letter written by Lord Trevelyan, who had overall responsibility for famine relief. The boorish tone of the opening comments about 'these Irish' is explicitly offensive. Trevelyan's generalised insults reflect the **depth of prejudice and suspicion** felt towards an entire population, who are 'Idle as trout in light'. Such ruthless disregard is further underlined by the image of the official blood-red seal. The proposed solutions – 'toil' or hard labour building roads 'going nowhere' – could hardly be more cynical and are all the more ironic coming from the 'Relief Committee'.

Stanza two (**like stanzas four and six**) is italicised and introduces another speaker, the authoritative voice of a consultant doctor. The unidentified voice quoting statistics to an unnamed woman is casually impersonal. The situation becomes clearer as the poem continues: the medical expert is discussing the woman's failure to have children. Boland portrays him as insensitive and patronising: 'anything may have caused it'. His tone becomes increasingly **unsympathetic as he dismisses her disappointment**: 'You never will, never you know'. He almost seems to take delight in repeating the word 'never'. The doctor's final comments are as severe as some of the remarks made by any of the British officials: 'take it well woman, grow/your garden, keep house'.

In stanza three, the poet herself imagines the terrible experiences of the famine victims. The language used to describe their struggle is disturbing: 'Sick, directionless they worked fork'. Prominent **harsh-sounding consonants**, especially 'c' and 'k' in such phrases as 'blood their knuckles on rock', emphasise the suffering. The alarming suggestion of cannibalism ('each eyed – /as if at a corner butcher – the other's buttock') is a reminder of how people were driven beyond normal standards of civilised human behaviour.

Stanza five focuses on the prevalence of death throughout the long famine years. Attitudes harden as widespread disease becomes commonplace. The poet's direct description, steady rhythm and resigned tone combine to reflect the awful reality of the times: 'they will work tomorrow without him'. Boland illustrates the **breakdown of communities** with the tragic example of one 'typhoid pariah' abandoned to die a lonely death without anyone to 'pray by his death rattle'.

This great human catastrophe is made all the more pathetic in **stanza seven**, which begins with an excerpt from Colonel Jones's response to Trevelyan: 'It has gone better than we expected'. **The offhand tone is self-satisfied** as he reports that the road-building schemes have succeeded in their real purpose of controlling the peasant population ('the wretches'). The horrifyingly detached admission – without the slightest sense of irony – of allowing the starving to 'fester' while 'we march the corn/to the ships' is almost beyond comprehension. The colonel's matter-of-fact comment about seeing 'bones/out of my carriage window' is a final reminder of the colossal gulf between the powerful and the powerless.

In the **final stanza**, Boland's **own feelings of revulsion** bring her back to the present when she sums up the 'Barren' reality of the childless woman 'never to know the load/of his child'. The famine road is reintroduced as a common symbol for the shared tragedies of both the victims of mass starvation and infertility. The final rhetorical question leaves us to consider important issues of authority and the abuse of power, whatever the circumstances.

ANALYSIS

'Eavan Boland uses evocative symbols to address important issues.' Discuss this statement in relation to 'The Famine Road', supporting your points with suitable quotation or reference.

Sample Paragraph

The deserted famine road in Boland's poem is a haunting symbol through which we can examine aspects of power and powerlessness. The poet blends two narratives, one of a country road in the 1840s and the other of a modern-day visit to a doctor, in a series of dramatic scenes. Lord Trevelyan and the doctor abuse their power. Trevelyan's offensive comments, 'these Irish', 'Idle as trout in light', set the tone. This ignorance is mirrored in the doctor's response to his infertile patient, 'You never will, never you know'. The harsh repetition of 'never' hammers home the awful truth to the unfortunate woman. Severe remedies are handed out to both the famine workers and the woman: the workers will 'toil' to build roads 'going nowhere', the woman will 'grow/your garden, keep house' for a non-existent family. The superior, patronising attitude of those in charge is captured in snippets of direct speech, 'It has gone better than we expected', 'but take it well woman'. Boland often focuses on the marginalised in society. None of the famine victims' voices are heard in this poem, and this omission emphasises their lack of power and their vulnerability. Instead, the 'wretches work till they are quite worn'. The alliterative 'w' stresses the futile never-ending effort. The workers cannot produce food to feed themselves, the barren woman cannot carry a child. Nothing changes. The concluding rhetorical question invites us to consider the abuse of power by those in authority and the raw tragedy of the victims through the image of the famine road.

Examiner's Comment

This top grade response traces the two interconnected narratives, focusing on the dramatic significance of these events. The similar tones of those in charge are well explored: Trevelyan's 'offensive' remarks are mirrored in 'the doctor's response to his infertile patient'. An interesting point is made about the omission of the victims' voices. Expression is controlled and confident throughout.

CLASS/HOMEWORK EXERCISES

1. To what extent does 'The Famine Road' show Eavan Boland's sympathies for the outsiders and the marginalised in society? Refer to the text in your answer.

2. Eavan Boland makes effective use of several dramatic techniques in 'The Famine Road'. Discuss this view, supporting your points with close reference to the poem.

SUMMARY POINTS

- Dramatic recreation of famine suffering and exploitation.
- Updated comparison with the experience of an infertile woman.
- Authentic language, descriptive details, stark imagery, symbols.
- Sound effects echo the harsh, cynical atmosphere.

4 THE SHADOW DOLL

They stitched blooms from the ivory tulle
to hem the oyster gleam of the veil.
They made hoops for the crinoline.

Now, in summary and neatly sewn –
a porcelain bride in an airless glamour –   5
the shadow doll survives its occasion.

Under glass, under wraps, it stays
even now, after all, discreet about
visits, fevers, quickenings and lusts

and just how, when she looked at   10
the shell-tone spray of seed pearls,
the bisque features, she could see herself

inside it all, holding less than real
stephanotis, rose petals, never feeling
satin rise and fall with the vows   15

I kept repeating on the night before –
astray among the cards and wedding gifts –
the coffee pots and the clocks and

the battered tan case full of cotton
lace and tissue-paper, pressing down, then   20
pressing down again. And then, locks.

'a porcelain bride'

Eavan Boland   19

Glossary

A shadow doll was sent to the bride-to-be in Victorian times by her dressmaker. It consisted of a Victorian figurine under a dome of glass modelling the proposed wedding dress.

1 *tulle:* fine net fabric.
2 *oyster:* off-white colour.
3 *crinoline:* hooped petticoat.
8 *discreet*: careful to avoid embarrassment by keeping confidences secret; unobtrusive.
9 *quickenings*: sensations; a woman's awareness of the first movements of the child in the womb.
12 *bisque*: unglazed white porcelain.
14 *stephanotis*: scented white flowers used for displays at both weddings and funerals.

INITIAL RESPONSE

1. What type of language is used to describe the doll? Do you consider it beautiful or stifling, or both? Illustrate your response with reference to the poem.
2. Do you think marriage has changed for the modern bride? Refer to the last two stanzas in your answer.
3. Choose two phrases from the poem that you found particularly interesting. Explain the reasons for your choice.

STUDY NOTES

'The Shadow Doll' is from the 1990 collection of poems, *Outside History*. *The shadow doll wore a model of the wedding dress for the bride-to-be. Boland uses the doll as a symbol to explore the submission and silence surrounding women and women's issues by placing the late twentieth century and Victorian times side by side.*

The **first two stanzas** describe the doll vividly, with her 'ivory tulle' and 'oyster gleam'. The 'porcelain doll' is a **beautiful, fragile object**, but the 'ivory' and 'oyster' colours are lifeless. Passivity and restriction are being shown in the phrase 'neatly sewn'. The **pronoun 'it'** is used – the woman is seen as an object, not a real flesh-and-blood human being. The community is described in the preparations: 'They stitched', 'They made'. Are they colluding in the constraint? The phrase 'airless glamour' conveys an allure that has been deprived of life-giving oxygen. The occasion of the marriage is long gone, but the doll remains as a reminder, a shadow of what was.

The **language of containment** and imprisonment is continued in **stanza three**: 'Under glass, under wraps'. The doll is silent and 'discreet'; it knows but does not tell. The bride would have kept the doll throughout her life, so the doll would have been present at all major events such as marriage, childbirth, sickness, longings, 'visits, fevers, quickenings and lusts'. These experiences are not explored in poetry, which is why women and their issues are 'outside history'. They are neither recorded nor commented on.

Stanza four sees the **pronoun change to 'she'** as the poet imagines the Victorian bride considering her own wedding: 'she could see herself/inside it all'. It is as if she becomes like the doll, assuming a mask of 'bisque features' and unable to feel real life: 'holding less than real/stephanotis', 'never feeling/satin rise and fall with the vows'. The only remnant of her life is the silent doll. **Stanza five** ends with the word 'vows', and this is the link into the **next stanza**, which is a view from the twentieth-century bride where the pronoun changes to 'I'. The poet is 'repeating' the same vows as the Victorian bride. Are these entrapping and imprisoning women? Like the Victorian bride, the modern bride is surrounded by things ('cards and wedding gifts'), yet she is 'astray' (**stanza six**), with the same **sense of disorientation** coming over her. Is she feeling this because she is losing her individual identity as she agrees to become part of a couple?

Stanza seven increases the **feelings of restriction** when the suitcase is described as 'battered', and there is the added emphatic repetition of 'pressing down'. Finally, the single monosyllable '**locks**' clicks the poem to an end. The **onomatopoeic sound** echoes through the years as Boland voices the silence in the depressing ending. Little has changed from Victorian times for women.

ANALYSIS

'Boland's poems often end on a bleak note.' Discuss how 'The Shadow Doll' reflects this statement. Illustrate your response with reference to the text.

Sample Paragraph

The onomatopoeia of the monosyllabic word 'locks' echoes with frightening intensity at the end of the poem 'The Shadow Doll'. It suggests to me the clang of a prison door as the prisoner is locked in and denied freedom. This poem explores the nature and meaning of marriage for women. It starts with the description of the Victorian doll with its wedding dress, which seems to become a stifling mask fitted on a living, breathing woman, 'airless glamour', 'Under glass', 'under wraps'. The modern bride is 'astray'. Marriage is shown as confining and silencing, 'discreet'. The repetition of the phrase 'pressing down' has an almost nightmarish sense of claustrophobia. Both the Victorian bride and the modern bride are surrounded by objects, 'seed pearls', 'stephanotis', 'the cards and wedding gifts'. I find it strange that there is no mention of the prospective groom, or friends or families. Instead there is a growing sense of isolation and intimidation culminating in the echoing phrase 'And then, locks'. What or who is locked in? What or who is locked out?

Examiner's Comment

This short response carefully considers the effect of the poem's ending and Boland's exploration of the theme of marriage as a repressive and restricting force in women's lives. The candidate also touches on interesting questions about the narrow views expressed in the poem. A real sense of individual engagement is evident, particularly in the comment about the final two rhetorical questions. Top-grade standard.

CLASS/HOMEWORK EXERCISES

1. 'In her poetry, Boland uses concrete images to explore themes.' In your opinion, how valid is this statement? Use reference to 'The Shadow Doll' in your answer.

2. In 'The Shadow Doll', Boland succeeds in highlighting the experience of women in patriarchal societies. Discuss this view using close reference to the poem.

SUMMARY POINTS

- Themes include the changing nature of marriage and the oppression of women.
- Effective concrete details, symbolism, confinement imagery, repetition.
- Dreamlike sense of disorientation.
- Varying tones – reflective, sympathetic, critical and hopeful.

5 WHITE HAWTHORN IN THE WEST OF IRELAND

I drove West
in the season between seasons.
I left behind suburban gardens.
Lawnmowers. Small talk.

Under low skies, past splashes of coltsfoot, 5
I assumed
the hard shyness of Atlantic light
and the superstitious aura of hawthorn.

All I wanted then was to fill my arms with
sharp flowers, 10
to seem, from a distance, to be part of
that ivory, downhill rush. But I knew,

I had always known
the custom was
not to touch hawthorn. 15
Not to bring it indoors for the sake of

the luck
such constraint would forfeit –
a child might die, perhaps, or an unexplained
fever speckle heifers. So I left it 20

stirring on those hills
with a fluency
only water has. And, like water, able
to re-define land. And free to seem to be –

for anglers, 25
and for travellers astray in
the unmarked lights of a May dusk –
the only language spoken in those parts.

'the superstitious aura'

Glossary

Hawthorn is a flowering tree that blossoms in springtime. It is associated with fairytales and superstitions in Irish folklore. People believed that it was unlucky to cut hawthorn or to keep it indoors.
2   *the season*: between spring and summer.
5   *coltsfoot*: wild plant with yellow flowers.
6   *assumed*: became part of.
7   *Atlantic light*: unsettled weather causes the light to vary.
8   *superstitious aura*: disquiet associated with hawthorn stories.
20 *heifers*: cows which have not yet had calves.

INITIAL RESPONSE

1. Describe the poet's changing mood as she travels from her suburban home to the West. Refer to the text in your answer.

2. There are many beautiful images in the poem. Choose two that you find interesting and briefly explain their appeal.

3. What is the significance of the white hawthorn? What might it symbolise? Refer closely to the poem in your answer.

STUDY NOTES

In this poem, the folklore associated with hawthorn in rural Ireland is seen as symbolic of an ancient 'language' that has almost disappeared. Boland structures her themes around the image of a journey into the West. It seems as though she is hoping to return to her roots in the traditional landscape of the West of Ireland.

The poem opens on a conversational note. Boland's clear intention is to leave the city behind: 'I drove West/in the season between seasons'. Her tone is determined, dismissing the **artificial life of suburbia** ('Lawnmowers. Small talk.') in favour of the freedom awaiting her. **Stanza one** emphasises the poet's strong desire to get away from her cultivated suburban confines, which seem colourless and overly regulated. The broken rhythm of **line 4** adds to the abrupt sense of rigidity.

This orderly landscape is in stark contrast with the world of 'Atlantic light' Boland discovers on her journey. **Stanzas two and three** contain **striking images of energy and growth**. The 'splashes of coltsfoot' suggest a fresh enthusiasm for the wide open spaces as she becomes one with this changing environment. The prominent sibilant 's' underpins the rich stillness of the remote countryside.

She seems both fearful and fascinated by the hawthorn's 'superstitious aura'. The experience is similar to an artist becoming increasingly absorbed in the joy of painting. Run-on lines and the frequent use of the pronoun 'I' accentuate our appreciation of the **poet's own delight** in 'that ivory, downhill rush'.

Stanzas four and five focus on the mystery and superstition associated with hawthorn in Irish folk tradition. Boland's awareness of the **possible dangers** check her eagerness as she considers the stories: 'a child might die, perhaps'. The poet is momentarily caught between a desire to fill her arms with these wild flowers and her own disquieting belief in the superstitions. Eventually, she decides to follow her intuition and respect the customs of the West: 'So I left it'.

The personification ('stirring') of the hawthorn in **stanza six** reinforces Boland's regard for this unfamiliar landscape as a living place. The poet's imagination has also been stirred by her journey. In comparing the hawthorn to water, she suggests its elemental power. Both share a natural 'fluency' which can shape and 're-define land'.

The poet links the twin forces of superstition and landscape even more forcibly in **stanza seven**. They defy time and transcend recorded history. The hawthorn trees give the poet a **glimpse of Ireland's ancient culture**. Although nature remains elusive, Boland believes that for outsiders like herself – visiting 'anglers' and tourists – it is 'the only language spoken in these parts'. The poet's final tone is one of resignation as she accepts that she can never fully understand Ireland's unique landscape or the past.

ANALYSIS

'Boland uses a variety of poetic techniques to create poems which allow readers to contemplate the beauty and mystery of nature.' Discuss this statement, with particular reference to 'White Hawthorn in the West of Ireland'.

Sample Paragraph

Eavan Boland creates vivid word pictures of two contrasting landscapes, the ordered urban and the wild rural. In the first stanza the poet dismisses the uniform urban landscape, full of 'Lawnmowers. Small talk'. She decisively sets off on her journey, 'I left behind suburban gardens'. Suddenly the vista opens out to the big western skyline, full of variable weather, 'the hard shyness of Atlantic light'. The magic of the countryside is encapsulated in the 'superstitious aura of hawthorn'. The lush assonance of this line's broad vowels contrasts abruptly with the sharp sounds of the town's descriptive details. The short lines of the first stanza are replaced by long run-on lines mirroring the energy of nature, 'that ivory downhill rush', and the poet's delight, 'All I wanted then was to fill my arms/with sharp flowers'. But there is another aspect to nature foreshadowed in the adjective, 'sharp'. Cutting the hawthorn is considered bad luck in the countryside and Boland respects the local tradition, 'So I left it'. She, like the other tourists, 'anglers' and 'travellers' may enjoy, but not fully understand the wild beauty of nature, 'the only language spoken in those parts'. Because of Boland's remarkable poetic skills, readers are left longing for and puzzling over nature's beauty, 'astray in /the unmarked lights of a May dusk'.

Examiner's Comment

This answer focuses on how aspects of Boland's style contribute to communicating her message that nature may be appreciated but never entirely understood. A developed discussion encompasses the poet's use of varying tones and sound effects: 'The lush assonance of this line's broad vowels contrast sharply with the sharp sounds of the town's descriptive details'. Accurate quotation supports the discussion throughout. A confident top grade standard.

CLASS/HOMEWORK EXERCISES

1. What do you think Eavan Boland has learned from her journey to the West of Ireland? Refer to the poem in your answer.

2. Boland makes effective use of both visual and aural imagery to celebrate the Irish landscape in this poem. Discuss this statement, using close reference to the text.

> **SUMMARY POINTS**
>
> - Beauty of the native landscape and Irish traditions are central themes.
> - Contrast between urban and rural landscapes.
> - Reflective tone reveals the poet's personal feelings and attitudes.
> - Vivid visual imagery, free rhythm, striking onomatopoeia and sibilant effects.

6 OUTSIDE HISTORY

There are outsiders, always. These stars –
these iron inklings of an Irish January,
whose light happened

thousands of years before
our pain did: they are, they have always been   5
outside history.

They keep their distance. Under them remains
a place where you found
you were human, and

a landscape in which you know you are mortal.   10
And a time to choose between them.
I have chosen:

out of myth into history I move to be
part of that ordeal
whose darkness is   15

only now reaching me from those fields,
those rivers, those roads clotted as
firmaments with the dead.

How slowly they die
As we kneel beside them, whisper in their ear.   20
And we are too late. We are always too late.

28 POETRY FOCUS

'These stars'

Glossary

2 *inklings*: slight idea or suspicion; clues.
6 *history*: record or account of past events and developments; the study of these.
13 *myth*: tale with supernatural characters; untrue idea or explanation; imaginary person; story with a germ of truth in it.
17 *clotted*: soft, thick lumps formed.
18 *firmaments*: sky or heavens.

INITIAL RESPONSE

1. How are the stars 'outsiders'? Do you think they are an effective symbol for those who are marginalised and regarded as of no importance? Discuss, using reference from the poem.

2. Has the poet succeeded in moving 'to be/part of that ordeal'? Look carefully at the imagery and language in the poem.

3. Explain the significance of the last stanza of the poem: 'How slowly they die/As we kneel beside them, whisper in their ear./And we are too late. We are always too late'. In your opinion, has the poet's dilemma been resolved?

STUDY NOTES

'Outside History' was written in 1990 as part of a collection of poems that were arranged to reflect the changing seasons. This poem is set in January. Boland believes that it is important to remember the experiences of those who have not been recorded in history. These are the outsiders, 'the lost, the voiceless, the silent' to whom she gives a hauntingly beautiful voice.

Lines 1–6. The poem opens with an **impersonal statement**: 'There are outsiders, always'. The poet is referring to those who have not been recorded in history. The stars are also outsiders, standing outside and above human history. At their great distance, they are shown as cold and distant ('iron', 'Irish January'). They have a permanence and longevity that are in contrast to human life: 'whose light happened/thousands of years before/our pain did'. The run-on line suggests the light that travels thousands of years to reach us. The phrase 'outside history' is placed on its own to emphasise how the stars do not belong to human history.

Lines 7–10. The poet stresses **the aloneness of the stars**: 'They keep their distance'. They don't want to be involved. Now she turns to 'you', a member of the human race, and places 'you' in context with the words 'place' and 'landscape'. This is where 'you found/you were human' and 'mortal'. Unlike the stars; 'you' are a suffering member of the human race who is subject to ageing and death. The line 'And a time to choose between them' could refer to choosing between the perspective of the stars, i.e. remaining at an uninvolved distance, or the perspective of a member of the human race, i.e. involved and anguished.

Lines 11–18. The phrase 'I have chosen' marks a **turning point** in the poem. Boland has made a deliberate decision, **moving away from 'myth'** and tradition. She felt that myth obscures history. She regarded figures like Caitlin Ni Houlihan and Dark Rosaleen, female symbols for Ireland, as 'passive', 'simplified' and 'decorative' emblems in male poems. For the poet, history was laced with myths, which, in her opinion, were as unreal, cold and distant as the stars are from reality. She regarded these mythic emblems as false and limiting, 'a corruption'. Boland is trying to achieve a sense of belonging and wholeness by unwinding the myth and the stereotype. She wanted reality rather than the glittering image of the stars: 'out of myth into history I move to be/part of that ordeal'.

Just as the stars' light travelled vast distances to reach us, so the darkness of unwritten history is travelling to reach her 'only now'. The run-on stanza again suggests great distances that had to be covered for the poet to connect with past history. There follows a description that suggests the **Irish famine**: 'those fields', 'those rivers', 'those roads' which were covered with 'the dead'. The paradoxical phrase 'clotted as/firmaments' uses the language of the stars to describe the numberless bodies strewn everywhere as a result of the famine. This condensed image evokes a poignant sense of the soft mounds of victims lying as numberless as the stars. The full stop after 'the dead' reinforces the finality of death.

Lines 19–21. The last stanza changes to the collective 'we'. Is this referring to the Irish people accepting responsibility for **honouring the dead** and connecting and being part of history? The rite of contrition is being said: 'As we kneel beside them, whisper in their ear'. It was believed that the person's soul would go to rest in heaven as they had made their peace with God, but the repetition of the last line stresses that the words of comfort have come 'too late'. The people don't know they are being honoured by the poet. Nevertheless, the poem stands as a testament to them and their unrecorded history. Has Boland changed her attitude from the beginning of the poem: 'There are outsiders, always'? Has she brought them in from the cold sidelines, including them into history? Or has she and 'we' left it too late?

ANALYSIS

'Eavan Boland's poetry gives a haunting voice to the marginalised and dispossessed in society.' Discuss this statement, with particular reference to Boland's poem, 'Outside History'.

Sample Paragraph

In our modern affluent world, there are many marginalised people. A stark statement opens the poem, 'There are outsiders, always', reminiscent of Christ's statement that the poor are always with us. I found the symbol of the stars effective because they represented the cold distance the outsiders must feel as they look in, but don't belong, 'they have always been/ outside history'. The sympathetic tone and the alliterative phrase, 'iron inklings of an Irish January' evocatively capture the predicament facing marginalised people. The stars show no human empathy with the dispossessed, 'They keep their distance'. But Boland has 'chosen' to embrace her humane side. She will be 'part of that ordeal' in order to give a voice to those forgotten, 'whose darkness is/ only now reaching me'. The run-on stanza indicates how long it has taken. She gives them an unforgettable voice, recalling their tragic story, 'those roads clotted as/ firmaments with the dead'. The blunt verb 'clotted' resounds with the obscenity of what happened to the unknown victims, evoking anonymous mounds of earth where they lay. Respect and dignity are suggested in the sibilant lines, 'How slowly they die/ As we kneel beside them, whisper in their ear', as the last rites are recited. The poem ends with the melancholy realisation, 'And we are too late'. They won't know that they are being remembered. The dispossessed may not, but Boland has given them a voice – both to the present and future generations.

Examiner's Comment

As part of a full essay this perceptive reading of Boland's poem addresses the task directly in a series of accurately referenced arguments. Excellent use of quotation throughout supports the thoughtful discussion points. Expression is also clear and impressive, 'But Boland has chosen to embrace her humane side'. An informed exploration of the poet's language also ensures the top grade standard.

CLASS/HOMEWORK EXERCISES

1. Does 'Outside History' make a compelling case on behalf of voiceless and marginalised people? Support your answer with close reference to the text of the poem.

2. In your opinion, what does the dominant tone throughout the poem reveal about Eavan Boland as a person? Support your answer with close reference to the text.

SUMMARY POINTS

- Key themes – exclusion of the marginalised.
- Boland's distrust of myth, history and stereotypes.
- Varying tones – reflective, regretful, didactic.
- Effective use of repetition, striking imagery.

7 THE BLACK LACE FAN MY MOTHER GAVE ME

It was the first gift he ever gave her,
buying it for five francs in the Galeries
in pre-war Paris. It was stifling.
A starless drought made the nights stormy.

They stayed in the city for the summer. 5
They met in cafés. She was always early.
He was late. That evening he was later.
They wrapped the fan. He looked at his watch.

She looked down the Boulevard des Capucines.
She ordered more coffee. She stood up. 10
The streets were emptying. The heat was killing.
She thought the distance smelled of rain and lightning.

These are wild roses, appliquéd on silk by hand,
darkly picked, stitched boldly, quickly.
The rest is tortoiseshell and has the reticent, 15
clear patience of its element. It is

a worn-out, underwater bullion and it keeps,
even now, an inference of its violation.
The lace is overcast as if the weather
it opened for and offset had entered it. 20

The past is an empty café terrace.
An airless dusk before thunder. A man running.
And no way now to know what happened then –
none at all – unless, of course, you improvise:

The blackbird on this first sultry morning, 25
in summer, finding buds, worms, fruit,
feels the heat. Suddenly she puts out her wing –
the whole, full, flirtatious span of it.

'And no way now to know what happened then'

Glossary

2 *Galeries*: Paris store.
13 *appliquéd*: trimming.
15 *tortoiseshell*: clear decorative material.
15 *reticent*: reserved, restrained.
17 *bullion*: treasure.
24 *improvise*: make up, imagine.
28 *flirtatious*: enticing, playful.
28 *span*: extent, measure.

INITIAL RESPONSE

1. The setting is important in this poem. Briefly explain what it contributes to the atmosphere, referring to the text in your answer.

2. Comment on the effect of the short sentences and irregular rhythms in the first three stanzas.

3. Did you like this poem? Give reasons for your response, referring to the text of the poem in your answer.

STUDY NOTES

Set in pre-war Paris in the 1930s, the incident that occurs is the giving of a gift, a black lace fan that the poet's father gave to her mother. A fan was usually seen as a sign of romantic love and desire. However, its significance here is never entirely explained to us. Maybe this is in recognition of our inability to fully understand other people's relationships or to recall the past and the effect it has on us, although we may attempt to. Boland's poem is one of those attempts.

Stanza one begins on a narrative note as the poet recreates a pivotal moment in her parents' lives back in the 1930s. **The fan was a special symbol of young love** and was important because it was 'the first gift' from her father to her mother. Other details of the precise cost and the 'stifling' weather add to the importance of the occasion. Although the Parisian setting is romantic, the mood is tense. Their courtship is framed in a series of captured moments, as though Boland is flicking through an old photo album.

In **stanzas two and three**, short sentences and the growing unevenness of the rhythm add to this cinematic quality: 'They met in cafés. She was always early'. The hesitant relationship between the lovers is conveyed repeatedly through their nervous gestures: 'He looked at his watch', 'She stood up'. Boland builds up the tension through references to the heat wave: 'the distance smelled of rain and lightning'. The image might also suggest the **stormy nature of what lay ahead** for the couple.

Stanzas four and five focus on the elegant lace fan in **vivid detail**. Boland notes its decorative qualities, carefully embroidered with the most romantic 'wild roses' and fine 'tortoiseshell'. She seems fascinated by the painstaking craft ('stitched boldly') involved in creating this beautiful token of love. But the **poet's appreciation of the fan becomes diminished** with guilt. The tortoiseshell has suffered 'violation' at the expense of the gift. In Boland's mind, the delicate colours decorating the fan came from 'a worn-out, underwater bullion'. The tone is suddenly downbeat as the thought throws a shadow ('The lace is overcast') on her parents' relationship.

In **stanza six**, the poet returns to the romantic Parisian drama of the 'empty café terrace', but admits that she can never know what really happened that fateful evening in the 'airless dusk before thunder'. Instead, she must 'improvise' it. But at least the romantic moment is preserved in her imagination. Not for the first time, however, there is an underlying suggestion of the reality of relationships over time, and the balance of joy and disappointment that is likely. For Boland, the fan is only a small part of her parents' story. Perhaps she realises that **the past can never be completely understood**.

The striking image of a blackbird dominates the **final stanza**. The poet returns to the present as she observes the bird 'in summer, finding buds'. The movement of the blackbird's wing is an unexpected link with the black lace fan all those years ago. While the souvenir is old, its significance as a symbol of youthful romance can still be found elsewhere. For the first time, **Boland now seems**

to understand the beauty of her parents' love for each other. The last lines are daring and appear to describe both the blackbird and her mother as a young girl holding her new gift: 'Suddenly she puts out her wing –/the whole, full, flirtatious span of it'. The energetic pace of the lines combine with the alliterative sounds and sibilant music to produce a real sense of celebration at the end.

ANALYSIS

'Eavan Boland takes a balanced, unsentimental view of relationships.' To what extent is this true of 'The Black Lace Fan My Mother Gave Me'? Support your answer with reference to the poem.

Sample Paragraph

This poem is not a typical love poem. It is out of the ordinary in ways. The poet does not try to glorify the relationship when they first met. Indeed, they seem unsure of each other. The poet tries to work out the story behind their relationship by looking at the lace fan. She imagines the intense heat of that summer in Paris: 'It was stifling'. References to the weather hint at an uncomfortable relationship: 'The heat was killing'. Boland might be referring indirectly to the future problems in the couple's marriage over the years. The fact that the Second World War was about to break out is also a bad sign. Having said that, the gift of the fan is a symbol of the attraction the couple felt. It is a traditional image of true romance. The poet shows the reality of the relationship by noting the unsentimental details: 'He was late', 'She stood up'. There was nervousness and excitement when they were first infatuated with each other, but their love was to change over time. She also compares the fan to a blackbird's wing which excites the poet. This gives us a final impression that Boland is happy to imagine the youthful love between her parents back in the 1930s. In a way, the poem is as much about the love Boland herself feels for her parents as about their love.

Examiner's Comment

This paragraph focuses well on the way love is presented throughout the poem. The answer would have been improved by a less note-like commentary at the beginning. Good use is made of suitable quotations and this top grade response is well-rounded off with an effective point about the poet's own enduring love for her parents.

CLASS/HOMEWORK EXERCISES

1. Comment on Eavan Boland's use of symbolism in this poem, referring to the text in your answer.

2. What does Boland's poem reveal about her parents' relationship? Support the points you make with reference to both the subject matter and language use in the poem.

SUMMARY POINTS

- Themes include romantic love and changing family relationships.
- Striking language – central symbol of the fan, dramatic image of the blackbird.
- Evocative atmosphere of 1930s Paris.
- Vivid detail; varying tones – reflective, nostalgic, realistic.

8 THIS MOMENT

A neighbourhood.
At dusk.

Things are getting ready
to happen
out of sight.   5

Stars and moths.
And rinds slanting around fruit.

But not yet.

One tree is black.
One window is yellow as butter.   10

A woman leans down to catch a child
who has run into her arms
this moment.

Stars rise.
Moths flutter.   15
Apples sweeten in the dark.

'this moment'

Glossary

7   *rinds*: peels.

INITIAL RESPONSE

1. Choose either one visual or one aural image from the poem, and briefly comment on its effectiveness. Support your answer by referring to the text.

2. Comment on how Boland manages to create drama within the poem.

3. What do you think is the central theme in the poem? Refer closely to the text in your answer.

STUDY NOTES

In this short lyric poem, Eavan Boland captures the experience of a passing moment in time. It is clear that she is moved by the ordinariness of suburban life, where she glimpses the immeasurable beauty of nature and human nature. The occasion is another reminder of the mystery and wonder of all creation, as expressed by the American poet Walt Whitman, who wrote, 'I know of nothing else but miracles'.

The poem's **opening lines** introduce a suburban area in any part of the world. Boland pares the scene down to its essentials. All we learn is that it is dusk, a time of transition. The atmosphere is one of quiet intensity. Full stops break the rhythm and force us to evaluate what is happening. Although we are presented with an **anonymous setting**, it seems strangely familiar. The late evening – especially as darkness falls – can be a time for reflecting about the natural world.

The stillness and dramatic anticipation intensify further in **lines 3–8**. Something important is about to happen 'out of sight'. Boland then considers some of nature's wonders: 'Stars and moths'. In the twilight, everything seems mysterious, even 'rinds slanting around fruit'. The poet's eye for detail is like that of an artist. The rich, sensory image of the cut fruit is exact and tactile. She uses simple language precisely to create a **mood of natural calmness** that is delayed for a split second ('But not yet').

There is time for two more **vivid images** in **lines 9–10**. The startling colour contrast between the 'black' tree and the window that is 'yellow as butter' has a cinematic effect. The simile is homely, in keeping with the domestic setting. The repetition of 'One' focuses our attention as the build-up continues. Again, Boland presents the sequence of events in a series of brief glimpses. It is as if she is marking time, preparing us for the key moment of revelation.

This occurs in **lines 11–13**. The central image of the mother and child intuitively reaching out for each other is a powerful symbol of unprompted love. It is every bit as wonderful as any of life's greatest mysteries. The three lines become progressively condensed as the child reaches her mother. The syntax suggests their eagerness to show their love for each other. Boland's decision to generalise ('A woman' and 'a child') emphasises the **universal significance** of 'this moment'. The crucial importance of people's feelings transcends time and place.

There is a slight tone of anti-climax about the **last three lines**. However, Boland rounds off her description of the moment by placing it within a wider context. The constant expression of family love is in harmony with everything else that is beautiful in nature. This feeling is suggested by the recurring sibilant 's' sounds and the carefully chosen verbs ('rise', 'flutter' and 'sweeten'), all of which celebrate the excitement and **joy of everyday human relationships**.

ANALYSIS

'Eavan Boland's poetry deals effectively with important contemporary issues.' Discuss this statement, with particular reference to her poem, 'This Moment'.

Sample Paragraph

Eavan Boland sets her poem in a contemporary setting, a Dublin suburb at dusk. The short, pithy lines, 'A neighbourhood./At dusk', set a modern, minimalist tone for this anonymous, yet familiar scene which is played out across countless estates worldwide. The mystery of this transition time between day and night is caught in the economical run-on lines, 'Things are getting ready/to happen/out of sight'. In this 'not yet' moment, the mysterious powers and actions of nature are observed, 'And rinds slanting around fruit'. The verb 'slanting' vividly suggests the unfurling movement of nature's growth. Yet, I also feel there is a slight tinge of danger, reminding me of the serpent in the Garden of Eden waiting to pounce. Her painterly eye precisely captures this moment at dusk, the silhouetted tree, the window lit by its electric lamp, 'One tree is black./One window is yellow as butter'. Suddenly a child runs into a waiting mother's arms, 'A woman leans down to catch a child'. The general terms used emphasise the universal significance of this experience of a child returning to the security of a loving mother's arms. The tension of the moment is relaxed as if nature exhales, all is now in its rightful place. A series of gentle verbs: 'rise', 'flutter' and 'sweeten' chart its peaceful movement. Boland's poem describes a common social issue – how in this uncertain modern world, every parent heaves a sigh of relief when a child returns safely to the security of the family home.

Examiner's Comment

This competent response addresses both the theme and style of the poem. A developed discussion deals with Boland's use of free verse and economical language. An interesting personal reading of the poem is given in the line, 'I also feel there is a slight tinge of danger...' This well written, successful answer engages closely with the body of the poem. Top grade standard.

CLASS/HOMEWORK EXERCISES

1. Comment on the poet's tone in 'This Moment'. Refer to the text in your discussion.

2. A sense of intense mystery is often found in Boland's poetry. To what extent is this true of 'This Moment'? Support your answer with close reference to the poem.

SUMMARY POINTS

- Themes include the mystery of nature and the beauty of loving relationships.
- Effective use of simple language and succinct dramatic style.
- Vivid, sensuous imagery; sibilant and assonant effects.
- Varying moods – subdued, reflective, celebratory.

THE POMEGRANATE

The only legend I have ever loved is
the story of a daughter lost in hell.
And found and rescued there.
Love and blackmail are the gist of it.
Ceres and Persephone the names.   5
And the best thing about the legend is
I can enter it anywhere. And have.
As a child in exile in
a city of fogs and strange consonants,
I read it first and at first I was   10
an exiled child in the crackling dusk of
the underworld, the stars blighted. Later
I walked out in a summer twilight
searching for my daughter at bed-time.
When she came running I was ready   15
to make any bargain to keep her.
I carried her back past whitebeams
and wasps and honey-scented buddleias.
But I was Ceres then and I knew
winter was in store for every leaf   20
on every tree on that road.
Was inescapable for each one we passed.
And for me.
           It is winter
and the stars are hidden.   25
I climb the stairs and stand where I can see
my child asleep beside her teen magazines,
her can of Coke, her plate of uncut fruit.
The pomegranate! How did I forget it?
She could have come home and been safe   30
and ended the story and all
our heart-broken searching but she reached
out a hand and plucked a pomegranate.
She put out her hand and pulled down

the French sound for apple and 35
the noise of stone and the proof
that even in the place of death,
at the heart of legend, in the midst
of rocks full of unshed tears
ready to be diamonds by the time 40
the story was told, a child can be
hungry. I could warn her. There is still a chance.
The rain is cold. The road is flint-coloured.
The suburb has cars and cable television.
The veiled stars are above ground. 45
It is another world. But what else
can a mother give her daughter but such
beautiful rifts in time?
If I defer the grief I will diminish the gift.
The legend will be hers as well as mine. 50
She will enter it. As I have.
She will wake up. She will hold
the papery flushed skin in her hand.
And to her lips. I will say nothing.

'my child asleep'

Glossary

The pomegranate (from a French word meaning an apple with many seeds) is a pulpy oriental fruit.

5 *Ceres and Persephone*: mythological figures. Ceres was the goddess of earth and motherhood. Persephone was her beautiful daughter who was forced by Pluto to become his wife and was imprisoned in Hades, the underworld. Ceres was determined to find Persephone and threatened to prevent anything from growing on the earth until she was allowed to rescue her daughter. But because Persephone had eaten sacred pomegranate seeds in Hades, she was condemned forever to spend part of every year there.

9 *city of fogs*: London, where the poet once lived.

18 *buddleias*: ornamental bushes with small purple flowers.

48 *rifts*: gaps, cracks.

49 *defer*: delay.

INITIAL RESPONSE

1. Boland conveys a clear sense of the city of London in this poem. How does she succeed in doing this? Refer closely to the text in your answer.

2. From your reading of this poem, what do you learn about the relationship between the poet and her own daughter? Refer to the text in your answer.

3. Comment on the poet's mood in the last five lines of the poem.

STUDY NOTES

In the poem, narrated as one unrhymed stanza, Boland explores the theme of parental loss by comparing her own experiences as a mother and daughter with the myth of Ceres and Persephone. Although it is a personal poem, it has a much wider relevance for families everywhere.

Boland presents this exploration of the mother–child relationship as a dramatic narrative. In the **opening lines**, the poet tells us that she has always related to 'the story of a daughter lost in hell'. This goes back to her early experience as 'a child in exile' living in London. Her **sense of displacement** is evident in the detailed description of that 'city of fogs and strange consonants'. Like Persephone trapped in Hades, Boland yearned for home. But the myth has a broader relevance to the poet's life – she 'can enter it anywhere'. Years later, she recalls a time when, as a mother, she could also identify with Ceres, 'searching for my daughter'.

Lines 13–18 express the intensity of Boland's feelings for her child: she was quite prepared 'to make any bargain to keep her'. The **anxious tone** reflects the poet's awareness of the importance of appreciating the closeness between herself and her teenage daughter while time allows. She expresses her maternal feelings through rich natural images: 'I carried her back past whitebeams'.

But she is also increasingly aware that both she and her daughter are ageing. This is particularly evident in **line 20**, as she anticipates an 'inescapable' change in their relationship: 'winter was in store for every leaf'.

Line 24 marks a defining moment ('It is winter') for them both. Observing her daughter asleep in her bedroom, Boland now sees herself as Ceres and the 'plate of uncut fruit' as the pomegranate. This marks the realisation that **her child has become an adult**. The poet imagines how different it might have been had Persephone not eaten the fruit – 'She could have come home' and ended all the 'heart-broken searching'. But Persephone deliberately made her choice, a decision that is emphasised by the repeated mention of her gesture ('she reached/out a hand', 'She put out her hand'). Significantly, Boland is sympathetic: 'a child can be/hungry'.

In **line 42**, the poet considers alerting her daughter ('I could warn her') about the dangers and disappointments that lie ahead. **Harsh imagery** suggests the difficulties of modern life: 'The rain is cold. The road is flint-coloured'. Boland wonders if 'beautiful rifts in time' are the most a mother can offer. Such delaying tactics may only postpone natural development into adulthood.

In the end, she decides to 'say nothing'. There is a clear sense of resignation in the **final lines**. The poet accepts the reality of change. Boland's daughter will experience the same stages of childhood and motherhood as the poet herself: 'The legend will be hers as well as mine'. This truth is underlined by the recurring use of 'She will', a recognition that her daughter's destiny is in her own hands. The **poem ends on a quietly reflective note** as Boland respectfully acknowledges the right of her daughter to mature naturally and make her own way in life.

ANALYSIS

'Eavan Boland's use of mythical references vividly illuminates her own personal experiences.' Discuss this statement, with particular reference to Boland's poem, 'The Pomegranate'.

Sample Paragraph

In my view, Eavan Boland has been very successful in blending her own life as a child and mother with Persephone and Ceres. The fact that she uses an ancient legend adds a touch of mystery to the theme of mother–daughter relationships. This gives the poem a universal quality. First, she compares herself to Persephone, the exiled child in London where the stars were 'blighted'. This links the grimy city life to the underworld of Hades. But Boland is more concerned with the present and her fears of losing her own daughter who is growing up fast. By describing her fears through the old story of Ceres, she increases our understanding of how anxious she was feeling. Both parents were 'searching' desperately. Together, the legend and the true life story of the poet and her reluctance to come to terms with her daughter growing up really show how parents have to let go of their children and give them the freedom to make their own mistakes and learn for themselves. Most parents find it hard to give their children freedom. Overall, the mythical references emphasis the universality of Boland's natural feelings for her daughter. I thought they were very effective in conveying the poem's central theme.

Examiner's Comment

There are some very good points here in response to a challenging question. Although the answer shows personal engagement, it could be rooted more thoroughly in the text through a more extensive use of quotation. Some sentences are overlong and the expression is repetitive at times (with overuse of the words 'fears' and 'freedom'). Points would need to be more developed to achieve the top grade.

CLASS/HOMEWORK EXERCISES

1. What image of Eavan Boland herself emerges from this poem? Refer closely to the text in your answer.

2. Boland manages to create a series of powerfully evocative moods throughout this poem. Discuss this statement, supporting your answer with close reference to the text.

SUMMARY POINTS

- Boland considers the complexity of mother-daughter relationships.
- Striking images – nature, family and the difficulties of modern life.
- Mythical references reflect a timeless, universal sense of loss.
- Tones vary – empathetic, anxious, resigned.

10 LOVE

Dark falls on this mid-western town
where we once lived when myths collided.
Dusk has hidden the bridge in the river
which slides and deepens
to become the water   5
the hero crossed on his way to hell.

Not far from here is our old apartment.
We had a kitchen and an Amish table.
We had a view. And we discovered there
love had the feather and muscle of wings   10
and had come to live with us,
a brother of fire and air.

We had two infant children one of whom
was touched by death in this town
and spared: and when the hero   15
was hailed by his comrades in hell
their mouths opened and their voices failed and
there is no knowing what they would have asked
about a life they had shared and lost.

I am your wife.   20
It was years ago.
Our child was healed. We love each other still.
Across our day-to-day and ordinary distances
we speak plainly. We hear each other clearly.

And yet I want to return to you   25
on the bridge of the Iowa river as you were,
with snow on the shoulders of your coat
and a car passing with its headlights on:

I see you as a hero in a text –
the image blazing and the edges gilded – 30
and I long to cry out the epic question
my dear companion:

Will we ever live so intensely again?
Will love come to us again and be
so formidable at rest it offered us ascension 35
even to look at him?

But the words are shadows and you cannot hear me.
You walk away and I cannot follow.

'comrades in hell'

Glossary

1. *mid-western town*: Iowa, a state in the US. Boland attended the prestigious Iowa Writers' Workshop in 1979 and lived there for a while with her family.
2. *myths*: fictitious tales with supernatural characters and events.
6. *hero*: Aeneas was a hero in the *Aeneid*. He visited the underworld by crossing the River Styx where he saw his dead companions, but they could not communicate with him.
8. *Amish*: strict American religious sect that makes functional, practical furniture without decoration.
31. *epic*: great, ambitious.
35. *formidable*: very impressive.

INITIAL RESPONSE

1. This poem is an open and honest meditation on the nature of love. Write your own personal response to it, referring to the text in your answer.

2. Do you think the use of the Aeneas myth is effective? Give reasons, using the poem as evidence for your point of view.

3. Explain the significance of the last section of the poem: 'But the words are shadows and you cannot hear me./You walk away and I cannot follow'. In your opinion, is this a positive or negative ending?

STUDY NOTES

'Love' is part of a sequence of poems called 'Legends' in which Boland explores parallels between myths and modern life. She records her personal experience of young love in Iowa at a time when tragedy touched the family, when her youngest daughter was seriously ill and came close to death. This is interwoven with the myth of Aeneas returning to the underworld. The narrative poem explores the nature of human relationships and how they change over time. It also shows the similarity of human experience down through the ages.

Lines 1–6. The poem opens in darkness, **remembering the past**. Her personal experience was in 'this mid-western town' in Iowa, and the poem connects this with the myth of Aeneas visiting the underworld. Aeneas crosses the bridge on the River Styx to reach Hades, the land of the Shades ('the hero crossed on his way to hell'). Boland and her husband were also experiencing their own hell as they visited their very sick little girl in hospital.

Lines 7–12 These lines give us a **clear, detailed picture of their external ordinary life**: 'a kitchen', 'an Amish table', 'a view'. The poem is written in loose, non-rhyming stanzas, which suits reminiscences. Their internal emotional life is shown in the **striking metaphor** 'love had the feather and muscle of wings'. Love was beating, alive, vibrant. The word 'feather' suggests it could soar to great heights, while 'muscle' signifies that it was a powerful emotion. This natural, graceful love was palpable, substantial, elemental, 'a brother of fire and air'.

Lines 13–19. The **personal drama** of the sick daughter who 'was touched by death' is recalled. But Boland did not lose her child. The verb 'spared' links us with the myth again. Aeneas is in the underworld, but because his comrades are shadows, they cannot ask the questions they are longing to ask about the life they once shared. The moment of communication is lost: 'there is no knowing what they would have asked'.

Lines 20–36. Now the poet meditates on the **changing nature of love**. The 'we' becomes 'I' – 'I am your wife'. Do they, as husband and wife, communicate as deeply as they did before? Her tone is crisp and matter-of-fact, almost businesslike. She wants to recapture the intensity of their love and shared times, when she saw her husband as 'a hero in a text'. In her memory of him, he is outlined by the cars' lights as they pass on the bridge. Described as 'blazing' and 'gilded', he is contrasted to the darkness of the night, as Aeneas is contrasted with the darkness of the underworld. She is longing to experience that special time, that transcendence, again.

Rhetorical questions are posed at the end: 'Will we ever live so intensely again?' The inference is no. She can imagine asking these questions about the life they shared together, but she cannot actually articulate them. This is **similar to Aeneas' dilemma** – his comrades long to ask questions about the life they shared with him, but 'their voices failed'. Neither Boland nor the 'comrades' could express their strong feelings; neither can ask the questions they want to ask. The words of the questions remain unformed, unspoken, 'shadows'.

Lines 37–38. The poem ends with a two-line stanza in which she accepts that the **gap cannot be bridged**: 'You walk away and I cannot follow'. There is a real sense of loss and resignation in Boland's final tone.

ANALYSIS

This poem is about memory. How does the poet explore the theme? Refer either to the content and style in your answer. Illustrate your response with reference to the poem.

Sample Paragraph

By blending myth and personal experience, Boland gives her poems a true sense of universality. But she also blends timelines, the past and the present tenses to give a quality of timelessness to her work. In 'Love', the immediacy and freshness of a potent memory is captured by her use of the present tense: 'Dark falls', 'the bridge … slides and deepens/to become the water', 'here is our old apartment'. The recent past is shown in the past tense as she recalls what they had: 'We had a kitchen and an Amish table./We had a view', 'love … had come to live with us', 'We had two infant children'. In the past they had a life together which was lived very intensely. Are they missing any of this now? The tense then changes to the present as Boland states her identity: 'I am your wife'. I notice that it is the partnership she is referring to, not her role as mother. Here she honestly and openly explores her concerns about the changing nature of love. Their moment of crisis is over: 'Our child was healed'. She itemises a list: 'We speak', 'we hear'. They 'love each other still'. But a note of longing is heard in 'I want' and the future tense 'Will we?' Realistically she appraises the current situation and notes 'words are shadows', 'you cannot hear me', 'You walk away', 'I cannot follow'. The intense personal nature of their love has changed. Like Aeneas' comrades, she cannot voice her question ('voices failed'), and her husband, like Aeneas, cannot hear. The changing tenses add a timeless quality to the experience of memory, as time shared is recalled. The poem ends with the never-changing realisation that time cannot be relived.

Examiner's Comment

An unusual approach is taken as the response focuses on the use of tenses as a stylistic feature to communicate theme: 'The changing tenses add a timeless quality to the experience of memory'. There is evidence of close reading of the poem and effective use of quotation throughout. Expression is varied and fluent. This assured response, e.g. 'The poem ends with the never-changing realisation that time cannot be relived', merits the highest grade.

CLASS/HOMEWORK EXERCISES

1. 'When myths collided.' Do you consider Boland's use of myths in her work effective in exploring her themes? Discuss, referring to the poems on your course.

2. The poem, 'Love', illustrates Boland's subtle skill in conveying significant universal truths through her exploration of personal relationships. Discuss this view, supporting your points with close reference to the text.

SUMMARY POINTS

- The changing nature of romantic love is a central theme.
- References to Greek mythology used to explore parallels with modern life.
- Use of detailed description, striking metaphors, rhetorical questions.
- Contrasting tones of relief, reflection and resignation.

LEAVING CERT SAMPLE ESSAY

'Boland's reflective insights offer fresh perspectives on a variety of universal themes.' To what extent do you agree or disagree with this statement? Support your answer with reference to both the subject matter and language use in the poetry of Eavan Boland on your course.

Marking Scheme Guidelines

Candidates are free to agree and/or disagree with the statement, but they should engage with how the poet's reflections offer 'fresh perspectives on a variety of universal themes'. Reward responses that include clear analysis of both themes and language use (though not necessarily equally) in Boland's poetry.

Indicative material:
- Explorations of the changing aspects of love and relationships.
- Refreshing celebration of natural beauty and tradition.
- Intense engagement with the marginalised and dispossessed.
- Subversive attitude to women's experience in a patriarchal world.
- Challenging views on Irishness, conflict, myth and history.
- Striking imagery emphasises thoughts and emotions.
- Varying moods/tones convey renewed understanding and empathy.

Sample Essay
(Boland's reflections offer fresh perspectives)

1. *Eavan Boland is a distinctive Irish poet whose work ranges widely over basic themes and issues which relate to the lives of very many people. She writes movingly about love, family relationships, conflict and the experience of being marginalised. Her poems are often thought-provoking – particularly when she explores the treatment of women in society. For me, Boland's observations have provided new outlooks on many important issues.*

2. *Several poems, including 'The Shadow Doll' and 'The Famine Road', contrast past and present eras to examine how women have been expected to behave in a predominantly patriarchal world. In 'The Shadow Doll', Boland focuses on an object associated with Victorian weddings – a small porcelain doll in an enclosed glass case. The precise descriptive details of a 'porcelain bride in an airless glamour' suggest Boland's understanding of how young women were once viewed in marriage. She emphasises the idea of oppression and even suffocation. The poet's precise language highlights a sense of imprisonment – 'stitched blooms', 'hoops', 'neatly sewn'. The hesitant rhythm and repetition of 'Under glass, under wraps' adds to the notion of helplessness. In some ways, the symbolism seems a little too obvious for modern*

readers who are more aware of sexist attitudes, but I believe that there are still great pressures on girls to look and act in particular ways. The doll is obviously unreal, but nonetheless frightening. The final lines are almost surreal as Boland recalls that on the night before her own wedding, she herself felt strangely objectified, 'astray among the cards and wedding gifts'. Increasingly aware of becoming entrapped, the poem ends with a series of highly disturbing images – 'pressing down again. And then locks'.

3. Boland often challenges society's patriarchal attitudes, reminding readers that women are expected to conform to the norms of a male-dominated context. Although 'The Famine Road' is primarily concerned with the callous treatment of Ireland's starving people during the mid-19th century, the poet also links their suffering to the lives of infertile women in today's world. Interlinked with the 19th-century voices, Boland introduces the modern voice of an insensitive doctor who curtly dismisses the infertile patient he is treating: 'take it well woman, grow/your garden, keep house'. The stark experience of famine victims and the disappointment of being unable to have a child are effectively illustrated by the shared image of the famine road. The realities of suffering and loss are universal and timeless.

4. As Eavan Boland lived in Ireland during the Troubles of the 1970s, it is not surprising that she writes about the tragic violence of that period. For a young person nowadays, that whole era seems distant and unreal. However, in 'Child of our Time', the poet presents a startling reminder of the tragic reality of conflict by commemorating a baby killed in the 1974 Dublin bombing. Boland dedicates the poem to a friend's baby who had died in infancy. What I found of greatest interest is the way the entire poem celebrates the precious quality of every child's life. The tone varies from tender sympathy to bitter anger, emphasising the responsibility adults have to protect innocent children.

5. The early lines demand that the older generation should create 'order' out of the 'discord' resulting from the unfortunate child's 'murder'. Boland's voice is formal and measured, laying the blame on society at large – 'We who should have known'. The inclusive pronoun involves the reader directly. Soft, gentle sound effects, such as 'rhymes for your waking, rhythms for your sleep', reflect the simple world of childhood. However, the poem's increasingly reverential tone builds to a prayerful conclusion hoping that the child's short life will affect future generations, so that people find 'a new language'. In one way, Boland is giving readers a lead here by speaking out clearly against those who have lost respect for human life. This short dramatic poem challenges us to value every individual.

6. 'This Moment' and 'White Hawthorn in the West of Ireland' are both reflective poems which encourage readers to consider the beauty and mystery of nature. In the short lyric, 'This Moment', the poet focuses on the wonder of time itself when 'Things are getting ready/to happen'. The setting – 'a neighbourhood' – could be anywhere. Vivid details of the natural world, such as 'Stars and moths', create a mood of

heightened anticipation – the shock of each moment of being alive. The final image – 'A woman leans down to catch a child' – is a simple but powerful symbol of universal love, highlighting perhaps the single most important aspect of human life. Such an insight is typical of Eavan Boland who also captures the strange beauty of the Irish landscape in 'White Hawthorn in the West of Ireland'. Describing a journey from Dublin to the West, she is able to link the wild natural vegetation – 'sharp flowers' – with traditional Irish superstitions. The hawthorn is part of the native landscape and culture – a reminder that our identity is defined by many different forces.

7. *I have always found a quietly graceful quality in Boland's writing. Her measured observational poems often make a dramatic impact. Her short narratives have an unsettling intensity which makes the reader think more deeply about important aspects of life. In particular, she writes with great honesty and insight about Irish identity and the female experience.*

(approx. 885 words)

Examiner's Comment

A very well-structured top grade essay which addresses the question confidently. Points are developed effectively and illustrated by apt quotations and references. Expression is also highly impressive and well-controlled: 'The hesitant rhythm and repetition of "Under glass, under wraps" add to the notion of helplessness'. Some examples of the varying tones would have highlighted the discussion in paragraph 4. Good use is made of cross references in paragraph 6. The close analysis of the poet's language is to be commended – particularly in Paragraphs 2 and 5.

MARKING SCHEME
P = 15/15
C = 15/15
L = 15/15
M = 5/5
Total = 50/50

SAMPLE LEAVING CERT QUESTIONS ON BOLAND'S POETRY

(45/50 MINUTES)

1. 'Eavan Boland addresses contemporary modern-day issues through effective comparisons from history and mythology.' Discuss this statement, supporting your answer with reference to the poems by Boland on your course.

2. 'Boland makes effective use of evocative language to address issues which are both personal and private.' Discuss this statement, supporting your answer with reference to the poetry of Eavan Boland on your course.

3. 'Boland's poetry gives an honest account of the female experience with delicacy and precision.' Support your answer with reference to the poetry of Eavan Boland on your course.

Sample Plan (Q2)

'Eavan Boland deals with issues which are both private and personal, but which also have a universal appeal.' Discuss this statement. Support your answer with reference to the poems by Boland on your course.

- Intro: A personal response is required referring to both subject matter and style. Both tasks, the private and personal and the universal dimensions of her poetry, should be explored.

- Point 1: 'Child of Our Time' – personal response to newspaper picture of fireman carrying dead child after bomb given widespread resonance by saying all of us need to find 'a new language'. Personal tone both compassionate and admonishing. Use of formal language suited to elegy and prayer.

- Point 2: 'The Pomegranate' – deals with the relationship between mother and daughter, particularly the wrenching moment of separation despite the mother's worry of no longer being able to protect her child. This personal situation is directly linked to the myth of Persephone and Ceres, giving it a timeless, universal dimension.

- Point 3: 'Love' also uses a myth, Aeneas and the underworld, to portray a personal experience which has universal appeal.

- Point 4: 'The War Horse' – metaphorical poem about attitudes to war. Rigid, controlled couplets show the suburban desire for order. The epic title broadens the appeal of the poem. The blending of past and present, blurs the boundaries of time.

- Point 5: 'This Moment' – a moment in suburbia, at dusk, recollected with painterly precision. The collective experience is shown through the use of general terms and details enabling a universal significance to the private event.

- Conclusion: Boland refers to specific personal moments or events and gives them a widespread interest by linking them with mythology, by changing tones and by her vivid visual descriptions. Her poetry often transcends the particular to become general.

Sample Essay Plan (Q2)

Develop one of the above points into a paragraph.

Sample Paragraph: Point 3

By interweaving myth with a personal story, Boland creates poetry that becomes universally appealing. She uses this technique in the poem 'Love'. Here the story of the hero Aeneas, who goes to the underworld where his dead comrades are, is interwoven with an actual story of Boland's, when her daughter was seriously ill. In each there is a hero, Aeneas and Boland's husband. Each has their own trauma to deal with. Aeneas cannot hear what 'his comrades in hell' want to ask, as their 'voices failed'. The questions they wanted to ask 'about a life they had loved and shared' will never be known. Similarly, Boland is unable to ask about a life she and her husband had known as she feels unable to voice the question, 'Will we ever live so intensely again?' They had lived in this way when one of their children was 'touched by death in this town and spared.' Often in times of tragedy, people are capable of great things. To Boland, her husband was 'a hero in a text.' Although their feelings for each other are unchanged ('We love each other still'), she longs for the love they once shared. It was an almost ecstatic, spiritual experience. But, just as Aeneas is never asked questions by his comrades, so her husband is never asked her question. Instead the 'words are shadows'. Once again, a domestic event is transformed into a wider arena by entangling it with a myth, the story of Aeneas crossing the river Styx.

Examiner's Comment

As part of a full essay answer, this is a highly impressive top grade paragraph that gives a personal response firmly rooted in the text. The paragraph focuses on the use of myth by Boland to explore the wider dimensions of domestic situations. Impressive vocabulary makes this a very successful effort, 'a domestic event is transformed into a wider arena by enmeshing it with a myth.'

LAST WORDS

'Eavan Boland's work continues to deepen in both humanity and complexity.'

Fiona Sampson

'Memory, change, loss, the irrecoverable past – such are the shared condition of humankind, with which she scrupulously engages.'

Anne Stevenson

'Poets are those who ransack their perishing mind and find pattern and form.'

Eavan Boland

PAUL DURCAN

1944–

'That's what poetry is about: getting out of your miserable self and opening your eyes.'

Paul Durcan is one of modern Ireland's foremost and most prolific poets. He is known for his controversial, comic and deeply moving poems. An outspoken critic of his native country, he has traced its emergence from the repressions of the 1950s to the contradictions of the present day.

Born in Dublin in 1944, Durcan spent much of his childhood with relatives in County Mayo. He was educated at University College Cork, where he studied archaeology and medieval history. In 1967, he met Nessa O'Neill. The couple later married and had two daughters. The marriage ended in 1984.

Among Durcan's many poetic influences are Eliot, Hopkins and Kavanagh. Significantly, his first solo collection of poetry, *O Westport in the Light of Asia Minor*, won the Patrick Kavanagh Award in 1975.

A variety of voices can be heard throughout Durcan's distinctive work, by turns hilarious, humane and heartbreaking. He uses many different forms, including dramatic monologues, ballads, mock news reports, songs and even prayers. His poetry can be surreal, mystical, passionate and ironic.

The subject matter of Paul Durcan's poems ranges widely, from explorations of cultural change in contemporary Ireland to intimate studies of family relationships. He is constantly observing the world around him, challenging authority and expressing human vulnerability. Many of the narrative poems he writes are autobiographical, often filled with black humour and satirical jibes. They seem to be carefully designed for oral appreciation.

To find out more about Paul Durcan, or to hear readings of his poems, you could do a search of some of the useful websites available such as YouTube, bbc.co.uk and poetryarchive.org or access additional material on this page of your eBook.

Prescribed Poems — HIGHER LEVEL

❶ 'Nessa'
This deeply personal poem is centred around swimming, an extended metaphor conveying both the delights and dangers of falling in love. The hypnotic rhythm used throughout the poem reflects the intensity of Durcan's relationship with his wife: 'that was a whirlpool,/And I very nearly drowned'. — 60

❷ 'The Girl with the Keys to Pearse's Cottage'
This poem addresses aspects of Irish identity, belonging and the instability of place. In this narrative poem of love and loss, the central character, Cáit Killann, is a powerfully sad and realistic symbol of Irish emigration, an ironic reminder of what has become of Pádraic Pearse's idealistic dreams. — 64

❸ 'The Difficulty that is Marriage'
In this short, introspective reflection, Durcan suggests that while true love is not free of problems, it can still endure despite all the obstacles. After considering his relationship with his wife, the poet ends on a note of heightened romanticism: 'If it were with you, I should live for ever'. — 69

❹ 'Wife Who Smashed Television Gets Jail'*
Durcan sometimes uses a mock journalistic style, particularly in his humorous critiques of Irish society. This poem is divided into two sections: the first 21 lines in the voice of the husband who cannot understand his wife's distaste for television, and the final five-line report of the judge's verdict on the case. — 74

❺ 'Parents'*
This poem raises interesting questions about parent–child communication, a recurring theme in Paul Durcan's work. Characteristically, some of the poet's perceptions ('A child's face is a drowned face') have a deeply disturbing quality, which convey shock as well as intensity. — 78

❻ '"Windfall", 8 Parnell Hill, Cork'
This long poem recounts both the happiness of family love and domesticity and the bitter consequences of a marriage. The intensity of the pain of separation is searing as Durcan discloses the disintegration of important relationships: 'The most subversive unit in society is the human family'. — 82

7 **'Six Nuns Die in Convent Inferno'**
In this lengthy narrative poem about a fire that destroyed a Dublin convent in 1986, Durcan characteristically transforms the details of the tragedy into an extended exercise in spiritual reflection. The elderly nun who narrates the moving story of this disaster reveals the personal choices she had made and her memories of happier times: 'fluttering up and down the beach'.   92

8 **'Sport'***
Another painfully autobiographical poem in which Durcan recalls a football match from his youth and explores the troubled relationship he had with his father. With disarming honesty, the poet accepts the unhappy estrangement between father and son: 'More than anybody it was you/I wanted to mesmerise'.   102

9 **'Father's Day, 21 June 1992'**
On a crucial train journey from Dublin to Cork, the poet confronts the erosive effects of time on his role as a husband and father. The poem alternates between tragicomedy, surreal scenes and moments of devastating self-awareness. By the end of this poignant journey, however, Durcan accepts that he no longer has any reason to celebrate Father's Day.   108

10 **'The Arnolfini Marriage'**
This dramatic monologue was inspired by the famous Jan Van Eyck oil painting, which is believed to represent a rich Italian merchant and his wife. Durcan assumes the personas of the married couple, 'We are the Arnolfinis', as they reflect on marriage and their good fortune. Characteristically, boundaries are blurred throughout the poem and we are left to guess at the poet's real feelings.   114

11 **'Rosie Joyce'**
Durcan has often used travel as a metaphor for reflection or soul-searching. In this upbeat poem celebrating the birth of his granddaughter, he remembers a car journey he took in May 2001 from Mayo to Dublin: 'Never before had I felt so fortunate'. Along the way, images of landscape and movement reveal his newfound sense of optimism.   120

12 **'The MacBride Dynasty'**
This poem relates the time Durcan's mother made a personal journey back to her hometown to introduce her young son, 'The latest addition' to the family dynasty, to her uncle's famous wife, Maud Gonne. Throughout the poem, underlying tensions in the prominent MacBride family are exposed.   128

13 **Three Short Poems: 'En Famille, 1979', 'Madman', 'Ireland 2002'**   133

1. NESSA

I met her on the first of August
In the Shangri-La Hotel,
She took me by the index finger
And dropped me in her well.
And that was a whirlpool, that was a whirlpool,   5
And I very nearly drowned.

Take off your pants, she said to me,
And I very nearly didn't;
Would you care to swim? she said to me,
And I hopped into the Irish Sea.   10
And that was a whirlpool, that was a whirlpool,
And I very nearly drowned.

On the way back I fell in the field
And she fell down beside me,
I'd have lain in the grass with her all my life   15
With Nessa:
She was a whirlpool, she was a whirlpool,
And I very nearly drowned.

O Nessa my dear, Nessa my dear,
Will you stay with me on the rocks?   20
Will you come for me into the Irish Sea
And for me let your red hair down?
And then we will ride into Dublin City
In a taxi-cab wrapped up in dust.
Oh you are a whirlpool, you are a whirlpool,   25
And I am very nearly drowned.

'And that was a whirlpool'

Glossary

2 *Shangri-La*: legendary location often used in a similar context to the Garden of Eden to represent a hidden paradise. The Shangri-La Hotel was located in Dalkey, Co. Dublin.

3 *index finger*: forefinger, pointer finger, trigger finger; often used to make a warning gesture.

5 *whirlpool*: swirling body of water produced by the meeting of opposing currents.

20 *on the rocks*: a phrase describing a drink served with ice cubes; also refers to a disaster at sea.

INITIAL RESPONSE

1. What impression of Nessa do you get from reading the poem? Refer to the text in your answer.

2. Comment on the effectiveness of the poet's use of the whirlpool image.

3. Write your own personal response to the poem, highlighting the impact it made on you.

STUDY NOTES

This well-known love poem comes from Paul Durcan's second collection, O Westport in the Light of Asia Minor *(1975). The poet has said that he first met Nessa O'Neill in the bar of the Shangri-La Hotel in Dalkey when he was at a wedding reception there in August 1967. Soon afterwards, the couple moved to London and married. 'Nessa' includes elements of the* aisling *(dream vision) poetry tradition, which dates from late 17th-century Gaelic literature, when Ireland was often represented by an enchanting female figure. Durcan's poem is centred around swimming, an extended metaphor conveying both the delights and dangers of falling in love.*

The poem's title and dramatic **opening lines** emphasise the significance of meeting Nessa 'on the first of August'. This date also marks the traditional Celtic harvest festival, a time for celebrations and arranging marriages. The Irish term *Lughnasa* even echoes Nessa's own name. From the outset, Durcan's first-person presentation associates the woman who was to be his soul mate with mythology. Their introduction 'In the Shangri-La Hotel' seems a suitably exotic setting, suggesting the close spiritual union the couple would share. However, **line 3** foreshadows the uncertainty of romance as the poet recalls being led 'by the index finger'. Durcan uses the poem's central **metaphor of swimming to express exhilaration and risk-taking**. The lovers' intimacy is evoked in the erotic image of the wishing well, 'a whirlpool' in which he 'very nearly drowned'. The repetition and insistent rhythm of **line 5** reflects the continuing fascination of this unforgettable turning point in the poet's life.

The tone is a mixture of colloquial intimacy and self-mocking incantation. From the outset, Durcan highlights Nessa's power to enchant. His **wry humour** is apparent in the self-deprecating comments about his initial nervousness: 'Take off your pants, she said to me,/And I very nearly didn't'. The breathless enthusiasm of their first encounter is evident in lively phrasing: 'I hopped into the Irish Sea' (**line 10**). The poet's signature use of refrain forces the reader to appreciate the personal upheaval caused by his relationship with Nessa.

Line 13 marks a noticeable change of mood. Durcan focuses on the aftermath ('the way back') of that first swim when Nessa 'fell down beside me'. The **enduring remorse of knowing and losing love** is clear in the regretful line 'I'd have lain in the grass with her all my life'. The contrasting brevity and precise lyrical simplicity of **line 16** ('With Nessa') is almost immediately undermined by the stark realisation of the whirlpool symbol as the poet faces the reality of love's impermanence. The poem's **richly textured final section** is particularly tender: 'O Nessa my dear, Nessa my dear' (**line 19**). Durcan delicately repeats his wife's name. Ironically, his plaintive desire for her to 'stay with me on the rocks' reveals a yearning for a marriage that was inevitably doomed. The poet's powerful vision of Nessa encompasses elements of both dreams and nightmares. Imagining her as an idealised heroic creature ('for me let your red hair down'), he wonders if she can still be with him in the sea. The heart-rending fantasy is abruptly replaced by a darker image of the couple journeying through Dublin 'In a taxi-cab wrapped up in dust' (**line 24**). An unmistakable sense of death – coupled with the acceptance of lost love – is tinged with the notion that their kindred spirits are united forever.

The hypnotic rhythm of the last two lines brings the poet's reflection of that special day when he met his beloved Nessa up to date. Using the present tense verb in the refrain, Durcan emphasises the ongoing and relentless hurt of the relationship breakdown: 'I am very nearly drowned'. Such **an honest expression of emotion and personal vulnerability** is characteristic of the poet. It has been said that the tragedy at the heart of Paul Durcan's writing is that he cannot accept tragedy. This is undoubtedly the case in 'Nessa', leaving readers with the lasting impression of a man who is still profoundly shocked by the enduring power of romantic love.

ANALYSIS

'What often defines Paul Durcan's poetry is an underlying sense of failure in personal relationships.' Do you agree with this view? Give reasons for your response, referring to Durcan's poem 'Nessa'.

Sample Paragraph

While Paul Durcan's poem, 'Nessa', is primarily a loving tribute to his ex-wife, it is also a warning that love doesn't always last. The suggestion of a relationship failing is suggested in the first stanza when Durcan describes their 'whirlpool' romance. This dramatic image indicates the wildness of their feelings and that they were taking a chance marrying. A whirlpool is exciting, but also precarious. Durcan uses the refrain at the end of each stanza to reinforce the idea of being unsuccessful in love. Looking back on their marriage, he seems to be really reprimanding himself for his own carelessness. As though he took love for granted when he 'hopped into the Irish Sea'. I think he blames the failure of the relationship on himself, as suggested by the phrase 'I fell'. Durcan's tone of longing – 'Will you stay with me on the rocks?' – is very well expressed in this tragic poetic metaphor. Nessa is pictured as a beautiful and mysterious woman whose 'red hair' mesmerised the poet. The end really brings out the tragic disappointment of the couple's separation as Durcan makes it clear that the distress still exists – 'you are a whirlpool'. His tone at the end is of anguish and disillusionment. The loss of true love of each other will remain with him forever.

Examiner's Comment

A focused personal response that addresses the question directly and traces the progress of thought in the poem. The critical discussion touches on several interesting aspects relating to the predominant sense of failure. Supportive quotes are integrated effectively into the answer. Impressive expression, overall, ensures that this is a top grade response.

CLASS/HOMEWORK EXERCISES

1. 'Durcan's inventive poetry is filled with dramatic tension.' Discuss this statement in relation to 'Nessa'.

2. Paul Durcan's personal relationships have often been described as power struggles. Discuss this view with particular reference to the poem 'Nessa'.

SUMMARY POINTS

- Personal exploration of the intense experience of romantic love.
- Effective use of extended swimming/whirlpool metaphor.
- Dramatic atmosphere; varying tones – nostalgic, regretful.
- Hypnotic rhythm; emphatic refrain, memorable visual/cinematic effects.

THE GIRL WITH THE KEYS TO PEARSE'S COTTAGE

to John and Judith Meagher

When I was sixteen I met a dark girl;
Her dark hair was darker because her smile was so bright;
She was the girl with the keys to Pearse's Cottage;
And her name was Cáit Killann.

The cottage was built into the side of a hill;   5
I recall two windows and cosmic peace
Of bare brown rooms and on whitewashed walls
Photographs of the passionate and pale Pearse.

I recall wet thatch and peeling jambs
And how all was best seen from below in the field;   10
I used sit in the rushes with ledger-book and pencil
Compiling poems of passion for Cáit Killann.

Often she used linger on the sill of a window;
Hands by her side and brown legs akimbo;
In sun-red skirt and moon-black blazer;   15
Looking toward our strange world wide-eyed.

Our world was strange because it had no future;
She was America-bound at summer's end.
She had no choice but to leave her home –
The girl with the keys to Pearse's Cottage.   20

O Cáit Killann, O Cáit Killann,
You have gone with your keys from your own native place.
Yet here in this dark – El Greco eyes blaze back
From your Connemara postman's daughter's proudly mortal face.

'El Greco eyes blaze back'

Glossary

3 **Pearse's Cottage**: Pádraic Pearse, Irish teacher and political activist who was one of the leaders of the 1916 Easter Rising, owned a small cottage in Rosmuc, Connemara. Pearse believed that the key to national identity and independence was knowledge of the language.
6 **cosmic**: endless, universal.
9 **jambs**: wooden doorframes.
11 **rushes**: marsh plants.
11 **ledger-book**: book used to keep records.
14 **akimbo**: standing confidently.
23 **El Greco**: Spanish Renaissance painter famous for his fantastical portraits.

INITIAL RESPONSE

1. Why, in your opinion, is it important that the poem's setting is a cottage that belonged to Pádraic Pearse? Use reference from the text to support your views.

2. Describe the atmosphere of country life that the poet creates in lines 5–10.

3. Select one image from the poem that you find particularly interesting. Briefly explain your choice.

STUDY NOTES

'The Girl with the Keys to Pearse's Cottage' was published in Paul Durcan's first poetry collection, O Westport in the Light of Asia Minor, *in 1975. Themes of identity, belonging and the instability of place are frequently addressed in Durcan's work. The concept of home is a recurring concern. In this case, the poet narrates a poem of love and loss which includes some elements of the traditional Irish ballad. The poetic voice incorporates both the experiences of the poet's 16-year-old self and his mature adult attitude to the painful legacy of emigration.*

The poem's **opening lines** immediately bring the reader back to a bittersweet moment in Durcan's life: 'When I was sixteen I met a dark girl'. **The strong visual awareness and effective use of repetition** ('dark', 'dark hair', 'darker') suggest the native Irish colouring of the young girl. Her dazzling smile is captured in the long line that culminates with the monosyllabic adjective 'bright', perhaps mirroring sudden sunshine bursting from the clouds over Western Ireland. We learn that the young woman held the 'keys to Pearse's Cottage'. Had she the means to unlock the secret of his house as well as enabling visitors to enter there? Reverently, the narrator reveals the identity of his lost love: 'And her name was Cáit Killann'.

The **second stanza** describes Pearse's cottage in remarkable detail: 'built into the side of a hill'. Durcan draws the reader into a romanticised place of 'cosmic peace'. He makes effective use of alliteration to emphasise the **simplicity and lack of ostentation** of the two-bedroomed house, with its 'bare brown rooms' and 'whitewashed walls'. In stark contrast to this are the photographs of the fiery nationalist politician himself, 'the passionate and pale Pearse'.

Stanza three delves further into the poet's memory ('I recall wet thatch and peeling jambs') as the ordinary scene opens up its secrets under the poet's observant gaze. This is a place that is past its best days, tired and weary. Is this how the people of the countryside regarded their environment? The **personal autobiographical detail** is conveyed in the picture of the young poet who sits 'in the rushes with ledger-book and pencil'. Instead of creating accounts, he compiles 'poems of passion' for the girl he loves. Again, alliteration suggests the copious number of poems the infatuated young poet wrote. The naive awkwardness of expressing his feelings in a book dedicated to dry statistics reflects the engaging sincerity of youth.

In **stanza four**, Durcan lyrically recalls Cáit Killann's languid grace: 'she used linger on the sill of a window'. The slender vowel 'i' delineates her confident sensuous movements. Suddenly, the pen portrait erupts into colour – 'brown legs', 'sun-red skirt', 'moon-black blazer'. These compound words indicate both her extraordinary effect on the poet and also **her effortless harmony with the native environment**. The beautiful Cáit belongs here. She gazes 'wide-eyed' and innocent 'toward our strange world'. Readers are left to wonder what she is about to discover.

The adult poet's answer in the **penultimate stanza** is that 'Our world was strange because it had no future'. His tone is suddenly bitter in response to the bleak realisation that emigration engulfs this crumbling place. 'She was America-bound at summer's end', almost as if she were a migratory bird. The stark political reality becomes a personal experience: 'She had no choice but to leave her home'. **Durcan has always addressed public issues** and he leaves us in no doubt of his own deep awareness that Irish life is lived in transit. Our young migrants become the diaspora scattered around the globe.

The **final stanza** is defined by a grief-stricken poetic voice lamenting the departure of someone who is loved. The poet repeats Cáit's name tenderly. **Plaintive assonant sounds** echo the traditional mourning or keening that was once found in the West of Ireland: 'O Cáit Killann, O Cáit Killann'. Now that she has left her 'own native place', it is as though a young plant was roughly torn from the Irish soil and transplanted elsewhere to bloom. The poet clearly regards Ireland as a 'dark' country, yet the memory of Cáit's vivid 'El Greco eyes' remains and illuminates. In celebrating the alluring looks of the 'postman's daughter', Durcan has coloured the ordinariness of Connemara with the exotic fascination of international artistic beauty. El Greco, the Spanish painter, dared to view the world his way, sometimes representing it through exquisite portraits of intriguing women with shining eyes.

For Durcan, Cáit Killann also carried her own extraordinary light. The intensity of her gaze is conveyed in the explosive alliterative phrase 'blaze back' from her 'proudly mortal face'. Just like the poet, we mourn her loss. Through his use of metaphor, Durcan has transformed this native Irish girl into a striking icon. In addition, he has brought the reader to a different vantage point from which to view **the tragedy of emigration,** which is such an intrinsically Irish experience. Is this realistic viewpoint similar to the perspective from which Pearse's cottage might be perceived: 'all was best seen from below in the field'? Does something have to be viewed from a distance in order to understand it? Have we been brought to a moment of epiphany as we contemplate the sombre reality of exile? At any rate, Cáit Killann remains a powerfully sad and realistic symbol of Irish emigration, an ironic reminder of what has become of Pearse's idealistic dreams.

ANALYSIS

'In the poetry of Paul Durcan, reality is frequently shaped by the imagination.' Discuss this statement in relation to the poem, 'The Girl with the Keys to Pearse's Cottage'. Support your views with close reference to the text.

Sample Paragraph

Durcan's keen observation of mundane detail, 'wet thatch', 'peeling jambs', 'bare brown rooms', 'whitewashed walls', etc., all root the poem firmly in the reality of rain-soaked Connemara. All is calm, 'cosmic peace', on the surface. Yet bubbling beneath this seeming ordinariness, strong feelings flow, portrayed vividly in the photographs of the 'passionate and pale Pearse' who once inhabited this place. The longing of a sixteen-year-old boy for the beautiful 'postman's daughter' can be sensed as he sat 'in the rushes' while 'Compiling poems of passion' for her. The girl of the 'sun-red skirt' and 'moon-black blazer' is brought into another world through Durcan's inspired reference to her 'El Greco eyes'. The ordinary is opened up by his inventive metaphor. The Spanish painter, El Greco, saw things in a unique way – exactly like Cáit, 'Looking toward our strange world wide-eyed'. She seems surprised or perplexed at what she sees, perhaps because she is being forced to leave her native land, 'America-bound at summer's end'. Despite the sacrifice of the 1916 Rising, of which Pearse was a leader, this country is still unable to support its own people. But is the girl truly gone? Does her spirit still remain 'in this dark' as her eyes 'blaze back'? From my reading of the poem, I believe that she exists only in the poet's memory. Suddenly the reality of this little place in the West of Ireland has been formed by the imagination of the poet to represent the tragedy of emigration.

Examiner's Comment

A good personal response which engages well with the poem. Carefully considered terms, such as 'inventive' and 'inspired', indicate a sustained focus on addressing the question directly. Overall, the expression is very well managed, particularly the first sentence. Accurate quotations are effectively integrated into the critical discussion. A highly successful top grade response.

CLASS/HOMEWORK EXERCISES

1. 'Paul Durcan's poetry is often concerned with the world of the Irish countryside that has now disappeared.' Discuss this statement in relation to 'The Girl with the Keys to Pearse's Cottage'. Support the points you make with reference to the text.

2. Durcan's poems address both personal and public themes. To what extent is this true of 'The Girl with the Keys to Pearse's Cottage'? Support your answer with reference to the text.

SUMMARY POINTS

- Prominent themes include idealism, national identity, home, exile, love and loss.
- Evocative images of Irish rural life and female beauty.
- Variety of tones – nostalgic, angry, sad.
- Effective use of autobiographical detail, symbolism, irony, repetition.

THE DIFFICULTY THAT IS MARRIAGE

We disagree to disagree, we divide, we differ;
Yet each night as I lie in bed beside you
And you are faraway curled up in sleep
I array the moonlit ceiling with a mosaic of question marks;
How was it I was so lucky to have ever met you? 5
I am no brave pagan proud of my mortality
Yet gladly on this changeling earth I should live for ever
If it were with you, my sleeping friend.
I have my troubles and I shall always have them
But I should rather live with you for ever 10
Than exchange my troubles for a changeless kingdom.
But I do not put you on a pedestal or throne;
You must have your faults but I do not see them.
If it were with you, I should live for ever.

'a mosaic of question marks'

Glossary

Difficulty: challenge, complication, problem.
Marriage: formal union of a couple; a close blend or mixture of two things.
4   *array*: adorn, arrange in an impressive way.
4   *mosaic*: pattern, montage.
6   *pagan*: unbeliever, atheist.
6   *mortality*: humanity, transience, death.
7   *changeling*: transient, secretly exchanged.
9   *troubles*: afflictions, difficulties.
11 *exchange*: swap, substitute.
12 *pedestal*: raised platform, exalted position.
13 *faults*: failings, weaknesses.

INITIAL RESPONSE

1. Why, in your opinion, would Paul Durcan regard marriage as a difficulty? Refer to the poem to support your response.

2. Choose one image from the poem that you thought was particularly effective and explain your choice.

3. Would you consider the poet to be realistic or romantic in his view of marriage? Refer to the text in your answer.

STUDY NOTES

Paul Durcan published 'The Difficulty that is Marriage' in his collection Teresa's Bar *(1976). In considering his relationship with his wife, the poet's lyrical voice clearly reflects his intense personal romanticism. He observes and explores a small everyday event, a married couple sharing a bed together, but who are estranged from each other. Reflecting on his upbringing, Durcan once said, 'We were educated to believe that women were, on the one hand, untouchable and pure and on the other hand, that they were the source of all evil … women represent and embody freedom … living in much closer harmony with their true selves.' The title of this very personal poem suggests that while true love is not immune from problems, it will endure despite such obstacles.*

The **opening line** of this dramatic monologue is broken into abrupt staccato sections by its frequent punctuation marks and the deadening alliterative letter 'd': 'We disagree to disagree, we divide, we differ'. Durcan cleverly pinpoints the destructive conflict in a marriage as two separate individuals try to live as part of a couple. In this case, they cannot even agree that they can disagree. Instead, they are distinct, they deviate, they argue. After this turmoil of daily married life, three run-on lines smoothly convey, in unforced conversational tones, the stillness of the marriage bed: 'each night as I lie in bed beside you'. But while the couple are physically present in the one space, mentally and emotionally they are worlds apart. She is 'faraway curled up in sleep', content and at peace with herself. In contrast, the poet is lying awake, thinking, wondering, questioning. **Durcan's strong visual sensibility is evident** in the descriptive 'I array the moonlit ceiling with a mosaic of question marks'. The image has the immediacy of a snapshot coupled with surrealism as the reader views the ceiling bathed in the romantic moonlight patterned with the question marks of uncertainties: 'How was it I was so lucky to have ever met you?' Is the relationship broken into countless pieces by constant soul-searching and argument? Is the poet trying to reassemble the fragments into an ideal shape? The world with which he is so familiar seems to be undermined by such secret moments of human doubt and disbelief.

Durcan has always portrayed himself as an admirer of women, and on numerous occasions has cast his wife, Nessa, in her heroic role as someone to be admired, the one person who provides stability in his insecure life. In **line 6**, he expresses the male pain of never doing well enough, criticising his own character: 'I am no brave pagan proud of my mortality'. He is not an audacious savage delighted with his transient humanity. The self-deprecating tone changes to one of deep romanticism in his declaration that he would live forever 'on this changeling earth' if he could be 'with you, my sleeping friend'. There is a strong underlying sense that the poet feels uncomfortable in this world. In Irish folklore, a changeling refers to a child who has been secretly exchanged by the fairies for the parents' real child.

Line 9 reveals the dark side of Durcan's personality, 'I have my troubles', which is a common Irish euphemism for serious problems. Durcan has spoken of being committed by his family, against his will, to a range of psychiatric treatments, including electric convulsive therapy. He subsequently suffered from depression and has admitted, 'I think I came out of it with a kind of melancholia.' **Is the poet casting himself here in the role of sacrificial victim?** His father, with whom he had a difficult relationship, predicted that he would never be free of misfortune: 'Nemesis will follow you all the days of your life.' Is this why Durcan sees this earth as a 'changeling' place? Three words resonate: 'changeling', 'exchange' and 'changeless'. Is he willing to swap his longing for peace if he can always be with his beloved? 'But I should rather live with you for ever/Than exchange my troubles for a changeless kingdom'.

Paradoxically, while the poet denies that he exaggerates his feelings for his wife by exalting her 'on a pedestal or throne' (**line 12**) as if she were a saint or queen, at the same time he appears to worship her. He declares that 'You must have your faults', yet disarmingly admits, 'but I do not see them'. This short, introspective poem concludes with a statement of heightened romanticism: 'If it were with you, I should live for ever'. The **reverential tone** suggests a strong sense of the spiritual fulfilment he receives from their relationship. Yet although this poem shows such high regard for his wife, Durcan remains the leading man throughout, demanding to be noticed despite all his charming self-criticism. Alternatively, it is possible to read the poem more generously in the light of another of the poet's statements: 'Heaven is other people: a house where there are no women and children is a very empty house.'

ANALYSIS

'Paul Durcan has the gift of being able to make something out of nothing.' Discuss this statement with reference to his poem 'The Difficulty that is Marriage'. Support the points you make with reference to the text.

Sample Paragraph

'The Difficulty that is Marriage' explores the deep gulf between couples and the challenges they face. This is a universal theme that very many people can relate to. The obstacles to a successful relationship are vividly conveyed in the alliterative, broken opening line, 'We disagree to disagree, we divide, we differ'. The couple engage in aggressive, complicated wordplay as they attempt to score points off each other. The woman's ability to be content with herself is evident in the simple phrase, 'faraway curled up in sleep'. In contrast, the man's anxiety is revealed in the cleverly constructed imaginative line, 'I array the moonlit ceiling with a mosaic of question marks'. Ironically, this married couple appear close, but really inhabit different universes. Durcan addresses a crucial issue, the reality of complicated human relationships. Using the direct language of genuine emotion, the husband longs to be 'with you for ever'. We are left wondering if, instead of outlining differences, did the poet convey these feelings to his partner? Or can he only address her like this because she is his 'sleeping friend'? I wonder did he ever tell her 'How was it I was so lucky to have ever met you'? Or did he just paint patterns on the ceiling? Perhaps this is the real difficulty of marriage, no one really knows for certain what the other is thinking or feeling. Durcan skilfully presents an ordinary occurrence, a married couple at night, one awake, one asleep, and creates a very important something out of a very mundane nothing.

Examiner's Comment

This is a competent response to a challenging question. There is a good personal approach throughout which shows engagement with the poem: 'We are left wondering if, instead of outlining differences, did the poet convey these feelings to his partner?' Among several interesting points is the focus on the complexity of relationships: 'no-one really knows for certain what the other is thinking or feeling'. Effective use is made of accurate quotation. Expression is also clear and well controlled. A highly successful answer.

CLASS/HOMEWORK EXERCISES

1. 'Poetry has to be fundamentally cinematic, painterly and musical.' Discuss this view in relation to Durcan's poem 'The Difficulty that is Marriage'. Refer closely to the text in your answer.

2. In your opinion, what does Paul Durcan's poem reveal about his married relationship? Support the points you make with close reference to the text.

SUMMARY POINTS

- Explores the trials and triumphs of married relationships.
- Characteristically candid and emotional poetic voice.
- Tones vary – detached, personal, reflective, sardonic, reverential, loving.
- Dramatic monologue, contrast, exaggerated visual images.

4   WIFE WHO SMASHED TELEVISION GETS JAIL

'She came home, my Lord, and smashed in the television;
Me and the kids were peaceably watching *Kojak*
When she marched into the living room and declared
That if I didn't turn off the television immediately
She'd put her boot through the screen;   5
I didn't turn it off, so instead she turned it off –
I remember the moment exactly because Kojak
After shooting a dame with the same name as my wife
Snarled at the corpse – Goodnight, Queen Maeve –
And then she took off her boots and smashed in the television;   10
I had to bring the kids round to my mother's place;
We got there just before the finish of *Kojak*;
(My mother has a fondness for *Kojak*, my Lord);
When I returned home my wife had deposited
What was left of the television into the dustbin,   15
Saying – I didn't get married to a television
And I don't see why my kids or anybody else's kids
Should have a television for a father or mother,
We'd be much better off all down in the pub talking
Or playing bar-billiards –   20
Whereupon she disappeared off back down again to the pub.'
Justice O'Brádaigh said wives who preferred bar-billiards to family television
Were a threat to the family which was the basic unit of society
As indeed the television itself could be said to be a basic unit of the family
And when as in this case wives expressed their preference in forms of
    violence   25
Jail was the only place for them. Leave to appeal was refused.

'peaceably watching *Kojak*'

Paul Durcan 75

Glossary

1 *my Lord*: official form of address to a judge in court.
2 *Kojak*: American TV crime drama starring Telly Savalas. The series was popular in Ireland during the mid-1970s.
9 *Queen Maeve*: legendary Irish queen with a colourful reputation.
20 *bar-billiards*: group table game in which short cues are used.
26 *appeal*: review to challenge a court sentence.

INITIAL RESPONSE

1. In your opinion, what is the main point or message of this poem? Refer to the text in your response.

2. Comment on Durcan's use of irony throughout the poem, supporting the points you make with reference to the text.

3. Write a paragraph outlining your own feelings in response to this poem. Refer to the text in your answer.

STUDY NOTES

In his hard-hitting critiques of Irish society, one of Paul Durcan's signatures is the poem written as pseudo-reportage, where an unlikely event is depicted in a seemingly journalistic style. Humour has always been an essential component of the distinctive Durcan style. This poem is divided into two sections: the first 21 lines in the voice of the husband and the final five-line report of the judge's opinion and verdict. The poet's father was a circuit court judge.

The news headline title and matter-of-fact simplicity of the **opening lines** increase their dramatic impact. There is an instantaneous quality to the initial evidence presented by the aggrieved husband who acts as a witness in the matter of his wife's prosecution, protesting that at the moment the act of violence occurred, 'Me and the kids were peaceably watching *Kojak*'. Unable to see the irony of viewing a violent TV drama, the man is immediately **ridiculed and mocked** by Durcan. His assertive wife is identified as 'Queen Maeve' solely because the husband describes Kojak as 'shooting a dame with the same name' (**line 8**). This instantly associates her with one of the great legendary symbols of female power – a queen of Connaught in the Ulster Cycle of Irish myths. However, in the real patriarchal world of Durcan's Ireland, the modern Maeve is merely seen as a deranged troublemaker.

The husband proceeds to condemn himself further by boasting that instead of taking his wife seriously, he has still not come to terms with the interruption to one of his favourite TV programmes.

It is unsurprising to learn that he rushes off to seek comfort from his mother, who shares his 'fondness for *Kojak*' (**line 13**). However, aggressive as his wife's actions may be, it soon becomes clear that it is **her words and attitudes that serve to justify her condemnation**. As the story unfolds, Durcan slips effortlessly from the real to the surreal, often to inspired comic effect. When the distressed husband returns home, he discovers that his wife has dumped 'What was left of the television into the dustbin' (**line 15**).

In direct opposition to her uncommunicative husband and children, she boldly states: 'I don't see why my kids or anybody else's kids/Should have a television for a father or mother' (**lines 17–18**). **Durcan's bizarre humour is laced with unsmiling undertones**. For him, TV violence and escapism compete with the less glamorous facts of real life. As a result, any interference with the illusions that television creates can now be treated as serious crimes. The reader's sympathy for the eponymous wife is further generated by exposing the dramatic delusions of the male judge.

In the poem's **final lines**, the satire becomes much more intense. Durcan undermines the astounding moral certainty in the arrogant speech delivered by 'Justice O'Brádaigh', who declares that 'the television itself could be said to be a basic unit of the family' (**line 24**). The unashamed verdict promotes the idea that **virtual violence has a rightful place at the heart of family life**, a reason for the judge to state that 'Jail was the only place' for transgressors such as Maeve, who will not be allowed to challenge her sentence since 'Leave to appeal was refused'. The snarling tone of such a dismissive ruling is in keeping with Justice O'Brádaigh's prevailing mindset of disdainful self-delusion.

What sustains the tragicomic structure of this poem is Durcan's skilful depiction of the contrasting characters who are party to the scene: the precious husband, his frustrated wife and the condescending judge. Significantly, the wife herself is never directly heard. **Durcan is uncompromising in exposing negative attitudes towards voiceless women** – especially women who dare to resist the bounds of rigid expectations. His disapproval of the conventional pieties of Ireland's conspiratorial, male-dominated society is characteristic of his poetry. However, a close reading of 'Wife Who Smashed Television Gets Jail' reveals that it is not the medium of television, but its abuse, that Durcan calls into question. As usual, in addressing such cultural issues, the poet entertains and gives pause for thought.

ANALYSIS

'Paul Durcan's deep sense of outrage is often evident in his poetry.' Discuss this view in relation to 'Wife Who Smashed Television Gets Jail', using references from the poem to support your answer.

Sample Paragraph

Paul Durcan has a reputation for producing what appear to be light-hearted poems, but his anger is never far from the surface. This is true of 'Wife Who Smashed Television Gets Jail' where he confronts society's ignorance and hypocrisy. The idea of a wife being taken to court by a man who gives more attention to his TV seems ridiculous, but the real point is that women have very little power. I could easily imagine Durcan's anger at the man's superior tone – 'Me and the kids were peaceably watching *Kojak*'. Even his comment about the detective 'shooting a dame' is a reminder that it's a man's world, both on TV and in real life. Underneath the absurd courthouse scene, Durcan barely conceals his rage that men – the husband, the TV hero and the influential judge – all represent a macho world. I thought the last line – 'Leave to appeal was refused' – summed up the poet's appreciation of how women in Irish society are marginalised. Durcan also makes effective use of the mock newspaper style. The serious courtroom atmosphere almost convinced me to take what was happening seriously. The poet seems to be saying that it is nearly impossible not to be part of the patriarchal culture that prevents many women from expressing the view that emotions and communication are more important than escapist TV violence. The outrage was present throughout the poem especially during the comic scenes.

Examiner's Comment

This is a clearly focused personal response showing good engagement with the poem. The focus on the dominance of male characters provided worthwhile support. Valuable use was also made of suitable references – particularly the *Kojak* quotation which was very effective. Expression was well controlled throughout. In-depth analysis secures a top grade.

CLASS/HOMEWORK EXERCISES

1. 'Humour and surrealism are Durcan's most powerful satirical weapons.' Discuss this statement with reference to the poem 'Wife Who Smashed Television Gets Jail'.

2. Durcan has been described as a 'feminist writer'. Based on your reading of this poem, do you agree or disagree with this view? Support your answer with reference to the text.

SUMMARY POINTS

- Durcan criticises aspects of Irish patriarchal society.
- Effective use of irony, surreal humour.
- Satirical exaggeration, comic journalistic writing style.
- Varying tones – ridicule, sympathy, outrage.

5 PARENTS

A child's face is a drowned face:
Her parents stare down at her asleep
Estranged from her by a sea:
She is under the sea
And they are above the sea: 5
If she looked up she would see them
As if locked out of their own home,
Their mouths open,
Their foreheads furrowed –
Pursed-up orifices of fearful fish –   10
Their big ears are fins behind glass
And in her sleep she is calling out to them
    Father, Father
    Mother, Mother
But they cannot hear her: 15
She is inside the sea
And they are outside the sea.
Through the night, stranded, they stare
At the drowned, drowned face of their child.

'And in her sleep she is calling out to them'

Glossary

3 *Estranged*: separated.
9 *furrowed*: wrinkled.
10 *Pursed-up orifices*: open-shaped mouths.
18 *stranded*: abandoned.

INITIAL RESPONSE

1. Write a paragraph giving your own immediate reaction to reading 'Parents'. Refer to the poem in your answer.

2. Select one image from the poem that you find particularly unsettling and briefly explain your choice.

3. Using reference to the text, comment on the poem's dramatic features.

STUDY NOTES

'Parents' was published in Paul Durcan's 1978 collection, Sam's Cross. *The poem raises interesting questions about parent–child communication, a recurring theme in Durcan's work. Characteristically, some of the poet's perceptions have a disturbing quality which convey shock as well as intensity.*

The poem's opening metaphor – 'A child's face is a drowned face' – has a startling effect. The devastating image represents every parent's greatest fear and introduces an **overwhelmingly anxious mood** that will dominate the entire poem. Durcan develops the sea metaphor in **lines 2–3**, creating a desperate scene of helplessness, as the parents can only stare down at their precious child, 'Estranged from her by a sea'. The lack of intimate communication – symbolised by the impenetrable ocean – is a central theme. There is something unsettling about the parents' realisation that they are already detached from their newborn child and that they can never know her as much as they would wish.

Lines 4–5 reflect their sense of shock at the unfathomable gulf that exists between them and the child: 'She is under the sea/And they are above the sea'. The separate lines and contrasting prepositions emphasise the obstacle. Repetition and a deliberate rhythm further underline Durcan's sombre tone. For the first time in the poem, the child's perspective is presented when she imagines her parents being 'locked out of their own home' (**line 7**). Just as she is no longer within the security of the womb, they are also leading independent lives. Her growing understanding of the world is described in a series of increasingly distorted images. The 'furrowed' looks on her parents' foreheads are unnerving. The **surreal underwater sequence** becomes even more grotesque when Durcan compares the concerned adult expressions to 'Pursed-up orifices of fearful fish'. To the confused and frightened infant, the parents' ears are 'fins behind glass'.

Through **lines 12–14**, the developing drama of the parent–child exchange becomes all the more poignant. Durcan's dark vision of the child's distressed cry for attention ('Father, Father/Mother, Mother') transcends the moment and highlights the trauma of unfulfilled relationships between parents and children, lasting perhaps throughout entire lifetimes. For the poet, however, there is no denying the harsh fact of disconnection revealed in **line 15**: 'But they cannot hear her'. An overpowering mood of desolation dominates the poem. The subdued tone and ironic alliteration echo **Durcan's sad acceptance that there will always be barriers between parents and children.** Throughout his writing career, the poet has explored his own troubled relationships, particularly with his father, who was a stern and distant figure.

There is a restrained **sense of resignation** in **lines 16–19**. Durcan repeats the stark truth about separation between individuals, contrasting the child 'inside the sea' with her parents, who are 'outside'. The final elegiac mood is achieved by the exaggerated illustration of the ever-watchful parents, who are left 'stranded', faced with the challenge of coming to terms with the 'drowned, drowned face of their child'. The repetition of 'drowned' in the long final line leaves readers thinking of the many questions raised in this short poem. As always, Durcan has addressed important issues, not just about how individual human beings interact, but about the mystery of life itself.

ANALYSIS

'Paul Durcan writes well about detachment and isolation.' Discuss this view, with particular reference to 'Parents'. Refer closely to the text in your response.

Sample Paragraph

Durcan addresses interesting aspects of human experience in his poetry, and this is certainly the case in 'Parents'. The poem focuses on one set of unnamed parents and their young child, but takes a very negative view of the relationship. From the start, the parents are disconnected from their baby daughter, imagining that her sleeping face is 'a drowned face'. Their imagined fear of her death immediately suggests that her life is outside of their control. Durcan uses shocking sea images all through the poem to show the lack of close contact with the child who appears to be 'under the sea'. This gap exists between them and they can never know her completely. Their panic is conveyed very effectively in nightmarish terms. The child sees them as alien, almost intimidating, like 'fearful fish'. She calls to them but 'they cannot hear her'. I felt this was a really heartbreaking moment, especially as the poet repeated her frantic words, 'Father, Father/Mother, Mother'. The separation they feel in never fully communicating is seen at the end of the poem where the parents are 'stranded' – another sea image – 'Through the night'. This tragic insight into the distances between people is reinforced in the last line by the repetition of 'drowned' – a final reminder of detachment and alienation.

Examiner's Comment

A successful response which tackles the question directly. Suitable references and quotations sustain the focused discussion of Durcan's treatment of isolation. There is some good personal engagement, particularly in the final sentence. The answer traces the development of thought in the poem very effectively, using the poet's succession of shocking images. Expression is varied and assured throughout, guaranteeing a top grade.

CLASS/HOMEWORK EXERCISES

1. 'Durcan's most compelling poems often raise significant questions about the complexity of human relationships.' To what extent is this true of 'Parents'? Support your answer with reference to the poem.

2. Durcan's poetic voice has been noted for its insistent, hypnotic rhythms. To what extent is this the case in 'Parents'? Support your answer with close reference to the text.

SUMMARY POINTS

- Durcan raises penetrating questions about parent-child relationships.
- Contrasting moods/tones – anxious, serious, intense, poignant, resigned.
- Striking and sustained visual imagery of the sea – distorted, unnerving.
- Effective use of powerful language and free rhythm.

6 'WINDFALL', 8 PARNELL HILL, CORK

But, then, at the end of day I could always say –
Well, now, I am going home.
I felt elected, steeped, sovereign to be able to say –
I am going home.
When I was at home I liked to stay at home;   5
At home I stayed at home for weeks;
At home I used sit in a winged chair by the window
Overlooking the river and the factory chimneys,
The electricity power station and the car assembly works,
The fleets of trawlers and the pilot tugs,   10
Dreaming that life is a dream which is real,
The river a reflection of itself in its own waters,
Goya sketching Goya among the smoky mirrors.
The industrial vista was my Mont Sainte-Victoire.
While my children sat on my knees watching TV   15
Their mother, my wife, reclined on the couch
Knitting a bright-coloured scarf, drinking a cup of black coffee,
Smoking a cigarette – one of her own roll-ups.
I closed my eyes and breathed in and breathed out.

It is ecstasy to breathe if you are at home in the world.   20
What a windfall! A home of our own!
Our neighbours' houses had names like 'Con Amore',
'Sans Souci', 'Pacelli', 'Montini', 'Homesville'.
But we called our home 'Windfall'.
'Windfall', 8 Parnell Hill, Cork.   25
In the gut of my head coursed the leaf of tranquillity
Which I dreamed was known only to Buddhist Monks
In lotus monasteries high up in the Hindu Kush.
Down here in the dark depths of Ireland,
Below sea level in the city of Cork,   30
In a city as intimate and homicidal as a Little Marseilles,
In a country where all the children of the nation
Are not cherished equally
And where the best go homeless, while the worst
Erect block-house palaces – self-regardingly ugly –   35
Having a home of your own can give to a family
A chance in a lifetime to transcend death.

At the high window, shipping from all over the world
Being borne up and down the busy, yet contemplative, river;
Skylines drifting in and out of skylines in the cloudy valley;
Firelight at dusk, and city lights;
Beyond them the control tower of the airport on the hill –
A lighthouse in the sky flashing green to white to green;
Our black-and-white cat snoozing in the corner of a chair;
Pastels and etchings on the four walls, and over the mantelpiece
'Van Gogh's Grave' and 'Lovers in Water';
A room wallpapered in books and family photograph albums
Chronicling the adventures and metamorphoses of family life:
In swaddling clothes in Mammy's arms on baptism day;
Being a baby of nine months and not remembering it;
Face-down in a pram, incarcerated in a high chair;
Everybody, including strangers, wearing shop-window smiles;
With Granny in Felixstowe, with Granny in Ballymaloe;
In a group photo in First Infants, on a bike at thirteen;
In the back garden in London, in the back garden in Cork;
Performing a headstand after First Holy Communion;
Getting a kiss from the Bishop on Confirmation Day;
Straw hats in the Bois de Boulougne, wearing wings at the seaside;

Mammy and Daddy holding hands on the Normandy Beaches;
Mammy and Daddy at the wedding of Jeremiah and Margot;
Mammy and Daddy queuing up for *Last Tango in Paris*;
Boating on the Shannon, climbing mountains in Kerry;
Building sandcastles in Killala, camping in Barley Cove;
Picnicking in Moone, hide-and-go-seek in Clonmacnoise;
Riding horses, cantering, jumping fences;
Pushing out toy yachts in the pond in the Tuileries;
The Irish College revisited in the Rue des Irlandais;
Sipping an *orange pressé* through a straw on the roof of the Beaubourg;
Dancing in Père Lachaise, weeping at Auvers.
Year in, year out, I pored over these albums accumulating,
My children looking over my shoulder, exhilarated as I was,
Their mother presiding at our ritual from a distance –
The far side of the hearthrug, diffidently, proudly.
Schoolbooks on the floor and pyjamas on the couch –
Whose turn is it tonight to put the children to bed?

Our children swam about our home
As if it was their private sea,
Their own unique, symbiotic fluid
Of which their parents also partook.
Such is home – a sea of your own –   80
In which you hang upside down from the ceiling
With equanimity, while postcards from Thailand on the mantelpiece
Are raising their eyebrow markings benignly:
Your hands dangling their prayers to the floorboards of your home,
Sifting the sands underneath the surfaces of conversations,   85
The marine insect life of the family psyche.
A home of your own – or a sea of your own –
In which climbing the walls is as natural
As making love on the stairs;
In which when the telephone rings   90
Husband and wife are metamorphosed into smiling accomplices,
Both declining to answer it;
Initiating, instead, a yet more subversive kiss –
A kiss they have perhaps never attempted before –
And might never have dreamed of attempting   95
Were it not for the telephone belling.
Through the bannisters or along the bannister rails
The pyjama-clad children solemnly watching
Their parents at play, jumping up and down in support,
Race back to bed, gesticulating wordlessly: 100
The most subversive unit in society is the human family.

We're almost home, pet, almost home...
Our home is at...
I'll be home...
I have to go home now...   105
I want to go home now...
Are you feeling homesick?
Are you anxious to get home?...
I can't wait to get home...
Let's stay at home tonight and...   110
What time will you be coming home at?...
If I'm not home by six at the latest, I'll phone...
We're nearly home, don't worry, we're nearly home...

But then with good reason
I was put out of my home: 115
By a keen wind felled.
I find myself now without a home
Having to live homeless in the alien, foreign city of Dublin.
It is an eerie enough feeling to be homesick
Yet knowing you will be going home next week; 120
It is an eerie feeling beyond all ornithological analysis
To be homesick knowing that there is no home to go home to:
Day by day, creeping, crawling,
Moonlighting, escaping,
Bed-and-breakfast to bed-and-breakfast; 125
Hostels, centres, one-night hotels.

Homeless in Dublin,
Blown about the suburban streets at evening,
Peering in the windows of other people's homes,
Wondering what it must feel like 130
To be sitting around a fire –
Apache or Cherokee or Bourgeoisie –
Beholding the firelit faces of your family,
Beholding their starry or their TV gaze:
Windfall to Windfall – can you hear me? 135
Windfall to Windfall...
We're almost home, pet, don't worry anymore, we're almost home.

'Lovers in Water'

Glossary

Windfall: something good received unexpectedly; something the wind has blown down.

3 *elected, steeped, sovereign*: slang terms for being very lucky.

7 *winged*: high-backed chair; capable of flight.

11 *life is a dream*: play by the Spanish playwright Calderon, which deals with the problems of distinguishing between illusion and reality.

13 *Goya*: Spanish romantic painter whose works contain a subversive imaginative element.

13 *smoky mirrors*: a reference to a painting by Goya of a Spanish king with his family containing an image of Goya himself in a dark mirror looking out at the viewer. The message is one of underlying corruption and decay.

14 *Mont Sainte-Victoire*: beautiful French mountain often painted by Paul Cézanne.

27 *Buddhist Monks*: monks who live a simple meditative life. They believe that married couples should respect each other's beliefs and privacy.

28 *lotus*: sacred. The lotus refers to an exotic water lily and to a fruit that causes dreamy forgetfulness.

28 *Hindu Kush*: mountain range stretching from Afghanistan to Pakistan, meaning 'Kills the Hindu', a reference to the many Indian slaves who perished there from harsh weather conditions.

31 *Marseilles*: oldest city in France, a Mediterranean port that suffered many sieges and where 'La Marseillaise', the French national anthem, came from. It had a colony of famous artists and is now a gateway for immigrants from the African continent.

35 *block-house palaces*: a disparaging reference to new high-rise buildings that sprang up in modern Ireland.

46 *'Van Gogh's Grave'*: Vincent van Gogh (1853–90) is a famous Dutch post-Impressionist painter who suffered, like Durcan, from depression. He was a tortured soul who lived for his art.

46 *'Lovers in Water'*: a reference to a painting by modern artist Francine Scialom Greenblatt that refers to a private place made public.

49 *swaddling*: strips of cloth wrapped around a newborn child to calm it; also a reference to how the infant Jesus is described in the gospel account.

61 *Last Tango in Paris*: romantic movie (1972) about a love affair that ends in tragedy.

68 *Beaubourg*: small, stylish hotel in Paris.

69 *Père Lachaise*: largest cemetery in Paris, containing the graves of many famous people.

69 *Auvers*: village where Van Gogh lived.

78 *symbiotic*: safe, secure; similar to the natural pre-birth environment.

82 *equanimity*: composure, calmness.

83 *benignly*: compassionately, favourably.

86 *psyche*: consciousness; soul.

91 *metamorphosed*: changed.

91 *accomplices*: partners – usually in crime.

93 *subversive*: unsettling, rebellious.

100 *gesticulating*: gesturing dramatically.

116 *keen*: sharp, biting.

118 *alien*: unfamiliar, strange.

119 *eerie*: scary, unnatural.

121 *ornithological*: scientific study of birds.

132 *Apache*: Native American tribe from Arizona.

132 *Cherokee*: Native American tribe from the southern United States.

132 *Bourgeoisie*: conservative middle class, chiefly concerned with wealth.

INITIAL RESPONSE

1. In your opinion, what is Durcan's central theme or point in this poem? Briefly explain your response.

2. The poet uses conversational language throughout the poem. What effect do you think this has on the reader?

3. Comment on the tone of the concluding line, 'We're almost home, pet, don't worry anymore, we're almost home'. Does the poet really believe this or is there a darker meaning?

STUDY NOTES

'"Windfall", 8 Parnell Hill, Cork' was published in Paul Durcan's collection The Berlin Wall Café *(1985). It chronicles not only the happy domesticity Durcan enjoyed in his marriage with his wife, Nessa, and their two daughters, but also the bitter consequences of the break-up of that marriage for the poet. The intensity of the pain of separation is searing as the ex-husband unflinchingly discloses the disintegration of his relationship. Paul Durcan has commented, 'Hardly a day goes by that I don't think about our marriage ... I put the breakdown of our marriage down to my stupidity.'*

The **opening line** is written in the conditional tense and expresses a possibility for the future. The poet used to be able to say, 'Well, now, I am going home', as if all the ills of the world could be left outside when he retreated to his one safe place of contentment. Durcan explains how good he felt that he could make that statement: 'I felt elected, steeped, sovereign'. He felt chosen, 'steeped' in luck, free and dominant. But there is a note of regret here, clearly suggesting that he can no longer return home. The importance of home is emphasised by continual repetition: 'When I was at home I liked to stay at home;/At home I stayed at home for weeks'. From his privileged position in his 'winged chair', the poet could survey the familiar sights of the city port, 'the river and the factory chimneys'. He meditates, 'Dreaming that life is a dream which is real'. For Durcan, however, reality becomes uncertain, unfocused, 'The river a reflection of itself in its own waters'.

His mind turns to a painting by Goya where the painter has depicted himself in a 'smoky' mirror behind a group of people peering out at the viewer. The industrial vista of Cork seems every bit as important for the poet as Mont Sainte-Victoire was for another artist, Paul Cézanne. A happy picture of domesticity soon replaces the fluid, unsettling river images. We see Durcan and his family forming a secure, close-knit group: 'my children sat on my knees watching TV'. It is a picture of indolence. Their mother is described separately, as if not quite belonging to this unit. In contrast to the poet, she is much more engaged, 'Knitting', 'drinking', 'Smoking'. But Durcan is oblivious and blissfully happy in his comfortable habitat: 'I closed my eyes and breathed in and breathed out'.

Section two (line 20) conveys the heights of emotion, 'ecstasy', felt when an individual is at ease in the right place, 'at home in the world'. The poet describes this as a 'windfall', something good that has been received unexpectedly. The tone is complacent – almost cynical – when he recalls the names of his neighbours' homes: 'Con Amore' (with love), 'Sans Souci' (without worries), 'Homesville'. Some other houses are called after popes, suggesting the controlling religious influence on the local community. Durcan points out that he and his wife were above all that – 'But we called our home "Windfall"', as though nature itself had provided this haven for his family. Already there is an underlying suggestion that he took too much for granted. He still feels a sense of deep serenity in the depths of his being, 'the leaf of tranquillity', known only to the ascetic monks who lived in Asia's remote mountain ranges.

The exotic image of 'lotus monasteries' evokes the **idealised state of wistful forgetfulness** enjoyed both by the monks and the poet himself. But this restful dreamscape is rudely torn apart by the shocking reality of bourgeois Ireland's 'dark depths'. Cork city is 'intimate', private and personal, but also 'homicidal', murderous, just like the subversive city of Marseilles, where the French Revolution started. Characteristically, Durcan makes a bitter reference to the Irish Constitution, which had not fulfilled its promises and instead produced 'a country where all the children of the nation/Are not cherished equally'. He ridicules the greed of the rising moneyed classes and their 'block-house palaces'. This section concludes **(lines 36–37)** that 'Having a home of your own' allows a family to 'transcend death'. Some of the poet's ancestors had once been evicted from their holding in County Mayo. Durcan has said that in his own family, 'There was only one value and that was money.'

The dreamy sight of changing skies opens the poem's **third section (line 38)**. Tall ships are 'drifting in and out of skylines in the cloudy valley'. **Family harmony appears to reign**: 'Our black-and-white cat snoozing in the corner of a chair'. The living room is filled with pictures and old photo albums that record in detail the changes in family life over two generations. But another disturbing note is struck as the poet describes early pictures of himself 'Face-down in a pram, incarcerated in a high chair'. Durcan was once regarded by his own relations as the black sheep of the family and at one time he was even confined to a mental institution. As he studies the albums, he feels betrayed by the false expressions: 'shop-window smiles'. The seemingly random collection of memories ranges widely over significant times and various places at home, at school and on holiday. The young Durcan is seen behaving wildly, 'Performing a headstand after First Holy Communion'. Yet he seems more forlorn than bitter. Is the concluding image, 'wearing wings at the seaside', a reference to his innocence or his wish to escape?

The **fourth section (line 59)** continues with a hypnotic refrain, 'Mammy and Daddy'. Is the poet now openly sneering at the irony of these misleadingly happy photos? He has placed himself centre stage of two family units, as though watching himself growing from childhood to parenthood. For years, he has 'pored over these albums' with his children, who seem equally 'exhilarated' by these glimpses into the past. It is yet another irony that the 'hearthrug' – which used to signify domestic warmth – is now a symbol of the void at the heart of the house. Strangely, **his wife is excluded**, almost sidelined as the adult in the scene coolly looking on, 'presiding'. The poet's wife is described as self-effacing, but she looks on 'proudly'. Does the poet now consider that he made the mistake of taking her for granted? She was the family breadwinner while Durcan remained at home caring for their two children and writing. He has since said, 'I sometimes think Nessa missed out. She was out working while I was with the girls'. At times, the tone wavers between condemnation and remorse, with the conflicting preoccupations of the couple's time together remaining unresolved. In the midst of the rough and tumble of family life, 'Schoolbooks on the floor and pyjamas on the couch', her cool voice echoes, 'Whose turn is it tonight to put the children to bed?'

An allegorical **dream scene** reveals the spiritual and emotional aspects of ordinary family life in **section five (line 76)**: 'Our children swam about our home/As if it was their private sea'. Their idyllic, unrestrained happiness is caught in the image of the 'symbiotic fluid' of which everyone 'partook'. Durcan believed that home was a place where one could be at liberty without consequences, even hanging 'upside down from the ceiling/With equanimity'. However, the sibilant line 'Sifting the sands underneath the surfaces of conversations' sounds a warning note. Is someone scrutinising, negatively reviewing? The couple are happy when they are partners in crime, 'smiling accomplices', preferring to continue kissing rather than answer the phone. There are signs that the poet could only relate to his wife when she was not behaving as a responsible adult. Meanwhile, the children watch their 'parents at play' sharing another 'subversive kiss' before running 'wordlessly' to bed. But from his intense study of the 'family psyche', Durcan has learned that **the challenges of an intimate relationship can be destructive**. His ringing assertion that 'The most subversive unit in society is the human family' abruptly contradicts any nostalgic homesickness he may have been experiencing.

In the **sixth section (line 102)**, a reassuring parental voice is heard: 'We're almost home, pet, almost home'. The poet follows up with a litany of everyday phrases, some hanging unfinished, and all containing the word 'home'. It is as if this ubiquitous term – the crucial concept of 'home' and belonging – highlights the **overwhelming sense of security and safety he associates with family life**: 'If I'm not home by six at the latest, I'll phone…' The comforting tone concludes this short section as if Durcan himself and his family have almost made it 'home'. As always, the immediacy of his poetic voice resonates with readers, reinforcing the universal importance of close family relationships.

Inevitably, however, all the celebration of domesticity – whether real or imagined – is shattered in the **penultimate section (line 114)**: 'But then with good reason/I was put out of my home'. The poet no longer refers to 'our home', as in the previous section, but to 'my home'. Does he think he has an absolute right to be there? Durcan frankly admits that he was expelled 'with good reason'. But what was this reason – depression, alcoholism, a refusal to mature? Is he assuming the manipulative posture of the bad boy, disarmingly admitting his faults so that he will be immediately forgiven?

There is more than a hint of self-pity in the claim that he was finally brought down 'By a keen wind'. Is this sharp, biting force really his wife? Typically self-absorbed, the poet goes on to describe his experience of being without a home. He now has to live in the 'alien, foreign city of Dublin', a frightening, disorienting experience. He has discovered how strange it is to be 'homesick' and regards it as totally unnatural, 'beyond all ornithological analysis' if 'there is no home to go home to'. **Short lines effectively convey the aimless wanderings of a homeless man.** 'Day by day' he spends his time 'creeping, crawling,/Moonlighting, escaping'. What a contrast to his previous idyllic existence, when he was in control of his home in his 'winged chair', surveying his own 'Mont Sainte-Victoire' with his happy children on his knees. Now he moves restlessly from 'Bed-and-breakfast to bed-and breakfast;/Hostels, centres, one-night hotels'.

The poem's bittersweet **final section (line 127)** refers again to a 'Windfall', but now the word is said with bitter irony. It no longer refers to his comfortable home, but to himself as a rootless object 'Blown about the suburban streets at evening'. Longingly, he peers 'in the windows of other people's homes,/Wondering what it must feel like/To be sitting around a fire'. This basic experience is enjoyed by all races and societies, 'Apache or Cherokee' or the middle-class 'Bourgeoisie'. They all have the privilege of looking at their families' faces illuminated by firelight, whether they gaze at the stars or the TV screen. The poet now resembles a distressed vessel that had been cast adrift. He is calling frantically for assistance: 'can you hear me?' At this point, the calming tones of a parent return, tenderly reassuring a distracted child: 'We're almost home, pet, don't worry anymore, we're almost home'. Is this longing so deeply ingrained in Durcan that he takes refuge in convincing himself that it is still a possibility? Or is the reality the awful truth that he can never again go back to '"Windfall", 8 Parnell Hill, Cork'?

ANALYSIS

'Paul Durcan charms readers with his self-critical revelations while concealing his own self-centredness.' Discuss this statement in relation to the poem '"Windfall", 8 Parnell Hill, Cork'. Refer closely to the text in your response.

Sample Paragraph

In this poem, Paul Durcan charms us by presenting memorable images of cosy domesticity, 'my children sat on my knees watching TV', 'Our children swam about our home'. I did feel sympathy for him when I heard his graphic account of homelessness, 'creeping and crawling' as though he was unwanted, going from one anonymous place to another, 'Hostels, centres, one-night hotels'. He appears rootless, a windfall, belonging nowhere, 'Blown about the suburban streets at evening'. But his admission of being 'put out' of his home 'with good reason' seems as if he is condemning himself just to get pity. His wife is seen busily 'Knitting'. She is 'presiding' while the poet and his children look at old pictures of him 'Dancing' in a Paris graveyard. She is the breadwinner and the adult in the relationship, 'Whose turn is it tonight to put the children to bed?' Is he placing his wife in the role of a person who didn't understand him? I believe that his wife was becoming frustrated, 'Sifting the sands underneath the surfaces of conversations'. She snapped and finally refused to accept her husband's selfish behaviour. In my opinion, this poem is not really about Durcan's home, but about himself. He does attempt to hide his self-centred character. At the same time, I still feel sorry for him. He ends up as a very lonely man who has lost all, reduced to the pitiful state of peering into other people's homes and who can never say 'Well, now, I am going home'.

Examiner's Comment
The paragraph touches on interesting aspects of how the poet appears to readers and there is a good attempt at addressing the crucial relationship between Durcan and his wife. Points are well illustrated with accurate quotation. There is a basic attempt at personal engagement: 'At the same time, I still feel sorry for him'. However, note-like commentary weakens the response: 'He ends up as a lonely man who has lost all'. Although the task is addressed, the quality of expression lowers the mark to a good middle grade.

CLASS/HOMEWORK EXERCISES

1. 'In many of his poems, Paul Durcan relishes conflict and exhibitionism.' Discuss this statement in relation to '"Windfall", 8 Parnell Hill, Cork'. Support the points you make with suitable reference.

2. Based on your reading of this poem, describe Durcan's views on Irish family life. Support your answer with close reference to the text.

SUMMARY POINTS

- Key themes – domestic family happiness and the pain of broken relationships.
- Autobiographical/personal details; intense rhythms.
- Varying tones – reflective, ironic, celebratory, wistful, regretful, self-critical.
- Effective use of repetition, vivid images/metaphors.

7 SIX NUNS DIE IN CONVENT INFERNO

To the
happy memory of six Loreto nuns
who died
between midnight and morning of
2 June 1986

I

We resided in a Loreto convent in the centre of Dublin city
On the east side of a public gardens, St Stephen's Green.
Grafton Street – the *paseo*
Where everybody *paseo*'d, including even ourselves –
Debouched on the north side, and at the top of Grafton Street,   5
Or round the base of the great patriotic pebble of O'Donovan Rossa,
Knelt tableaus of punk girls and punk boys.
When I used pass them – scurrying as I went –
Often as not to catch a mass in Clarendon Street,
The Carmelite Church in Clarendon Street   10
(Myself, I never used the Clarendon Street entrance,
I always slipped in by way of Johnson's Court,
Opposite the side entrance to Bewley's Oriental Café),
I could not help but smile, as I sucked on a Fox's mint,
That for all the half-shaven heads and the martial garb   15
And the dyed hair-dos and the nappy pins
They looked so conventional, really, and vulnerable,
Clinging to warpaint and to uniforms and to one another.
I knew it was myself who was the ultimate drop-out,
The delinquent, the recidivist, the vagabond,   20
The wild woman, the subversive, the original punk.
Yet, although I confess I was smiling, I was also afraid,
Appalled by my own nerve, my own fervour,
My apocalyptic enthusiasm, my other-worldly hubris:
To opt out of the world and to   25
Choose such exotic loneliness,
Such terrestrial abandonment,
A lifetime of bicycle lamps and bicycle pumps,
A lifetime of galoshes stowed under the stairs,
A lifetime of umbrellas drying out in the kitchens.   30

I was an old nun – an agèd beadswoman –
But I was no daw.

I knew what a weird bird I was, I knew that when we
Went to bed we were as eerie an aviary as you'd find
In all the blown-off rooftops of the city:
Scuttling about our dorm, wheezing, shrieking, croaking,
In our yellowy corsets, wonky suspenders, strung-out garters,
A bony crew in the gods of the sleeping city.
Many's the night I lay awake in bed
Dreaming what would befall us if there were a fire:
No fire-escapes outside, no fire-extinguishers inside;
To coin a Dublin saying,
We'd not stand a snowball's chance in hell. Fancy that!
It seemed too good to be true:
Happy death vouchsafed only to the few.
Sleeping up there was like sleeping at the top of the mast
Of a nineteenth-century schooner, and in the daytime
We old nuns were the ones who crawled out on the yardarms
To stitch and sew the rigging and the canvas.
To be sure we were weird birds, oddballs, Christniks,
For we had done the weirdest thing a woman can do –
Surrendered the marvellous passions of girlhood,
The innocent dreams of childhood,
Not for a night or a weekend or even a Lent or a season,
But for a lifetime.
Never to know the love of a man or a woman;
Never to have children of our own;
Never to have a home of our own;
All for why and for what?
To follow a young man – would you believe it –
Who lived two thousand years ago in Palestine
And who died a common criminal strung up on a tree.

As we stood there in the disintegrating dormitory
Burning to death in the arms of Christ –
O Christ, Christ, come quickly, quickly –
Fluttering about in our tight, gold bodices,
Beating our wings in vain,
It reminded me of the snaps one of the sisters took
When we took a seaside holiday in 1956
(The year Cardinal Mindszenty went into hiding
In the US legation in Budapest.

He was a great hero of ours, Cardinal Mindszenty,
Any of us would have given our right arm
To have been his nun – darning his socks, cooking his meals,
Making his bed, doing his washing and ironing.) 75
Somebody – an affluent buddy of the bishop's repenting his affluence –
Loaned Mother Superior a secluded beach in Co. Waterford –
Ardmore, along the coast from Tramore –
A cove with palm trees, no less, well off the main road.
There we were, fluttering up and down the beach, 80
Scampering hither and thither in our starched bathing-costumes.
Tonight, expiring in the fire, was quite much like that,
Only instead of scampering into the waves of the sea,
Now we were scampering into the flames of the fire.

That was one of the gayest days of my life, 85
The day the sisters went swimming.
Often in the silent darkness of the chapel after Benediction,
During the Exposition of the Blessed Sacrament,
I glimpsed the sea again as it was that day.
Praying – daydreaming really – 90
I became aware that Christ is the ocean
Forever rising and falling on the world's shore.
Now tonight in the convent Christ is the fire in whose waves
We are doomed but delighted to drown.
And, darting in and out of the flames of the dormitory, 95
Gabriel, with that extraordinary message of his on his boyish lips,
Frenetically pedalling his skybike.
He whispers into my ear what I must do
And I do it – and die.
Each of us in our own tiny, frail, furtive way 100
Was a Mother of God, mothering forth illegitimate Christs
In the street life of Dublin city.
God have mercy on our whirring souls –
Wild women were we all –
And on the misfortunate, poor fire-brigade men 105
Whose task it will be to shovel up our ashes and shovel
What is left of us into black plastic refuse sacks.
Fire-brigade men are the salt of the earth.

Isn't it a marvellous thing how your hour comes
When you least expect it? When you lose a thing,
Not to know about it until it actually happens?
How, in so many ways, losing things is such a refreshing experience,
Giving you a sense of freedom you've not often experienced?
How lucky I was to lose – I say, lose – lose my life.
It was a Sunday night, and after vespers
I skipped bathroom so that I could hop straight into bed
And get in a bit of a read before lights out:
Conor Cruise O'Brien's new book *The Siege*,
All about Israel and superlatively insightful
For a man who they say is reputedly an agnostic –
I got a loan of it from the brother-in-law's married niece –
But I was tired out and I fell asleep with the book open
Face down across my breast and I woke
To the racket of bellowing flame and snarling glass.
The first thing I thought was that the brother-in-law's married niece
Would never again get her Conor Cruise O'Brien back
And I had seen on the price-tag that it cost £23.00:
Small wonder that the custom of snipping off the price
As an exercise in social deportment has simply died out;
Indeed a book today is almost worth buying for its price,
Its price frequently being more remarkable than its contents.

The strange Eucharist of my death –
To be eaten alive by fire and smoke.
I clasped the dragon to my breast
And stroked his red-hot ears.
Strange! There we were, all sleeping molecules,
Suddenly all giving birth to our deaths,
All frantically in labour.
Doctors and midwives weaved in and out
In gowns of smoke and gloves of fire.
Christ, like an Orthodox patriarch in his dressing gown,
Flew up and down the dormitory, splashing water on our souls:
Sister Eucharia; Sister Seraphia; Sister Rosario;
Sister Gonzaga; Sister Margaret; Sister Edith.
If you will remember us – six nuns burnt to death –
Remember us for the frisky girls that we were,
Now more than ever kittens in the sun.

II

When Jesus heard these words at the top of Grafton Street
Uttered by a small, agèd, emaciated, female punk
Clad all in mourning black, and grieving like an alley cat, 150
He was annulled with astonishment, and turning round
He declared to the gangs of teenagers and dicemen following him:
'I tell you, not even in New York City
Have I found faith like this.'

That night in St Stephen's Green, 155
After the keepers had locked the gates,
And the courting couples had found cinemas themselves to die in,
The six nuns who had died in the convent inferno,
From the bandstand they'd been hiding under, crept out
And knelt together by the Fountain of the Three Fates, 160
Reciting the Agnus Dei: reciting it as if it were the torch song
Of all aid – Live Aid, Self Aid, Aids, and All Aid –
Lord, I am not worthy
That thou should'st enter under my roof;
Say but the word and my soul shall be healed. 165

'six nuns burnt to death'

Glossary

- *Inferno*: uncontrollable fire, conflagration.
- 3 *paseo*: pedestrian area where people can take a leisurely stroll.
- 5 *Debouched*: emerged into the open.
- 6 *O'Donovan Rossa*: Jeremiah O'Donovan Rossa (1831–1915) was a prominent Irish Republican. Durcan refers to his large stone memorial as a 'pebble'.
- 7 *tableaus*: groups posing as though in a theatrical freeze.
- 15 *martial garb*: military-style clothes.
- 18 *warpaint*: heavy make-up.
- 20 *recidivist*: undesirable character.
- 24 *apocalyptic*: ruinous.
- 24 *hubris*: excessive pride or arrogance.
- 32 *daw*: jackdaw, noisy crow.
- 34 *aviary*: enclosure or large cage for birds.
- 47 *schooner*: fast sailing ship.
- 48 *yardarms*: parts of a mast from which sails are hung.
- 49 *rigging*: ropes and other supports for sails.
- 50 *Christniks*: fans of Jesus; a pun on the word 'Beatniks'.
- 54 *Lent*: six-week period of penance leading up to Easter in Christian liturgy.
- 60 *young man*: a reference to Jesus.
- 68 *snaps*: photographs.
- 70 *Cardinal Mindszenty*: József Mindszenty (1892–1975), leader of the Catholic Church in Hungary. He was jailed for opposing communism.
- 76 *affluence*: wealth, privileged circumstances.
- 87 *Benediction*: Catholic religious service of blessing.
- 88 *Exposition of the Blessed Sacrament*: prayerful part of Catholic devotion to the Blessed Sacrament (the consecrated bread and wine believed to be the real presence of Jesus Christ).
- 96 *Gabriel*: angel who served as God's messenger.
- 97 *Frenetically*: frantically, wildly.
- 118 *Conor Cruise O'Brien*: prominent Irish politician, writer and academic (1917–2008).
- 120 *agnostic*: religious sceptic.
- 132 *Eucharist*: Thanksgiving; refers to the Mass and Holy Communion (the consecrated bread and wine).
- 134 *dragon*: mythical creature representing fire.
- 136 *molecules*: body particles.
- 141 *Orthodox patriarch*: leader of the Eastern Orthodox Church, the second largest Christian Church in the world.
- 149 *emaciated*: skinny, skeletal.
- 152 *dicemen*: street performers, mime artists.
- 160 *Fountain of the Three Fates*: St Stephen's Green statue of the Three Fates or Graces controlling human destiny.
- 161 *Agnus Dei*: Lamb of God (Latin), referring to Christ, a contemplative prayer.
- 162 *Live Aid, Self Aid*: popular charities.
- 162 *Aids*: acquired immune deficiency syndrome, a syndrome caused by human immunodeficiency virus (HIV).

INITIAL RESPONSE

1. Based on your reading of the poem, what is your impression of convent life in Ireland? Refer to the text in your answer.

2. Briefly describe Durcan's attitude to the nuns and their way of life. Is he always sympathetic to them? Explain your response.

3. Choose one short section of the poem that you consider particularly dramatic and rich in imagery. Discuss the poet's language use, commenting on its effectiveness.

STUDY NOTES

Paul Durcan has a reputation for being an incisive social commentator. His journalistic approach ranges widely over contemporary events, defining him as a poet of the present moment. But the poet is never content with mere reportage. This long narrative poem about a fire that destroyed a Dublin convent in 1986 characteristically transforms the details of the tragedy into an extended exercise in spiritual reflection. He focuses on one elderly nun who narrates the story of this disaster and reveals the personal choices she had made and her memories of happier times.

Durcan's poems are predominantly narrative in form, but they often combine incidents, impressions and flights of fancy. In this case, the title juxtaposes the dramatic newspaper heading, 'Six Nuns Die in Convent Inferno', with the poignant memorial celebrating the women who dedicated their lives to Christ. What is most evident in the **opening lines** of Part I is the spirited voice of the nun who provides a short history of the Loreto convent where she 'resided'. The **gentle, self-deprecating humour** of the sisters joining the Grafton Street crowds and 'scurrying' past punks who 'Knelt' indicates a lively sense of irony.

The narrator is particularly amused by the displays of youthful rebelliousness she notices: 'the half-shaven heads' and 'dyed hair-dos' (**lines 15–16**). She is also convinced that **her 'subversive' choice of vocation** makes her 'the ultimate drop-out'. In retrospect, she is still shocked by her decision to 'opt out of the world' and follow the religious life in all its 'exotic loneliness'. But despite the long 'lifetime' of 'bicycle pumps' and 'umbrellas drying out', she always understood the significance of her alternative calling as a nun: 'I knew what a weird bird I was' (**line 33**). From her 'agèd beadswoman' perspective, stooped and dressed in black, she is able to imagine how she must appear to outsiders, who might compare her eccentric appearance in full religious habit to 'a daw' – not that any criticism dampens her enthusiasm. Durcan develops the bird metaphor – 'we were as eerie an aviary as you'd find', suggesting the enclosed convent environment.

The speaker's **reflections become increasingly surreal** when she recalls occasional fears ('what would befall us if there were a fire') and the accompanying prospect of a 'Happy death'. Durcan uses a dramatic sailing image to bring to mind the thought of being accidentally killed while 'sleeping at the top of the mast/Of a nineteenth-century schooner'. His attitude to the nuns, encompassing both admiration and astonishment, shows how closely he himself identifies with these unusual women who have 'Surrendered the marvellous passions of girlhood'. He also acknowledges the contribution made by the Loreto nuns in Ireland to providing spiritual guidance and education. Their essential work is compared to the sailors who 'stitch and sew the rigging and the canvas'. The poet's trademark repetition emphasises their sacrifice and isolation: 'Never to have children … Never to have a home of our own' (**lines 57–58**).

Many of Durcan's more loosely structured poems are composed by 'cutting' and 'reassembling' various narrative scenes. In **line 63**, the speaker remembers the 'disintegrating dormitory' and the terrifying ecstasy of 'Burning to death in the arms of Christ'. Amid the chaos – accentuated by exclamatory language – there is **the unsettling sense of souls desperate to emerge as angels**: 'Beating our wings in vain'. In another sudden change of space and time, the narrator associates this crucial moment with an earlier experience when the nuns 'took a seaside holiday in 1956'. The nostalgia for a simpler, old-fashioned era is apparent in the innocent hero worship of Cardinal Mindszenty and the youthful pleasures of carefree times, 'scampering into the waves'. However, the fond memory is short-lived and the secluded beach abruptly becomes the raging fire that consumed the sisters: 'Now we were scampering into the flames'.

Nevertheless, the elation experienced by the speaker during moments of devout prayer is expressed in terms of the 'day the sisters went swimming'. Durcan uses the nun's elegiac recollection to emphasise the central importance of unconditional Christian faith. Her **visionary account** equates Christ with all of the natural world, including 'the fire in whose waves/We are doomed but delighted to drown' (**lines 93–94**). A touch of black humour is added to her portrait when she imagines the 'boyish' angel Gabriel, 'Frenetically pedalling his skybike'. Her childlike sincerity is also obvious when she worries about the 'poor fire-brigade men' and the loss of a book she borrowed from her niece – 'it cost £23.00'.

Throughout the poem, Durcan promotes the radical Christian values of charity, piety and the achievement of sanctity through suffering, all virtues epitomised in Christ's own life on earth. The nun who narrates this tragic story readily accepts her fate as God's will: 'The strange Eucharist of my death' (**line 132**). In trying to make sense of the horrific event, the poet interweaves an ingenious series of random insights ('all sleeping molecules') and nightmarish images ('I clasped the dragon to my breast'). The inferno itself is personified, dramatising this central moment of Christian renewal – the paradoxical transition into the spiritual afterlife from earthly existence, 'giving birth to our deaths'. But we are never allowed to forget that at the heart of this sacrifice is the reality of human loss: 'six nuns burnt to death'. As the individual names are recorded precisely, readers can share **Durcan's tender and sad compassion**. The narrator's modest request – to be remembered as 'the frisky girls that we were' (**line 146**) – is particularly moving. Characteristically playful to the end, she chooses a universal image of childhood innocence to describe her vision of eternal happiness: 'Now more than ever kittens in the sun'.

The 18 lines that make up Part II of the poem are told as third person narrative. The didactic tone echoes countless gospel stories. Durcan imagines the aftermath of the tragedy, with Jesus relocated to Grafton Street, where he is humbled by the story of the grieving nun, now in the persona of 'a small, agèd, emaciated, female punk' (**line 149**). His shocked reaction ('annulled with astonishment') reflects the poet's well-documented objections to current Catholic teaching on aspects of marriage breakdown. Within this framework, linking the six nuns' deaths to the vulnerability of some women today, **Durcan achieves a bizarre satirical effect**. But while he mocks Ireland's conservative Catholic lawmakers, he shows the highest regard for the unshakable faith of individuals, such as the victims of the convent fire.

The poem ends as it began, back in St Stephen's Green, where a final dramatic scenario is played out under cover of darkness. Trancelike, the dead nuns kneel 'by the Fountain of the Three Fates' happily chanting the Agnus Dei (**line 161**) 'as if it were the torch song' at an outdoor music festival. **The words of this Communion prayer are spoken in preparation for the Divine encounter** – sentiments that are entirely in keeping with the faith of the six Loreto sisters. Durcan's tone of conviction and use of italics reflect the significance of recognising human unworthiness and the acceptance of divine healing love.

From the outset, the poet has venerated the nuns who lost their lives, articulating their religious impulses in particular. The poem's surreal and theatrical elements broaden our understanding of Durcan's subject matter, increasing the clarity of **his imaginative vision**. In blending psychological and physical impressions, he has managed to translate the sensational newspaper story of the inferno into an incisive exploration of individual religious experience.

ANALYSIS

'Durcan's unique poetic voice is particularly evident in his elegies for victims.' Discuss this view based on your reading of 'Six Nuns Die in Convent Inferno', supporting the points you make with reference to the poem.

Sample Paragraph

Paul Durcan's poetry is always accessible and his distinctive voice is evident in the tragic poem, 'Six Nuns Die in Convent Inferno'. Religious topics are often found in Durcan's writing. This elegy shows his great sympathy for the victims of the 1986 fire, but also shows their deaths in the true religious sense. The nuns are now with God. The rambling anecdotal style is typical of Durcan. His narrator is one of the nuns who died, a jolly person, still childish and mischievous. She sees herself as a comic character and refers to the O'Donovan Rossa memorial as 'the patriotic pebble'. I liked the way her personality was gradually revealed, showing that she was never disappointed with life. She saw death – even the terrible inferno – as a 'very strange Eucharist', a release. The poem wandered in and out of times in her life, mixing the fire scene with her everyday walks around Stephen's Green and vivid memories of a holiday in Tramore. Durcan always uses names to create a sense of place. His respect for the nuns was obvious in his use of prayers. The whole poem paid tribute to the nuns' deep faith, suggesting that they are more or less obsessed with religion. Durcan's conclusion was dreamlike, showing the spirits of the six nuns celebrating their entry to Heaven through a vivid image of dancing in the dark. I thought the tribute was sincere without being sentimental, another good feature of Paul Durcan's poems.

Examiner's Comment

This fresh response shows clear personal engagement with the poem: 'I liked the way her character was gradually revealed'. The answer touches on several interesting points – focusing particularly well on characteristics of Durcan's style, for example his anecdotal approach and use of place names. The expression is satisfactory, but more use could be made of supportive quotations (and some are slightly inaccurate). Falls just below the top grade.

CLASS/HOMEWORK EXERCISES

1. 'Durcan makes good use of surrealistic effects in addressing religious themes.' Discuss this statement based on your reading of 'Six Nuns Die in Convent Inferno'. Support the points you make with reference to the poem.

2. Based on your reading of this poem, describe Paul Durcan's views on Irish family life. Support your answer with close reference to the text.

SUMMARY POINTS

- Narrative of the fire tragedy becomes an extended spiritual reflection.
- Key themes include personal choices, sacrifice, faith, the religious life.
- Fragmented, theatrical structure; striking images – realistic, surreal.
- Varying tones – ironic, compassionate, satirical, critical.

SPORT

There were not many fields
In which you had hopes for me
But sport was one of them.
On my twenty-first birthday
I was selected to play   5
For Grangegorman Mental Hospital
In an away game
Against Mullingar Mental Hospital.
I was a patient
In B Wing.   10
You drove all the way down,
Fifty miles,
To Mullingar to stand
On the sidelines and observe me.

I was fearful I would let down   15
Not only my team but you.
It was Gaelic football.
I was selected as goalkeeper.
There were big country men
On the Mullingar Mental Hospital team,   20
Men with gapped teeth, red faces,
Oily, frizzy hair, bushy eyebrows.
Their full forward line
Were over six foot tall
Fifteen stone in weight.   25
All three of them, I was informed,
Cases of schizophrenia.

There was a rumour
That their centre-half forward
Was an alcoholic solicitor   30
Who, in a lounge bar misunderstanding,
Had castrated his best friend
But that he had no memory of it.
He had meant well – it was said.
His best friend had had to emigrate   35
To Nigeria.

To my surprise,
I did not flinch in the goals.
I made three or four spectacular saves,
Diving full stretch to turn
A certain goal around the corner,
Leaping high to tip another certain goal
Over the bar for a point.
It was my knowing
That you were standing on the sideline
That gave me the necessary motivation –
That will to die
That is as essential to sportsmen as to artists.
More than anybody it was you
I wanted to mesmerise, and after the game –
Grangegorman Mental Hospital
Having defeated Mullingar Mental Hospital
By 14 goals and 38 points to 3 goals and 10 points –
Sniffing your approval, you shook hands with me.
'Well played, son.'

I may not have been mesmeric
But I had not been mediocre.
In your eyes I had achieved something at last.
On my twenty-first birthday I had played on a winning team
The Grangegorman Mental Hospital team.
Seldom if ever again in your eyes
Was I to rise to these heights.

'I had achieved something'

Glossary

Sport: an activity involving effort and skill in which an individual or team compete; also refers to a person who behaves in a good way in response to teasing or defeat.
1 *fields*: pitches, areas, disciplines.
7 *away game*: played at an opponent's place, seen as an advantage to the opposing team.
14 *observe*: examine, consider, scrutinise.
27 *schizophrenia*: long-term mental disorder with symptoms including emotional instability, detachment from reality and withdrawal into self.
32 *castrated*: removed testicles; deprived of power, made docile.
38 *flinch*: cower, dodge, shy away.
46 *motivation*: reasons to act and be enthusiastic.
50 *mesmerise*: fascinate, captivate.
54 *Sniffing*: snorting, showing contempt for.
56 *mesmeric*: brilliant, hypnotic.
57 *mediocre*: only average, amateurish, ordinary.

INITIAL RESPONSE

1. Based on an initial reading of the poem, what is your impression of Paul Durcan's father? Refer closely to the text in your response.

2. Trace the changing tones of voice as the poem progresses. Support your answer with appropriate reference.

3. Are you sympathetic or not to the character of Durcan himself that emerges from the poem? Refer to the text to support the points you make.

STUDY NOTES

'Sport' is from Paul Durcan's collection Daddy, Daddy, for which he was awarded the Whitbread Prize (1990). This poem is painfully autobiographical, as he not only recalls a difficult time in his youth, but also explores the troubled relationship he had with his father. Durcan has remarked: 'My father would say, "Paul is a sissy. Come on, be a man." I was aware of his deep disappointment.'

The poet's father was a judge in the circuit court. He was an introverted man, apparently ill-suited to the legal profession. Nevertheless, Durcan shared 'many rich moments' with him in early childhood. But in the mid-1950s, 'the picture darkened' when the young Durcan was about 10. Paul began to receive beatings and there was pressure about exam performance. He contracted a serious bone disease at 13, which ended his athletic career. Because of difficulties with his behaviour in his late teens, members of his wider family had him committed to a mental hospital.

The poem **opens** candidly, with Durcan addressing his father directly. He immediately registers an acute awareness of his father's disappointment with him in many areas: 'There were not many fields/In which you had hopes for me/But sport was one of them'. Sometimes, when men find it hard to communicate, they can relate through sport. They can express their emotions as they discuss the winning or losing of a match without being considered odd. The Gaelic football game Durcan recalls was played on his twenty-first birthday, the day he becomes a man. In **line 6, the chilling context of this occasion** is revealed. It was an 'away game' between the inmates of 'Grangegorman Mental Hospital' and 'Mullingar Mental Hospital'. Durcan is 'a patient/In B Wing', a vulnerable individual. He acknowledges his father's efforts to attend the match, driving 'Fifty miles,/To Mullingar to stand/On the sidelines'. The inference is that the father was never really involved in the poet's life. Durcan also suggests his father's judgemental character when he is described as coming to 'observe me'. It is almost as if his son was a laboratory specimen. The curt tone clearly indicates that **his father's attendance was far from supportive**.

Nevertheless, there is no denying the son's extreme anxiety to impress: 'I was fearful I would let down/Not only my team but you' (**lines 15-16**). The young man was obviously keen to please his father in this unlikely Gaelic match, where he had been 'selected as goalkeeper'. Durcan's fondness for dark humour is evident in his exaggerated description of the opposition players. The Mullingar team had 'gapped teeth, red faces,/Oily, frizzy hair, bushy eyebrows'. They scarcely seemed human. **Odd details reflect the poet's visual alertness**. The opposing team consisted of 'big country men' whose 'full forward line/Were over six foot tall/Fifteen stone in weight'. These three suffered from schizophrenia, a withdrawal from reality into fantasy. As if the situation was not surreal enough already, Durcan recounts the 'rumour' (**line 28**) about another member of the Mullingar team, 'an alcoholic solicitor' who had mindlessly 'castrated his best friend'. Readers are left with an uneasy sense of absurd comedy based on uncontrollable male violence.

As for the game itself, the poet is amazed by his own performance: 'To my surprise,/I did not flinch in the goals'. The dramatic jargon of sports writing is used, perhaps self-mockingly, to describe his exploits on the field of play, making 'spectacular saves' that were at 'full stretch'. Action-packed verbs convey his tremendous agility – 'Diving', 'Leaping' – and all for the approval of his father, 'knowing/That you were standing on the sideline'. Durcan makes a revealing comment in **line 47** that **both artists, such as himself, and sportsmen must have absolute motivation** – 'That will to die'. They will give their all and risk everything in their desire to succeed.

The young man's need to make an impact on his father accelerates: 'it was you/I wanted to mesmerise'. Characteristically, the overwhelmingly decisive triumph of Durcan's team is recorded with mock-heroic pride: '14 goals and 38 points to 3 goals and 10 points'. Despite this great triumph, however, the father's minimal response, his monosyllabic ruling, is less than enthusiastic: 'Well played, son'. There is no embrace. Instead, a formal handshake takes place. The disappointment of the young man contrasts with the emotionally stilted father 'Sniffing … approval'. Is he suggesting that his son is merely satisfactory, damning him with faint praise? Of course, we see everything from the son's perspective. During the early 1960s, a father's function in Irish society was to fund and guide his family. Overt displays of affection were not common between parents and children, especially sons. Is Durcan's forensic examination of the father–son relationship almost as unhealthy as his father's scrutiny of him? Are both tragically locked into damaging behavioural attitudes?

In the poem's concluding section, Durcan ruefully admits, 'I may not have been mesmeric' (**line 56**). Yet he also asserts 'But I had not been mediocre' and had indeed 'achieved something at last'. The phrase 'at last' forcefully expresses how intensely aware the poet is of his father's lack of confidence in him. After all, he had accomplished something, playing on a 'winning team'. It was, however, a mental hospital patients' team. Does this matter greatly to the father – and to the son? **The poem ends on a poignant note**: 'Seldom if ever again in your eyes/Was I to rise to these heights'. Dark shadows of family relationships were cast by the father's continuing disappointment. The son is still devastated about what it means to be a man and always to feel not quite good enough. As the poet himself has stated elsewhere, even though the father 'loved books', it was always clear that 'the more it looked like I was going to be a writer, the more he was against it'.

ANALYSIS

'Durcan's poetry is not just revealing, it also has a shockingly frank quality.' Discuss this statement in relation to the poem 'Sport'. Refer closely to the text in your answer.

Sample Paragraph

The highly personal poem 'Sport' comes from Durcan's collection *Daddy, Daddy*, whose title is a reference to the American poet Sylvia Plath's cry to her father, 'Daddy, daddy, you bastard, I'm through'. I think the lines in 'Sport' are almost as shocking. They convey, in a frank manner, the longing of the young son for his father's approval. Durcan reveals his lack of confidence in lines such as, 'I was fearful I would let down/Not only my team but you'. He was willing, as Christ was, to make the ultimate sacrifice for his father, 'That will to die'. Like most young men, he desperately wanted to 'mesmerise' his uncommunicative father. The urgent tone seems to me to suggest the spellbinding effect he wishes to make on him. I thought the father's lukewarm response was hurtful, especially when he shook hands and uttered the cold words 'Well played, son'. The poet does not shy away from disclosing that just as his father stood on 'the sidelines' to 'observe' him, he now appears obsessed with studying his father and is still trying to understand him after so many years. I believe he feels just as let down by his father's behaviour as his father is by his: 'But I had not been mediocre'. His continuing disappointment mirrors his father's feelings towards him as he sadly notes in the run-on concluding lines of the poem, 'Seldom if ever again in your eyes/Was I to rise to these heights'. Durcan is actually quite brave to detail the awkward relationship he had with his father with such devastating honesty.

Examiner's Comment

A well-written paragraph that uses suitable reference to outline the poet's central theme, the difficult father-son relationship. The use of pertinent descriptive terms, such as 'uncommunicative', 'lukewarm' and 'devastating', helps to define their strained relationship. There is clear evidence throughout of close engagement with the poem: 'I believe he feels just as let down by his father's behaviour as his father is by his'. A highly successful response which merits the top grade.

CLASS/HOMEWORK EXERCISES

1. 'Paul Durcan blends fact, fiction and fantasy to create a realistic view of the world.' Discuss this viewpoint in relation to the poem, 'Sport'. Support your opinions with close reference to the text.

2. In your opinion, what kind of relationship did the poet have with his father? Support your answer with close reference to the poem, 'Sport'.

SUMMARY POINTS

- Characteristically personal exploration of a complex father-son relationship.
- Effective use of tragicomedy, mock-heroism and irony.
- Tone varies – casual, sad, comic, self-mocking.
- Revealing narrative/descriptive details, lively verbs.

FATHER'S DAY, 21 JUNE 1992

Just as I was dashing to catch the Dublin–Cork train,
Dashing up and down the stairs, searching my pockets,
She told me that her sister in Cork wanted a loan of the axe;
It was late June and
The buddleia tree in the backyard   5
Had grown out of control.
The taxi was ticking over outside in the street,
All the neighbours noticing it.
'You mean that you want me to bring her down the axe?'
'Yes, if you wouldn't mind, that is –'   10
'A simple saw would do the job, surely to God
She could borrow a simple saw.'
'She said that she'd like the axe.'
'OK. There is a Blue Cabs taxi ticking over outside
And the whole world inspecting it,   15
I'll bring her down the axe.'
The axe – all-four-and-a-half feet of it –
Was leaning up against the wall behind the settee –
The fold-up settee that doubles as a bed.
She handed the axe to me just as it was,   20
As neat as a newborn babe,
All in the bare buff.
You'd think she'd have swaddled it up
In something – if not a blanket, an old newspaper,
But no, not even a token hanky   25
Tied in a bow round its head.
I decided not to argue the toss. I kissed her goodbye.

The whole long way down to Cork
I felt uneasy. Guilt feelings.
It's a killer, this guilt.   30
I always feel bad leaving her
But this time it was the worst.
I could see that she was glad
To see me go away for a while,
Glad at the prospect of being   35
Two weeks on her own,
Two weeks of having the bed to herself,

Two weeks of not having to be pestered
By my coarse advances,
Two weeks of not having to look up from her plate
And behold me eating spaghetti with a knife and fork.
Our daughters are all grown up and gone away.
Once when she was sitting pregnant on the settee
It snapped shut with herself inside it,
But not a bother on her. I nearly died.

As the train slowed down approaching Portarlington
I overheard myself say to the passenger sitting opposite me:
'I am feeling guilty because she does not love me
As much as she used to, can you explain that?'
The passenger's eyes were on the axe on the seat beside me.
'Her sister wants a loan of the axe …'
As the train threaded itself into Portarlington
I nodded to the passenger 'Cúl an tSúdaire!'
The passenger stood up, lifted down a case from the rack,
Walked out of the coach, but did not get off the train.
For the remainder of the journey, we sat alone,
The axe and I,
All the green fields running away from us,
All our daughters grown up and gone away.

110 POETRY FOCUS

'the train threaded itself into Portarlington'

Glossary

Father's Day: an important family occasion in honour of male parenting, traditionally celebrated on the third Sunday of June.
5 *buddleia tree*: colourful flowering shrub; butterfly bush.
23 *swaddled*: wrapped.
25 *token*: symbolic, nominal.
27 *argue the toss*: dispute the issue.

35 *prospect*: expectation.
38 *pestered*: bothered.
39 *coarse advances*: unrefined sexual demands.
53 *Cúl an tSúdaire*: Irish name for Portarlington (literally 'back of the tanner', referring to the tannery once located there). Durcan might well be making a snide comment about the town's humble origins.

INITIAL RESPONSE

1. In your opinion, what does the poem's first stanza reveal about the relationship between the poet and his wife? Refer closely to the text in your answer.

2. Select one image (or line) that has a surreal or bizarre impact in the poem. Briefly explain your choice.

3. Comment on the significance of the poem's final line: 'All our daughters grown up and gone away'.

STUDY NOTES

Because so much of his poetry has been autobiographical, Durcan's insecure relationships are already widely known. 'Father's Day, 21 June 1992' is taken from A Snail in my Prime *(1993) and recounts a crucial train journey when the poet confronts the adverse effects of time on his role as a husband and father. Typically, the poem alternates between tragicomedy, surreal scenes and devastating self-awareness. The abrupt changes of tone and mood are likely to be disconcerting for readers, who can never be completely sure about the poet's true feelings.*

In the anecdotal **opening lines**, Durcan assumes the persona of a slightly befuddled figure 'dashing' about the house. From the outset, there are suggestions of marriage difficulties, particularly in his petulant account of his wife's attitude towards him: 'She told me that her sister in Cork wanted a loan of the axe'. Everyone involved in this uneasy family drama seems slightly eccentric. **Durcan often finds grim humour in the most unexpected circumstances**. Is he suggesting that his sister-in-law is dangerously deranged? The poet's mention of the garden shrub that is now 'out of control' adds to the unstable atmosphere. Could this be a reference to his officious wife and her sister? Or is the marriage itself veering close to crisis? Meanwhile, the waiting taxi is 'ticking over', another possible symbol of the explosive domestic situation.

The strained exchange between the couple (**lines 9–16**) illustrates their barely concealed frustration with each other. Although the poet is reluctant to bring an axe on public transport, his wife is politely insistent: 'if you wouldn't mind'. She seems to be a strangely disembodied presence, reflecting the considerable lack of communication in the marriage. In choosing to do as he is asked on this occasion – 'I decided not to argue the toss' – Durcan indicates a history of marital disagreements. Almost as a defence mechanism to block out the truth about a relationship under threat, **Durcan's description of the scene becomes increasingly trancelike**. He exaggerates the importance of the axe – 'all-four-and-a-half feet of it' – comparing it to 'a newborn babe' (**line 21**). The simile has a poignant association with happier times, when his infant children represented what was truly meaningful about Father's Day. In a blurred state of distorted memories and nostalgic self-pity, the poet personifies the axe and wonders why it could not have been 'swaddled' or at least gift-wrapped with 'a bow round its head'.

Durcan's small domestic narrative develops in the poem's **second stanza**. On the train journey from Dublin to Cork, his tone is much more reflective as he laments his guilty mood: 'I always feel bad leaving her'. Acknowledging that his wife is 'glad' to be alone, he indulges in mock-serious self-recrimination. Not only will she will welcome a fortnight's break from his 'coarse advances', but she will no longer have to endure his irritating table manners, 'eating spaghetti with a knife and fork' (**line 41**). Whether such overstated self-accusation is totally sincere is, of course, open to question. At any rate, whatever humour that exists is soon replaced with **the stark reality of loss** that is at the heart of the poet's unhappiness: 'Our daughters are all grown up and gone away'. This heartbreaking admission, enhanced by broad assonant effects, provides a momentary explanation for the couple's failing marriage. However, in a sudden change in tone, the poet recalls another comic occasion when his young wife was pregnant and almost got trapped in the fold-up settee. Ironically, the memory does not lessen the deep sense of disappointment that he is experiencing.

The poem's **third stanza** is set at Portarlington Station, where Durcan seems overwhelmed by profound feelings of sorrow. However, the normality of his situation quickly turns into an anarchic event. In a dreamlike sequence, the poet imagines confiding in another passenger about his guilt 'because she does not love me/As much as she used to'. **The surreal sense of disorientation grows** when the encounter is viewed from the perspective of the stranger, whose 'eyes were on the axe on the seat beside me'. Needless to say, when Durcan calls out the station name in Irish, 'Cúl an tSúdaire', the frightened passenger leaves the coach as quickly as possible. Again, the farcical episode is underpinned with underlying heartbreak. In the **final lines**, we see a broken human being abandoned in a bizarre world of utter isolation: 'we sat alone,/The axe and I'. The ending is particularly lyrical, evoking the sadness of innocent times gone forever: 'All the green fields running away from us'. Durcan often uses the metaphor of travel to express significant changes in his life. The train journey to Cork is a remarkably sombre one, depicting a forlorn man who is still struggling to come to terms with the effects of time and the devastating fact that 'All our daughters' are 'grown up and gone away'. The concluding mood is one of estrangement and desolation. Durcan is only too aware that he no longer has a reason to celebrate Father's Day.

ANALYSIS

'Father's Day, 21 June 1992' is one of Paul Durcan's most personal and revealing poems. What aspects of the poem affected you most?

Sample Paragraph

After studying 'Father's Day, 21 June 1992', I had mixed feelings. In some ways, the poem is a desperately sad memory of the time when Durcan realised his marriage was ending. The cold conversation about bringing an axe to Cork was only amusing on the surface. The couple seemed like strangers and Durcan isn't in the mood for another argument – 'I decided not to argue the toss'. The mood in the family home is awkward. The discussion about bringing an axe on the train seems ludicrous, but it's difficult not to have sympathy for both the poet and his wife. There is a distance between them, evident in the ironic comment, 'I kissed her goodbye'. For me, the most moving part of the poem is Durcan's acknowledgement 'Our daughters are all grown up and gone away'. The serious tone, slow rhythm of this long thoughtful line, filled with mournful assonance, emphasises the poet's essential depression. He now accepts that there is nothing to keep his marriage alive and the poem's concluding lines left me genuinely sympathetic. Father's Day has lost all meaning for Durcan. The image of 'All our green fields running away from us' is very appropriate. As he looks out of the train window, the beauty of the Irish countryside is out of reach for the ageing poet. I thought this was a very moving symbol of his empty life – and I felt it was in keeping with the elegiac mood throughout this memorable poem.

Examiner's Comment

A very good personal response, showing true engagement with the poem: 'the poem's concluding lines left me genuinely sympathetic'. The focus throughout is on the emotional interaction with the poet's experience of failure and loss. Effective use was made of supportive quotes. Expression is also clear and varied: 'The serious tone and the slow rhythm of this long thoughtful line, filled with mournful assonance, emphasises the poet's essential depression'. In-depth analysis merits the top grade.

CLASS/HOMEWORK EXERCISES

1. 'The use of humour in Paul Durcan's poems provides revealing insights into his complex personal relationships.' Discuss this view, with particular reference to 'Father's Day, 21 June 1992'.

2. Trace the changing tones in the poem, 'Father's Day, 21 June 1992'. Support your answer with close reference to the text.

SUMMARY POINTS

- Durcan considers the destructive impact of time on his role as husband and father.
- Dislocated dreamlike atmosphere, heightened drama, edgy dialogue.
- Effective use of travel metaphor, irony, surreal scenes.
- Contrasting tones of discomfort, dark humour, reflection and resignation.

THE ARNOLFINI MARRIAGE

after Jan Van Eyck

We are the Arnolfinis.
Do not think you may invade
Our privacy because you may not.

We are standing to our portrait,
The most erotic portrait ever made, 5
Because we have faith in the artist

To do justice to the plurality,
Fertility, domesticity, barefootedness
Of a man and a woman saying 'we':

To do justice to our bed 10
As being our most necessary furniture;
To do justice to our life as a reflection.

Our brains spill out upon the floor
And the terrier at our feet sniffs
The minutiae of our magnitude. 15

The most relaxing word in our vocabulary is 'we'.
Imagine being able to say 'we'.
Most people are in no position to say 'we'.

Are you? Who eat alone? Sleep alone?
And at dawn cycle to work 20
With an Alsatian shepherd dog tied to your handlebars?

We will pause now for the Angelus.
Here you have it:
The two halves of the coconut.

'We are the Arnolfinis'

Glossary

The Arnolfini Marriage: Painted by the Dutch artist Jan Van Eyck in 1434 and regarded as a masterpiece, it has become a well-known symbol of marriage yet it retains its mystery.

1 *Arnolfinis*: Generally believed to represent the Italian merchant Giovanni and his wife Constanza, possibly in their home in the Flemish city of Bruges, perhaps undertaking a civil marriage ceremony. It was commissioned a year after Constanza died.
2 *invade*: infringe, violate, intrude on.
3 *privacy*: undisturbed time, secrecy.
5 *erotic*: sensual, suggestive.
6 *faith*: complete trust.
7 *To do justice*: to be fair and reasonable.
7 *plurality*: range, various meanings, truth.
8 *barefootedness*: In 15th-century Flanders, it was traditional to remove shoes for a wedding ceremony. This emphasised the marriage rite's blessedness and inviolability.
12 *reflection*: light thrown back from a surface; image formed by a reflection; a serious thought.
15 *minutiae*: small, precise details.
15 *magnitude*: greatness, importance.
22 *Angelus*: Christian devotional prayers commemorating the announcement to Mary that she was going to give birth to Jesus, the son of God.
24 *coconut*: fruit of the coconut palm, consisting of a hard fibrous husk and white inner core.

INITIAL RESPONSE

1. Based on your reading of the poem, do you think that the speakers are trying to shock or discomfort the reader? Briefly explain your views.

2. What, in your opinion, is Durcan's attitude towards the Arnolfinis? Refer to the poem in your answer.

3. Select one image from the poem that you found particularly interesting. Comment on its effectiveness.

STUDY NOTES

Paul Durcan's poetry collection Give Me Your Hand *(1994) was inspired by paintings in London's National Gallery. He has taken some of the most famous paintings in the world and interpreted them with his own distinctive poetic voice. We see the artwork 'through the prism of his imagination' as he projects himself into the famous characters of the paintings, slipping in and out of the pictures and 'sending us on flights of our own'. 'The Arnolfini Marriage' was inspired by the Jan Van Eyck oil painting, which is believed to represent a rich Italian merchant and his wife. It was painted in Bruges in 1434, 'in its own way new and revolutionary … For the first time in history, the artist became the perfect eye-witness'.*

The **opening line** of this dramatic monologue simply states, 'We are the Arnolfinis', a confident declaration by an assured, well-to-do couple. Durcan assumes their persona. The regular form of the poem – eight three-line stanzas – mirrors the orderly composition of the portrait. The speakers issue a stern warning to the reader: 'Do not think you may invade/Our privacy because you may not'. The formal tone contains more than a suggestion that Durcan is casting a satirical eye on the prim couple. Although this painting has become a famous symbol of marriage, representing the Arnolfinis in the intimate environment of their home, it conceals as much as it reveals. It is, however, an utterly convincing picture of a room as well as the people who inhabit it. Argument rages over the original painting, but the most recent view suggests that the couple are Giovanni and Constanza Arnolfini. Some critics maintain that the woman is simply holding up her full-skirted dress in the contemporary fashion. Although the wife looks pregnant, there are no recorded children for this couple. In the painting, the man's hand is raised as if taking an oath. Is it a record of a marriage contract in the form of a painting? **Durcan is clearly fascinated – both by the questions raised and by the answers we will never know**, since we cannot 'invade' the couple's 'privacy'.

The announcement at the start of the **second stanza** is also intriguing: 'We are standing to our portrait'. It is as if they are taking up position in readiness for military action. Is the poet suggesting that marriage can also have its share of conflict? Nonetheless, the speakers describe the painting as the 'most erotic portrait ever made'. It is certainly a sensual, stimulating picture celebrating the couple's sexual relationship as well as the sanctity of marriage. Throughout **stanza three**, Durcan emphasises the faith the Arnolfinis have in the artist's ability 'To do justice to the plurality' of their married lives. **There are many aspects to a man and woman saying 'we'.** A chance of having children, 'Fertility', is now possible. The challenge of living together as man and wife, 'domesticity', must now be faced. The removal of shoes, 'barefootedness', could suggest the vulnerability of laying bare one's soul to another in an intimate relationship. Going barefoot also means landing on the forefoot, the centre of gravity. This guarantees optimum balance and increased stability – but is this true for every marriage?

In **stanza four**, the Arnolfinis assert that they want the artist to 'do justice' and be objective in his depiction of their 'bed/As being our most necessary furniture'. It is central to their marriage. They hope the artist will execute a work of integrity, 'to our life as a reflection'. They want a true likeness. **Durcan's fondness for the surreal** becomes evident in the **fifth stanza** with the introduction of a more disturbing image: 'Our brains spill out upon the floor'. Does this suggest the suppressed aggression within the relationship? Meanwhile, the little dog, usually a symbol of loyalty, is sniffing 'The minutiae of our magnitude', the small details that reveal the couple's sense of their importance. In the **sixth stanza**, the repetition of 'we' shows the complacency of the couple now that they are man and wife: 'The most relaxing word in our vocabulary is "we"'. They luxuriate in their ability to say it: 'imagine being able to say "we"'. Then they realise that most people are not so fortunate – 'are in no position to say "we"'. Durcan has used the process of repetition to develop this thought. But is he also thinking about his own marriage and that he never expected it to fail?

The tone of the **seventh stanza** sharply challenges us with the uncomfortable question: 'Are you?' The solitary state of the reader is highlighted by the emphatic 'Who eat alone? Sleep alone?' Durcan sketches some of the mundane routines of modern life for people who 'at dawn cycle to work'. **What a contrast to the opulence of the Arnolfinis.** He uses another surreal image ('an Alsatian shepherd dog tied to your handlebars') to perhaps exaggerate the insecurity of our contemporary world.

In the **last stanza**, the couple 'pause now for the Angelus'. This Christian act of devotion commemorates the occasion when the angel Gabriel declared to Mary that she was to conceive the son of God: 'blessed is the fruit of thy womb, Jesus'. Here is the good news, the possibility of redemption. A final dreamlike image is presented when the two figures in the portrait are seen as 'The two halves of the coconut'. Is Durcan laughing at the Arnolfinis? Or does this naive metaphor refer to the Hindu custom of breaking a coconut at a wedding to ensure the blessing of the gods? In some other societies, the coconut is regarded as the tree that provides all the necessities of life. As always, the poem (like the Van Eyck painting) shows and conceals equally. Once again, **boundaries are blurred** as the reader is challenged to view the accepted norms relating to married life in a different way.

ANALYSIS

'Durcan's poetry celebrates plurality of perspective.' Discuss this statement in relation to the poem 'The Arnolfini Marriage'. Refer closely to the text in your response.

Sample Paragraph

In 'The Arnolfini Marriage', Paul Durcan, in my opinion, clearly demonstrates the important role the artist adopts in showing how necessary it is to hold more than one view on things, 'we have faith in the artist/To do justice to the plurality'. I think Durcan wants us to consider this portrait of the Arnolfinis as a symbol of marriage and all it entails. Is it a battlefield, 'We are standing to our portrait'? Is it a contented, cosy state, 'The most relaxing word in our vocabulary is "we"'? This poem reminds me of the cult of celebrity in our times. We see someone's image and we feel we know this person intimately. Durcan warns us of this, one-sided view, 'Do not think you may invade/our privacy'. Although we see these people in the most intimate of settings, beside a bed with the curtains drawn open, we do not know the real purpose of the painting. The poet recognises a number of meanings in the picture: a record of a civil marriage, a wish for a fertile marriage or a memorial to a dead wife. A surreal image concludes the poem, 'two halves of the coconut'. Is this a dismissive reference to the self-important couple? Is it a reference to a blessing of a wedding? As usual, the nonconformist Durcan has succeeded in showing us that there are many ways to view someone or something. He has challenged our fixed notions of the way things are. After all, who goes to work with 'an Alsatian shepherd dog tied' to a bicycle? The puzzles in the poem show the complexity of humanity. He has raised many interesting questions with this 'reflection'.

Examiner's Comment

Overall, a well-focused response that addresses a demanding question. There is effective use of quotation throughout and some good personal engagement with the poem. Apart from an over-reliance on questions, the paragraph offers several interesting discussion points about Durcan's perspective. The focus on addressing the task ('He has challenged our fixed notions of the way things are.') in the question merits the top grade.

CLASS/HOMEWORK EXERCISES

1. 'Durcan does verbally what painting does visually.' Discuss this view, using suitable reference to the poem 'The Arnolfini Marriage'.

2. Some of Durcan's poems are known for their strange, dreamlike quality. To what extent is this true of 'The Arnolfini Marriage'? Support your response with close reference to the text.

SUMMARY POINTS

- Dramatic monologue where Durcan assumes the personas of the rich married couple.
- Effective use of repetition, questions, suggestion.
- Characteristic fondness for distorted/surreal description.
- Contrasting tones – formal, reflective, challenging.

ROSIE JOYCE

I

That was that Sunday afternoon in May
When a hot sun pushed through the clouds
And you were born!

I was driving the two hundred miles from west to east,
The sky blue-and-white china in the fields 5
In impromptu picnics of tartan rugs;

When neither words nor I
Could have known that you had been named already
And that your name was Rosie –

Rosie Joyce! May you some day in May 10
Fifty-six years from today be as lucky
As I was when you were born that Sunday:

To drive such side-roads, such main roads, such ramps, such roundabouts,
To cross such bridges, to by-pass such villages, such towns
As I did on your Incarnation Day. 15

By-passing Swinford – Croagh Patrick in my rear-view mirror –
My mobile phone rang and, stopping on the hard edge of P. Flynn's highway,
I heard Mark your father say:

'A baby girl was born at 3.33 p.m.
Weighing 7 and a 1/2 lbs in Holles Street. 20
Tough work, all well.'

II

That Sunday in May before daybreak
Night had pushed up through the slopes of Achill
Yellow forefingers of Arum Lily – the first of the year;

Down at the Sound the first rhododendrons 25
Purpling the golden camps of whins;
The first hawthorns powdering white the mainland;

The first yellow irises flagging roadside streams;
Quills of bog-cotton skimming the bogs;
Burrishoole cemetery shin-deep in forget-me-nots;

The first sea pinks speckling the seashore;
Cliffs of London Pride, groves of bluebell,
First fuchsia, Queen Anne's Lace, primrose.

I drove the Old Turlough Road, past Walter Durcan's Farm,
Umbrella'd in the joined handwriting of its ash trees;
I drove Tulsk, Kilmainham, the Grand Canal.

Never before had I felt so fortunate
To be driving back into Dublin city;
Each canal bridge an old pewter brooch.

I rode the waters and the roads of Ireland,
Rosie, to be with you, seashell at my ear!
How I laughed when I cradled you in my hand.

Only at Tarmonbarry did I slow down,
As in my father's Ford Anglia half a century ago
He slowed down also, as across the River Shannon

We crashed, rattled, bounced on a Bailey bridge;
Daddy relishing his role as Moses,
Enunciating the name of the Great Divide

Between the East and the West!
We are the people of the West,
Our fate to go East.

No such thing, Rosie, as a Uniform Ireland
And please God there never will be;
There is only the River Shannon and all her sister rivers

And all her brother mountains and their family prospects.
There are higher powers than politics
And these we call wildflowers or, geologically, people.

Rosie Joyce – that Sunday in May
Not alone did you make my day, my week, my year
To the prescription of Jonathan Philbin Bowman – 60

Daymaker!
Daymaker!
Daymaker!

Popping out of my daughter, your mother –
Changing the expressions on the faces all around you – 65
All of them looking like blue hills in a heat haze –

But you saved my life. For three years
I had been subsisting in the slums of despair,
Unable to distinguish one day from the next.

III

On the return journey from Dublin to Mayo 70
In Charlestown on Main Street
I meet John Normanly, organic farmer from Curry.

He is driving home to his wife Caroline
From a Mountbellew meeting of the Western Development Commission
Of Dillon House in Ballaghadereen. 75

He crouches in his car, I waver in the street,
As we exchange lullabies of expectancy;
We wet our foreheads in John Moriarty's autobiography.

The following Sunday is the Feast of the Ascension
Of Our Lord into Heaven: 80
Thank You, O Lord, for the Descent of Rosie onto Earth.

'There is only the River Shannon'

Glossary

6 *impromptu*: spontaneous, spur-of-the-moment.
15 *Incarnation Day*: Rosie's day of birth, seen by Durcan as blessed.
16 *Croagh Patrick*: Co. Mayo mountain and place of religious pilgrimage.
17 *P. Flynn's highway*: satirical reference to an impressive new road in the constituency of a former government minister, Padraig Flynn.
20 *Holles Street*: Dublin maternity hospital.
24 *Arum Lily*: colourful flower.
25 *the Sound*: the small village of Achill Sound on Achill Island.
25 *rhododendrons*: vivid shrubs that flower in springtime.
26 *whins*: gorse; wild bushes with yellow flowers.
27 *hawthorns*: thorny hedgerow bushes that usually have white flowers.
29 *Quills of bog-cotton*: stems of sedge plants with flower heads resembling tufts of cotton.
31 *sea pinks*: grass-like stalks with pink flowers.
32 *London Pride*: long-stemmed evergreen plant that flowers in pale pink clusters.
33 *fuchsia*: widely cultivated bush with brilliant deep purplish-reddish colours.
33 *Queen Anne's Lace*: tall plant with fern leaves and bright white flowers.
39 *pewter*: dark grey-coloured metal.
44 *Ford Anglia*: brand of family car.
46 *Bailey bridge*: small temporary bridge.
47 *relishing*: delighting in, appreciating.
47 *Moses*: Biblical figure and religious prophet chosen by God to lead the Jewish people out of slavery.
57 *geologically*: geographically, in natural history.
60 *Jonathan Philbin Bowman*: journalist and broadcaster.
61 *Daymaker*: Durcan repeats a comment used by Philbin Bowman about people who made him feel more cheerful.
68 *subsisting*: struggling to live.
78 *wet our foreheads*: colloquial expression for having a celebratory drink (based on baptising a newborn child).
78 *John Moriarty*: Irish philosopher and mystic.
79 *Feast of the Ascension*: important Christian day commemorating the bodily ascension of Jesus into heaven.

INITIAL RESPONSE

1. Based on your reading of Section I of the poem, describe Paul Durcan's mood as he drives to Dublin. Support your answer with reference to the text.

2. What does Durcan reveal about his attitude to Ireland in Section II? In your response, use suitable reference to the poem.

3. Vivid imagery is a recurring feature of this poem. Select one image that you consider particularly striking and comment briefly on your choice.

STUDY NOTES

'Rosie Joyce' (taken from Paul Durcan's 2004 collection, The Art of Life) celebrates the birth of the poet's granddaughter. Her arrival into the world represents a wonderful new beginning in the poet's life. He has frequently used the motif of travel to signify self-renewal, opportunities to reflect on change and emotional development. In this case, Durcan recalls a car journey he took in May 2001 from County Mayo to Dublin. Along the way, images of landscape and movement reveal his newfound sense of optimism.

The casual, narrative opening of Section I is typical of so many of Durcan's autobiographical poems. There is a nostalgic quality to the description of that golden Sunday afternoon: 'a hot sun pushed through the clouds' (**line 2**). Rosie's birth is immediately symbolised through images drawn from the world of nature. **The idyllic setting reflects Durcan's euphoric tone** perfectly. Breathless exclamatory phrasing ('And you were born!') and the repetition of the child's name convey the poet's immense joy. Run-on lines underpin the insistent rhythm. It is Rosie's 'Incarnation Day' (**line 15**), a special occasion on which the poet feels truly blessed.

Driving 'two hundred miles from west to east', Durcan is intensely aware of the newness of nature that is reflected all around him. Seeing the world through a child's eyes, he takes great delight in listing everything he notices: 'such side-roads, such main roads, such ramps, such roundabouts'. His deeply satisfying sense of freedom to travel through the country at large is palpable. By persistently naming local places ('By-passing Swinford – Croagh Patrick in my rear-view mirror'), **Durcan acknowledges their equally distinctive importance**. He recounts the crucial details of the telephone message alerting him of Rosie's birth. The simple facts recording the baby's weight and time of birth – 'A baby girl was born at 3.33 p.m.' (**line 19**) – contrast sharply with Durcan's highly emotional response.

Section II focuses on the Irish landscape in summertime. Durcan highlights the colourful diversity and energy of an island in bloom: 'Yellow forefingers of Arum Lily – the first of the year' (**line 24**). **The sense of regeneration is everywhere**: 'the first rhododendrons', 'first hawthorns', ' first yellow irises'. Repetition suggests the widespread growth and the careful choice of forceful verbs ('powdering', 'skimming', 'speckling') adds to our understanding of the vivid power of nature at its height. Everywhere he looks, Durcan sees the shrubs and flowers celebrating Rosie's birth – even the graveyard at Burrishoole is 'shin-deep in forget-me-nots' (**line 30**). The poet mentions more of the place-names on his cross-country route: 'the Old Turlough Road, past Walter Durcan's Farm'. The intimacies of setting and the poet's enthusiastic voice carry into reflections of his excitement: 'Never before had I felt so fortunate' (**line 37**). Indeed, his great desire to be with Rosie seems almost Biblical: 'I rode the waters and the roads of Ireland'.

The poet's careful observation of rural villages reminds him of a journey he once took 'half a century ago'. During that earlier drive, he remembers his father 'relishing his role as Moses' as he named the River Shannon as 'the Great Divide/Between the East and the West' (**lines 48–49**). Durcan takes the opportunity of his granddaughter's birth to present his own view: 'No such thing, Rosie, as a Uniform Ireland'. The poet develops his plea for tolerance and acceptance by emphasising the diversity of the country's geography: 'There is only the River Shannon and all her sister rivers/And all her brother mountains'. With simple clarity ('There are higher powers than politics'), **the poet dismisses the boundaries of class, religion and gender that have often divided Irish people**. After emphatically expressing devotion to his '*Daymaker*' granddaughter, Durcan names Rosie as his personal saviour in a tone that is manifestly reverential: 'you saved my life. For three years/I had been subsisting in the slums of despair' (**lines 67–68**).

In Section III, the mood is much more subdued as the poet recounts details of his 'return journey from Dublin to Mayo'. The daily social routines that mark small communities are illustrated by the chance meeting in Charlestown between Durcan and an old friend, an 'organic farmer from Curry'. Somewhat typically of Irish people's behaviour, their encounter is not without its awkward nuances: 'He crouches in his car, I waver in the street' (**line 76**). Before long, however, the two men share a drink in honour of the new baby. They discuss the life of Co. Kerry poet and philosopher, John Moriarty. This seemingly mundane moment represents what is best about Ireland's cultural and communal identity. **Rosie Joyce has now been accepted into her new natural and spiritual environment.** The cycle of life and death continues. In the poem's **final lines**, Durcan returns to his earlier religious mood with a formal offering of thanksgiving for his granddaughter's life. The motif becomes deliberately whimsical and prayer-like, building to a high point: 'Thank you, O Lord, for the Descent of Rosie onto Earth'.

ANALYSIS

'Paul Durcan frequently uses journeys as a metaphor for reflection or soul-searching.' To what extent do you agree with this statement? Support your answer with reference to the poem.

Sample Paragraph

Paul Durcan's love of travel is clearly evident in 'Rosie Joyce'. Journeys are often metaphors for new insights into life. His car journey from Mayo to visit his infant grand-daughter in Dublin gives him the perfect opportunity. He welcomes her into the world and begins to think deeply about what it means to be Irish. In the early lines, Durcan reflects on how lucky he is to be able to love a new family member. Everything on the route fills him with joy – and his upbeat tone is emphatic as he drives past 'such villages, such towns'. The variety and energy of nature thrills him. But the journey also reminds him of his youth when his father would tell him how the River Shannon was the 'Great Divide/ Between the East and the West'. However, Durcan no longer agrees and his message to his grand-daughter is a resounding one: 'No such thing, Rosie, as a Uniform Ireland'. The trip across country has given the poet a chance to clarify his own views on the diverse Ireland that Rosie will discover. I thought Durcan's description of our small island as a place of great scenic variety was the central idea in the poem – 'There is only the River Shannon and all her sister rivers/ And all her brother mountains'. He is welcoming the child into a pluralist Ireland – where he accepts all its cultural diversity. He sees people as being equal, above politics and other such labels. For Durcan, the two hundred mile trip has been enlightening. On a personal note, he sees the child as bringing joy to his spirit – 'you saved my life'. The sincerity of Durcan's reverential tone is quite moving. His journey has been physical and spiritual – one of great happiness and discovery – a glimpse of how the first Christians felt when they celebrated the birth of Jesus.

Examiner's Comment

This clearly written and incisive response focuses effectively on the significance of the poet's journey – both on a personal and cultural level. Useful quotations support key discussion points and the expression is very well handled (although dashes are slightly over-used). There is also some very good engagement with the poem, especially when discussing Durcan's powerful varied tones: 'The sincerity of Durcan's reverential tone is quite moving'. A top grade response.

CLASS/HOMEWORK EXERCISES

1. 'Durcan's poems can be challenging at times, but they provide a singularly refreshing view of Ireland.' Discuss this view with particular reference to 'Rosie Joyce'. Support the points you make with reference to the poem.

2. Paul Durcan's poems have been described as diary entries which reveal the poet's private life. Discuss this view with particular reference to the poem, 'Rosie Joyce'.

SUMMARY POINTS

- Characteristically introspective exploration of regeneration.
- Effective use of the extended travel metaphor.
- Detailed description, recurring images of movement, landscape, birth.
- Contrasting moods and tones of delight, reflection and resignation.

THE MACBRIDE DYNASTY

What young mother is not a vengeful goddess
Spitting dynastic as well as motherly pride?
In 1949 in the black Ford Anglia,
Now that I had become a walking, talking little boy,
Mummy drove me out to visit my grand-aunt Maud Gonne   5
In Roebuck House in the countryside near Dublin,
To show off to the servant of the Queen
The latest addition to the extended family.
Although the eighty-year-old Cathleen Ni Houlihan had taken to her bed
She was keen as ever to receive admirers,   10
Especially the children of the family.
Only the previous week the actor MacLiammóir
Had been kneeling at her bedside reciting Yeats to her,
His hand on his heart, clutching a red rose.
Cousin Séan and his wife Kid led the way up the stairs,   15
Séan opening the door and announcing my mother.
Mummy lifted me up in her arms as she approached the bed
And Maud leaned forward, sticking out her claws
To embrace me, her lizards of eyes darting about
In the rubble of the ruins of her beautiful face.   20
Terrified, I recoiled from her embrace
And, fleeing her bedroom, ran down the stairs
Out onto the wrought-iron balcony
Until Séan caught up with me and quieted me
And took me for a walk in the walled orchard.   25
Mummy was a little but not totally mortified:
She had never liked Maud Gonne because of Maud's
Betrayal of her husband, Mummy's Uncle John,
Major John, most ordinary of men, most
Humorous, courageous of soldiers,   30
The pride of our family,
Whose memory always brought laughter
To my grandmother Eileen's lips. 'John,'
She used cry, 'John was such a gay man.'
Mummy set great store by loyalty; loyalty   35
In Mummy's eyes was the cardinal virtue.
Maud Gonne was a disloyal wife
And, therefore, not worthy of Mummy's love.
For dynastic reasons we would tolerate Maud,
But we would always see through her.   40

'the ruins of her beautiful face'

Glossary

1 *vengeful*: vindictive.
1 *goddess*: deity, powerful creature.
2 *Spitting*: hissing.
2 *dynastic*: old established family superiority.
5 *Maud Gonne*: English-born Irish revolutionary who had a stormy relationship with W.B. Yeats. She married Major John MacBride, with whom she had one son.
9 *Cathleen Ni Houlihan*: Cathleen is an old woman of Ireland who mourns the loss of her four provinces, which have been taken by the English. Maud Gonne played her in Yeats's famous play.
12 *MacLiammóir*: Micheál MacLiammóir, a flamboyant English-born Irish actor.
13 *Yeats*: famous Irish poet who celebrated Maud Gonne in his poetry throughout his life.
15 *Cousin Séan*: Séan MacBride was Maud and Major John's only son. He went on to win a Nobel Peace Prize.
19 *lizards*: reptiles with rough, prickly skin.
21 *recoiled*: jumped back, flinched.
23 *wrought-iron*: tough form of iron fashioned into swirling shapes.
26 *mortified*: embarrassed, uncomfortable.
28 *Uncle John*: Major John MacBride was the uncle of Paul Durcan's mother. He was executed by the British for his part in the 1916 Rising.
36 *cardinal*: greatest, essential.
37 *disloyal*: treacherous, unfaithful.
39 *tolerate*: endure, accept.
40 *see through*: see the reality, realise the truth about.

INITIAL RESPONSE

1. From your reading of the poem, briefly describe Durcan's attitude to Maud Gonne when he was taken to meet her.

2. Surreal imagery is a feature of Paul Durcan's poetry. Choose one surreal image from the poem that made an impact on you and discuss its effectiveness.

3. Comment on Durcan's use of repetition in this poem. Support your answer with reference to the text.

STUDY NOTES

'The MacBride Dynasty' was published in Paul Durcan's 2007 collection, The Laughter of Mothers. *These poignant poems commemorate his mother, Sheila MacBride Durcan. They contrast sharply with the many withering poems about his father, Judge John Durcan. The poet's mother was the niece of one of the renowned martyrs of 1916, Major John MacBride, the husband of Maud Gonne. This poem relates the time Durcan's mother made a personal journey back to her hometown to introduce her young son, ('The latest addition' to the family dynasty), to her uncle's famous wife.*

The **opening lines** dramatically pose an intriguing question with mock solemnity: 'What young mother is not a vengeful goddess/Spitting dynastic as well as motherly pride?' The epic reference suggests the angry response to a slur on the family name. **The MacBrides regarded themselves as a family of significance** in the Mayo region, as can be seen from the poem's title. They were a dynasty, a prominent and powerful family who retained their power and influence through several generations. If an injustice is perceived to have been done to one of the family, the other members close ranks against the outsider. The onomatopoeic verb 'Spitting' graphically depicts the mythical outrage of the young mother. Precise details root the visit to 'grand-aunt Maud' firmly in reality: 'In 1949 in the back Ford Anglia'. At that time, most people in Ireland could not afford to own a car. Broad-vowelled assonance ('walking, talking') mimics the babbling of the five-year-old Durcan as the proud mother drives to Roebuck House to show off her young son to Maud. A sly reference is made to Gonne's autobiography, *A Servant of the Queen*, which refers to a vision she had of the Irish queen of old, Cathleen Ni Houlihan. The reference is also ironic since Gonne was an Irish nationalist who rejected the British queen.

The lengthy run-on **line 9** describes how the 80-year-old Maud had 'taken to her bed'. Is there a suggestion that she is a self-indulgent woman? She is referred to as the mythical character she played in Yeats's drama. In this personal narrative, **Durcan seems to be slowly dismantling the popular image of Maud Gonne** as a beautiful young woman, the feminist Irish activist loved by Yeats. Her vanity is obvious: 'She was keen as ever to receive admirers'. The rarefied, overly dramatic world she existed in is cleverly demonstrated by the intimate anecdote showing the famous Irish actor MacLiammóir on his knees at her bedside, 'clutching a red rose' while reciting the poetry of Yeats to her. Is the tone slightly disapproving? The formal, almost regal atmosphere of the house is captured in the description of how 'Cousin Seán and his wife Kid led the way up the stairs' as the door was opened and the arrival of Durcan's mother was announced. But the young Durcan is no MacLiammóir. He does not pay court, but runs away, terrified at this monster 'sticking out her claws' and whose 'lizards of eyes' flitted quickly about. With this bizarre image, the leading lady of nationalistic politics is reduced to a crumbling wreck as the devastation of her beauty by the cruel hand of time is laid bare: 'In the rubble of the ruins of her beautiful face' (**line 20**). The alliteration stresses the poignancy of this devastating portrait.

Maud Gonne's relationship with the MacBrides was intricate. She had turned down Yeats's offers of marriage and had married Major John in Paris in 1903. When the marriage ended, she made allegations of domestic violence. She raised her son in Paris until MacBride's execution and then returned to Ireland. The run-on lines (**lines 21–25**) convey the alarm of a little boy terrified out of his wits until his uncle calms him down with a 'walk in the walled orchard'. The long vowel 'a' and the gentle 'w' alliteration produce a soothing effect. **Line 26** carefully records his mother's subtle reaction to his behaviour: 'a little but not totally mortified'. **Was she secretly glad that her little son had not behaved well to a woman she did not respect?** The poet candidly reveals the source of his mother's distaste for Gonne: her 'Betrayal of her husband'. In contrast, a much more favourable picture is painted of Major John, not only through the poet's voice, but also his mother's. He is the 'pride of our family'. His light-heartedness is also noted: 'he 'always brought laughter/To my grandmother Eileen's lips'.

Durcan's ability to capture Irish speech is shown in **line 35**: 'Mummy set great store by loyalty'. The admirable characteristic is repeated: 'loyalty/In Mummy's eyes was the cardinal virtue'. But Maud had committed the cardinal sin of being 'a disloyal wife', for which there is no forgiveness. The repetition of the word 'Mummy' – delivered in a highly sarcastic tone – shows how the poet is influenced by his mother's judgement that Maud was 'not worthy of Mummy's love'. **Is Durcan also critical of his intolerant mother**, who adopts a superior attitude to the infamous Maud? Once again, the underlying MacBride tensions are exposed. The family ('we') would accept her grudgingly, but only 'For dynastic reasons'. The chilling qualification is in the **final line**: 'But we would always see through her'. History might well be fooled by Maud's mythical status, but the family knew what she truly was. Has Durcan succeeded in debunking another official state myth? No person or thing is immune to criticism or satirical comment. As a challenging poetic voice, he has always 'seen through' falseness. He believes language in Ireland has been abused 'by poets as much as by gunmen and churchmen'. Is he also criticising Yeats?

ANALYSIS

Paul Durcan is regarded as the 'Public Poet'. How is this shown in the poem 'The MacBride Dynasty'? Refer closely to the poem in your response.

Sample Paragraph

From the title of the poem to the slyly humorous last line, Durcan captures what others miss. He does not shy away from questioning popular, widely accepted beliefs. In this poem, he exposes not only the power struggles within a self-important family, the 'MacBride Dynasty', but also he reveals the real Maud Gonne as she is in the ill-health and arrogance of her later years, 'She was keen as ever to receive admirers'. The poet publicly deals with private matters and personally comments on some famous Irish public figures. The one-sided stance adopted by the MacBride family is clear for all to see in the flattering portrait of 'Uncle John'. His mother's critical attitude to the 'disloyal' Maud is revealed. She would 'tolerate' this woman, but only for 'dynastic reasons'. The poet reveals the elderly Maud Gonne to the public gaze, 'In the rubble of the ruins of her beautiful face'. Her power to influence has disappeared. In a way, she is a pathetic figure. She is now seen as a reptile with 'claws' and 'lizards of eyes darting about'. The absurdity between reality and image is being exposed through this fantasy. She is no longer the woman Yeats worshipped. A great myth has been exposed to the public. Now, not only Durcan and his mother, but we too can 'see through' and are not fooled by the artifice of 'a red rose'. In 'The MacBride Dynasty', Durcan has dared to express the unthinkable.

Examiner's Comment
This is a very good attempt at addressing a challenging question. There is close engagement with the poem: 'The absurdity between reality and image is being exposed through this fantasy', and a clear thematic response. Overall, points are effectively supported by useful reference and quotation. Ideas are expressed fluently throughout: 'The poet deals publicly with private matters'. A very high standard which deserves the top grade.

CLASS/HOMEWORK EXERCISES

1. 'Poetry is a form of entertainment, but it is not cheap.' Discuss this statement made by Durcan in relation to the poem 'The MacBride Dynasty'. Support your views with suitable reference to the text.

2. Durcan's poetic voice often goes beyond critical comment and can even become cruel on occasion. Discuss this view, supporting your answer with particular reference to 'The MacBride Dynasty'.

SUMMARY POINTS

- Autobiographical/anecdotal poem commemorating the poet's family.
- Dramatic opening, bizarre scenes, dark humour.
- Effective use of authentic speech patterns.
- Use of photographic imagery, run-on lines, assonance, repetition.
- Contrasting tones – critical, sardonic, reflective, sarcastic.

THREE SHORT POEMS

Paul Durcan's enigmatic two-line poems are sharp and epigrammatic. They are also characteristic of his richly textured work in accommodating his contradictory responses to Ireland and to personal relationships. Durcan's intense poetry often focuses on memories of loneliness. Even when he is being ironic, the essential bleakness of his poetic vision is still evident.

EN FAMILLE, 1979

Bring me back to the dark school – to the dark school of childhood:
To where tiny is tiny, and massive is massive.

'En Famille, 1979' almost appears to be a cry for help, as though the poet has never come to terms with the traumatic effects of his earliest experiences. The 'dark school' presents **a disturbing metaphor of his boyhood** and the force of his most intimate hopes and fears. Repetition and the exaggerated extremes of 'tiny' and 'massive' suggest childhood innocence. Durcan's use of the French title phrase (meaning 'with one's family' or 'at home') is heartbreakingly poignant. Yet he remains obsessed with the past. His unsettled childhood, particularly his painful relationship with his father, has marked much of his poetry.

MADMAN

Every child has a madman on their street:
The only trouble about *our* madman is that he's our father.

'Madman' offers further evidence that Paul Durcan's **poetry can encompass nightmares as well as dreams**. Despite this poem's humorous whimsy and surface levity, there is something harrowing about the admission. Terms such as 'madman' are often used casually. Within the immediate family context, however, the word takes on a much greater personal significance. Durcan's short poem raises interesting questions about our own perception of 'madness' and its effects on individuals.

IRELAND 2002

Do you ever take a holiday abroad?
No, we always go to America.

'**Ireland 2002**' is typical of those small 'nutshell poems' that aim to encapsulate a given period of recent history or define Irish contemporary life. The piece is usually read as a **trenchantly satirical criticism of the country's moneyed classes**, for whom America isn't considered 'abroad'. It could also refer to Ireland's history of emigration to the United States and that our diaspora no longer seems foreign. The poem is a reminder of how Ireland has become so culturally influenced by US fashions and attitudes over recent times. Durcan's glib tone echoes the self-absorbed nature of complacent Celtic Tiger Ireland at its height.

PAUL DURCAN: THE PUBLIC POET

Paul Durcan has always assumed the role of the public poet. Whether questioning Irish politics or simply documenting his day-to-day encounters with shopkeepers and bank clerks, his poems essentially attempt to capture what most people seem to miss.

Throughout his long career, Durcan has given mesmerising poetry recitals of his work to audiences in Ireland and internationally. He seems to enjoy the role of poet-as-storyteller and his readings have been extraordinarily popular. He has also recorded and released readings of his poems.

He has said, 'People have called me a performance poet – a phrase I deeply dislike. But to me, it's another part of the work – or rather, the fulfilment of it. The poem has to work on the page, but it has to be spoken as well.'

The poet's objections to being categorised are understandable. Such labels take away from the serious themes he explores and his inventive use of language. He is widely recognised for his authentic sense of Irish speech.

Surrealism is one of his most powerful satirical devices. Seemingly random flights of fantasy are recurring features of his narrative poems, highlighting incongruities between reality and an imaginary – often a bizarre – world. While such surreal scenes can be highly comic and entertaining, the poet's underlying sense of outrage can sometimes break through his verbal control.

Durcan himself has an expressive voice that rises and falls with emotion, always displaying perfect timing. He whispers some lines, sings others. He has even been known to shout. It all adds up to the powerful impact of his public readings.

'Durcan's mastery of tone, his manic confidentiality, his blithe expositions of the seemingly unthinkable, his hypnotic repetitions of what other poets would hardly dare utter once ... give an air of audacious authority unique in contemporary poetry.'

Brendan Kennelly

LEAVING CERT SAMPLE ESSAY

'Paul Durcan's poetry dares to explore the hidden areas of life in a confidential yet authoritative manner.'
Discuss this view, supporting your response with suitable reference to the poems by Durcan on your course.

Marking Scheme Guidelines

Candidates are free to agree and/or disagree with the statement. The key terms ('dares to explore the hidden areas of life' and 'confidential yet authoritative manner') should be addressed either explicitly or implicitly. Evidence of genuine engagement with the poems should be rewarded. Allow for a wide range of approaches in the answering.

Indicative material:

- Provocative treatment of key themes, such as history, love, family
- Convincing treatment of compelling personal disclosures
- Addresses revealing aspects of intimate relationships and identity
- Confident plurality of perspectives challenge views of readers
- Repetition as a powerful process for epiphany and self-discovery
- Sense of place and community adds authenticity
- Effective use of surreal imagery, symbolism, colloquial language, etc.

Sample Essay

(Durcan's poetry dares to explore the hidden areas of life)

1. Paul Durcan probes dark, bitter themes of contemporary Irish life, emigration and strained relationships. His meditations and monologues challenge the accepted views on Irish life as he keenly observes and elusively slides into surreal images to examine this odd world of ours. Like one of his favourite poets, Kavanagh, he sees the extraordinary in the ordinary and he enables readers to view life, as his character Cáit does, 'Looking toward our strange world wide-eyed'.

2. The poet addresses the sombre reality of emigration in 'The Girl with the Keys to Pearse's Cottage'. The young Irish girl's future was 'America-bound at summer's end'. This was no fun-filled adventure, no world-exploring gap year. 'She had no choice but to leave her home'. She was so much part of her landscape with her 'sun-red skirt and moon-black blazer', yet she is torn from her native environment. Her intriguing character is caught in the surprising alliterative image, 'El Greco eyes blaze back'. The piercing eyes, so similar to the exotic Spanish painter's portraits, illuminate the darkness felt by the poet at his personal loss. I was urged by the poet to view Ireland's history of exile as the shocking reality that after all the sacrifices of 1916, this country cannot support its own. Durcan bitterly laments his loss with the repetitive phrase, 'O Cáit Killann, O Cáit Killann'. I was convinced by his obvious frustration in his

account of the hidden tragedy of emigration which pulls people from their homes and shatters families.

3. Durcan is not afraid to expose intimate family relationships in all their complexities. 'Sport' explores the troubled relationship he had with his father. The devastation he experienced as a young man desperately attempting to impress his father is evident in the bleak phrases 'I was fearful I would let you down', 'Seldom if ever again in your eyes/Was I to rise to these heights'. Durcan had just played a game of football on the side of Grangegorman Mental Hospital to which he had been committed. The poet's efforts in this game is described in the typically heightened language of sports writing, 'I did not flinch', 'spectacular saves', 'Diving at full stretch'. However, he was met by his father 'Sniffing' his 'approval' as he coldly 'shook hands' with his son. I felt the aching longing of the poet to be regarded and praised, 'I may not have been mesmeric/But I had not been mediocre'. Durcan made me realise the hurt that is caused by the lack of close communication between family members. He is deeply hurt because he feels he is never quite good enough.

4. Marriage is successfully scrutinised in several of Durcan poems, including 'The Arnolfini Marriage', after the famous Dutch painting of a self-assured couple. He uses the language of military combat, 'We are standing to our portrait' to suggest that marriage can be a battle of wills. The vulnerability of this intimate relationship is conveyed by the detail of the couple's bare feet, 'barefootedness'. Durcan shows the complacent contentment of the married couple basking in the embrace of their togetherness, 'The most relaxing word in our vocabulary is "we"'. A series of sharp staccato questions blast out as the poet questions 'Who eat alone? Sleep alone?' – contrasting the individual life of the reader with the cosy intimacy of the two Arnolfinis. In presenting different views on married life, the poet challenged me to look again at the accepted norms of marriage.

5. Characteristically, Durcan spares neither himself nor the reader when he exposes the shocking consequences of a marriage break-up. 'Nessa' examines his personal relationship with his wife through the extended metaphor of a whirlpool, which is at once exciting and dangerous. Nessa is described as if she were an enchantress in an old Irish aisling leading the hopelessly devoted lover away, 'She took me by the index finger'. Her intoxicating attraction is echoed in the poet's hypnotic phrase, 'She was a whirlpool, she was a whirlpool'. The poem's central metaphor is a powerful literary device for reflecting on the contradictions of married life. Once again, Durcan is showing us contrasting views of romantic love. There is the thrill and exhilaration of Nessa seducing him, 'for me let your red hair down'. But there is also the destruction of the individual self, 'And I very nearly drowned'. The poem ends with a series of poignant questions reflecting Durcan's deep sense of loss – 'Will you stay with me on the rocks', 'Will you come for me into the Irish Sea'. This honest expression of emotion and admission of personal vulnerability act as a reminder that serious relationships can be overwhelming. The poet made me question whether love, no matter how romantic, should require the total sacrifice of self.

6. *Paul Durcan, with audacious authority, has stirred up accepted views by peering under the stones of society's accepted norms on such universal themes as emigration and relationships. He has allowed me to see the familiar world in a new light which enabled me to question and challenge. His 'bittersweet clowning' has produced intimate poems which truly reveal the essential oddness at the heart of the everyday secret areas of life.*

(approx. 865 words)

Examiner's Comment

A solid top-grade answer showing some clear personal interaction with Durcan's poetry. Generally focused on addressing the question. Most main points are dealt with effectively and there is good use of apt quotation. Some of the poems discussed, such as 'Sport', would have benefitted from a more thorough treatment of the striking techniques (e.g. varying tones and irony) that are used to expose the poet's preoccupations.

MARKING SCHEME
P = 13/15
C = 12/15
L = 13/15
M = 5/5
Total = 43/50

SAMPLE LEAVING CERT QUESTIONS ON DURCAN'S POETRY

(45/50 MINUTES)

1. 'Paul Durcan's poetry reflects a broad range of powerful feelings communicated through thought-provoking imagery.' Do you agree with this assessment of his poetry? Your answer should focus on the poet's themes and the way he expresses them. Support the points you make with suitable reference to the poems by Durcan on your course.

2. 'Durcan's vision of life is conveyed in poems that are both satirical and self-critical.' Discuss this statement, supporting your answer with suitable reference to the poetry of Durcan on your course.

3. 'The poetry of Paul Durcan explores the tensions of modern life in an inventive and insightful fashion.' Write a response to this statement, supporting your points with reference to the poems by Durcan on your course.

Sample Essay Plan (Q1)

'Paul Durcan's poetry reflects a broad range of powerful feelings communicated through thought-provoking imagery.' Do you agree with this assessment of his poetry? Your answer should focus on the poet's themes and the way he expresses them. Support the points you make with suitable reference to the poems by Durcan on your course.

- Intro: Identify the elements of the question to be addressed ('broad range of powerful feelings', 'thought-provoking imagery'). Introduce Durcan as a searingly honest poet who lays himself bare in the exploration of strong emotions arising from personal experiences. Communicates different aspects of the situations through precise and surreal imagery delivered in a variety of tones.

- Point 1: Despair and frustration at the common Irish experience of emigration, 'The Girl with the Keys to Pearse's Cottage'. Arresting image 'El Greco eyes blaze back' captures the essence of the girl and highlights the poet's deep yearning.

- Point 2: Fear of change is emphasised in '"Windfall", 8 Parnell Hill, Cork'. Different aspects of home are examined in similes such as 'a city as intimate and homicidal as a Little Marseilles'.

- Point 3: The challenge of being oneself when in a troubled relationship is shown in his deep disappointment at the cold response of his father in 'Sport'. An image of precise detail conveys the moment 'Sniffing your approval'.

- Point 4: Durcan is joyful as he is deeply moved by the lasting power of love in 'Nessa'. The image of a whirlpool expresses the excitement and danger of a close romantic relationship.

- Point 5: Bizarre imagery and a variety of tones allow Durcan to explode icons and myths in 'The MacBride Dynasty'.

- Conclusion: The sensitive poet, Durcan, illuminates our complex world, challenging us to view and reconsider its multifaceted aspects.

Sample Essay Plan (Q1)

Develop one of the above points into a paragraph.

Sample Paragraph: Point 5

The disapproving feeling of Paul Durcan's mother towards her relative, Maud Gonne, and her pride in her own family is provocatively conveyed in the poem 'The MacBride Dynasty'. Maud Gonne was a revered figure in early 20th-century Irish history, beloved of the poet W.B. Yeats and wife of Major John MacBride, a patriot of the 1916 Rising. She was greatly admired and the 'actor MacLiammóir/ Had been kneeling at her bedside reciting Yeats to her'. Through two intimate perspectives, Durcan's mother's and his five-year-old self, a different picture of this symbolic woman emerges. The young Durcan's terror of this iconic woman is revealed through surreal imagery. He cruelly paints a devastating portrait of the once-beautiful Maud, 'sticking out her claws/To embrace me, her lizards of eyes darting about'. Through this monstrous imagery, Durcan challenges the accepted view of this famous woman. A similarly negative portrait of Maud is shown through the dismissive comment delivered at the conclusion of the poem, 'But we would always see through her'. She had been viewed and judged by the family as unworthy because of her behaviour towards her husband, the relative of Durcan's mother who 'set great store by loyalty' and Maud had not matched up. The cutting tone of this line slashes through the veneer of Maud's greatness.

Examiner's Comment

As part of a full essay, this solid response is very well-rooted in the text. Quotes are integrated effectively and expression is both varied and assured throughout: 'Durcan's terror of this iconic woman is revealed through surreal imagery', 'The cutting tone of this line slashes through the veneer of Maud's greatness'. Lively expression and a clear focus on the task guarantee a top grade.

LAST WORDS

'His songs celebrate our small mercies and tender decencies in a world that favours the corrupt.'

Paula Meehan

'He makes particularly engaging poems out of passing conversations - "You're looking great – are you going to a wedding?"/"Oh God no – I'm coming back from a wake."'

Deirdre Collins

'Like all first-class comedians, he is deadly serious.'

Terry Eagleton

ROBERT FROST

1874–1963

'A poem begins in delight and ends in wisdom.'

One of the great 20th-century poets, Robert Frost is highly regarded for his realistic depictions of rural life and his command of American colloquial speech. His work frequently explores themes from early 1900s country life in New England, often using the setting to examine complex social and philosophical ideas. Nature is central to his writing. While his poems seem simple at first, they often transcend the boundaries of time and place with metaphysical significance and a deeper appreciation of human nature in all its beauty and contradictions. Despite many personal tragedies, he had a very successful public life. It is ironic that such a calm, stoical voice emerged from his difficult background. At times bittersweet, sometimes ironic, or often marvelling at his surroundings, Frost continues to be a popular and often-quoted poet. He was honoured frequently during his lifetime, receiving four Pulitzer Prizes.

To find out more about Robert Frost, or to hear readings of his poems, you could do a search of some of the useful websites available such as YouTube, bbc.co.uk and poetryarchive.org or access additional material on this page of your eBook.

Prescribed Poems — HIGHER LEVEL

Note that Frost uses American spellings in his work.

❶ 'The Tuft of Flowers'*
One of Frost's best-loved works, this poem describes how a simple clump of wild flowers succeeds in uniting two separate people. The poem illustrates Frost's technique of bringing readers through an everyday rustic experience to reveal a universal truth. — **144**

❷ 'Mending Wall'*
Repairing a damaged wall between his neighbour and himself, Frost considers the theme of community and fellowship, and wonders if 'Good fences make good neighbors'. — **149**

❸ 'After Apple-Picking'
Set on his New England farm at the end of the apple harvest, Frost meditates on the nature of work, creativity and of what makes a fulfilled life. Characteristically, the poem is thought-provoking and open to many interpretations. — **154**

❹ 'The Road Not Taken'
Another of Frost's most popular poems. Using the symbol of a remote country crossroads, the poet dramatises the decisions people face in life – and the consequences of their choices. — **159**

❺ 'Birches'
The sight of some forest birches excites Frost's imagination to associate childhood games of swinging on the trees with the process of writing poetry. The poem has been seen as an expression of Frost's own philosophical outlook on life. — **164**

6 **'Out, Out—'***
This affecting poem is based on an actual story of a serious chainsaw accident.
Despite the tragedy, Frost leaves readers in no doubt of life's grim reality: 'It goes on'.   **169**

7 **'Spring Pools'**
In this captivating lyric poem, the fragile beauty and transience of the pools give
Frost an acute awareness of the natural cycle of growth, decay and renewal.   **174**

8 **'Acquainted with the Night'**
This short lyric depicts the dark, alienating side of urban life. Familiar themes include
the passing of time and lack of communication. In metaphorical terms, Frost also
explores 'the dark night of the soul'.   **177**

9 **'Design'**
Frost's sonnet, depicting nature as volatile and terrifying, addresses the possibility
of an underlying plan or design for the universe.   **182**

10 **'Provide, Provide'**
Another poem that deals with some of Frost's favourite themes – time, old age
and independence. For Frost, however, the only certainty or constant in life is change.   **186**

1 THE TUFT OF FLOWERS

I went to turn the grass once after one
Who mowed it in the dew before the sun.

The dew was gone that made his blade so keen
Before I came to view the levelled scene.

I looked for him behind an isle of trees;   5
I listened for his whetstone on the breeze.

But he had gone his way, the grass all mown,
And I must be, as he had been,–alone,

'As all must be,' I said within my heart,
'Whether they work together or apart.'   10

But as I said it, swift there passed me by
On noiseless wing a bewildered butterfly,

Seeking with memories grown dim o'er night
Some resting flower of yesterday's delight.

And once I marked his flight go round and round,   15
As where some flower lay withering on the ground.

And then he flew as far as eye could see,
And then on tremulous wing came back to me.

I thought of questions that have no reply,
And would have turned to toss the grass to dry;   20

But he turned first, and led my eye to look
At a tall tuft of flowers beside a brook,

A leaping tongue of bloom the scythe had spared
Beside a reedy brook the scythe had bared.

The mower in the dew had loved them thus,   25
By leaving them to flourish, not for us,

Nor yet to draw one thought of ours to him,
But from sheer morning gladness at the brim.

The butterfly and I had lit upon,
Nevertheless, a message from the dawn, 30

That made me hear the wakening birds around,
And hear his long scythe whispering to the ground,

And feel a spirit kindred to my own;
So that henceforth I worked no more alone;

But glad with him, I worked as with his aid, 35
And weary, sought at noon with him the shade;

And dreaming, as it were, held brotherly speech
With one whose thought I had not hoped to reach.

'Men work together,' I told him from the heart,
'Whether they work together or apart.' 40

'his long scythe whispering'

Glossary

Tuft: cluster, bunch.
1 turn: upturn; toss grass to dry it out.
3 keen: sharp; effective.
6 whetstone: stone used for sharpening scythes.
18 tremulous: trembling or nervous.
22 brook: stream.
23 scythe: implement used for cutting grass or hay.
29 lit upon: discovered.
33 kindred: closely related to.

INITIAL RESPONSE

1. Describe the dominant mood in lines 1–10 of the poem.

2. Choose two images from the poem that you found particularly interesting and effective. Briefly explain your choice in both cases.

3. Would you describe the poem as uplifting? Give reasons for your answer.

STUDY NOTES

The poem describes how a simple, uncut clump of wild flowers can unite two separate people. It is one of Frost's best-loved works and typifies his technique of bringing readers through an everyday rustic experience to reveal a universal truth – in this case about alienation, friendship and communication. The poem consists of 20 rhymed couplets written in strict verse. Frost once remarked that 'writing without structure is like playing tennis without a net'.

The narrative voice in the **opening section** of the poem is relaxed, in keeping with the unhurried rhythm. Frost's initial tone is low-key and noncommittal. The speaker has gone out to turn the grass so that it can dry. Someone else had mowed it earlier 'in the dew before the sun'. **Lines 5–6** reveal the speaker's sense of solitude and isolation; the unnamed mower has 'gone his way'. This leads him to consider **the loneliness of the scene and of human experience**. The introspective mood becomes more depressed as the poet searches for his fellow worker. Figurative descriptions of the 'levelled scene' and 'an isle of trees' add to the atmosphere of pessimism as the speaker implies that he must also be 'alone'. For Frost, this is the essential human experience for all, 'Whether they work together or apart'.

The poem's **second section** is marked by the sudden appearance of a 'bewildered butterfly'. After fluttering 'round and round' looking for the 'resting flower' that gave it such delight the day before, it then flies close to the speaker: 'on tremulous wing came back to me'. The adjective 'tremulous' suggests fragility and a **new sense of excited anticipation in the air**. The butterfly seems to reflect the speaker's 'questions that have no reply'. Perhaps they have both enjoyed great happiness in the past. The butterfly eventually turns and leads the speaker to a 'tall tuft of flowers beside a brook' that have escaped the mower's scythe – not by accident, but because 'he had loved them' and left them to flourish out of 'sheer morning gladness'.

The significance of the meadow flowers and the brook cannot be overlooked, because here the **mood suddenly changes to optimism**. The presence of the mysterious butterfly establishes communication between the early-morning mower and the narrator. Frost suggests this connection with his vivid description of the spared flowers as 'a leaping tongue of bloom'. In the **final section**, the speaker and the butterfly 'lit upon,/Nevertheless, a message from the dawn'. With images such as the 'wakening birds around' and a 'spirit kindred to my own', we might assume that this 'message' could indeed be one of human friendship and communal love.

The ending is paradoxical: 'Men work together ... Whether they work together or apart'. However, **Frost believed in spiritual presence and was inspired by an overwhelming sense of fellowship**. Although apart, the speaker and the absent mower are working with a shared appreciation of nature's beauty and a common commitment to a better world. The poem could also be interpreted biographically, since Frost had lost several of his loved ones and may well have written it as an emotional outlet. Even though his family members were deceased, he remains close to them in spirit. Whatever the poet's intention, readers should draw their own conclusions from the poem.

ANALYSIS

In your view, is 'The Tuft of Flowers' a dramatic poem? Refer closely to the text in your answer.

Sample Paragraph

I liked Frost's poem 'The Tuft of Flowers' for many reasons – one of which was its dramatic storyline. It has been described as a lyrical soliloquy. The narrative element is there from the start. The first mower mentioned seems a mysterious character who got me wondering. The central character (poet) is obviously close to nature as he goes about his work turning the grass. His inner drama interests me most, as his attitude changes from loneliness at the beginning to happiness and companionship. The two moods contrast dramatically. First, the sadness of 'I looked for him', 'I listened for his whetstone' and 'brotherly speech' and then the more sociable 'Men work together'. The clear, vivid imagery is also dramatic, especially the butterfly's flight – 'On noiseless wing' – and the description of the small outcrop of flowers – 'a leaping tongue of bloom'. Frost sets his poems in the secluded New England landscape and this provides a beautiful setting for what are deep meditations about the important questions in life – 'questions that have no reply'. The rhythm or movement of the poem quickens in the final lines as the poet expresses his positive view of life – 'Men work together'. I thought this was the ideal way to round off this quietly dramatic poem.

Examiner's Comment
A very well controlled answer focusing on some key dramatic elements, such as the use of the character's 'inner drama' and 'lyrical soliloquy'. Good personal interaction and commentary. References were handled effectively and points were clearly presented: 'The rhythm or movement of the poem quickens in the final lines as the poet expresses his positive view of life – "Men work together"'. A highly successful top grade response.

CLASS/HOMEWORK EXERCISES

1. In your opinion, what is Frost's main theme or message in 'The Tuft of Flowers'? Refer closely to the text of the poem in your answer.

2. 'The poetry of Robert Frost is known for its simple, everyday language.' To what extent is this evident in 'The Tuft of Flowers'? Support your answer with reference to the poem.

SUMMARY POINTS

- Typically narrative style – from the poet's own personal experience.
- Human fellowship and how humans can learn from nature are central themes.
- Contrasting moods – pessimism changes to optimism.
- Rhyming couplets create unity and help in expressing the poet's ideas.
- Effective use of onomatopoeia, rich imagery and symbolism.

2 MENDING WALL

Something there is that doesn't love a wall,
That sends the frozen-ground-swell under it,
And spills the upper boulders in the sun;
And makes gaps even two can pass abreast.
The work of hunters is another thing: 5
I have come after them and made repair
Where they have left not one stone on a stone,
But they would have the rabbit out of hiding,
To please the yelping dogs. The gaps I mean,
No one has seen them made or heard them made, 10
But at spring mending-time we find them there.
I let my neighbor know beyond the hill;
And on a day we meet to walk the line
And set the wall between us once again.
We keep the wall between us as we go. 15
To each the boulders that have fallen to each.
And some are loaves and some so nearly balls
We have to use a spell to make them balance:
'Stay where you are until our backs are turned!'
We wear our fingers rough with handling them. 20
Oh, just another kind of outdoor game,
One on a side. It comes to little more:
There where it is we do not need the wall:
He is all pine and I am apple orchard.
My apple trees will never get across 25
And eat the cones under his pines, I tell him.
He only says, 'Good fences make good neighbors.'
Spring is the mischief in me, and I wonder
If I could put a notion in his head:
'Why do they make good neighbors? Isn't it 30
Where there are cows? But here there are no cows.
Before I built a wall I'd ask to know
What I was walling in or walling out,
And to whom I was like to give offense.
Something there is that doesn't love a wall, 35
That wants it down.' I could say 'Elves' to him,
But it's not elves exactly, and I'd rather
He said it for himself. I see him there,

Bringing a stone grasped firmly by the top
In each hand, like an old-stone savage armed. 40
He moves in darkness as it seems to me,
Not of woods only and the shade of trees.
He will not go behind his father's saying,
And he likes having thought of it so well
He says again, 'Good fences make good neighbors.' 45

'Something there is that doesn't love a wall'

Glossary

1 *Something there is that doesn't love a wall*: ice and frost dislocate walls (also a pun on the poet's name).
4 *abreast*: side by side.
27 *Good fences make good neighbors*: one reading is that a strong fence protects by keeping people apart.
36 *Elves*: small supernatural beings, often malevolent.

INITIAL RESPONSE

1. In your opinion, what is it that doesn't love a wall? Support your answer with reference to the poem.

2. There are two speakers in the poem. Which one is the wiser, in your view? Refer to the text in your answer.

3. Point out two examples of humour in the poem and comment on how effective they are in adding to the message of 'Mending Wall'.

STUDY NOTES

This popular poem of Robert Frost's was written in 1913 and appears first in his second collection, 'North of Boston'. When the land was being cleared for agriculture, the stones gathered were made into walls. Frost said this poem 'contrasts two types of people'. President John F. Kennedy asked Frost to read this poem to Khrushchev, Russia's leader at the time of the Cuban Missile Crisis, when there was a possibility of another world war. The Berlin Wall was a symbol of the cold relations between Russia and the US. Imagine the leaders listening to the line 'I'd ask to know/What I was walling in or walling out'.

'Mending Wall' was responsible for building a picture of Frost as an ordinary New England farmer who wrote about normal events and recognisable settings in simple language. **Line 1** is mysterious: 'Something there is that doesn't love a wall'. **A force is at work to pull down the barriers** people insist on erecting. The speaker repairs the holes in the wall left by hunters: 'I have come after them and made repair'. But there are other holes in the wall, though 'No one has seen them made or heard them made'. In a yearly ritual, 'at spring mending-time', the poet and his neighbour meet to carry out repairs. Each looks after his own property as they walk along: 'To each the boulders that have fallen to each'. But a tone of coldness creeps into the poem amid this neighbourly task, with the repetition of how the wall has separated them at all times: 'set the wall between us', 'keep the wall between us'.

It is a difficult task, as the stones fall off as quickly as they are placed: 'Stay where you are until our backs are turned!' The **good-humoured banter** of the workers comes alive in the humorous remark, and readers feel as if they are there in New England watching the wall being repaired. The light-hearted mood is continued in **line 21** as the poet describes the activity as an 'outdoor game'. Then he comments that they don't even really need the wall where it is: 'He is all pine and I am apple orchard'. The poet jokes that his apple trees cannot go over and eat his neighbour's pine cones. His neighbour then speaks: 'Good fences make good neighbors'. He comes across as a serious type, quoting old sayings, in **contrast** to the mischievous poet: 'Spring is the mischief in me'. Frost is allying himself with the turbulent force that is pushing through the land, creating growth and pulling down walls. The neighbour is shown as one who has accepted what has been said without question, one who upholds the status quo.

In **line 31**, the poet poses questions to himself and wishes he could say to his neighbour, 'Why do they make good neighbours?' **He then wonders what a wall is keeping in and keeping out**. He also wonders what is pulling down the wall. He mockingly suggests 'Elves', then discounts that. Frost presents his rather uncommunicative neighbour in a series of unflattering images: 'an old-stone savage armed', 'He moves in darkness'. Is the poet saying that we must question received wisdom and not blindly follow what we are told? The neighbour, who accepts, is presented as a figure of repression who 'moves in darkness'. He just repeats 'Good fences make good neighbors' like a mantra. Is the poet suggesting that there are some people who derive comfort from just remaining the same, who do not welcome change ('He will not go behind his father's saying')?

The tone of the poem changes as the easy, neighbourly sociability of a shared task is replaced by a **feeling of tension**, first in the effort to keep the tumbling wall upright, and then in the opposite attitudes of the two neighbours – the mischievous, questioning poet and the taciturn, unquestioning neighbour 'like an old-stone savage'. The desire for human co-operation is often stopped, not by outside circumstances, but by a lack of desire on the part of the people involved. This is the poet commenting on human dilemmas. The easy-going, almost ruminative tone of someone musing to himself is written in blank verse, unrhymed iambic pentameter. The colloquial conversational phrases are all tightly controlled throughout this thought-provoking poem.

ANALYSIS

'Frost's deceptively simple poems explore profound truths about life.' Discuss this statement in relation to the poem 'Mending Wall'.

Sample Paragraph

I think Frost has very successfully given us a picture of two opposite personalities in this poem. The moody neighbour who doggedly walks on his side of the wall, 'We keep the wall between us both as we go', is vividly described. Here is a person who accepts what was told to him without question 'Good fences make good neighbors'. It is as if he is reciting the two-times tables. This is fact. There is no need to question. He is comfortable and secure in his traditional mindset. 'He will not go behind his father's saying'. He almost mindlessly repeats it. The poet describes him in unflattering terms, referring to him as 'an old stone-armed savage'. He also states that he was one who moved 'in darkness'. Frost does not agree with this unquestioning attitude of his neighbour's. It is not only a wall which divides these two, there is a completely different mindset. The poet has a lively personality, making jokes as they work, 'Stay where you are until our backs are turned', regarding the work as a game. However, he is not lightweight, as he asks the fundamental question about any boundary, 'I'd ask to know/What I was walling in or out'. He also asks the rather sensitive question about who he was likely to give offence to, with his wall. The neighbour has no such finer feeling, and is portrayed as someone who keeps on going in the same route as always. This apparently simple poem, written in blank verse, sticks in the reader's mind long after the reading. Frost has written a poem which is hard to get rid of. We are left wondering, are walls natural or necessary? Must we break down barriers to live as good neighbours? What if we are over-run?

Examiner's Comment

A solid response exploring the distance between contrasting personalities, a traditionalist and a maverick. Points are well developed through a fluent use of language, 'It is as if he is reciting the two-times tables. This is fact'. The questions towards the end show a lively engagement with the poem. However, the response is slightly marred by inaccurate quoting: 'an old stone-armed savage', 'walling in or out'. This prevents the answer achieving the highest grade.

CLASS/HOMEWORK EXERCISES

1. Comment on Frost's use of imagery. Do you find it effective? Refer closely to the text in your answer.

2. 'Frost's poems often have a universal significance and raise interesting questions about human relations.' To what extent do you agree or disagree with this view? Support your answer with reference to 'Mending Wall'.

SUMMARY POINTS

- Key themes include community, fellowship, boundaries and borders.
- Characteristic use of accessible, everyday language and humorous touches.
- Effective use of symbolism, slow-moving rhythm and unrhymed blank verse.
- Variety of tones: narrative, relaxed, interrogative, apprehensive and reflective.

3 AFTER APPLE-PICKING

My long two-pointed ladder's sticking through a tree
Toward heaven still,
And there's a barrel that I didn't fill
Beside it, and there may be two or three
Apples I didn't pick upon some bough.   5
But I am done with apple-picking now.
Essence of winter sleep is on the night,
The scent of apples: I am drowsing off.
I cannot rub the strangeness from my sight
I got from looking through a pane of glass   10
I skimmed this morning from the drinking trough
And held against the world of hoary grass.
It melted, and I let it fall and break.
But I was well
Upon my way to sleep before it fell,   15
And I could tell
What form my dreaming was about to take.
Magnified apples appear and disappear,
Stem end and blossom end,
And every fleck of russet showing clear.   20
My instep arch not only keeps the ache,
It keeps the pressure of a ladder-round.
I feel the ladder sway as the boughs bend.
And I keep hearing from the cellar bin
The rumbling sound   25
Of load on load of apples coming in.
For I have had too much
Of apple-picking: I am overtired
Of the great harvest I myself desired.
There were ten thousand thousand fruit to touch,   30
Cherish in hand, lift down, and not let fall.
For all
That struck the earth,
No matter if not bruised or spiked with stubble,
Went surely to the cider-apple heap   35
As of no worth.
One can see what will trouble
This sleep of mine, whatever sleep it is.

Were he not gone,
The woodchuck could say whether it's like his   40
Long sleep, as I describe its coming on,
Or just some human sleep.

'Toward heaven still'

Glossary

7   *Essence*: scent.
10 *glass*: ice.
12 *hoary*: covered in frost.
20 *russet*: reddish-brown.
22 *ladder-round*: a rung or support on a ladder.
34 *stubble*: remnant stalks left after harvesting.
40 *woodchuck*: groundhog, a native American burrowing animal.

INITIAL RESPONSE

1. Select one image that evokes the hard, physical work of apple-picking. Comment on its effectiveness.

2. What do you understand lines 27–29 to mean?

3. Write a short personal response to this poem.

STUDY NOTES

The poem is a lyrical evocation of apple harvesting in New England. Frost takes an ordinary experience and transforms it into a meditative moment. Harvesting fruit soon becomes a consideration of how life has been experienced fully but with some regrets and mistakes. Frost chose not to experiment but to use traditional patterns, or as he said, he preferred 'the old-fashioned way to be new'. 'After Apple-Picking' is not free verse, but it is among Frost's least formal works, containing 42 lines varying in length, a rhyme scheme that is also highly irregular and no stanza breaks.

The speaker in the poem (either Frost himself or the farmer persona he often adopted) feels himself drifting off to sleep with the scent of apples in the air. He thinks of the ladder he has left in the orchard still pointing to 'heaven'. Is the poet suggesting that his work has brought him closer to God? The slow-moving rhythm and broad vowel sounds ('two-pointed', 'bough', 'drowsing') in the **opening lines** reflect his **lethargic mood**. Although he seems close to exhaustion, he is pleased that the harvest is complete: 'But I am done with apple-picking now'. Ironically, his mind is filled with random thoughts about the day's work. The drowsy atmosphere is effectively communicated by the poet's mesmerising description: 'Essence of winter sleep is on the night'.

This dream-like state releases Frost's imagination and he remembers the odd sensation he felt while looking through a sheet of ice he had removed earlier from a drinking trough. While the memory is rooted in reality, it appears that he has experienced the world differently: 'I cannot rub the strangeness from my sight'. As he is falling asleep, he is conscious that his dreaming will be associated with **exaggerated images of harvesting**: 'Magnified apples appear and disappear' (**line 18**). The poet emphasises the sensuousness of what is happening. The vivid apples display 'every fleck of russet' and he can feel the pressure of the 'ladder-round' against his foot. He hears the 'rumbling sound' of the fruit being unloaded. The images suggest abundance: 'load on load of apples', 'ten thousand thousand'. Frost's use of repetition, both of evocative sounds and key words, is a prominent feature of the poem that enhances our appreciation of his intense dream.

Physically and mentally tired, the poet also relives the anxiety he had felt about the need to save the crop from being 'bruised or spiked with stubble', and not to lose them to 'the cider-apple heap'. In the poem's **closing lines**, which seem deliberately vague and distorted, Frost wonders again about the nature of consciousness: 'This sleep of mine, whatever sleep it is'. Like so many of his statements, the line is rich in possible interpretations. For some critics, the poem appears to be exploring the art and craft of writing. Others take a broader view, seeing it as a metaphor for how human beings live their lives. The poet's own final thoughts are of the woodchuck's winter retreat, before he eventually surrenders to his own mysterious 'sleep'.

'After Apple-Picking' is typical of Frost's work. Despite the apparent cheerfulness of much of the writing, it has **undertones of a more sober vision of life**. As always, there is a thoughtful quality to the poem. The reference to the approach of winter hints at the constant presence of mortality. Frost's question about what kind of sleep to anticipate suggests untroubled oblivion or possibly some kind of renewal, just as the woodchuck reawakens in the springtime after its long hibernation.

ANALYSIS

'Frost's work has a surface cheerfulness which belies a more serious vision of life.' Discuss this statement in relation to the poem, 'After Apple-Picking'. Support your answer with reference to the poem.

Sample Paragraph

In his famous dramatic monologue, 'After Apple-Picking', Robert Frost creates a mood of otherworldliness. At the start, his accurate description of the orchard is realistic. But some of the poem seems symbolic – such as the mention of the ladder pointing to heaven which might suggest Frost's religious feelings. The setting is calm and the poet feels tired but satisfied after his demanding physical work – 'there's a barrel that I didn't fill'. But his tiredness soon makes his mood more dreamy – 'Essence of winter sleep is on the night'. The sibilance and slender vowels add to this languid atmosphere. I could trace a growing surreal quality to the poem as Frost drifts in and out of consciousness, remembering flashes of his work picking the apples – 'The scent of apples: I am drowsing off'. He mentions 'sleep' repeatedly, reflecting his deep weariness. The rhythm is slow and irregular, just like his confused thoughts about the apples he harvested or damaged. At times he is troubled, recalling his worries that some of the fruit would be 'bruised'. By the end of the poem, he is in a dream-like state, equally obsessed with apple-picking and his own need for sleep. He even wonders about 'whatever sleep it is'. As he drifts off, he thinks of the animals that sleep through the winter and compares himself to the woodchuck. I think this kind of whimsical mood reflects his great interest in nature and is a characteristic of this great American poet.

Examiner's Comment

This is a very well written and accomplished answer that ranges widely and shows some close personal engagement: 'I could trace a growing surreal quality to the poem as Frost drifts in and out of consciousness, remembering flashes of his work'. There is an assured sense of the central mood and this is supported with apt quotations. Interesting references to Frost's style ensure the highest grade.

CLASS/HOMEWORK EXERCISES

1. Comment on the effectiveness of the poem's imagery in appealing to the senses. Refer closely to the text in your answer.

2. "Many of Frost's poems appear simple, but often have layers of underlying meanings.' Discuss this view, with particular reference to 'After Apple-Picking'.

SUMMARY POINTS

- Subject matter considers creativity, human achievement and the cycle of life.
- Dreamlike atmosphere and contrasting tones – peaceful, nostalgic, regretful.
- Rich sensory imagery and symbolism convey underlying themes.
- Effective use of repetition, sibilance and assonance throughout.

4 THE ROAD NOT TAKEN

Two roads diverged in a yellow wood,
And sorry I could not travel both
And be one traveler, long I stood
And looked down one as far as I could
To where it bent in the undergrowth;   5

Then took the other, as just as fair,
And having perhaps the better claim,
Because it was grassy and wanted wear;
Though as for that, the passing there
Had worn them really about the same,   10

And both that morning equally lay
In leaves no step had trodden black.
Oh, I kept the first for another day!
Yet knowing how way leads on to way,
I doubted if I should ever come back.   15

I shall be telling this with a sigh
Somewhere ages and ages hence:
Two roads diverged in a wood, and I—
I took the one less traveled by,
And that has made all the difference.   20

'where it bent in the undergrowth'

Glossary

1 *diverged*: separate and go in different directions.
5 *undergrowth*: small trees and bushes growing beneath larger trees in a wood.
7 *claim*: attraction, entitlement.

INITIAL RESPONSE

1. In your opinion, is this a simple poem or does it have a more profound meaning? Outline your views, supporting them with relevant quotation.

2. Select one image from the poem that you consider particularly effective or interesting. Briefly justify your choice.

3. Frost has been described as someone who 'broods and comments on familiar country things … catching a truth in it'. In your view, what is the tone of this poem? Does it change or remain the same?

STUDY NOTES

One of Frost's most popular poems, it was the first published in the collection 'Mountain Interval' (1916). It was inspired by his friend, the poet Edward Thomas. Frost told Thomas, 'No matter which road you take, you'll always sigh, and wish you'd taken another'. Frost also said he was influenced by an event which happened to him at a crossroads after a winter snowstorm in 1912. He met a figure, 'my own image', who passed silently by him. Frost wondered at 'this other self'. The poem dramatises the choices we make in life and their consequences.

Huge themes are summarised in a simple narrative in this poem. In the **first stanza**, the speaker stands in a wood in autumn where two roads run off in different directions. He has to make a decision – which one will he take? The roads are 'about the same', so the emphasis is not on the decision, but on the **process of decision-making and its consequences**. The speaker decides that he cannot see where the first road is leading ('it bent in the undergrowth'), so he chooses the other one, though it is unclear why. The reference to the 'yellow wood' suggests that the poet is mature enough to realise the consequences of his decision. He won't have this opportunity again: 'I doubted if I should ever come back.' The beautiful image of the 'yellow wood' conjures up a picture of the autumn in New England, but it also has a deeper meaning and is tinged with regret. A person can't do everything in life; choice is part of the human condition.

Frost has said, 'I'm not a nature poet. There's always something else in my poetry.' Here, in this simple act, he is **exploring what it means to be human** and dramatises the decision-making process. There is the human desire to avoid making a decision ('sorry I could not travel both') and the consideration of the possible choices ('long I stood/And looked down one as far as I could'). The **regular rhyme scheme** mirrors the poet looking this way and that as he tries to decide which to choose (abaab, cdccd, efeef, ghggh). The unusual rhyme also underlines the unusual choice made. Frost felt that 'the most important thing about a poem ... is how wilfully, gracefully, naturally entertainingly and beautifully its rhymes are'.

Then, in **stanza two**, **he makes the decision**: he 'took the other one'. Why? Was it because it 'was grassy and wanted wear'? Is this someone who is individualistic and likes to do something different to the crowd? Does this suggest a desire for adventure? Then the poet becomes increasingly mischievous. When he sent the poem to his friend, Edward Thomas, Frost wrote: 'I don't know if you can get anyone to see the fun of the thing without showing them.' After pointing out the difference between the two roads, he now declares that they were not so different: 'the passing there/Had worn them really about the same'.

In the **third stanza**, he continues to **point out the similarity of the two roads**, which 'equally lay'. So is the idea that if you choose the less conventional route in life, you may not end up having adventures? The reader is now as confused as the poet was when trying to decide what to do. The second great truth is then revealed: no matter what we get, we always want what we don't have. The regret is palpable in the emphatic 'Oh, I kept the first for another day!' But there won't be another day, because time marches on and we cannot return to the past; we can only go on, as 'way leads on to way'.

In **stanza four**, the poet realises in **hindsight** that he will tell of this day in the future, 'ages and ages hence', though why 'with a sigh'? Has his choice resulted in suffering? Frost's own personal life was littered with suffering and tragedy. Does the repetition of 'I' and the inclusion of the dash suggest that the poet is asserting his maverick individuality as he resolutely declares: 'I took the one less traveled by,/And that has made all the difference'? Do you think he feels he made the right choice for himself? This common experience of choice and decision-making is caught succinctly in this simple narrative. It sounds like a person thinking aloud; the language seems ordinary. Yet upon closer examination, we become aware of the **musical sound effects**. The repeated 'e' sound, coupled with the sibilant 's' sounds ('it was grassy') and alliteration ('wanted wear') convey a calm, deliberating voice. Here is Frost's 'sound of sense'. This poem is inclusive rather than exclusive, as it invites the reader to share in the poet's decision-making.

ANALYSIS

'Frost uses traditional form not in an experimental way, but adapted to his purpose.' Discuss this statement with reference to 'The Road Not Taken'. Quote in support of your answer.

Sample Paragraph

Frost takes traditional subject matter similar to the Romantics, nature and man's relationship with nature, and tells us, 'There's plenty to be dark about, you know. It's full of darkness.' He forms his poems not in an experimental way, but in a deliberate way which suits his purpose. He uses iambic pentameter, a traditional metre used by Shakespeare, as it most closely resembles the English speaking voice, and it is an ironic, sceptical voice, 'yet knowing how way leads on to way', which resonates in 'The Road Not Taken'. The structure of the poem follows the deliberating process, as first the speaker tries to avoid making a choice, then considers the alternatives, 'long I stood'. The decision is made and almost immediately there is a sense of regret: 'Oh, I kept the first for another day'. The use of an unusual rhyme scheme adds to the excluded feel of the speaker. This is someone to whom individuality and self-sufficiency matters: 'I took the one less traveled by,/And that has made all the difference'. The rhyme scheme of the first stanza is abaab. The unusual rhyme scheme mirrors the unusual choice the poet made. Frost believed in the 'sound of sense', as he tells us that we can know what is going on even through a closed door by the sound, not necessarily the meaning of words. Consider the line, 'Because it was grassy and wanted wear'. The alliteration and the sibilance suggest an almost idyllic wilderness. So Frost structures the form of his poems for a purpose. In this poem the rhyme scheme mimics the glancing this way and that as the speaker tries to decide what route to take. These are some of the ways Frost uses form for a purpose, rather than experimenting just for its own sake.

Examiner's Comment

This thoroughly developed answer shows a deep sense of engagement, particularly the discussion on the poetic voice: 'an ironic, sceptical voice, "Yet knowing how way leads on to way"'. Points on style range widely and clearly demonstrate an understanding of Frost's skill in using structure, rhyme and sound effects. Expression is also excellent throughout. The well-sustained focus and integrated quoting ensure that the standard reached the highest grade.

CLASS/HOMEWORK EXERCISES

1. Frost's ambition was to 'write a few poems it will be hard to get rid of'. Do you think he succeeded? Refer to the poem 'The Road Not Taken' in your response.

2. 'The ending of "The Road Not Taken" has often been described as ambiguous and inconclusive.' Discuss this view, with particular reference to the poem.

SUMMARY POINTS

- Key themes – the natural world and the consequences of making choices in life.
- The autumnal setting provides a suitable context for this simple narrative.
- Reflective tone and characteristically simple language throughout.
- Effective use of emphatic rhyme and appealing musical sibilant effects.

5 BIRCHES

When I see birches bend to left and right
Across the lines of straighter darker trees,
I like to think some boy's been swinging them.
But swinging doesn't bend them down to stay
As ice storms do. Often you must have seen them   5
Loaded with ice a sunny winter morning
After a rain. They click upon themselves
As the breeze rises, and turn many-colored
As the stir cracks and crazes their enamel.
Soon the sun's warmth makes them shed crystal shells   10
Shattering and avalanching on the snow crust—
Such heaps of broken glass to sweep away
You'd think the inner dome of heaven had fallen.
They are dragged to the withered bracken by the load,
And they seem not to break; though once they are bowed   15
So low for long, they never right themselves:
You may see their trunks arching in the woods
Years afterwards, trailing their leaves on the ground
Like girls on hands and knees that throw their hair
Before them over their heads to dry in the sun.   20
But I was going to say when Truth broke in
With all her matter-of-fact about the ice-storm,
I should prefer to have some boy bend them
As he went out and in to fetch the cows—
Some boy too far from town to learn baseball,   25
Whose only play was what he found himself,
Summer or winter, and could play alone.
One by one he subdued his father's trees
By riding them down over and over again
Until he took the stiffness out of them,   30
And not one but hung limp, not one was left
For him to conquer. He learned all there was
To learn about not launching out too soon
And so not carrying the tree away
Clear to the ground. He always kept his poise   35
To the top branches, climbing carefully
With the same pains you use to fill a cup
Up to the brim, and even above the brim.

Then he flung outward, feet first, with a swish,
Kicking his way down through the air to the ground.   40
So was I once myself a swinger of birches.
And so I dream of going back to be.
It's when I'm weary of considerations,
And life is too much like a pathless wood
Where your face burns and tickles with the cobwebs   45
Broken across it, and one eye is weeping
From a twig's having lashed across it open.
I'd like to get away from earth awhile
And then come back to it and begin over.
May no fate willfully misunderstand me   50
And half grant what I wish and snatch me away
Not to return. Earth's the right place for love:
I don't know where it's likely to go better.
I'd like to go by climbing a birch tree,
And climb black branches up a snow-white trunk   55
Toward heaven, till the tree could bear no more,
But dipped its top and set me down again.
That would be good both going and coming back.
One could do worse than be a swinger of birches.

'birches bend to left and right'

Glossary

1 *birches*: deciduous trees with smooth, white bark.
7 *click*: tapping sound made by the branches when they touch.
9 *crazes their enamel*: cracks the ice on the trees.
10 *crystal shells*: drops of melting ice on branches.
11 *avalanching*: collapsing.
14 *bracken*: fern leaves.
31 *limp*: loose; wilted.
39 *swish*: whoosh.
50 *willfully*: deliberately.

INITIAL RESPONSE

1. Choose one image from the poem that you found particularly interesting or effective. Briefly explain your choice.

2. Comment on Frost's use of contrast in the poem.

3. Do you find the poet's overall outlook optimistic or pessimistic? Refer to the text in your answer.

STUDY NOTES

'Birches' was published in 1915, and like so much of Robert Frost's popular work, there is far more happening within the poem than first appears. The poem has been viewed as an important expression of his philosophical outlook on life. With its formal perfection, its opposition of the internal and external worlds and its occasional dry wit, it is one of the best examples of everything that is interesting and engaging about Frost's poetry.

The opening description of the leaning birches is interesting, as Frost compares them to the 'straighter darker trees'. The scene immediately brings him back to his childhood and he likes to think that 'some boy's been swinging them'. This tension between what has actually happened and what the poet would like to have happened – between the real world and the world of the imagination – runs through much of the poem. Throughout **lines 1–20**, he wonders why the birches are bent 'to left and right'. He accepts that the true reason is because of the ice weighing them down. The poet's **precise, onomatopoeic language** – particularly the sharp 'c' effect in 'cracks and crazes their enamel' – echoes the tapping sound of the frozen branches. Vivid, sensual imagery brings the wintry scene to life: 'crystal shells', 'snow crust', 'withered bracken'. Frost's conversational tone is engaging: 'You'd think the inner dome of heaven had fallen'. Characteristically, he adds a beautiful simile, comparing the bent branches 'trailing their leaves on the ground' to girls who are drying their cascading hair in the sunshine.

In the poem's second section (**lines 21–40**), Frost resists the accurate explanation ('Truth') for the bent trees, preferring to interpret the scene imaginatively. He visualises a lonely boy ('too far from town to learn baseball') who has learned to amuse himself among the forest birches. In simple, factual terms, the poet describes the boy as he 'subdued his father's trees'. We are given a sense of his youthful determination to 'conquer' them all until 'not one was left'. His persistence teaches him valuable lessons for later life. Swinging skilfully on the trees, the boy learns 'about not launching out too soon'. Readers are left in no doubt about the rich **metaphorical significance of the birches**. In highlighting the importance of 'poise' and 'climbing carefully', Frost reveals his belief in discipline and artistry as the important elements of a successful life ('to fill a cup/Up to the brim'). Such symbolism is a common feature of his writing.

Lines **41–59** are more nostalgic in tone. Frost recalls that he himself was once 'a swinger of birches' and extends the metaphor of retreating into the world of imagination and poetry. The similarities between climbing birches and writing poetry become more explicit: 'I'd like to get away from earth'. However, he stresses that he does not wish for a permanent escape because 'Earth's the right place for love'. Is this what poets do when they withdraw into their imaginations and reflect on reality in an attempt to explore the beauty and mystery of life? They are dreamers, idealists. The birch trees are similarly grounded, but they also reach '*Toward* heaven'. The emphatic image (the italics are Frost's) suggests his continuing aspiration for **spiritual fulfilment through the poetic imagination**: 'That would be good both going and coming back'. Frost ends his poem by stating his satisfaction with overcoming challenges and benefiting from the desire to achieve by writing: 'One could do worse than be a swinger of birches'.

ANALYSIS

'Frost's search for spiritual fulfilment is effectively captured through detailed description.' Discuss this statement in relation to the poem, 'Birches'. Support your discussion using accurate referencing from the text.

Sample Paragraph

Frost's detailed use of language makes 'Birches' one of the poet's most accessible poems. The simple images and colloquial expression create a natural connection between the poet and his readers. I very much liked the closely observed descriptions of the ice-covered branches: 'the sun's warmth makes them shed crystal shells'. The sibilance here adds to the beauty of the language. There are so many impressive images in the poem. Using onomatopoeia, Frost captures the subtle sounds of the forest in the bitter weather. The trees 'click upon themselves'. The poet obviously loved nature and had a keen eye for its beauty. I also liked his comparison of the trail of leaves to the 'girls on hands and knees that throw their hair'. It was dramatic, fresh and unusual. The boy's movement playing on the trees is dynamic: 'Then he flung outward, feet first, with a swish'. Near the end of the poem, Frost describes a harsher side of the forest when 'your face burns and tickles with the cobwebs'. As someone who spent my childhood in the country, I could relate to this tactile image. For me, Frost is a wonderful writer whose poems give a clear sense of the New England landscape. 'Birches' is a very successful piece of description, mainly due to the poet's precise choice of words and the vivid imagery.

Examiner's Comment

This paragraph showed a good knowledge of the text and a clear personal appreciation of Frost's writing skills: 'The sibilance here adds to the beauty of the language'. However, the response does not fully address the task and there is little reference to the 'search for spiritual fulfillment'. This weakens the answer, which does not achieve the highest grade..

CLASS/HOMEWORK EXERCISES

1. In your opinion, what is the central theme or message in 'Birches'? Support your answer with reference to the text.

2. 'While Frost's poetry contains elements of suffering, there are also moments of comfort and joy in his work.' To what extent is this true of 'Birches'? Support your answer with reference to the poem.

SUMMARY POINTS

- Central themes include childhood, creativity, imagination and escapism.
- Motion of swinging can be seen as a metaphor for transcending harsh realities.
- Recurring contrasts: light/darkness, love/pain, life/death, Heaven/Earth.
- Effective use of descriptive details, striking images, sibilance and assonance.
- Tones vary: reflective, nostalgic, philosophical.

6 'OUT, OUT—'

The buzz saw snarled and rattled in the yard
And made dust and dropped stove-length sticks of wood,
Sweet-scented stuff when the breeze drew across it.
And from there those that lifted eyes could count
Five mountain ranges one behind the other   5
Under the sunset far into Vermont.
And the saw snarled and rattled, snarled and rattled,
As it ran light, or had to bear a load.
And nothing happened: day was all but done.
Call it a day, I wish they might have said   10
To please the boy by giving him the half hour
That a boy counts so much when saved from work.
His sister stood beside them in her apron
To tell them 'Supper.' At the word, the saw,
As if to prove that saws knew what supper meant,   15
Leaped out at the boy's hand, or seemed to leap—
He must have given the hand. However it was,
Neither refused the meeting. But the hand!
The boy's first outcry was a rueful laugh,
As he swung toward them holding up the hand,   20
Half in appeal, but half as if to keep
The life from spilling. Then the boy saw all—
Since he was old enough to know, big boy
Doing a man's work, though a child at heart—
He saw all spoiled. 'Don't let him cut my hand off—   25
The doctor, when he comes. Don't let him, sister!'
So. But the hand was gone already.
The doctor put him in the dark of ether.
He lay and puffed his lips out with his breath.
And then—the watcher at his pulse took fright.   30
No one believed. They listened at his heart.
Little—less—nothing!—and that ended it.
No more to build on there. And they, since they
Were not the one dead, turned to their affairs.

'Sweet-scented stuff when the breeze drew across it'

Glossary

'Out, Out—': phrase from a speech which Macbeth, King of Scotland, made on hearing of the death of his wife and when he was surrounded by enemies. He was commenting on the brevity and fragility of life: 'Out, out brief candle. Life's but a walking shadow' (Shakespeare).

4 **lifted eyes**: reference to Psalm 21 – 'I will lift up mine eyes unto the hills' – but the people here don't. The sunset is ignored.

6 **Vermont**: a state in New England, America.

28 **ether**: form of anaesthetic.

INITIAL RESPONSE

1. What kind of world is shown in the poem? Consider the roles of adults and children. Refer to the text in your response.

2. In your opinion, why does the poet tell the story in chronological order? How does it affect your understanding of the story?

3. Comment on the use of colloquial language in the poem. Refer closely to the text in your answer.

STUDY NOTES

Based on an actual event that occurred in 1910, the poem refers to a tragic accident when the son of a neighbour of Frost's was killed on his father's farm. By chance, he had hit the loose pulley of the sawing machine and his hand was badly cut. He died from heart failure due to shock. The event was reported in a local paper.

This **horrifying subject matter**, the early violent death of a young boy, was, in Frost's opinion, 'too cruel' to include in his poetry readings. The title, which is a reference to a speech from Shakespeare's *Macbeth*, is a telling comment on how tenuous our hold on life is. The scene is set on a busy timber yard: 'a world of actual hard, rattling, buzz saw, snarling action' (Seamus Heaney). **In line 1**, Frost's rasping onomatopoeic sounds give a vivid sound picture of the noisy, dangerous yard. The **long, flowing, descriptive lines** paint a picture of a place full of menace and physical reality where work has to be done. But there is beauty in the midst of this raw power: 'Sweet-scented stuff when the breeze drew across it'. The soft sibilant 's', the assonance of the long 'e' and the compound word 'Sweet-scented stuff' all go to show the surprising beauty to be found in the midst of the practical 'stove-length sticks of wood'.

The **surroundings are also beautiful**, if only the people would look up. But they, unlike the poet, are unaware of 'Five mountain ranges one behind the other/Under the sunset far into Vermont', as their focus is on the work. The repetition of the verbs 'snarled and rattled, snarled and rattled' mimic the action of the repeated sawing. The detail 'As it ran light, or had to bear a load' shows how the saw pushed through the wood to get it cut, then lightly ran back through the cut. Line 9 tells us that the day was 'all but done'. A foreshadowing of the impending tragedy is given in 'I wish they might have said'. This is the only time in the whole poem when the personal pronoun 'I' is used. The poet's compassionate understanding for the young boy is evident as he explains how much it matters to a boy to be given precious time off from such hard work: 'That a boy counts so much'. The colloquial language in **line 10**, 'Call it a day', brings the reader right into this rural scene, rooting the poem in ordinary day-to-day life. The irony shimmers from the line, for soon there will be no more days for the boy.

A domestic detail adds to the reality of this scene as the boy's sister appears 'in her apron/To tell them "Supper."' In this central episode in **line 14**, the saw suddenly becomes personified, as if it too 'knew what supper meant'. The **jagged language**, 'Leaped out at the boy's hand, or seemed to leap—', reminds us of the jagged teeth of the saw as it seeks its prey. The mystifying accident is referenced in 'seemed to'. How could it have happened? 'He must have given the hand.' The helplessness of the victim, the boy, is shown: 'Neither refused the meeting'. We are reminded of someone almost paralysed into inaction at the split second of a horrific accident. Was this destiny? Is the poet adversely commenting on the mechanisation of farming, or on the practice of getting a boy to do a man's job? **All the attention is now focused on the hand**: 'But the hand!' The pity of the event is palpable in this climactic phrase.

The boy's reaction is chilling and poignant. He holds up the hand, 'spilling' its life blood. He pathetically asks for help, begging his sister not to let the doctor amputate his hand: 'Don't let him'. Now the poet interjects: 'So.' What more is to be said? It is like a drawn-out breath after the tension of the awful accident. The harsh reality is there for all to see: 'the hand was gone already'. The boy realised this when he 'saw all'. Without the use of his hands, there would be no man's work for him any more: 'He saw all spoiled'.

The closing section in lines **27-31** shows the details of the medical help: the 'dark of ether', the boy's breath 'puffed'. Now **the lines break up into fragments** as the terrible final act of the tragedy unfolds: 'No one believed'. The heartbeats ebbed away: 'Little—less—nothing!' There are echoes of the Macbeth speech when Macbeth says, 'It is a tale told by an idiot … signifying nothing'. The **sober reality hits home**: 'and that ended it'. The realisation that there is now no future for the boy is grasped: 'No more to build on there'. Frost has said that the reality of life is that 'it goes on'. And so the people there, because they were not the one dead, 'turned to their affairs'. No matter what horror happens in life, a new day comes. Neither the people nor the poet are being callous and unfeeling. Seamus Heaney calls it the 'grim accuracy' of the poem's end. The long line length also signals the return to normality.

The tone in this narrative poem shades from the anger and menace of the saw, to the calm of the beautiful rural countryside, to the wistful wishes of the poet and on to the fear and horror of the accident. In the end, Frost's ironic tone gives way to the cold fear of the finality of death, when all is changed forever.

ANALYSIS

Seamus Heaney commented, 'Here was a poet who touched things as they are, somehow.' Discuss this statement with reference to the poem 'Out, Out—'.

Sample Paragraph

This poem touched me deeply, as it reminded me of the Elton John song 'A Candle in the Wind', which he wrote for another young person whose life was cruelly snuffed out in a terrible accident, just like this young boy. Many people are horrified at the poet and the people at the end of the poem, as they 'turned to their affairs'. Yet this is what life is like; after an accident, people put the kettle on. This does not mean they don't care, it means that the reality of life is, as Frost once said, 'It goes on'. I think it was very brave of the poet to just say things as they are, rather than pretending that life is not dark sometimes. I also felt as if I were actually in the timber yard as the saw 'snarled and rattled' in Vermont. The detail of sound and smell, 'Sweet-scented stuff', brought me there. It reminded me of Kavanagh, our Irish poet, who could see beauty in the most ordinary places. Frost, it seems to me, is also commenting negatively on the practice of having a young boy perform a man's job. The wistful 'I wish they might have said' condemns those who insisted on getting the job finished at the expense of the boy. It was too much to ask of a 'big boy', a 'child at heart'. The reality of the boy's life fading away was vividly captured by the poet in the line 'Little—less—nothing!' The punctuation adds to the effect of the heartbeat becoming weaker and finally stopping. This poet dared to say what life is like. He 'touched things as they are'. He achieved this by his craftsmanship as a poet, and his compassionate eye as a human being.

Examiner's Comment

A thoughtful, personal exploration of the poem, using quotations that are carefully integrated into the answer, all of which results in a well-deserved top grade. Contemporary references illustrate the continuing relevance of Frost as a realistic voice. The point regarding Frost's skilful use of punctuation is well developed: 'The punctuation adds to the effect of the heartbeat becoming weaker and finally stopping'.

CLASS/HOMEWORK EXERCISES

1. It has been said that Frost's poems are 'little voyages of discovery'. Write a personal response to this poem, using quotations from the poem to support your answer.

2. 'Frost's poems are filled with disturbing reminders of life's harsh realities.' Discuss this view, with particular reference to 'Out, Out –'.

SUMMARY POINTS

- Key themes – life's unfairness and unpredictability of human existence.
- Highly dramatic poem, with characters facing a crisis in a particular setting.
- Powerful onomatopoeic effects: alliteration and assonance.
- Contrasting images – beautiful landscape, dangerous sawmill.

7 SPRING POOLS

These pools that, though in forests, still reflect
The total sky almost without defect,
And like the flowers beside them, chill and shiver,
Will like the flowers beside them soon be gone,
And yet not out by any brook or river,   5
But up by roots to bring dark foliage on.

The trees that have it in their pent-up buds
To darken nature and be summer woods—
Let them think twice before they use their powers
To blot out and drink up and sweep away   10
These flowery waters and these watery flowers
From snow that melted only yesterday.

'darken nature'

Glossary
2 *defect*: blemish; flaw.
5 *brook*: small stream.
6 *foliage*: plants; undergrowth.

INITIAL RESPONSE

1. What aspects of the spring pools are conveyed in the first stanza? Refer to the text in your answer.

2. Choose one image from the poem that you found particularly striking. Briefly explain your choice.

3. Write your own personal response to the poem.

STUDY NOTES

'Spring Pools' captures a moment at the end of winter during which the poet reflects on the natural cycle of growth, decay and renewal. Rain falls from the sky, settles in pools and is then drawn up into the trees. In recalling the origins of this beautiful lyric poem, Frost commented, 'One night I sat alone by my open fireplace and wrote "Spring Pools". It was a very pleasant experience, and I remember it clearly, although I don't remember the writing of many of my other poems.'

The poem's title seems to celebrate new growth and regeneration. Ironically, **stanza one** focuses mainly on the fragility of nature. As always, Frost's **close observation of the natural world is evident** from the start. The clear pool water mirrors the overhead sky 'almost without defect'. While the simple images of the forest and flowers are peaceful, there is no escaping the underlying severity of 'chill and shiver'. The entire stanza of six lines is one long sentence. Its slow-moving pace, repetition and assonant vowels ('pools', 'brook', 'roots') enhance the sombre mood. Pool water will be absorbed by the tree roots to enrich the leaves and create 'dark foliage' and water and flowers will all 'soon be gone'. Frost pays most attention to the interdependence within the natural world and the transience of the beauty around him.

In **stanza two**, the poet addresses the trees directly, warning them to 'think twice before they use their powers'. He personifies them as an intimidating presence, associating them with dark destructiveness and 'pent-up' energy to 'blot out and drink up and sweep away'. Such forceful language combines with a resurgent rhythm to emphasise the power of the trees. The **tone becomes increasingly regretful in the final lines**. We are left with another evocative image of how nature's beauty is subject to constant change: 'snow that melted only yesterday'.

Frost's **poem is typically thought provoking**, touching on familiar themes regarding the mysteries of nature and the passing of time. Some critics interpret 'Spring Pools' as a metaphor for the creative process – water has long been a symbol of inspiration. Frost's own writing is wonderfully controlled, in keeping with the sense of order within the natural world that he describes. Both stanzas mirror each other perfectly and the aabcbc rhyme scheme completes the fluency of the lines.

ANALYSIS

'Reflective consideration of nature is central in Frost's thought-provoking poetry.' Discuss this statement in relation to the poem 'Spring Pools'. Refer closely to the text in your response.

Sample Paragraph

There is a deep sense of loss going through much of Frost's poem 'Spring Pools'. It struck me first in the negative language of the opening stanza. Frost refers to the perfect sky 'without defect', implying that something might soon destroy the perfection. The peaceful setting of the winter flowers beside the pools is also spoiled when the poet points out that they 'chill and shiver'. The mood is downbeat – everything in nature will end inevitably and 'soon be gone'. The image of the trees ('dark foliage') adds to my sense of this depressing feeling. In the second part of the poem, Frost points out the irony of springtime as a season of decay just as much as of growth. To some degree, I think this is a realistic view, but it does take away from the joy of spring. The mood deteriorates as the poem continues. The trees are seen as agents of destruction, drying up the water from the pools and removing the flowers. They 'darken nature' – a dramatic way of summing up the overall mood of this poem.

Examiner's Comment

This focused paragraph uses quotations effectively to communicate the central mood of the poem, 'Frost refers to the perfect sky "without defect", implying that something might soon destroy the perfection'. Some further discussion of style, particularly tone and rhythm, would have added to the answer which just fails to achieve the top grade.

CLASS/HOMEWORK EXERCISES

1. In your view, what is the central theme or message of 'Spring Pools'? Refer closely to the poem in your answer.

2. 'One of Frost's great skills is the craftsmanship he displays in using sounds to convey meaning.' Discuss this statement, with particular reference to 'Spring Pools'.

SUMMARY POINTS

- Central themes include time itself and the cycle of life, death and renewal.
- Contrasting moods – serious, sombre, pensive and regretful.
- Rich, musical effects: assonance, sibilance and emphatic end-rhyme.
- Characteristic use of simple, accessible language and sensuous imagery.

8 ACQUAINTED WITH THE NIGHT

I have been one acquainted with the night.
I have walked out in rain—and back in rain.
I have outwalked the furthest city light.

I have looked down the saddest city lane.
I have passed by the watchman on his beat   5
And dropped my eyes, unwilling to explain.

I have stood still and stopped the sound of feet
When far away an interrupted cry
Came over houses from another street,

But not to call me back or say good-by;   10
And further still at an unearthly height
One luminary clock against the sky

Proclaimed the time was neither wrong nor right.
I have been one acquainted with the night.

'I have looked down the saddest city lane'

Glossary

12 *luminary clock*: moon; a real clock shining with reflected light; simply passing time.

13 *Proclaimed ... wrong nor right*: this ambiguous message that the clock brings leaves us with more questions than answers. Why is the time neither wrong nor right? For whom is it so? For what is the time neither right nor wrong?

INITIAL RESPONSE

1. Does the shape of the poem add to or subtract from the poem's message? Comment on how the stanzas are arranged. Refer to the text in your answer.

2. Is there a sense of climax or anticlimax in this poem? Look at the rhyme scheme, the prevalence of end-stopped lines and the repetition. Refer to the text in your answer.

3. Write your own personal response to the poem.

STUDY NOTES

'Acquainted with the Night' is a sonnet from Frost's collection of poetry called West-Ring Brook *(1928). Unusually for Frost, it is set in a bleak city rather than the countryside. This is one of Frost's darkest poems and portrays a solitary, isolated figure filled with despair. It is reminiscent of the Modernist poets, such as T. S. Eliot, or the American artist Edward Hopper, whose paintings frequently showed a solitary individual.*

The 20th century was a time of huge social upheaval and warfare, and was primarily focused on material progress rather than spiritual awareness. It was the century of the individual, rather than the community. Many people became alienated, lonely and confused. The certainty that institutions bring was lost, moral codes were abandoned and the traditional comforts of extended family and community began to disappear. The poem begins with a declaration: 'I have been one acquainted with the night'. It is a frank statement, rather like the declarations made at an AA meeting. It is also reminiscent of the Old Testament reference to **one who was despised and rejected by men**, a man of sorrows 'acquainted with grief'. The second line in this **first stanza** shows the direction that the poem will take. There are two journeys: the body travels outwards towards the edge of the city ('I have walked out in rain') while the mind travels inwards to the edge of the psyche ('and back in rain').

This **alienation is echoed in the form of the poem**, which is not a conventional 14-line sonnet (either three quatrains and a rhyming couplet, or an octet and sestet); here there is a terza rima format. The poet uses a three-line rhyming stanza, concluding with a rhyming couplet (aba, bcb, cdc, ded, ff). The terza rima was used by the great Italian poet Dante in his famous poem 'The Divine Comedy' to describe the descent into hell. Is Frost using this structure in his poem because he is describing his descent into his own private hell? (His life had included many personal tragedies.) Is he using this format because nothing is conventional any more? This is a highly personal poem, as it uses 'I' at the beginning of seven of its fourteen lines. The rhythm imitates a slow walking movement: 'I have outwalked the furthest city light'. The poet has now gone beyond the last visible sign of civilisation. The use of iambic pentameter is the metre closest to the speaking voice in English, and the measured flow underlines the poet's melancholy mood.

The **solemn, sombre mood** of overwhelming anxiety is shown in the long vowel sounds of the **second stanza**: 'I have looked down the saddest city lane'. The broad vowels 'a' and 'o' lengthen the line and show the world-weariness of one who has seen and experienced too much. Although it is set at night, the traditional time for romance and lovers, we are presented with never-ending rain and gloom. A listless mood is created by the repetition of 'I have'. The run-on line suggests the ongoing trudging of this weary man who is too caught up in his own dark thoughts to even bother communicating with the 'watchman'. He is 'unwilling to explain' and is jealously guarding his privacy. Is this walk symptomatic of his inner state? Can nothing penetrate this extreme loneliness?

The use of the run-on line continues in the **third stanza**. Frost comes to an abrupt stop on his journey as an 'interrupted cry' rings out across the **desolate urban landscape**. Who cried? Why? And why was the cry 'interrupted'? Is something awful happening to someone? We, and the poet, don't know. Can anything be done about it? No. The poet just remarks in the next stanza that it has nothing to do with him, 'not to call me back or say good-by'. This is the chilling aspect of living in a big city: the sense of just being another person nobody cares about. These others have no substance, being reduced to the 'sound of feet' or a 'cry'.

In the **fourth stanza**, the poet speaks of a 'luminary clock'. This could be the moon or a real clock that is reflecting light. Is it symbolic of time passing relentlessly? Why is it at an 'unearthly height'? Is it because time rules the human world and nothing can change this? The **final couplet** proclaims that the 'time was neither wrong nor right'. We are left wondering what the time was neither right nor wrong for – what was supposed to happen? There is a real **sense of confusion** here, and echoes of Hamlet's declaration that 'the time is out of joint'. The poem ends as it begins: 'I have been one acquainted with the night'. We have come full circle, though **nothing has been achieved**. We have experienced the darkness with the poet. There is no sense of comfort or guidance, only the realisation of a hostile world.

ANALYSIS

'Robert Frost writes dramatic lyrics of homelessness.' Discuss this statement in relation to the poem 'Acquainted with the Night'. Refer closely to the text in your response.

Sample Paragraph

The sense of homelessness is palpable in this unconventional sonnet of Robert Frost's. The individual in the poem seems to be always on his own, not connected either with family, friend or acquaintance, a real loner in a big anonymous city. The form of the poem mirrors this individualism. It is a maverick sonnet, just like in the great American tradition of cowboy films or gangster movies: the hero is the loner who never quite fits in. There is no network to comfort this man, no community to offer help and encouragement. This emphasis on self comes at a price. The hero does not want to engage, 'And dropped my eyes'. He wanders through town like the tumbleweed of old, with no roots to hold it still. The poem is like a mini drama as the main character plays out his exterior action: 'I have walked out in rain', and his interior journey, 'unwilling to explain'. The verbs carry the action of this sad man: 'outwalked', 'looked', 'passed by', 'stood', 'stopped'. This man is going nowhere. The setting is vividly realised as the bleak urban landscape is drawn with its endless rain and strange noises. So there is character, action, setting and mood. The music of this lyrical poem is the rhythm of a slow walk as the steady iambic pentameter tempo steps out a hypnotic beat: 'I have outwalked the furthest city light.' The broad vowels add to this sombre music as the poem grinds on relentlessly: 'I have looked down the saddest city lane'. This is indeed dark mood music, as the drawn-out vowel sounds 'lane', 'explain', 'beat' and 'feet' tap out the despair of this lonely man. So, in conclusion, I do agree with the statement that 'Acquainted with the Night' is indeed a dramatic lyric of homelessness.

Examiner's Comment

This paragraph addresses the three elements of the question ('homelessness', 'dramatic' and 'lyric'). The response shows a real appreciation of poetic technique, as the terms are not only explained, but are examined well in relation to the poem: 'The music of this lyrical poem is the rhythm of a slow walk as the steady iambic pentameter tempo steps out a hypnotic beat'. Assured expression throughout. A highly successful top grade answer.

CLASS/HOMEWORK EXERCISES

1. Seamus Heaney describes this poem as 'dark'. What type of darkness is there? Is it literal or metaphorical or both? Refer to the text in your answer.

2. 'The personal narrative voice in Frost's poems can give readers an added sense of realism.' Discuss this view, with particular reference to 'Acquainted with the Night'.

SUMMARY POINTS

- Time, loneliness and the breakdown of communication are key themes.
- Powerful evocation of the anonymous urban atmosphere.
- The darkness symbolizes a pervading sense of spiritual emptiness.
- Effective use of simple language, repetition, assonance and end-rhyme.

9 DESIGN

I found a dimpled spider, fat and white,
On a white heal-all, holding up a moth
Like a white piece of rigid satin cloth—
Assorted characters of death and blight
Mixed ready to begin the morning right,   5
Like the ingredients of a witches' broth—
A snow-drop spider, a flower like a froth,
And dead wings carried like a paper kite.

What had that flower to do with being white,
The wayside blue and innocent heal-all?   10
What brought the kindred spider to that height,
Then steered the white moth thither in the night?
What but design of darkness to appall?—
If design govern in a thing so small.

'a dimpled spider, fat and white'

Glossary

The poem's title refers to the argument that the natural design of the universe is proof of God's existence.
1. *dimpled*: indented.
2. *heal-all*: plant (once used as a medicine).
4. *blight*: disease in plants; evil influence.
6. *witches' broth*: revolting recipes used to cast spells.
12. *thither*: to there, to that place.
13. *appall*: horrify (to make pale, literally).

INITIAL RESPONSE

1. How important a part does the colour white play in this poem? Refer to the text in your answer.

2. Select one comparison from the poem that you consider particularly effective. Briefly explain your choice.

3. Describe the poet's tone in the octave. How does it compare with the tone in the sestet?

STUDY NOTES

'Design' explores our attempts to see order in the universe – and our failure to recognise the order that is present in nature. Frost's sonnet raises several profound questions. Is there a design to life? Is there an explanation for the evil in the world? The poet was fascinated by nature from a philosophical point of view. His choice of the traditional sonnet form allows him to address such an important theme in a controlled way.

In the **opening line**, Frost describes how he finds a 'dimpled spider, fat and white' on a flower, 'holding up a moth' it has captured. The adjective 'dimpled' usually has harmless connotations far removed from the world of arachnids, but in this context, and combined with the word 'fat', it suggests an unattractive image of venomous engorgement. The colour white (used four more times in this short poem) also tends to have positive overtones of innocence and goodness. But most spiders are brown or black, and purity here quickly gives way to pale ghastliness. Indeed, the **tone becomes increasingly menacing** as the octave proceeds. The unwary moth has been lured to its grizzly death on the 'white heal-all' flower, which makes the situation even more deceitful.

Frost's chilling similes reflect the deathly atmosphere. The hapless moth is held 'Like a white piece of rigid satin cloth'. The 'characters of death' in this grim drama are compared to the 'ingredients of a witches' broth'. **Lines 7–8** are particularly ironic. Frost then revises his view of the grotesque scene, seeing the **tragic coincidence** involving the 'snow-drop spider' and 'a flower like a froth'. While the images appear attractive, there is a lingering suggestion of gloom and ferocity.

The focus changes in the **sestet** as the tone grows passionately angry. Frost uses a series of **rhetorical questions demanding an explanation** for what he has witnessed: 'What had that flower to do with being white'? Is this implying that nature isn't so innocent after all? He reruns the sequence of events and wonders what 'steered the white moth thither in the night'. The possibility that such a catastrophic event might be part of a great 'design of darkness' appalls the poet. However, the poem's final line ('If design govern in a thing so small') is the most intriguing of all. The word 'if' leaves the possibility that there is no grand plan for the universe, that it is all accidental. Whether predestination or chance is the more terrifying reality is left for readers to consider.

ANALYSIS

'Frost presents contrasting views on nature in his thought-provoking poetry.' Discuss this statement in relation to the poem 'Design'. Quote accurately to support your views.

Sample Paragraph

In his poem 'Design', Robert Frost takes an ironic approach to nature. Unlike other poems (e.g. 'The Tuft of Flowers'), where he ends up being reassured by the beauty and mystery of his natural environment, 'Design' is decidedly disquieting. The first few lines describe a repulsive side of nature's basic law – kill or be killed. I found the image of the bloated spider quite revolting: 'fat and white'. The poet cleverly conveys a strong sense of the violence and death that takes place when nature begins 'the morning right'. Dead moths are routine – often in beautiful settings. Nature is full of such contradictions. The image of the moth like a 'white piece of rigid satin cloth' suggested the lining of a coffin and reminded me that we see signs of our own mortality all around us. At the same time, Frost seems to be realistic about nature. Even in violent situations, there are beautiful creatures. The 'dead wings' are compared to a graceful 'paper kite'. Under different circumstances, I could imagine a more attractive 'snow-drop' or the 'wayside blue' of a wild flower. Overall, I think the poet probably shows a less attractive side to nature in the poem, but it is not altogether bleak or depressing. I found his ideas interesting and liked the way he managed simple language to raise deep and disturbing questions about our natural world.

Examiner's Comment

A balanced response, demonstrating a good understanding of the poem. References and quotations were carefully chosen and used effectively. Genuine engagement, e.g. 'The image of the moth like a "white piece of rigid satin cloth" suggested the lining of a coffin and reminded me that we see signs of our own mortality all around us'. Varied, confident expression underpins the top grade standard.

CLASS/HOMEWORK EXERCISES

1. Sonnets often move from description to reflection ('sight to insight'). To what extent is this true of 'Design'? Refer closely to the poem in your answer.

2. 'Robert Frost often expresses complex ideas by using starkly contrasting images.' Discuss this statement, with particular reference to Frost's poem, 'Design'.

SUMMARY POINTS

- Sonnet form used to explore the dark unpredictability of nature.
- The poet challenges the belief of a divine design for the world.
- Variety of tones – ironic, disturbing, confrontational.
- Effective use of vivid imagery, startling contrasts and descriptive details.

10 PROVIDE, PROVIDE

The witch that came (the withered hag)
To wash the steps with pail and rag
Was once the beauty Abishag,

The picture pride of Hollywood.
Too many fall from great and good   5
For you to doubt the likelihood.

Die early and avoid the fate.
Or if predestined to die late,
Make up your mind to die in state.

Make the whole stock exchange your own!   10
If need be occupy a throne,
Where nobody can call *you* crone.

Some have relied on what they knew,
Others on being simply true.
What worked for them might work for you.   15

No memory of having starred
Atones for later disregard
Or keeps the end from being hard.

Better to go down dignified
With boughten friendship at your side   20
Than none at all. Provide, provide!

'once the beauty Abishag'

Robert Frost 187

Glossary

3 *Abishag*: beautiful young woman who comforted King David in his old age.
12 *crone*: witchlike; old, withered woman.
17 *Atones*: makes amends (for sin or wrongdoing).
20 *boughten*: bought.

INITIAL RESPONSE

1. Is the advice given in the poem to be taken seriously or humorously, or a mixture of both? Discuss, using reference from the poem to support your answer.

2. What elements in the poem resemble a fairytale or fable? Pick your favourite element and explain why you like it.

3. What conclusion, if any, does the poem come to? Do you agree or disagree with the view expressed? Refer to the text to support your view.

STUDY NOTES

This poem was written at the height of Frost's fame, in a collection called A Further Rage *(1936). It was based on a real woman he had seen cleaning steps. The poem contrasts with most of Frost's work, as the tone is bitter and the emphasis is on material success. The Great Depression, a time of mass unemployment in America, was taking place. Is Frost suggesting that self-sufficiency is the answer?*

The **first stanza** advises us to **plan for the future**. Why? A cold, bleak scene of a withered old woman doing a menial job of washing steps is given as a salutary picture of what happens if you don't provide. This is what happened to Abishag. The reference to the biblical character adds a timeless element – this is a truth for all generations. We don't know what is to be. In this poem, old age equals diminishing beauty and success.

In **stanza two**, the destructive element of time is stressed as the poem comes to the present, 'Hollywood'. Even in the dream factory, beauty does not last. The tone of the poem is one of **addressing a public audience**, as if at an evangelical rally: 'For you to doubt the likelihood'. Fortune is fickle, as we all know.

The poem now offers **mock advice: the only solution is to die young** ('Die early'). Images of icons hover in our minds of tragic, famous deaths of the young and beautiful, such as James Dean and Marilyn Monroe. In the **third stanza**, **the only other solution is to become wealthy** and 'die in state'.

An imperative verb, 'Make', in the **fourth stanza** shouts at us to grab material success: 'Make the whole stock exchange your own!' The exclamation mark captures the mood of exhortation that pervades this unusual poem of Frost's. The quaint image of the throne adds to the timeless element of this poem, as it is a universal symbol of power and wealth. Only political power, privilege and riches provide protection against the harsh reality of ageing. If 'you' don't want the same fate as Abishag, 'you' must be alert.

Independence was very important to Frost. Now, in **stanza six**, the poem cautions us that even if our early lives were wonderful, 'having starred', that memory is not a safeguard against the misfortune that might happen later in life. Black humour in the **final stanza** suggests, with wry, unsentimental honesty, that it is better to **buy friendship** ('boughten') than suffer loneliness at the end of life. Is this cynical view that bought friends are better than none realistic? The poem concludes with great urgency: 'Provide, provide!' Frost did not believe in a benevolent God ruling the universe, but rather takes the view that there is an indifferent God and we are subject to random darkness. This is not an affirmative poem.

Frost favoured **traditional poetic structures**, declaring that he was 'one of the notable craftsmen of this time'. Here the full rhyme of aaa, bbb, ccc, ddd, etc. does not seem strained. We hardly notice it in this carefully crafted poem of seven triplets. The rhythmic pattern of blank verse, i.e. four short–long beats, set against the irregular variations of colloquial speech gives this poem its energy. The use of the imperative for the verbs, especially 'Provide, provide', demands that the reader take this message on board. Frost presents **painful ideas** – in this instance a cynical view of fame and success – **in a controlled form**. He has said, 'The poems I make are little bits of order.'

ANALYSIS

'Poetry is a momentary stay against confusion.' Discuss this statement in relation to the poem 'Provide, Provide'. Use references from the text to support your views.

Sample Paragraph

The bleak, cold situation painted by Frost is very different from his other poems where a quiet, sensible speaking voice alerts us to the beauties of nature. Here the focus is on 'look out for your old age, as no one is going to want you'. I wonder if Frost was uncomfortable about his decision to commit himself to being famous? Did he, like so many contemporary stars today, find the whole fame business tacky and shallow? When he read this poem in public, he usually added a line, 'Or somebody else'll provide for you!/And how'll you like that?' He is condemning those who take 'handouts', social benefits. The poem is stating that change is the only certainty and vehemently exhorts us to get ourselves in order if we don't want to have a miserable time when looks and youth are gone. I like the mock serious tone in which this message is delivered: 'If need be occupy a throne,/Where nobody can call you crone'. I think this wry, dry, cynical tone appeals especially to today's reader who is saturated with this 'fame' issue. I also think that humour is very effective in delivering a message, particularly one as unpalatable as this. The airbrushed perfection of the groomed Hollywood stars is captured perfectly in the alliterative phrase: 'The picture pride of Hollywood'. Frost has arranged this line as carefully as the lighting technician has arranged the lighting of a star, so that all seems picture perfect. But the poet knew that this is not how it is – 'the end' is 'hard'. Frost said, 'If you suffer any sense of confusion in life, the best thing you can do is make little poems.' Here is the human's need for order in a terrifying universe.

Examiner's Comment

This lively, personal approach to a very challenging question effectively explores Frost's own personal circumstances, his views on poetry and life. In-depth discussion of Frost's style is satisfying – 'The airbrushed perfection of the groomed Hollywood stars is captured perfectly in the alliterative phrase: "the picture pride of Hollywood"'. Impressive vocabulary and confident expression throughout. A top grade answer.

CLASS/HOMEWORK EXERCISES

1. 'A poem begins in delight and ends in wisdom.' Is this a valid statement in relation to the poem 'Provide, Provide'? Use quotation from the poem in your explorations.

2. 'In many of his poems, Robert Frost reveals himself as neither an optimist nor a pessimist, but as a realist.' To what extent is this true of 'Provide, Provide'? Support your answer with reference to the poem.

SUMMARY POINTS

- Central themes – time's erosive power, transience and endurance.
- Characteristically simple, accessible language and colloquial speech.
- Range of tones: serious, light-hearted, mocking, ironic, cynical.
- Effective use of contrasting images, repetition.

LEAVING CERT SAMPLE ESSAY

'We enjoy poetry for its ideas and language.'
Using the above statement as your title, write an essay on the poetry of Robert Frost. Support the points by reference to the poetry of Robert Frost on your course.

Marking Scheme Guidelines
Expect candidates to deal with both elements of the question – ideas and language – but not necessarily separately. Take 'ideas' to mean themes, subjects, attitudes, issues and so on. Take 'language' to mean style, manner, phraseology, appropriate vocabulary, imagery, etc. The level of engagement with the poetry will serve as an implicit treatment of what 'we enjoy' in the poetry of Robert Frost.

Indicative material:
- Poet's views on life/experience.
- Habitual concerns in the poems.
- Elegant plainness of his expression.
- Typical patterns of imagery/language.
- Variety of registers in the texts, etc.

Sample Essay
(We enjoy Frost's poetry for its ideas and language)

1. How could you not enjoy the work of a man whose favourite book was Robinson Crusoe? Here is a quiet, sensible speaking voice dealing with human suffering, isolation, loneliness and our relations with the world around us. No wonder his poems were sent to inspire soldiers in the Second World War, or that he was chosen to speak at the inauguration of JFK. 'Mending Wall' deals with an annual event where two neighbours check and mend their boundary wall ritualistically each spring. The communal activity joins people, but this poem is also about gaps in understanding between people. The speaker delights in mischief, in contrast to his neighbour, who 'walks in darkness' because he is traditional and is content to repeat received wisdom from previous generations without question: 'Good walls make good neighbors'.

2. Civilisation needs boundaries and order. Respecting rules is necessary in society, otherwise there is chaos. We must respect equality, but also difference. Each remains on his own land, 'One on a side'. So Frost's single event contains a complex issue: boundaries connect and divide. The two neighbours can also be seen as reflecting the two contrasting facets of Frost – the wall toppler who delights in wildness, breaking rules, being disruptive; and the builder who abides by strict rules, form, grammar and the traditional structure of poems. Such insights are what attracts me to Frost's work.

3. I also enjoyed the idea that there is a force in nature that does not like the way men construct boundaries. When I think of the Native Americans who did not believe in land ownership but rather guardianship and care of Mother Earth, I agree that 'Something there is that doesn't love a wall'. I think it was a good poem to read to President Khrushchev, particularly at a time of the Cold War and the Iron Curtain: 'I'd ask to know what I was walling in or walling out'. The Romantic influence can be seen in the subject matter of 'The Road Not Taken'. Nature is the stimulus for an insight. This poem deals with decisions taken when young. We are all facing tough decisions now regarding study, points and careers and will we be like Frost's friend who inspired this poem, and regret decisions we have made? Will we be thinking of things that might have been: 'I shall be telling this with a sigh'? When we look at our classmates and know that we will all take different roads and may not meet again for quite some time, don't the lines 'Yet knowing how way leads on to way, I doubted if I ever should come back' ring very true?

4. Nature provides a beautiful but passive background to the horrific event in 'Out, Out—'. Frost never read this poem at his readings as he regarded it as too cruel. It was inspired by a newspaper account about a young boy whose hand was amputated by a saw as he was doing a man's job and who subsequently died. This reminded me of how Bob Geldof created Live Aid from an item of TV news. Like the Victorians, Frost believed that there was no benevolent God compassionately caring for the world. Terrible things happen. For me, the most shocking thing in this poem was not the chainsaw as it became an animal and devoured the boy's hand; rather it was how the onlookers who 'since they were not the one dead, turned to their affairs'. This is chilling. But Frost believed one thing about life: 'It goes on'. When I consider the tragic life Frost lived, I can see how he understood the importance of endurance, however cold it may seem.

5. Frost's simple subject matter covers complex issues: 'There's always something else in my poetry.' His language allows us access to them. He did not follow the fashion of the time. Instead, he adopted the persona of the New England farmer inspired by natural events. But underpinning the colloquial language is a strict adherence to traditional forms and patterning. To him, free verse was like 'playing tennis without a net'. He used blank verse and iambic pentameter, which has rhythm but not rhyme: 'Something there is that doesn't love a wall'. There is a tension between the ordinary subject matter and the colloquial voice, as it is constrained by poetic patterning.

6. Frost believed in the sound of a poem; he said poems rather than read them, believing the sound carried the meaning. I see this clearly in 'The buzz saw snarled and rattled in the yard'. The sound of this line suggests a menacing element in the midst of beauty. The dust is beautifully described as 'sweet-scented stuff when the breeze blew across it'. The gentle 's' sound conveys the harmony in the timber yard, in contrast to the strident sound of the saw. I also enjoyed Frost's use of drama in his poetry, the moment

of decision in 'The Road Not Taken' when he wrote: 'Two roads converged in a yellow wood' and the strange 'interrupted cry' in 'Acquainted with the Night' which left me wondering who had cried and why. No wonder I am just one of millions who enjoy Frost's poetic ideas and language.

(approx. 870 words)

Examiner's Comment

A detailed exploration of the question that includes well-developed points on both subject matter and style supported by succinct quotations. The essay ranged widely, covering Frost's adoption of various personae, his purposeful use of colloquial language and sound effects. Expression throughout was very impressive – varied and always confidently managed: 'But underpinning the colloquial language is a strict adherence to traditional forms and patterning'. A very assured response deserving the highest grade.

MARKING SCHEME
P = 15/15
C = 15/15
L = 15/15
M = 5/5
Total = 50/50

SAMPLE LEAVING CERT QUESTIONS ON FROST'S POETRY

1. 'Robert Frost's poetry has a contemporary feel, yet he uses traditional poetic techniques.' Discuss this statement, supporting your answer with reference to both the subject matter and style of the Frost poems on your course.

2. 'Frost's poetry makes a powerful impact on the reader both through his outlook and use of language and imagery.' To what extent do you agree or disagree with this view? Support your answer with suitable reference to the poetry by Frost on your course.

3. 'Robert Frost's poetry catches life by the throat.' Discuss this statement with reference to both the subject matter and language use in the poems by Frost on your course.

Sample Essay Plan (Q2)

'Frost's poetry makes a powerful impact on the reader both through his outlook and use of language and imagery.' To what extent do you agree or disagree with this view? Support your answer with suitable reference to the poetry by Frost on your course.

- Intro: Interesting themes, individualistic style. His fascination with nature and human nature. Favourite poem – 'The Road Not Taken'.

- Point 1: Family – background tragic, yet it is the still, calm voice which sounds from the poem. He extends the invitation, 'you come too', as he explores man's relationship with nature.

- Point 2: 'Sound of sense' – 'Writing with your ear to the voice'. Use of first person in 'Out, Out—'. Use of first person pronoun in 'The Road Not Taken'.

- Point 3: Formal rhyme – traditionalist, good craftsman, art deceptive, rhyme scheme in 'The Road Not Taken'. Terza rima in 'Acquainted with the Night'.

- Point 4: Metaphors – Doesn't force, allows the metaphors to speak for themselves, e.g. road is a metaphor for a life choice in 'The Road Not Taken'.

- Point 5: Other themes – natural world, endurance, ordinary life, etc.

- Conclusion: Wrote about ordinary people living ordinary lives. View of nature bleak. Aware of time and effect on human beings.

Sample Essay Plan (Q2)

Develop one of the above points into a paragraph.

Sample Paragraph: Point 5

The subject matter of Frost's poetry is rooted in the natural world. He believed that 'man has need of nature, but nature has no need of man'. But it was nature which was thought-provoking, a stimulus for the poet, leading to insight and revelation: 'A poem begins in delight and ends in wisdom.' This was in keeping with the Romantic poets, such as Wordsworth, and was in contrast to the Modernist movement that was in vogue at this time. They were urban poets who used classical references and were often obscure. Frost was and is accessible. He was influenced by current events – just like Geldof was inspired by a news item to create Live Aid, so Frost was inspired by a newspaper article to write the chilling poem of injured innocence, 'Out, Out—'. Frost believed in endurance: 'In three words I can sum up everything I've learned about life – it goes on.' He was influenced also by the Victorian poets like Hardy who did not believe in a world ruled by a benevolent God. Darkness erupts in a random manner with tragic consequences, as in 'Out, Out—'. He wrote about ordinary people living ordinary lives. But his view of the human condition was bleak and cold. He was aware of time and its effect on human beings.

Examiner's Comment

As part of a full essay answer, this exploration shows a real understanding of Frost's aims, his appreciation of nature and understanding of the human condition. Expressive language throughout, e.g. 'Darkness erupts in a random manner with tragic consequences' raises the answer to the top grade.

LAST WORDS

'Like a piece of ice on a hot stove, the poem must ride on its own melting.'

Robert Frost

'Robert Frost: the icon of the Yankee values, the smell of wood smoke, the sparkle of dew, the reality of farm-house dung, the jocular honesty of an uncle.'

Derek Walcott

'I'll say that again, in case you missed it first time round.'

Robert Frost

GERARD MANLEY HOPKINS

1844-89

'Every poet must be original.'

Gerard Manley Hopkins, a priest and poet, was born in Stratford, outside London, in 1844. Throughout his youth, Hopkins demonstrated excellent academic and artistic talent. In 1863 he began studying classics at Balliol College, Oxford, where he wrote a great deal of poetry. Hopkins converted to Catholicism and was later ordained a Jesuit priest in 1877. It was while studying for the priesthood that he wrote some of his best-known religious and nature poems, including 'The Windhover' and 'Pied Beauty'. His compressed style of writing, especially his experimental use of language, sound effects and inventive rhythms, combined to produce distinctive and startling poetry. In 1884 Hopkins was appointed Professor of Greek at University College, Dublin. He disliked living in Ireland, where he experienced failing health and severe depression. A devout and ascetic Jesuit, he was caught between his religious obligations and his poetic talent. In 1885 he wrote a number of the so-called 'terrible sonnets', including 'No worst, there is none', which have desolation at their core. Hopkins died of typhoid fever in June 1889 without ever publishing any of his major poems. He is buried in Glasnevin Cemetery.

INVESTIGATE FURTHER

To find out more about Gerard Manley Hopkins, or to hear readings of his poems, you could do a search of some of the useful websites available such as YouTube, bbc.co.uk and poetryarchive.org or access additional material on this page of your eBook.

Prescribed Poems   HIGHER LEVEL

1. 'God's Grandeur'
Hopkins' sonnet welcomes the power of the Holy Ghost to rescue people
from sin and hopelessness.   198

2. 'Spring'*
This poem celebrates the natural beauty of springtime. However, Hopkins
also regrets man's loss of innocence because of sin.   202

3. 'As Kingfishers Catch Fire, Dragonflies Draw Flame'
In recognising the uniqueness of everything that exists in the world, Hopkins
praises God as the unchanging source of all creation.   206

4. 'The Windhover'
This was one of Hopkins' favourite poems and describes a bird in flight. Its
powerful Christian theme focuses on the relationship between God and mankind.   210

5. 'Pied Beauty'
This short poem again celebrates the diverse delights of nature and human
nature, all of which owe their existence to a changeless Creator.   215

6. 'Felix Randal'
An engaging narrative poem about the life and death of one of Hopkins'
parishioners. At a deeper level, it celebrates the significance of living a
good Christian life.   219

7. 'Inversnaid'*
Another nature poem rejoicing in the unspoiled beauty of the remote
Scottish landscape. It concludes with the poet's heartfelt appeal to preserve
the wilderness.   224

8 **'I Wake and Feel the Fell of Dark, not Day'**
One of the 'terrible sonnets' in which Hopkins reveals his personal torment, self-disgust and despair. Some critics argue that the poet is attempting to renew his own religious faith. **228**

9 **'No Worst, There is None'**
Hopkins explores the experience of unbearable depression, guilt and the awful sense of feeling abandoned by God. Only sleep or death offer any relief. **232**

10 **'Thou Art Indeed Just, Lord, if I Contend'**
In this intensely personal poem, Hopkins wonders why good people suffer while the wicked seem to prosper. He ends by pleading with God to strengthen his own faith. **236**

1 GOD'S GRANDEUR

The world is charged with the grandeur of God.
  It will flame out, like shining from shook foil;
  It gathers to a greatness, like the ooze of oil
Crushed. Why do men then now not reck his rod?
Generations have trod, have trod, have trod;   5
  And all is seared with trade; bleared, smeared with toil;
  And wears man's smudge and shares man's smell: the soil
Is bare now, nor can foot feel, being shod.

And for all this, nature is never spent;
  There lives the dearest freshness deep down things;   10
And though the last lights off the black West went
  Oh, morning, at the brown brink eastward, springs –
Because the Holy Ghost over the bent
  World broods with warm breast and with ah! bright wings.

'nature is never spent'

Glossary

Hopkins' philosophy emphasised the uniqueness of every natural thing, which he called inscape. He believed that there was a special connection between the world of nature and an individual's consciousness Hopkins viewed the world as an integrated network created by God. The sensation of inscape (which the poet termed instress) is the appreciation that everything has its own unique identity. The concept is similar to that of epiphanies in James Joyce's writing.

1 *charged*: powered; made responsible.
2 *foil*: shimmering gold or silver.
4 *Crushed*: compressed from olives or linseed.
4 *reck his rod*: pay heed to God's power.
6 *seared*: scorched; ruined.
6 *bleared*: blurred.
6 *toil*: industrialisation.
8 *shod*: covered; protected.
9 *spent*: exhausted.
11 *last lights*: the setting sun.

INITIAL RESPONSE

1. Describe Hopkins' tone in the first four lines of this poem. Refer closely to the text in your answer.

2. How are human beings portrayed in the poem? Support your points with reference.

3. Select two unusual images the poet uses. Comment on the effectiveness of each.

STUDY NOTES

Hopkins wrote many Italian (or Petrarchan) sonnets (consisting of an octave and a sestet). The form suited the stages in the argumentative direction of his themes. Like many other Christian poets, he 'found' God in nature. His poetry is also notable for its use of sprung rhythm (an irregular movement or pace which echoed ordinary conversation). 'God's Grandeur' is typical of Hopkins in both its subject matter and style. The condensed language, elaborate wordplay and unusual syntax – sometimes like a tongue twister – can be challenging.

The poem's **opening quatrain** (four-line section) is characteristically dynamic. The **metaphor ('charged') compares God's greatness to electric power**, brilliant but hazardous. The visual effect of 'flame out' and 'shook foil' develops this representation of God's constant presence in the world. This image of oozing oil signifies a natural richness. The reference to electricity makes a subtle reappearance in **line 4**, where the 'rod' of an angry Creator is likened to a lightning bolt. The tone is one of energised celebration, but there is also a growing frustration: 'Why do men then now not reck his rod?' Hopkins seems mystified at human indifference to God's greatness.

The second quatrain is much more critical. We can sense the poet's own weariness with the numberless generations who have abandoned their spiritual salvation for the flawed material benefits of 'trade' and 'toil'. Hopkin's laboured repetition of 'have trod' is purposely heavy-handed. The internal rhymes of the negative verbs ('seared', 'bleared' and 'smeared') in **line 6** convey his deep sense of disgust at a world blighted by industry and urbanisation. **Man's neglect of the natural environment is closely linked to the drift away from God.** Hopkins symbolises this spiritual alienation through the image of the 'shod' foot out of touch with nature and its Creator.

However, in response to his depression, the mood changes in the **sestet** (the final six lines of the sonnet). Hopkins' tone softens considerably and is aided by the gentle, sibilant effect in **line 10**: 'There lives the dearest freshness deep down things'. As in many of his religious poems, he takes comfort in conventional Christian belief. For him, 'nature is never spent'. The world is filled with 'freshness' that confirms God's presence. This **power of renewal** is exemplified in the way morning never fails to follow the 'last lights' of dark night.

The reassuring image in the **last line** is one of God guarding the world and promising rebirth and salvation. The source of this constant regeneration is 'the Holy Ghost' (God's grace) who 'broods' over a dependent world with the patient devotion of a bird protecting its young. In expressing his faith and surrendering himself to divine will, the poet can truly appreciate the grandeur of God. The final exclamations ('Oh, morning' and 'ah! bright wings') echo Hopkins' **sense of euphoria**.

ANALYSIS

'Hopkins' original voice explores God's presence in this weary world.' Discuss this statement, with particular reference to the poem 'God's Grandeur'.

Sample Paragraph

Gerard Manley Hopkins uses the Petrarchan sonnet form to examine man's lack of awareness of the beauty of God's world. A dynamic alliterative metaphor dramatically opens the poem, 'The world is charged with the grandeur of God'. His power and brilliance are conveyed through condensed references to electricity, 'It will flame out, like shining from shook foil'. Yet man remains unconcerned at God's lightning bolt and does 'not reck his rod'. The tone in the second quatrain suggests the drudgery of man's mechanical world. The blight of industrialisation has 'smeared' God's glorious creation. The heavy repetition of the phrase 'have trod' coupled with the internally rhymed verbs ('seared' and 'bleared') show the horrendous effects of factories and urbanisation on both man and landscape. Hopkins, in an innovative image, suggests that man is no longer in touch with his natural environment, the 'shod' foot can no longer feel the earth. A gentler tone emerges in the sestet. Hopkins realises the power of nature to regenerate itself, 'nature is never spent'. Unusual word order and a gentle sibilant effect stresses this ability to renew, 'There lives the dearest freshness deep down things'. I was impressed with Hopkins' religious belief expressed in the lovely natural image of the bird protecting its young, 'the Holy Ghost over the bent/World broods with warm breast'. The cold man-made world which humans have created has now been replaced by the deeply satisfying awareness of God's glowing grace expressed in the final exclamation, 'ah! bright wings'.

Examiner's Comment

A very solid discussion on Hopkins' twin themes of God's power and man's indifference. There is a keen awareness of Hopkins' innovative use of language: 'A dynamic alliterative metaphor dramatically opens the poem'. Varied expressive language and accurate use of quotation also contribute to this top grade.

CLASS/HOMEWORK EXERCISES

1. Comment on Hopkins' use of sound in this poem. Refer closely to the text in your answer.

2. Hopkins is a poet of intense emotion, ecstasy and distress. Trace his expression of these emotions in your response. Support your answer with reference to the text.

SUMMARY POINTS

- Combination of conflicting emotions, ecstasy and distress.
- Natural world enlivened by God's presence.
- Assonance and alliteration emphasise despondency, man's neglect of natural environment associated with drift away from God.
- Belief in nature's ability to regenerate.
- Sonnet concludes with a benevolent image of Holy Ghost as benevolent mother bird.
- Tone becomes more reassuring in the sestet.

② SPRING

Nothing is so beautiful as spring –
   When weeds, in wheels, shoot long and lovely and lush;
   Thrush's eggs look little low heavens, and thrush
Through the echoing timber does so rinse and wring
The ear, it strikes like lightnings to hear him sing;   5
   The glassy peartree leaves and blooms, they brush
   The descending blue; that blue is all in a rush
With richness; the racing lambs too have fair their fling.

What is all this juice and all this joy?
   A strain of the earth's sweet being in the beginning   10
In Eden garden. – Have, get, before it cloy,
   Before it cloud, Christ, lord, and sour with sinning,
Innocent mind and Mayday in girl and boy,
   Most, O maid's child, thy choice and worthy the winning.

'that blue is all in a rush/With richness'

Glossary

2 *in wheels*: radiating out like spokes; rampant; pivoting movement.
2 *lush*: growing thickly, luxuriantly.
3 *Thrush's eggs*: songbird's eggs, which are light blue.
4 *rinse*: wash out with fresh water.
4 *wring*: to twist or squeeze; drain off excess water.
8 *have fair their fling*: the lambs are enjoying their freedom.
10 *strain*: a trace; streak; a segment of melody.
12 *cloud*: darken; depress.
13 *Mayday*: innocence of the young.
14 *Most:* the best choice.
14 *maid's child*: Jesus, son of Mary.

INITIAL RESPONSE

1. This poem opens with a confident statement. In your opinion, does the first section of the poem do justice to this declaration? Refer both to the style and content of the octet in your answer.

2. What is the mood in the second section of the poem? What reasons would you give for this change in the sestet? Use reference or quotation to support your point of view.

3. Hopkins preferred movement to stopping. What evidence for this statement is contained in the poem? Illustrate your response by referring to the expression and subject matter of the poem.

STUDY NOTES

'Spring' was written in May 1877. Hopkins had a special devotion to Mary, Queen of Heaven, and May is the month that is devoted to her. The poem was written after a holiday spent walking and writing poetry in Wales. He captures the exuberance of nature bursting into life.

The simple **opening sentence** in the first section, 'Nothing is so beautiful as spring', is a deliberately exaggerated statement (hyperbole) used to emphasise a feeling. This Petrarchan sonnet's **octet** starts with an **ecstatic account of the blooming of nature in spring**. As we examine the poet's use of language, we can understand why it should be heard rather than read. Here in the second line – 'When weeds, in wheels, shoot long and lovely and lush' – the alliteration of 'w' and 'l', the assonance of 'ee' and the slow, broad vowels 'o' and 'u' add to this description of abundant growth. We can easily imagine the wild flowers growing before our eyes, as if caught by a slow-motion camera, uncurling and straightening to reach the heavens.

The **energy of the new plants** is contained in the verb 'shoot'. Just as the plants are shooting from the fertile earth, so one word seems to sprout out of another in the poem, e.g. 'thrush' springing from 'lush'. Now we are looking down, carefully examining a delicately beautiful sight among the long grasses: 'Thrush's eggs look little low heavens'. Note the speckled appearance of the eggs, similar to the dappling of blue and white in the sky. The oval shape is like the dome of the heavens.

The poet's **breathless excitement** at the sight of Heaven on earth is caught by the omission of the word 'like'. Now we hear the song of the bird as the assonance of 'rinse' and 'wring' sings purely, cleansing our human ears with heavenly sounds. It has a powerful effect, like a bolt of lightning. The focus shifts to the gleam on the leaves of the pear tree, as its 'glassy' appearance is observed. Hopkins looked closely at objects to try to capture their essence (inscape). He once said, 'What you look hard at seems to look hard at you'.

Hopkins **pushes language** to its boundaries as nouns become verbs ('leaves' and 'blooms'). His unique style empowered modern poets to experiment to explore their own individuality. The sky seems to bend down to reach the growing trees: 'they brush/The descending blue'. The blueness of the sky is captured in the alliteration of 'all in a rush/With richness'. Meanwhile, newborn lambs are bounding happily, 'fair their fling'. This octet is a joyous exploration of a kaleidoscope of the colours, sounds and movement of spring. The poet's imagination soars as he strains language to encapsulate the immediacy of the moment.

In the **sestet**, **the mood becomes reflective** as the poet considers the significance of nature: 'What is all this juice and all this joy?' As he meditates, he decides it is 'A strain of the earth's sweet being', a fleeting snatch of melody from a perfect world 'In Eden garden', before it was sullied with sin. Hopkins **had a deep love of God**, especially as the Creator. His tone becomes insistent as he urges God to grasp the world in order to preserve it in its perfect state. The hard 'c' sound of 'cloy' and 'cloud' shows how the beauty will become stained and imperfect if Christ does not act swiftly. Hopkins desires virtue and purity: 'innocence', 'Mayday in girl and boy'. He refers to Christ as Mary's child ('O maid's child') as he attempts to persuade God that this world is worth the effort ('worthy the winning').

The regular rhyme scheme, cdcdcd, adds to the music of the poem as well as emphasising key words: 'joy', 'cloy', 'boy', 'beginning', 'Sinning', 'winning'. The poet was influenced by reading the medieval theologian Duns Scotus, who said that the material world was an incarnation of God. Thus Hopkins felt justified in his preoccupation with the material world, as it had a sacramental value.

ANALYSIS

'Hopkins uses poetry to speak of the glory of God.' Write a paragraph in response to this statement, using reference or quotation from 'Spring' to support your views.

Sample paragraph

Hopkins had felt uneasy loving the natural world or a friend in case it distracted him from loving God, which was the main focus of his life. But after reading the theologian Duns Scotus, who maintained that the material world was a representation of God, Hopkins felt if he loved nature, he was loving its creator. This had swayed his 'spirits to peace'. So in giving us the glorious octet of this poem 'Spring', with the weeds spiralling 'long and lovely and lush', the blue of the sky in 'a rush/With richness', the thrush's eggs like 'little low heavens', Hopkins is worshipping God. In the sestet he becomes more reflective as he more closely links the poem to the glory of God as he meditates on the meaning of all this 'juice' and 'joy'. He thinks we have seen a glimpse, 'A strain', of the earth before the Fall of Adam and Eve. He asks God to preserve the world in its sinless state. We also see his devotion to the Mother of God, Our Lady in this poem. The references to 'O maid's child' and 'Mayday' confirm this. May is the month associated with the worship of Mary, Queen of Heaven. Never since the 17th century has a poet given a deeper poetic expression to religious belief than Hopkins as he celebrates the abundant world of nature. I agree that 'nothing is so beautiful as spring'.

Examiner's Comment

This confident answer has noted some of the key influences on Hopkins (Duns Scotus) in his decision to glorify God in his poetry. Personal engagement with the poem is evident in the lively language, e.g. 'in giving us the glorious octet of this poem'. Expression throughout is clear and assured: 'He asks God to preserve the world in its sinless state'. The effective use of accurate quotation is central to this successful top grade response.

CLASS/HOMEWORK EXERCISES

1. Hopkins employs language in an energetic, intense and religious way. Do you agree? Use reference to the poem 'Spring' in your answer.

2. Hopkins is fascinated by the uniqueness of things. How does Hopkins convey the wonder of the individuality of an object through his use of language in this poem?

SUMMARY POINTS

- Euphoric declaration of beauty of nature.
- Jubilant tone, rush of energy, one word sprouts from another.
- Rich visual detail and stunning sound effects.
- Religious impulse, reflection on innocence, God's beauty in nature and man.
- Sonnet form – descriptive octet and reflective sestet.

3 AS KINGFISHERS CATCH FIRE, DRAGONFLIES DRAW FLAME

As kingfishers catch fire, dragonflies draw flame;
  As tumbled over rim in roundy wells
  Stones ring; like each tucked string tells, each hung bell's
Bow swung finds tongue to fling out broad its name;
Each mortal thing does one thing and the same: 5
  Deals out that being indoors each one dwells;
  Selves – goes itself; myself it speaks and spells,
Crying What I do is me: for that I came.

I say more: the just man justices;
  Keeps grace: that keeps all his goings graces;   10
Acts in God's eye what in God's eye he is –
  Christ. For Christ plays in ten thousand places,
Lovely in limbs, and lovely in eyes not his
  To the Father through the features of men's faces.

'dragonflies draw flame'

Glossary

1. *kingfishers*: brilliantly coloured birds that hunt small fish.
1. *dragonflies*: brightly coloured insects with transparent wings.
3. *tucked*: plucked.
4. *Bow*: rim of bell that makes a sound when struck.
7. *Selves*: (used as a verb) defining or expressing its distinctiveness.
9. *justices*: (as a verb) acting justly.
10. *Keeps grace*: obeys God's will.

INITIAL RESPONSE

1. Comment on the nature images in the poem's opening line.

2. Select two interesting sound effects from the poem and briefly explain the effectiveness of each.

3. 'Celebration is the central theme in this poem.' Write your response to this statement, supporting your answer with reference to the text.

STUDY NOTES

This sonnet is often cited as an example of Hopkins' theory of inscape, the uniqueness of every created thing as a reflection of God's glory. The poet believed that human beings had the uniqueness to recognise the divine presence in everything around us. This sonnet is written in an irregular ('sprung') rhythm that gives it a more concentrated quality.

The poem begins with two strikingly vivid images as Hopkins describes some of nature's most dazzling creatures. In **line 1**, he observes their vivid colour and dynamic movement (note the sharp alliteration and fast-paced rhythm) in the brilliant sunlight. The poet associates both the kingfisher and the dragonflies with fire. Aural images dominate **lines 2–4**. He takes great **delight in the uniqueness of existence** by listing a variety of everyday sounds: the tinkling noise of pebbles ('Stones ring') tossed down wells, the plucking of a stringed instrument and the loud ringing of a bell are all defined through their own distinctive sounds.

Hopkins is certain that the same quality applies to humans – 'Each mortal thing'. **We all express our unique inner selves**. Every individual does the same by presenting their inner essence (that dwells 'indoors'). The poet invents his own verb to convey how each of us 'Selves' (or expresses) our individual identity. The didactic tone of **lines 7–8** clearly reflects his depth of feeling, summed up by his emphatic illustration about our god-given purpose on earth: 'What I do is me: for that I came'.

Hopkins' enthusiasm ('I say more') intensifies at the start of the **sestet**. His central argument is that **people should fulfil their destiny by being themselves**. Again, he invents a new verb to illustrate his point: 'the just man justices' (good people behave in a godly way). Acting 'in God's eye' and availing of God's grace is our purpose on earth. The poet focuses on his belief that human beings are made in God's image and have the capacity to become like the omnipresent Christ.

Hopkins' **final lines** are filled with the devout Christian faith that God will redeem everyone who 'Keeps grace'. The poet repeatedly reminds us of the 'Lovely' personal relationship between God and mankind. It is Christ's presence within every human being that makes 'the features of men's faces' lovely in God's sight. Typically, Hopkins is convinced of the reality of Christ and the existence of the spirit world. He sees his own role as a 'kingfisher' catching fire – reeling in souls with his mystical poems of hope and spirituality.

Some critics have commented that the poem is too instructive and that Hopkins was overly concerned with getting across his message at the expense of method. The poet himself did not consider it a success. Yet there is no denying the poetic language of feeling and excitement in every line of the poem.

ANALYSIS

What aspects of this poem are typical of Hopkins' distinctive poetic style? Refer closely to the text in your answer.

Sample Paragraph

It seems to me that Hopkins the priest is the key speaker in 'As kingfishers catch fire'. To me, the poem is not as typical as 'Pied Beauty' or 'The Windhover'. However, his writing is unique. It is full of energy and unusual language patterns. It starts with lively images drawn from nature – 'As kingfishers catch fire, dragonflies draw flame'. In my opinion, no other poet on our course could write as precisely as this. There is an immediacy about his images that simply demands attention. The alliteration of 'f' and 'd' sounds suggest blinding flashes of colour, darting flames and dramatic movements – exactly what fish and insects do in their natural habitats. Hopkins uses very effective personification to show the vitality of the natural world – 'Stones ring'. He makes up new words of his own, such as 'justices'. Again, this is typical of his vibrant style. Hopkins does not bother with strict grammar either. He reduces sentences to childlike phrases to show his joy in being aware of the mystery of creation – 'For Christ plays in ten thousand places'. Even here, the alliteration adds energy to the rush of language. This is typical of so much of his poetry.

Examiner's Comment

This well-illustrated answer is somewhat narrowly focused, lacking development of points raised, e.g. 'Hopkins does not bother with strict grammar either'. More thorough engagement with the body of the poem is expected for a top grade. This note-like response, listing significant elements of Hopkins' style, comes short of the highest grade.

CLASS/HOMEWORK EXERCISES

1. Hopkins admitted that his poetry had an 'oddness' about it. Comment on his management of language in this poem. Refer closely to the text in your answer.

2. Hopkins uses the Petrarchan sonnet form of an octet (eight lines) and sestet (six lines) in this poem. How does the poet's treatment of his theme of wonder change in these two sections? Support your answer with close reference to the text.

SUMMARY POINTS

- Distinctive quality of everything in the natural world.
- Invents verb, 'selves', to suggest unique quality of nature and man.
- Aural imagery, onomatopoeia, use of everyday sounds, sprung rhythm.
- Compliance with God's will.

4 THE WINDHOVER

To Christ our Lord

I caught this morning morning's minion, king-
   dom of daylight's dauphin, dapple-dawn-drawn Falcon, in his riding
   Of the rolling level underneath him steady air, and striding
High there, how he rung upon the rein of a wimpling wing
In his ecstasy! then off, off forth on swing,   5
   As a skate's heel sweeps smooth on a bow-bend: the hurl and gliding
   Rebuffed the big wind. My heart in hiding
Stirred for a bird, – the achieve of, the mastery of the thing!

Brute beauty and valour and act, oh air, pride, plume here
   Buckle! AND the fire that breaks from thee then, a billion   10
Times told lovelier, more dangerous, O my chevalier!

   No wonder of it: sheer plod makes plough down sillion
Shine, and blue-bleak embers, ah my dear,
   Fall, gall themselves, and gash gold-vermilion.

'how he rung upon the rein of a wimpling wing'

Glossary

Windhover: a kestrel or small falcon; resembles a cross in flight.
1 *minion*: favourite; darling.
2 *dauphin*: prince, heir to French throne.
2 *dapple-dawn-drawn*: the bird is outlined in patches of colour by the dawn light, an example of Hopkins' use of compression.
4 *rung upon the rein*: circling movement of a horse at the end of a long rein held by a trainer; the sound of the bird pealing like a bell as it wheels in the sky.
4 *wimpling*: pleated.
6 *bow-bend*: a wide arc.
7 *Rebuffed*: pushed back; mastered.
7 *My heart in hiding*: the poet is afraid, unlike the bird.
10 *Buckle*: pull together; clasp; fall apart.
11 *chevalier*: medieval knight; Hopkins regards God as a knight who will defend him against evil.
12 *sheer plod*: back-breaking drudgery of hard work, similar to Hopkins' work as a priest.
13 *ah my dear*: intimate address to God.
14 *Fall, gall … gash*: a reference to the Crucifixion of Christ as He fell on the way to Cavalry, was offered vinegar and gashed by a spear on the cross.
14 *gold-vermilion*: gold and red, the colours of Christ the Saviour and also of the Eucharist, the Body and Blood of Christ which offers redemption.

INITIAL RESPONSE

1. In your opinion, has the poet been as daring in his use of language as the bird has been in its flight? Support your view by referring closely to the poem.

2. The sonnet moves from description to reflection. What does the poet meditate on in the sestet? Support your response by reference to the text.

3. Write your own personal response to the poem, referring closely to the text in your answer.

STUDY NOTES

'The Windhover' was Hopkins' favourite poem, 'the best thing I ever wrote'. It is dedicated to Christ, who died when he was thirty-three, and Hopkin was the same age when he wrote the poem in 1877. This is also the age when Jesuits are ordained. The poet celebrates the uniqueness of the bird and his own deep relationship with God the Creator.

The name of the bird comes from its custom of hovering in the air, facing the wind, as it views the ground for its prey. The opening lines of the **octet** are joyful and celebratory as Hopkins rejoices in the sight of the bird, 'daylight's dauphin'. The verb 'caught' suggests not just that the poet caught sight of the bird, but also that he 'caught' the essence of the bird on the page with words. This is an example of Hopkins' compression of language where he edges two meanings into one word or phrase.

Hopkins shaped language by omitting articles, conjunctions and verbs to express the energy of the bird, 'off forth on swing'. **Movement fascinated the poet**. The bird is sketched by the phrase 'dapple-dawn-drawn'. A vivid image of the flecks of colour on his wings (as the dawn light catches him) is graphically drawn here.

The **momentary freshness** is conveyed by 'this morning', with the bird in flight beautifully captured by the simile 'As a skate's heel sweeps smooth on a bow-bend'. The 's' sound mimics the swish of the skater as a large arc is traced on the ice. This curve is similar to the strong but graceful bend of a bow stretched to loose its arrow, with all its connotations of beauty of line and deadly strength.

In the **octet**, there is typical **energetic language**: 'how he rung upon the rein of a wimpling wing/ In his ecstasy!' This carries us along in its breathless description. It is not necessary for the reader to comprehend every word in order to appreciate the phrase's meaning. The word 'wimpling' refers to the beautiful, seemingly pleated pattern of the arrangement of the outstretched wings of the bird. The capital 'F' used for 'Falcon' hints at its symbolism for Christ. This very personal poem uses 'I' in the octet and 'my' in the sestet. Hopkins lavishes praise on the bird: 'dauphin' (young prince, heir) and 'minion' (darling). Run-on lines add to the poet's excitement. He acknowledges that the bird has what he does not possess: power, self-belief and grace ('My heart in hiding'). The lively rhyme, such as 'riding'/'striding', never becomes repetitive because of the varying line breaks. The octet concludes with Hopkins' admiration of 'the thing', which broadens the focus from the particular to the general. All of creation is magnificent.

This leads to the **sestet**, where **God the Creator becomes central to the poem**. The essence (inscape) of the bird is exposed: 'air, pride, plume here'. The bird is strong, brave, predatory, graceful and beautiful. The word 'Buckle' is paradoxical, as it contains two contradictory meanings: clasp together and fall apart. The bird is holding the line when it rides the rolling wind and falls apart as it swoops down on its prey. Capital letters for the conjunction 'AND' signal a moment of insight: 'the fire that breaks from thee'. The pronoun refers to God, whose magnificence is shown by 'fire'. The Holy Spirit is often depicted as a bird descending with tongues of flame. A soft tone of intimacy is then revealed: 'O my chevalier!' It is as if Hopkins wants God to act as the honourable knight of old, to take up his cause and fight on his behalf against his enemy. God will be Hopkins' defender against evil.

The **sestet** concludes with **two exceptional images**, both breaking apart to release their hidden brilliance. The ploughed furrow and the 'bluebleak embers' of coal both reveal their beauty in destruction: 'sillion/Shine', 'gash gold-vermilion'. Christ endured Calvary and crucifixion, 'Fall, gall … gash', and through his sacrifice, the 'Fall', achieved redemption for us. So too the priest embracing the drudgery of his service embraces his destiny by submitting to the will of God. In doing so, he reflects the greatness of God. Earthly glory is crushed to release heavenly glory. The phrase 'ah my dear' makes known the dominant force of Hopkins' life: to love God. The colours of gold and red are the colours of Christ the Saviour as well as the colours associated with the Eucharist, the Body and Blood of Christ. When Christians receive the sacrament of Holy Communion, they are redeemed. So, as the poem begins, 'dapple-dawn-drawn Falcon', it ends with 'gold-vermilion' in a triumph of glorious colour.

ANALYSIS

'Hopkins' intense reflections on Christ in his poetry are always conveyed with visual energy.' Discuss this statement, with particular reference to 'The Windhover'.

Sample Paragraph

In 'The Windhover', Hopkins uses the image of the falcon, which hovers in a cross-shape on the wind, as an emblem of Christ. Using strong images, the poet describes the bird's magnificent beauty, 'dapple-dawn-drawn', and its strength, 'rebuffed the big wind'. In the sestet, Hopkins calls God 'O my chevalier'. This gives me a vivid picture of a highly moral individual who was both strong-willed and who fought against evil. The verb 'Buckle' reminds me of the knight putting on his armour and stumbling in fierce battle. Christ also fell on the way to Cavalry where he was crucified – out of which a great glory was given to man, 'the fire that breaks from thee'. This sacrifice won our salvation. Hopkins felt it was right to focus on nature as it is a manifestation of the power and beauty of God. He believed that his vocation in life was to love God. In glorifying Him through the dramatic emblem of the windhover, he is glorifying divine creation, and therefore God Himself. The flash of red and gold, with which this visually powerful poem ends, 'gash gold-vermilion', reminds me that the lowly priest carrying out his ordinary duties is also revealing the beauty of God's creation. I think Hopkins' reflections on Christ add a real spiritual dimension to his poetry.

Examiner's Comment

Close reading of the poem is evident in this top grade personal response: 'The verb "Buckle" reminds me of the knight putting on his armour'. Quotations are very well used here to highlight Hopkins' commitment to his Christian faith, 'The flash of red and gold, with which the poem ends, "gash-gold-vermilion", reminds me that the lowly priest carrying out his ordinary duties is also revealing the beauty of God's creation'. Well-controlled language use throughout.

CLASS/HOMEWORK EXERCISES

1. How does Hopkins adapt the Petrarchan sonnet for his own purposes in 'The Windhover'? Use reference to the poem in your answer.

2. This profoundly personal poem commemorates the inimitable nature of the bird and the poet's intense relationship with God. For each of these aspects, pick an image from the poem which you considered particularly effective and explain why you have chosen that image.

SUMMARY POINTS

- Deeply personal poem, engaging opening.
- Relationship with God accentuated by poet's ability to see the divine in nature.
- Medieval chivalric imagery.
- Bird's movement depicted by alliteration and assonance.
- Optimistic ending, illustrated by 'blue-black' becoming 'gold-vermilion'.

5 PIED BEAUTY

Glory be to God for dappled things –
  For skies of couple-colour as a brinded cow;
    For rose-moles all in stipple upon trout that swim;
Fresh-firecoal chestnut-falls; finches' wings;
  Landscape plotted and pieced – fold, fallow, and plough;   5
    And all trades, their gear and tackle and trim.

All things counter, original, spare, strange;
  Whatever is fickle, freckled (who knows how?)
    With swift, slow; sweet, sour; adazzle, dim;
He fathers-forth whose beauty is past change: 10
        Praise him.

'skies of couple-colour'

Glossary

1 *Pied*: varied.
1 *dappled*: speckled, spotted.
2 *brinded*: streaked.
3 *rose-moles*: red-pink spots.
3 *stipple*: dotted.
4 *Fresh-firecoal chestnut falls*: open chestnuts bright as burning coals.
5 *pieced*: enclosed.
5 *fold*: sheep enclosure.
5 *fallow*: unused.
6 *trades*: farmwork.
6 *gear*: equipment.
6 *tackle*: implements.
6 *trim*: fittings.
7 *counter*: contrasting.
7 *spare*: special.
8 *fickle*: changeable.
10 *He*: God.
10 *fathers-forth*: creates.

INITIAL RESPONSE

1. In your view, what is the central theme in this poem? Refer to the text in your answer.

2. Discuss the poet's use of sound effects in the poem. Support your answer with quotations.

3. Choose two striking images from the poem and comment on the effectiveness of each.

STUDY NOTES

'Pied Beauty' is one of Hopkins' 'curtal' (or curtailed) sonnets, in which he condenses the traditional sonnet form. It was written in the so-called sprung rhythm that he evolved, based on the irregular rhythms of traditional Welsh verse. The poem's energetic language – particularly its sound effects – reflects Hopkins' view of the rich, abundant diversity evident within God's coherent creation.

The simplicity of the prayer-like **opening line** ('Glory be to God') is reminiscent of Biblical language and sets the poem's devotional tone. From the start, Hopkins displays a **childlike wonder** for all the 'dappled things' around him, illustrating his central belief with a series of vivid examples from the natural world.

Included in his panoramic sweep of nature's vibrant delights are the dominant blues and whites of the sky, which he compares to the streaked ('brinded') patterns of cowhide. The world is teeming with contrasting colours and textures, captured in **detailed images**, such as 'rose-moles all in stipple upon trout' and 'Fresh-firecoal chestnut-falls'.

For the exhilarated poet, everything in nature is linked. It is ironic, of course, that what all things share is their god-given individuality. In **line 4**, he associates broken chestnuts with burning coals in a fire, black on the outside and glowing underneath. In turn, the wings of finches have similar colours. Condensed imagery and compound words add even greater energy to the description.

Hopkins turns his attention to human nature in **lines 5–6**. The farmland features he describes reflect hard work and efficiency: 'Landscape plotted and pieced – fold, fallow, and plough'. The range of man's impact on the natural world is also worth celebrating, and this is reinforced by the orderly syntax and insistent rhythm. Human activity in tune with nature also glorifies God.

Hopkins' **final four lines** focus on the unexpected beauty of creation and further reveal the poet's passionate Christianity. As though overcome by the scale and variety of God's works – 'who knows how?' – the poet meditates on a range of contrasting adjectives ('swift, slow; sweet, sour; adazzle, dim'), all of which indicate the wonderful diversity of creation. As always, the alliteration gives an increased dynamism to this image of abundance and variety in nature.

The poem ends as it began – with a shortened version of the two mottoes of St Ignatius of Loyola, founder of the Jesuits: *Ad majorem Dei gloriam* (to the greater glory of God) and *Laus Deo semper* (praise be to God always). For Hopkins, God is beyond change. The Creator ('He fathers-forth') and all the 'dappled' opposites that enrich our ever-changing world inspire us all to 'Praise him'.

ANALYSIS

'Hopkins' appreciation of the energy present in the world is vividly expressed in his unique poetry.' Discuss this statement, with particular reference to 'Pied Beauty'.

Sample Paragraph

It seems to me that 'Pied Beauty' is more like a heartfelt prayer than an ordinary poem. It begins with the phrase 'Glory be to God' and continues to the final words 'Praise him'. In between, Hopkins lists a whole litany of examples of the variety of the 'dappled' natural environment, the 'brinded' patterns of cowhide, 'landscape plotted and pieced'. The pace of the poem is rapid as though he is in a rush to explain his astonishment: 'Fresh-firecoal chestnut-falls'. There is an overwhelming sense of God's mystery and greatness. This is partly due to the compound phrases, such as 'couple-colour' and 'rose-moles' which make us more aware of the varied appearances of natural things. The energetic rhythm builds to a climax in the last line. This is short, direct and almost breathless – just one simple monosyllabic phrase that sums up Hopkins' awareness of God's creation: 'Praise him'. From start to finish, I can easily appreciate Hopkins' personal sense of the overpoweringly beautiful world around him.

Examiner's Comment

A short well-focused response ranging over a number of interesting features of Hopkins' style, particularly his description of nature's energy: 'The pace of the poem is rapid, as though he is in a rush to explain his astonishment'. The rapidity of Hopkins' verse is effectively explored, particularly in the reference to the lead-up to the 'climax in the poem's final line'. A successful top grade standard.

CLASS/HOMEWORK EXERCISES

1. Compare and contrast the views expressed in 'Pied Beauty' with any other 'religious' poem by Hopkins from your course. Support your answer with reference to both poems.

2. In your opinion, how does Hopkins express his attitude towards God in this poem? Refer to his use of imagery and pay particular attention to the concluding four lines.

SUMMARY POINTS

- Condensed version (ten and a half lines) of traditional sonnet form (fourteen lines).
- Anthem of praise to God for nature's variety.
- Catalogue of vibrant examples of 'dappled beauty'. Effective use of compound words.
- Alliteration conveys how man's activities are in harmony with God's design.

6 FELIX RANDAL

Felix Randal the farrier, O he is dead then? my duty all ended,
Who have watched his mould of man, big-boned and hardy-handsome
Pining, pining, till time when reason rambled in it and some
Fatal four disorders, fleshed there, all contended?

Sickness broke him. Impatient he cursed at first, but mended   5
Being anointed and all; though a heavenlier heart began some
Months earlier, since I had our sweet reprieve and ransom
Tendered to him. Ah well, God rest him all road ever he offended!

This seeing the sick endears them to us, us too it endears.
My tongue had taught thee comfort, touch had quenched thy tears   10
Thy tears that touched my heart, child, Felix, poor Felix Randal;

How far from then forethought of, all thy more boisterous years,
When thou at the random grim forge, powerful amidst peers,
Didst fettle for the great grey drayhorse his bright and battering sandal!

'at the random grim forge'

Glossary

Felix Randal: the parishioner's name was Felix Spenser. 'Felix' in Latin means 'happy'. Randal can also mean a lowly, humble thing or trodden on.
1 *farrier*: blacksmith.
1 *O he is dead then*: reaction of priest at Felix's death.
2 *hardy-handsome*: compound word describing the fine physical appearance of the blacksmith.
4 *disorders*: diseases.
4 *contended*: competitively fought over Felix.
6 *anointed*: sacraments administered to the sick by a priest.
7 *reprieve and ransom*: confession; penance; communion; redemption from sin.
8 *Tendered:* offered.
8 *all road ever*: in whatever way (local dialect).
13 *random*: casual; irregular.
14 *fettle*: prepare.
14 *drayhorse*: big horse used to pull heavy carts.
14 *sandal*: type of horseshoe.

INITIAL RESPONSE

1. 'Hopkins is a poet who celebrates unique identities and experiences, their meaning and their value.' Discuss this statement with reference to the poem, illustrating your answer with quotations.

2. How does the octet differ from the sestet in this Petrarchan sonnet? Refer to theme and style in your response. Use quotations in support of your views.

3. Choose two aural images that you found interesting and give reasons for their effectiveness.

STUDY NOTES

'Felix Randal' was written in Liverpool in 1880. The poem contrasts with others such as 'Spring'. Hopkins had been placed as a curate to the city slums of Liverpool, 'a most unhappy and miserable spot', in his opinion. He didn't communicate successfully with his parishioners and he didn't write much poetry, except this one poem about the blacksmith who died of tuberculosis, aged thirty-one.

The opening of the **octet** identifies the man with his name and occupation, 'Felix Randal the farrier'. Then the poet shocks us with the priest's reaction: 'O he is dead then? my duty all ended'. On first reading, this sounds both dismissive and cold. However, when we consider that the death was expected and that the priest had seen all this many times, we realise that the line rings with authenticity and professional detachment. Also, in the face of the big events of life, we articulate our feelings with thoughtless, numbed remarks. For Hopkins, 'duty' was a sacred office. **The farrier is recalled in his physical prime**, using the alliteration of 'm', 'b' and 'h' in the phrase 'mould of man, big-boned and hardy-handsome'. The repetition of 'Pining, pining' marks his decline in health. His illness is graphically conveyed as his mental health deteriorated ('reason rambled') and the diseases attacked his body ('Fatal four disorders, fleshed there, all cotended'). The **illnesses took possession of the body** and waged a horrific battle to win supremacy, eventually killing Felix. The use of the word 'broke' is suitable in this context, as in the world of horses it refers to being trained. Is Felix trained ('broke') through suffering? His realistic reaction to the news – 'he cursed' – changes when he receives the sacraments ('being anointed'). Felix was broken but is now restored by 'our sweet reprieve and ransom', the healing sacraments. **The tone changes** with the personal pronoun. The priest–patient relationship is acknowledged: we, both priest and layperson, are saved by God. A note of resigned acceptance, almost an anti-climax, is evident in the line 'Ah well, God rest him all road ever he offended!' The use of the Lancashire dialect ('all road') by the priest shows a developing relationship between the two men.

The detached priest's voice resurfaces in the **sestet**: 'This seeing the sick'. This section of the sonnet focuses on **the reality of sickness** and its effects. Both the sick man and the priest received something from the experience. We respond to the sick with sympathy ('the sick endears them to us'), but we also appreciate ourselves and our own health more ('us too it endears') as we face another's mortality. The priest comforted the sick man with words ('My tongue') and the Last Sacraments, anointing by 'touch'. The priest becomes a father figure to 'child' Felix. Is there a suggestion that one must become like an innocent child to enter the kingdom of Heaven? The **tercet** (three-line segment) is intimate: 'thee', 'thy', 'Thy tears', 'my heart'. The **last tercet** explodes in a **dramatic flashback** to the energy of the young blacksmith in his prime, when there was little thought of death: 'How far from then forethought'. Onomatopoeia and alliteration convey the lifeforce (inscapes) of the young Felix, 'boisterous' and 'powerful amidst peers'.

Sprung rhythm adds to the force of the poem as the six main stresses are interspersed with an irregular number of unstressed syllables. Felix did a man's job at the 'grim forge' when he made the 'bright and battering sandal' for the powerful carthorse, magnificently captured in the assonance of 'great grey drayhorse'. The poem ends not with Felix in heavenly glory, but in his former earthly glory: 'thou … Didst fettle'. God has fashioned Felix through his suffering just as Felix had fashioned the horseshoe. Both required force and effort to bend them to the shape in which they can function properly. The poem is a celebration of God's creation of the man.

ANALYSIS

'Hopkins is a poet who celebrates unique identities and individual experiences, exploring their meaning and worth.' Discuss this statement in relation to one or more of the poems on your course, quoting in support of your points.

Sample Paragraph

In 'Felix Randal', Hopkins captures the unique essence of the man and his inscape, a great big strong man struck down by illness. He was 'big-boned and hardy-handsome', and the alliteration emphasises the magnificence of his physique. His understandable reaction to his own misfortune is caught in 'he cursed at first', the assonance echoing the deep guttural oaths. The repeated 'f' of 'Fatal four disorders, fleshed there' conveys the impossible odds stacked against the man. Here Hopkins has given us the unique identity of the man and his individual experience. He also gives us the rather dismissive voice of the weary priest: 'O he is dead then? my duty all ended'. Here is a man who has seen too much suffering. His use of the Lancashire dialect 'all road' shows how he has tried to enter the world of his parishioners, but he quickly reverts back to his professional capacity: 'This seeing the sick'. He has a strong belief that the sacraments he is offering will help: 'sweet reprieve and ransom'. So Hopkins also gives us the individual essence of the weary priest trying his best for the sick in his care. The poem leaves us feeling that the priest has received as much from the sick man as the sick man has received from the priest: 'Thy tears that touched my heart'. The experience broke through the cold exterior of the priest to reveal his human capacity for compassion. Felix's acceptance of his lot and the priest's acceptance of his lot both show the value of the experience.

Examiner's Comment

As part of a full essay answer, this paragraph has dealt comprehensively with the various elements of the question. The close attention to the poet's use of language, assonance and alliteration, enhances the answer. Real personal engagement with the poem is evident in the in-depth discussion of the priest's transition from tiredness to his regained 'professional capacity'. A highly successful answer which merits the top grade.

CLASS/HOMEWORK EXERCISES

1. Hopkins deals with suffering in his poetry. Has this any relevance to the modern reader? Use reference to 'Felix Randal' in your answer.

2. Hopkins gives a vivid portrait of the farrier. Discuss how his changing tone conveys his view of Felix Randal. Support your answer with close reference to the text.

SUMMARY POINTS

- Inscape (essence captured) of blacksmith in this Petrarchan Sonnet.
- 'Randal' suggests man's insignificance; glory only achieved through Christian faith.
- Sprung rhythm (many unstressed syllables) add to poem's energy.
- Simple everyday speech and colloquialisms root poem firmly in North of England.
- Final image is positive; 'b' sound accentuates energy.

7 INVERSNAID

This darksome burn, horseback brown,
His rollrock highroad roaring down,
In coop and in comb the fleece of his foam
Flutes and low to the lake falls home.

A windpuff-bonnet of fawn-froth   5
Turns and twindles over the broth
Of a pool so pitchblack, fell-frowning,
It rounds and rounds Despair to drowning.

Degged with dew, dappled with dew,
Are the groins of the braes that the brook treads through,   10
Wiry heathpacks, flitches of fern,
And the beadbonny ash that sits over the burn.

What would the world be, once bereft
Of wet and of wildness? Let them be left,
O let them be left, wildness and wet;   15
Long live the weeds and the wilderness yet.

'the fleece of his foam'

Glossary

Inversnaid is a remote area located near Loch Lomond in the Scottish Highlands.
1 *burn*: stream.
3 *coop*: hollow.
3 *comb*: moving freely.
4 *Flutes*: grooves; whistles.
6 *twindles*: spins.
7 *fell*: fiercely.
9 *Degged*: sprinkled about.
10 *groins of the braes*: sides of hills.
11 *heathpacks*: heather outcrops.
11 *flitches*: ragged tufts.
12 *beadbonny*: mountain ash tree with bright berries.
13 *bereft*: deprived.

INITIAL RESPONSE

1. From your reading of the first stanza, explain how the poet conveys the stream's energy.

2. Sound effects play a key part in the second and third stanzas. Choose two aural images that convey Hopkins' excited reaction to the mountain stream. Comment on the effectiveness of each.

3. Write your own personal response to the poem, referring closely to the text in your answer.

STUDY NOTES

'Inversnaid' was written in 1881 after Hopkins visited the remote hillsides around Loch Lomond. He disliked being in cities and much preferred the sights and sounds of the wilderness. The poem is unusual for Hopkins in that there is no direct mention of God as the source of all this natural beauty.

The **opening lines** of **stanza one** are dramatic. Hopkins compares the brown, rippling stream ('This darksome burn') to a wild horse's back. The forceful alliteration – 'rollrock highroad roaring' – emphasises the power of this small and dismal stream as it rushes downhill, its course directed by confining rocks. A sense of immediacy and energy is echoed in the **vigorous onomatopoeic effects**, including end rhyme ('brown', 'down'), repetition and internal rhyme ('comb', 'foam'). This is characteristic of Hopkins, as is his use of descriptive details, likening the foamy 'fleece' of the water to the fluted surface ('Flutes') of a Greek or Roman column.

Stanza two begins with another effective metaphor. The poet compares the yellow-brown froth to a windblown bonnet (hat) as the water swirls into a dark pool on the riverbed. The **atmosphere is light and airy**. Run-on lines reflect the lively pace of the noisy stream. However, the tone suddenly darkens with the disturbing image of the 'pitchblack' whirlpool which Hopkins sees as capable of drowning all in 'Despair'. The sluggish rhythm in **lines 7–8** reinforces this menacing mood.

Nature seems much more benign in **stanza three**. The language is softer sounding – 'Degged with dew, dappled with dew' – as Hopkins describes the steady movement of the water through 'the groins of the braes'. Enclosed by the sharp banks, the stream sprinkles nearby branches of mountain ash, aflame with their vivid scarlet berries. As always, Hopkins delights in the unspoiled landscape: 'Wiry heathpacks, flitches of fern,/And the beadbonny ash'. Throughout the poem, he has also used traditional Scottish expressions ('burn', 'braes') to reflect the lively sounds of the Highlands.

The language in **stanza four** is rhetorical. Hopkins wonders what the world would be like without its wild qualities. The tone is personal and plaintive: 'O let them be left, wildness and wet'. While repetition and the use of the exclamation add a sense of urgency, his plea is simple: let nature remain as it is. The final appeal – 'Long live the weeds and the wilderness yet' – is reminiscent of his poem 'Spring'. Once again, there is no doubting Hopkins' enthusiasm for the natural beauty of remote places and the sentiments he expresses are clearly heartfelt. Although written in 1881, the poem has obvious relevance for today's generation.

ANALYSIS

'Hopkins' deep appreciation of nature is a central feature of his striking poetry.' Discuss this statement, with particular reference to 'Inversnaid'.

Sample Paragraph

The most immediate thing that emerges about Hopkins is his extraordinary closeness to nature. This is evident in all his poems. He seems to have a heightened awareness of the sights and sounds of the remote mountain 'burn' in 'Inversnaid'. He details the colours of the water. It is 'darksome', 'horseback brown' and 'fawn-froth'. Hopkins is always excited by his natural environment. To him, the river is alive. It is 'roaring down'. He describes the Scottish rowan trees as 'the beadbonny ash', referring to their attractive red berries. Everything he says suggests his love for the natural world. In the last section of the poem, Hopkins openly states his fears for nature. He begs us to preserve the 'wildness and wet'. For him, all of nature deserves respect. He ends the poem with his own slogan, 'Long live the weeds and the wilderness'. Hopkins strikes me as being a lonely man who preferred the secluded Scottish hills where he could appreciate the natural world rather than being in a crowded city. Nature obviously inspired him and he seems to be deeply moved by the beauty of places such as Inversnaid. He repeats the words 'wet' and 'wildness' a number of times in the final lines, leaving us in no doubt about how much the natural landscape meant to him.

Examiner's Comment

Hopkins' awareness of the unruly aspects of nature is effectively explored: 'He details the colours of the water. It is "darksome"'. There is a convincing sense of close engagement with the body of the poem: 'Hopkins is always excited by his natural environment'. Accurate textual references and impressive, fluent expression ensure the top grade.

CLASS/HOMEWORK EXERCISES

1. In your opinion, does the poem 'Inversnaid' have relevance to our modern world? Support the points you make with reference to the text.

2. How does Hopkins reveal his intense love of nature in this poem? Refer to his subject matter and stylistic techniques in your response.

SUMMARY POINTS

- Celebration of nature's unruly beauty; unusually no reference to God.
- Colloquial Scots-English language locates poem in Scottish Highlands.
- Steady movement of water conveyed through onomatopoeic effects.
- Plea on behalf of unspoilt natural scenes.

8 I WAKE AND FEEL THE FELL OF DARK, NOT DAY

I wake and feel the fell of dark, not day.
What hours, O what black hours we have spent
This night! what sights you, heart, saw; ways you went!
And more must, in yet longer light's delay.
    With witness I speak this. But where I say   5
Hours I mean years, mean life. And my lament
Is cries countless, cries like dead letters sent
To dearest him that lives alas! away.

    I am gall. I am heartburn. God's most deep decree
Bitter would have me taste: my taste was me;   10
Bones built in me, flesh filled, blood brimmed the curse.
    Selfyeast of spirit a dull dough sours. I see
The lost are like this, and their scourge to be
As I am mine, their sweating selves; but worse.

'I wake and feel the fell of dark, not day'

Glossary

1. **fell**: threat; blow; knocked down; past tense of fall (fall of Adam and Eve cast into darkness); also refers to the mountain.
7-8. **dead letters sent / To dearest him**: communication which is of no use, didn't elicit a response.
9. **gall**: bitterness; anger; acidity; vinegar.
9. **deep decree**: command that cannot easily be understood.
11. **Bones built in me, flesh filled, blood brimmed the curse**: the passive tense of the verb might suggest how God created Man, yet Man has sinned.
12. **Selfyeast of spirit a dull dough sours**: yeast makes bread rise; Hopkins feels he cannot become good or wholesome.
13. **The lost**: those condemned to serve eternity in Hell with no hope of redemption, unlike the poet.

INITIAL RESPONSE

1. How is the oppressive atmosphere conveyed in this sonnet? Quote in support of your response.

2. How does the poem conclude, on a note of hope or despair? Illustrate your answer by referring closely to the text.

3. Comment on the use of alliteration to convey Hopkins' sense of dejection. Mention at least three examples.

STUDY NOTES

'I wake and feel the fell of dark, not day' was written in Dublin, where Hopkins was teaching at UCD and was burdened by a massive workload of examination papers. He was there for six years and had over 1,300 scripts a year to correct. After a long silence, he wrote the 'terrible sonnets'. Hopkins said of these, 'If ever anything was written in blood, these were.' This sonnet was discovered among his papers after his death.

The last three sonnets on the course are called the 'terrible sonnets'. They are similar to Frost's 'Acquainted with the Night'. Here Hopkins reaches the **darkest depths of bleak despair**. The sonnet opens in darkness and the only mention of light in the whole poem is 'light's delay' in **line 4**, as it is postponed. He wakes to the oppressive blow of the dark ('the fell of dark'), not to the brightness of daylight. The heaviness of depression is being described, the oppressive darkness which Adam woke to after his expulsion from the Garden of Eden. Hopkins and his soul have shared these 'black hours' and they will experience 'more'. It is not just hours they have spent in darkness, but 'years', 'life'.

The formal, almost Biblical phrase 'With witness I speak this' emphasises that what he has said is true. The hard 'c' sounds in 'cries countless' and the repetition of 'cries' keenly describe the **fruitless attempts at communication** ('dead letters'). There is no response: he 'lives alas! away'. We can imagine the poet in the deep dark of the night attempting to gain solace from his prayers to God ('dearest him'), but they go unanswered.

Hopkins feels this deep depression intensely. **Note the repetition of 'I'**: 'I wake', 'I speak', 'I say', 'I mean', 'I am gall', 'I am heartburn', 'I see', 'I am'. He is in physical pain, bitter and burning. The language might well refer to Christ's Crucifixion, when he was offered a sponge soaked in vinegar to drink, and pierced through his side. However, the poet recognises that it is God's unfathomable decision that this is the way it should be: 'God's most deep decree'. **The poet is reviled by himself** in **line 10**: 'my taste was me'. He describes how he was fashioned: 'Bones built in me, flesh filled, blood brimmed'. The alliteration shows the careful construction of the body by the Creator, but Hopkins is full of 'the curse'.

Could this sense of revulsion be related to original sin emanating from the fall of Adam and Eve? The deadening 'd' sound of 'dull dough' shows that there is no hope of rising. The body is tainted, soured. It does not have the capacity to 'Selfyeast', to resurrect or renew. Is it being suggested that Hopkins needs divine intervention? Is there an overtone of the bread of Communion, the wholesome Body of Christ? The scope of the poem broadens out at the end as the poet gains an **insight into the plight of others**. All those condemned to Hell are like this and in fact are worse off: 'but worse'. The horrific atmosphere of Hell is fixed in the phrase 'sweating selves'. For those 'lost', it is permanent. For Hopkins, perhaps it is just 'longer light's delay'. Some day **he will be redeemed**.

ANALYSIS

'Hopkins' poetry displays a deeply personal and passionate response to the human condition.' Discuss with reference to the poems on your course, illustrating your answer with relevant quotations.

Sample Paragraph

I was fascinated when reading about Hopkins' life to learn that he had to examine hundreds of scripts five or six times a year, and that his college lectures were conducted in uproar. He writes of a 'daily anxiety about work to be done', 'All impulse fails me'. Everyone can identify with this man suffering from depression. This is evident in 'I wake and feel the fell of dark, not day'. To me he is describing waking over and over again at night. The long vowel sounds in 'O what black hours' give an idea of the man tossing and turning, trying to sleep, his head in a whirl. Hopkins' personal and passionate relationship with God was the focus of his life. His passionate pleas to God, 'To dearest him', are useless, 'dead letters'. Usually God is written with a capital letter. I wonder if Hopkins is telling us that he doesn't even know how to address his Lord? So he is devastated and he uses the language of the Crucifixion to express that 'I am gall'. He, like all depressives, despises himself: 'the curse', 'dull dough'. The poem seethes with self-disgust. The only slight glimmer for the poet is that those condemned to Hell are in a worse situation 'and their scourge to be … their sweating selves; but worse'. Hopkins writes passionately about being human and the feeling of unworthiness. Sometimes people would say Hopkins is out of fashion, with his emphasis on sin and religion, but when I read of all the suicides today, I realise that Hopkins is describing a universal human condition, 'the deep night of the soul'.

Examiner's Comment
This is a mature personal response to the assertion that Hopkins reacts deeply and passionately to the human condition: 'The poem seethes with self-disgust'. There is also in-depth exploration of the poem's sound effects: 'The long vowel sounds in "O what black hours" give an idea of the man tossing and turning'. Vocabulary and expression are impressive, adding to a highly successful, top grade paragraph.

CLASS/HOMEWORK EXERCISES

1. 'Hopkins charts an extraordinary mental journey in the "terrible sonnets".' Give a personal response to this statement, quoting in support of your opinions.

2. Hopkins graphically explores his deep feeling of despair through light and dark imagery in 'I wake and feel the fell of dark, not day'. Pick one image of brightness and one of darkness which you considered effective and explain your choice.

SUMMARY POINTS

- Feeling of abandonment by God; spiritual suffering.
- Depressive's experience of waking into night vividly conveyed by imagery.
- Long vowel sounds and dragging repetition emphasise the prevailing darkness.
- Sense of self-disgust balanced by the poet's concluding empathy.

9 NO WORST, THERE IS NONE

No worst, there is none. Pitched past pitch of grief,
More pangs will, schooled at forepangs, wilder wring.
Comforter, where, where is your comforting?
Mary, mother of us, where is your relief?
My cries heave, herds-long; huddle in a main, a chief   5
Woe, world-sorrow; on an age-old anvil wince and sing –
Then lull, then leave off. Fury had shrieked 'No lingering!
Let me be fell: force I must be brief.'

O the mind, mind has mountains; cliffs of fall
Frightful, sheer, no-man-fathomed. Hold them cheap   10
May who ne'er hung there. Nor does long our small
Durance deal with that steep or deep. Here! creep,
Wretch, under a comfort serves in a whirlwind: all
Life death does end and each day dies with sleep.

'frightful, sheer, no-man-fathomed'

Glossary

1. *Pitched past pitch*: pushed beyond.
2. *pangs*: sudden pains.
2. *schooled at forepangs*: prepared by earlier sorrows.
3. *Comforter*: the Holy Spirit.
5. *main*: crowd.
8. *fell*: harsh; cruel.
8. *force*: perforce; therefore.
12. *Durance*: endurance; determination.
13. *whirlwind*: turmoil.

INITIAL RESPONSE

1. Comment on how Hopkins creates a sense of suffering and pessimism in the first four lines of the poem.

2. Discuss the effectiveness of the mountain images in lines 9–12.

3. In your opinion, is this a completely negative poem? Support your response by referring closely to the text.

STUDY NOTES

This Petrarchan sonnet was written in Hopkins' final years, at a time when he suffered increasingly from ill health and depression. It was one of a short series of sonnets of desolation, now known as the 'terrible sonnets' or 'dark sonnets'. In 'No worst, there is none', we see a man experiencing deep psychological suffering and struggling with his religious faith. The poem reveals a raw honesty from someone close to despair.

The **opening** is curt and dramatic, revealing the intensity of Hopkins' suffering: 'No worst, there is none'. He is unable to imagine any greater agony. The emphatic use of monosyllables in **line 1** reflects his angry frustration. Having reached what seems the threshold of torment, 'Pitched past pitch of grief', the poet dreads what lies ahead and the horrifying possibility that his pain ('schooled at forepangs') is likely to increase. The explosive force of the verb 'Pitched', combined with the harsh onomatopoeic and alliterative effects, heighten the sense of uncontrollable anguish. Both 'pitch' and 'pangs' are repeated, suggesting darkness and violent movement.

The rhythm changes in **line 3**. The three syllables of 'Comforter' slow the pace considerably. This is also a much softer word (in contrast to the harshness of the earlier sounds) and is echoed at the end of the line by 'comforting'. Hopkins' desolate plea to the Holy Spirit and the Virgin Mary emphasises his hopelessness: 'where, where is your comforting?' The tone, reminiscent of Christ's words on the Cross ('My God, why hast thou forsaken me?'), is both desperate and accusatory.

The poet likens his hollow cries for help to a herd of cattle in **line 5**. The metaphor highlights his lack of self-worth – his hopeless prayers 'heave' and 'huddle in a main'. He feels that his own suffering is part of a **wider universal 'world-sorrow'**. There is an indication here that Hopkins recognises that experiencing a crisis of faith can affect any Christian from time to time. This possibility is supported by the memorable image of the anvil being struck in **line 6**. He realises that the Christian experience involves suffering the guilt of sin and doubt to achieve spiritual happiness: 'on an age-old anvil wince and sing'.

But for the poet, any relief ('lull') from suffering is short lived. His unavoidable feelings of shame and the pain of remorse are hauntingly personified: 'Fury had shrieked'. Once again, the severe sounds and the stretching of the phrase 'No lingering!' over two lines reinforce the relentlessness of Hopkins' troubled conscience.

This tormented tone is replaced by a more reflective one in the opening lines of the **sestet**, where Hopkins moves from the physical world of his 'cries' into the metaphorical landscape of towering mountains, with their dark, unknown depths. This **dramatic wasteland**, with its 'no-man-fathomed' cliffs, is terrifyingly portrayed. The poet reminds us that the terror of depression and separation from God cannot be appreciated by those 'who ne'er hung there'. The terror of being stranded on the 'steep or deep' rock face cannot be endured for long.

In the **last two lines**, Hopkins resigns himself to the **grim consolation** that all the depression and pain of this world will end with death, just as everyday troubles are eased by sleep. The final, chilling image of the wretched individual taking refuge from the exhausting whirlwind is less than optimistic. There is no relief from the terrible desolation and Hopkins' distracted prayers have yet to be answered.

ANALYSIS

'Hopkins' deep despair is evident in the 'terrible sonnets'. Discuss this statement, with particular reference to 'No Worst , There is None'.

Sample Paragraph

At the start of 'No worst, there is none', the tone is totally despondent. The first sentence is short and snappy, emphasising that Hopkins has reached rock bottom. Hopkins was a manic depressive and obsessed with religion. He also had issues with sexuality. In many ways he was caught between his role as a Jesuit priest and his human desires. Rhetorical questions highlight his dependence on his religious faith – 'Comforter, where, where is your comforting?' This gives a heartfelt tone. Hopkins uses effective images which always make us feel sympathy for him, for example 'My cries heave, herds-long'. His tone is sorrowful and this is emphasised by the way he uses comparisons. The prayers he offers to Heaven are just useless words which he intones: 'My cries heave, herds-long'. He goes on to compare his sense of desperate danger from sin with being trapped on a steep mountain – 'O the mind, mind has mountains'. The use of the 'O' punctuation mark emphasises the tone of desperation. The end of the poem is even more negative. Hopkins obviously had issues with his own faith in God. He uses a strong tone of despair as he compares himself to a stranded wanderer finding shelter from a 'whirlwind'. His only comfort is sleep and eventually death, which will silence his inner pain. The last line emphasises his feelings of being tired with life – 'each day dies with sleep'. The tone is of complete hopelessness.

Examiner's comment

This response includes a number of relevant examples of the varying tones throughout. Accurate quotations are effectively used in support and there is some good engagement with the poem. The expression was slightly awkward in places: 'This gives a heartfelt tone' and there is overuse of the verb 'emphasises'. Although hard-working, the answer does not merit the highest grade.

CLASS/HOMEWORK EXERCISES

1. Write your own personal response to 'No worst, there is none'. Refer closely to the text in your answer.

2. The poet feels utterly abandoned by God in this poem. Trace the development of thought in 'No worst, there is none' and discuss how Hopkins uses vivid description to explore his negative feelings. Support your answer with close reference to the text.

SUMMARY POINTS

- Most despairing and bleakest of 'terrible sonnets'.
- Alarming metaphors and powerful sound effects reveal inner suffering.
- Ups and downs of man's spiritual journey suggested by mountain imagery.
- Slightly optimistic end, death brings end to suffering for man.

THOU ART INDEED JUST, LORD, IF I CONTEND

*Justus quidem tu es, Domine, si disputem tecum: verumtamen
justa loquar ad te: Quare via imporium prosperatur? &c.*

Thou art indeed just, Lord, if I contend
With thee; but, sir, so what I plead is just.
Why do sinners' ways prosper? And why must
   Disappointment all I endeavour end?
     Wert thou my enemy, O thou my friend,   5
   How wouldst thou worse, I wonder, than thou dost
Defeat, thwart me? Oh, the sots and thralls of lust
Do in spare hours more thrive than I that spend,
Sir, life upon thy cause. See, banks and brakes
Now leaved how thick! laced they are again   10
With fretty chervil, look, and fresh wind shakes
Them; birds build – but not I build; no, but strain,
Time's eunuch, and not breed one work that wakes.
Mine, O thou lord of life, send my roots rain.

'laced they are again/With fretty chervil, look'

Glossary

Latin quotation: Indeed you are just, O Lord, if I dispute with you; yet I would plead my case before you. Why do the wicked prosper?

1   The first lines of the poem are a version of a Latin quotation that is taken from the Bible.
1   *contend*: dispute; argue; challenge.
7   *sots*: drunkards.
7   *thralls*: slaves.
9   *brakes*: thickets; groves of trees.
11 *fretty*: fretted; interlaced; the herb chervil has lacy leaves.
11 *chervil*: garden herb; the 'rejoicing leaf'.
13 *Time's eunuch*: a castrated male, incapable of reproducing.

INITIAL RESPONSE

1. List the questions put to God. What tone is evident in each – anger, rebelliousness, reverence, resentment, trust, despair, etc.?

2. Is there a real sense of pain in the poem? At what point is it most deeply felt? How does the abrupt, jerky movement of the poem contribute to this sense of pain? Quote in support of your points.

3. Is the image of God in the poem stern or not? Do you think that Hopkins had a good or bad relationship with God? Illustrate your answer with reference to this poem.

STUDY NOTES

'Thou art indeed just, Lord, if I contend' was written in 1889 at a time of great unhappiness for Hopkins in Dublin. He had written in a letter that 'all my undertakings miscarry'. This poem is a pessimistic yet powerful plea for help from God. It was written three months before he died.

This sonnet opens with the **formal language of the courtroom** as the poet, in clipped tones, poses three questions in the **octet**. With growing frustration, he asks God to explain why sinners seem to prosper. Why is he, the poet, continually disappointed? If God was his enemy instead of his friend, how could he be any worse off? God, he allows, is just, but he contends that his own cause is also just. The language is that of a coherent, measured argument: 'sir', 'I plead'. This is a contrast to the twisted, tortured grammar of the 'terrible sonnets', which echoes the deep, dark despair of the poet.

However, in **lines 3–4**, 'and why must/Disappointment all I endeavour end?', the inversion of the natural order makes the reader concentrate on the salient point that 'Disappointment' is the 'end' result of all the work the poet has done. But **the tone remains rational**, as he points out to 'sir' that the worst doing their worse 'more thrive' than he does. But his frustration at his plight makes the line of the octet spill over into the sestet, as Hopkins complains that he has spent his life doing God's will ('life upon thy cause').

The **sestet** has the ring of the real voice breaking through as he urgently requests God to 'See', 'look'. Here is **nature busily thriving**, producing, building, breeding, growing. The movement and pace of continuing growth and regrowth is caught in the line 'Now leaved how thick! laced they are again'. The **alliteration** of 'banks and brakes', 'birds build' vividly portrays the abundance of nature, as does the **assonance** of 'fretty' and 'fresh'. **Flowing run-on lines** describe the surge of growing nature. Hopkins is the exception in this fertile scene. The negatives 'not', 'no', the punctuation of semi-colon and comma and the inversion of the phrase 'but not I build; no, but strain' depict the **fruitless efforts of the poet to create**. The terrible, dramatic, sterile image of 'Time's eunuch', the castrated male, contrasts the poet's unhappy state of unsuccessful effort with the ease of fruitful nature. Time is kind to nature, enabling it to renew, but the poet cannot beget one work: 'not breed one work that wakes'.

The **last line** of the poem pleads for help and rescue. An image of a drought-stricken plant looking for life-giving water is used to describe the poet's plight of unsuccessful poetic creativity. **He looks to the 'lord of life' for release**. Hopkins had written in one of his final letters, 'If I could produce work … but it kills me to be time's eunuch and never to beget'. It is intriguing that someone of such great faith can argue ('contend') so vehemently with God. Hopkins stretches the disciplined structure of the sonnet form to echo his frustration as he strains to create. He died unknown as a poet, his body of work not even mentioned in his obituary. But the irony is that he did create 'work that wakes'.

His friend, Robert Bridges, submitted some of his poems for an anthology of 19th century poetry and it attracted a favourable review which commented on how it possessed a 'poignant, even a passionate sincerity'. Thus, Hopkins finally found his place in the early 20th century, a time of innovation and technical experimentation. His 'roots' had been sent 'rain'.

ANALYSIS

'Hopkins' poetry deals with the theme that God's will is a mystery to us.' Discuss this statement, illustrating your response with relevant quotation from 'Thou art indeed just, Lord, if I contend'.

Sample Paragraph

How interesting to hear a man of great faith, a Jesuit priest, argue so openly and directly with God! As we see all the man-made and natural tragedies in the world, which of us has not thought, why has God allowed this to happen? Using the highly disciplined form of the sonnet, Hopkins charges

God with accusations in the form of questions. How is it that sinners 'prosper'? Why 'must/ Disappointment all I endeavour end?' The poet is frustrated, as we sometimes are; he does not know what is going on. God's will is a mystery to us. The tension at the centre of this sonnet is conveyed by Hopkins spilling the concerns of justice and morality into the sestet. He cannot contain himself. The mood of puzzlement continues in the sestet as he urgently points out ('See', 'look') how nature is thriving ('fretty chervil', 'birds build'). But he, in contrast, is not. He concludes with the striking image of himself as the sterile 'Time's eunuch', a castrated slave unable to produce. He makes one final plea to God to nourish his parched 'roots' with 'rain'. The alliteration of 'roots rain' aligns him with the fertile world of nature, 'banks and brakes'. God is the 'lord of life', his divine plan a mystery to us, but we have the capacity to pray to Him.

Examiner's Comment
Close reading of the text is evident here, particularly in the use of the rhetorical question, 'which of us has not thought, why has God allowed this to happen?' Assured use of language and accurate quotation: 'The mood of puzzlement continues in the sestet as he urgently points out ("See", "look") how nature is thriving ("fretty chervil", "birds build")'. This guarantees an impressive top grade.

CLASS/HOMEWORK EXERCISES

1. Hopkins' innovative stylistic techniques make his work accessible to the modern reader. How true is this of 'Thou art indeed just, Lord, if I contend'? Use reference to the poem in your answer.

2. Hopkins complains and questions throughout this poem. What conclusion does he reach in the end? Did you find this ending satisfactory or not? Give reasons for your opinion.

SUMMARY POINTS

- Deeply personal and direct address to God.
- Hurt and frustration as poet wrestles with his religious faith.
- Struggle to control anger and frustration.
- Effective use of alliteration and vivid imagery.
- Contrast between abundance of nature and man's infertility.
- Concluding prayer to enable creativity to blossom.

LEAVING CERT SAMPLE ESSAY

'The poetry of Gerard Manley Hopkins explores twin themes of nature and religion in an innovative and dramatic fashion.' Discuss this statement, supporting your answer with suitable reference to the poetry of Hopkins on your course.

Marking Scheme Guidelines
Candidates are free to agree and/or disagree with the statement. However, the key terms, 'themes of nature and religion' and 'innovative and dramatic fashion' should be addressed implicitly or explicitly. Reward responses that show clear evidence of personal engagement with the poems.

Indicative material:
- Provocative personal views on religion, the natural world, life.
- Experimental language – sound, imagery, symbolism, sprung rhythm.
- Christian themes – finding God in nature.
- Varying tones/moods; development of traditional poetic forms.
- Fresh approaches and originality, dramatic/descriptive power, etc.

Sample Essay

1. In my opinion, Hopkins is by far the most interesting and inventive of the poets I studied. As a Jesuit priest, it is hardly surprising that his personal faith in Catholicism is central to his poetry. He honestly and openly expressed himself through his poetry and that is an admirable quality. For much of the time, Hopkins focused on nature and the beauty of God's creation. His work raises questions about the Christian experience. We may not share his beliefs, but there is no doubting their sincerity. On a personal level, he openly confessed his own weaknesses. He is easy to identify with when he feels unworthy and hurt by God. His nature poems – always written in a distinctive dramatic style – are beautifully descriptive and give a great sense of the wonder of the natural world.

2. In the sonnet, 'Spring', Hopkins states his awe and admiration at the season of renewal. He begins with a confident arresting sentence which instantly grabs our attention. 'Nothing is so beautiful as spring'. This sense of immediacy lets us know that this is what Hopkins really believes. The urgent tone reflects his closeness to the growth that is taking place everywhere around him. Even the 'weeds in wheels shoot long and lovely and lush'. For Hopkins, all of nature is alive. This energy is echoed in the vigorous alliteration, suggesting the great range of wild plants growing untamed. Hopkins' fresh and condensed imagery seems to range over every aspect of nature – 'Thrush's eggs look little low heavens'. The simile associating the common shape and colour is filled with intensity, and introduces an early association between nature and the divine power responsible for creation. The octave continues with vibrant

descriptions of springtime – 'The glassy peartree', 'descending blue', 'the racing lambs'. For this poet, spring is overwhelming.

3. The sestet is typical of Hopkins in that he responds to the sights and sounds that he has just outlined, making sense of the world through his Christian beliefs. It is God who created 'all this juice and all this joy. Religious references dominate as he imagines his surroundings as 'Eden garden'. The tone becomes worshipful, almost prayer-like. He urges God to maintain this natural world in all its mystery and beauty – 'before it cloy'. Like other sonnets, 'Spring' concludes in a strong declaration of Hopkins's own faith, expressing the importance of virtue and purity – 'Innocent Mind and Mayday in girl and boy'. I found the ending visionary, as though the poet truly has a religious experience – and this was one of the most compelling aspects of Hopkins' poetry.

4. 'The Windhover' also addresses the themes of God and nature. Hopkins takes delight in the bird's dramatic flight amid 'the rolling level underneath him steady air'. The childlike syntax and powerful rhythm capture the kestrel's majestic movement. As usual, the poet's sound effects reinforce the bird's immense strength – 'morning's minion', 'daylight's dauphin', 'wimpling wing'. I was very impressed by the sheer control of such intensive language. The run-through lines in the octave emphasise the 'mastery' of the falcon and Hopkins' admiration for it. As with 'Pied Beauty' and 'God's Grandeur', the poet celebrates the unique beauty and wonder of existence. The final lines of 'The Windhover' recognise the birds as Hopkins' personal 'chevalier' – or champion – a dramatic symbol of God as a medieval knight who will save him.

5. While most of the Hopkins poems I have read are notable for the poet's unique use of language, 'Felix Randal' is a more biographical account of a hard-working Christian man who was a friend and a parishioner. Yet in telling the moving dramatic story of a simple blacksmith's life and death, the poet gets to the heart of what it means to be a good Christian. The farrier's anger when faced with serious illness – 'Impatient, he cursed at first' – is soon replaced by God's 'sweet reprieve and ransom'. Hopkins uses the poem as a parable, showing how every human being must come to terms with death. Another aspect of Christian life addressed in the poem is the priest's role bringing spiritual 'comfort'. But for me, what I liked most about 'Felix Randal' was the image of Hopkins himself as a sympathetic man who combined his official clerical duties with generous friendship towards the dying blacksmith – 'seeing the sick endears them to us'.

6. Religion and nature are very closely linked in Hopkins' poetry. Although the 'terrible sonnets' reveal the poet's doubts about his faith, he is always intent on strengthening his belief in God. For the most part, though, he clearly finds evidence of God's existence in the beauty and wonder of everyday natural

surroundings. 'Inversnaid' – describing a remote area of the Scottish Highlands characterises his great love for 'the weeds and the wilderness'. In many ways, as an outdoor enthusiast, I can relate to this. Hopkins has always reminded me of the freedom and beauty of rural landscapes – and that is one of the main reasons why his poems are so enjoyable.

(approx. 825 words)

Examiner's Comment

A very solid and impressive essay, showing some close personal interaction with Hopkins' poetry. Both aspects of the question (subject matter and writing style) were tackled confidently. The overview set out in the opening paragraph, combined with occasional cross references indicated a broad knowledge of key poems. Effective used of reference and accurate quotation throughout.

MARKING SCHEME
P = 14/15
C = 13/15
L = 14/15
M = 5/5
Total = 46/50

SAMPLE LEAVING CERT QUESTIONS ON HOPKINS' POETRY

(45/50 MINUTES)

1. 'Hopkins uses language in a startling and unique way.' Would you agree? Discuss this view, with reference to both the subject matter and language use in the poems by Hopkins on your course.

2. 'Hopkins' innovative poetry can range from delight to despair.' Discuss this statement with reference to both the themes and language use in the poems by Hopkins on your course.

3. 'The intensity of Hopkins' complex relationship with God is often reflected in the power of his poetic voice.' Discuss this view, with reference to both the subject matter and language use in the poems by Hopkins on your course.

Sample Essay Plan (Q1)

'Hopkins uses language in a startling and unique way.' Would you agree? Discuss this view, with reference to both the subject matter and language use in the poems by Hopkins on your course.

- **Intro:** A personal examination is required of the imaginative, innovative techniques used by the poet, and also a reference to their purpose. These include sound effects, vivid imagery, bending words, coining new ones.

- **Point 1:** 'Spring' – sound effects, alliteration, assonance, onomatopoeia, run-on lines, all reflect the exuberance of springtime.

- Point 2: 'Pied Beauty' – compound words suggest dappling effect and ecstatic elation. Similarly, 'Inversnaid' also uses compound phrases to convey euphoric expressions of joy in nature.

- Point 3: 'No worst there is none' – repetition recreates the fear of the poet as he descends into desolation as he feels abandoned by God.

- Point 4: 'The Windhover' – sprung rhythm, pushing many unstressed syllables into the line, creates a childlike enthusiasm. His patent sincerity moves us.

- Point 5: 'Felix Randal' – Contrasting views of the blacksmith and the priest suggested through alliteration, repetition, sprung rhythm, use of dialect and flashback.

- Conclusion: Like the Impressionists with paint, Hopkins with words bent his raw material into new shapes and textures so that the reader can experience the world from a unique and starling perspective.

Sample Essay Plan (Q1)
Develop one of the above points into a paragraph.

Sample Paragraph: Point 2
Hopkins loved movement rather than rest. This is evident from the poem 'Pied Beauty'. Alliteration – 'Fresh-firecoal', 'plotted and pieced', 'Fold, fallow'; assonance – 'finches' wings'; and compound words 'chestnut-falls' all celebrate the diversity of God's creation. This poem in particular reminds me of the Impressionist painters as they dabbed and speckled paint to recreate the varying light effects in nature. Hopkins uses his compound words in a similar way, 'couple-colour', 'rose-moles'. We sweep across the great patterns in nature which are 'adazzle', 'adim'. We see man working in harmony with nature, 'And all trades, their gear and tackle and trim.' There is a glorious orderly disorder, 'counter, original, spare, strange', in this 'dappled' place of God's creation, 'he fathers-forth'. Hopkins was a Jesuit and it was the custom for the Jesuit schools to start and finish their written work with praise to God. 'For the greater glory of God' is 'Glory be to God' while the ending 'Praise God always' is shortened to a more emphatic 'Praise Him'. Hopkins succeeds, in my opinion, in capturing the mystery, 'who knows what?' and the wonder, 'whose beauty is past change', of God's creation through his innovative techniques.

Examiner's Comment
As part of a full essay answer, this is a good personal response to Hopkins' techniques focusing on one of his trademarks, his use of compound words. An in-depth exploration is well supported with quotation. A top-grade answer.

LAST WORDS

'What you look hard at seems to look hard at you.'

G. M. Hopkins

Hopkins is more concerned with 'putting across his perceptions than with fulfilling customary expectations of grammar'.

Robert Bernard Martin

'Design, pattern, or what I am in the habit of calling inscape is what I above all aim at in poetry.'

G. M. Hopkins

JOHN KEATS

1795–1821

'I have loved the principle of beauty in all things.'

John Keats is one of the most widely recognised and loved English poets. Born in London in 1795, he was not expected to have poetic aspirations, considering his ordinary background. Nevertheless, from his earliest boyhood he had an acute sense of beauty, and in 1816, Keats passed his medical exams but chose to make a career as a poet. His first published poems included 'To One Who Has Been Long in City Pent' and 'On First Looking into Chapman's Homer'.

Keats is best known for his series of odes, filled with lush images of nature. These display a sure poetic instinct and a remarkable ability to appeal powerfully to the senses by the brilliance of his diction. Many of his poems are noted more for their strength of feeling than for thought, often reflecting the poet's intense inner conflicts.

In 1818, Keats first came into contact with the eighteen-year-old Frances (Fanny) Brawne, and a close friendship developed between them. In late 1819, they became engaged and he dedicated his sonnet 'Bright Star' to her. However, the relationship was cut short by the effects of consumption (tuberculosis). Despite various health and financial difficulties, this was Keats's most prolific writing period when he composed most of his famous odes.

As his medical condition worsened, he was advised to move to a warmer climate and in November 1820, he arrived in Rome. Unfortunately, Keats's health continued to deteriorate and he died there on 23rd February 1821.

John Keats's influence upon later poets has been immense. Generations of poetry lovers have been moved and inspired by his compelling use of language in addressing the significance of experience, imagination, art and illusion with penetrating thoughtfulness and without sentimentality. He is rightly regarded as perhaps the most talented poet of the English Romantic period.

The Romantic era was an artistic, literary, and intellectual movement that originated in Europe toward the end of the 18th and early 19th century. It was generally seen as a response to the logical, more restrained forms of literature composed in the earlier 'Age of Reason'. The Romantic poets promoted individualism, respect for nature, idealism, physical and emotional passion, and an interest in the mystic and supernatural.

Because of their theories of literature and life, prominent Romantic poets such as Keats, Wordsworth and Shelley, were drawn to lyric poetry; they even developed a new poetic form, often called the romantic meditative ode. These poets believed in intense feeling as an authentic source of aesthetic experience. They emphasised such emotions as unease, fear and wonder – especially when experienced in the awe-inspiring beauty of nature.

INVESTIGATE FURTHER

To find out more about John Keats, or to hear readings of his poems, you could do a search of some of the useful websites available such as YouTube, bbc.co.uk and poetryarchive.org or access additional material on this page of your eBook.

Prescribed Poems   HIGHER LEVEL

1 **'To One Who Has Been Long in City Pent'**
This Italian sonnet describes the delights of the English countryside while reflecting poignantly on the passing of time. Keats disliked living in the city and was firmly convinced about nature's restorative power.   **248**

2 **'Ode to a Nightingale'**
Unhappy with the real world, Keats attempts to escape into the ideal by entering the mysterious world of the nightingale's song. The poem begins by describing the song of an actual nightingale, but the bird quickly becomes a symbol of the immortality of nature. In the end, the poet is left with an intense self-awareness and returns to reality.   **252**

3 **'On First Looking into Chapman's Homer'** *
This Petrarchan sonnet conveys the sheer sense of excitement and wonder which Keats found after reading the ancient works of Homer. The poet uses dramatic imagery to describe the revelation of Chapman's English translation comparing it to an astronomer who has discovered a new planet, or to Cortez's first sighting of the Pacific Ocean.   **260**

④ 'Ode on a Grecian Urn'

Keats's famous ode explores the paradoxical relationship between the immortal world of art and transient reality. The enigmatic Grecian urn excites his imagination. It is a powerful symbol of timeless perfection which provokes by silently posing questions. The poem's conclusion, 'Beauty is truth, truth beauty', has often been viewed as the poet's personal philosophy on life.   **265**

⑤ 'When I Have Fears That I May Cease to Be'

In this Shakespearean sonnet, Keats expresses his fear of dying young before he has time to fulfil his potential. He also reflects on the transience of life, love and fame. The poem is a good example of Keats's use of archaic language and his distinctive musical sound effects.   **271**

⑥ 'La Belle Dame Sans Merci' *

A highly dramatic ballad set in the medieval era, this mysterious poem tells the tragic tale of a lovesick knight and his 'Beautiful Lady without Mercy'. The haunting story of love and loss in a bleak wintry landscape is dominated by images of death.   **275**

⑦ 'To Autumn'

Characteristically filled with wonderful images and sensuous detail, this celebrated poem describes the beauty of nature, highlighting autumn's abundant fruitfulness and ultimate decline. This is achieved through Keats's rich language, personification and evocative sound effects.   **281**

⑧ 'Bright Star, Would I Were Steadfast as Thou Art'

Another Shakespearean sonnet focusing primarily on the differences between eternity and mortality. As in many of his well-known odes, Keats is fascinated by the idea of a perfect, unchanging world – but is forced to accept that his dream is impossible.   **286**

1 TO ONE WHO HAS BEEN LONG IN CITY PENT

To one who has been long in city pent,
   'Tis very sweet to look into the fair
   And open face of heaven, – to breathe a prayer
Full in the smile of the blue firmament.
Who is more happy, when, with heart's content,   5
   Fatigued he sinks into some pleasant lair
   Of wavy grass, and reads a debonair
And gentle tale of love and languishment?
Returning home at evening, with an ear
   Catching the notes of Philomel, – an eye   10
Watching the sailing cloudlet's bright career,
   He mourns that day so soon has glided by:
E'en like the passage of an angel's tear
   That falls through the clear ether silently.

'the sailing cloudlet's bright career'

Glossary

Title: This reference closely echoes a line from John Milton's epic poem, 'Paradise Lost': 'As one who long in populous city pent'.
1 *pent*: confined, imprisoned.
4 *firmament*: sky.
6 *lair*: sheltered hideaway.
7 *debonair*: pleasing, sophisticated.
8 *languishment*: yearning, desire.
10 *Philomel*: legendary nightingale.
11 *cloudlet*: small cloud.
11 *career*: movement.
14 *ether*: upper air, atmosphere.

INITIAL RESPONSE

1. Describe the contrasting moods in the poem's octave and sestet. Support your answer with suitable reference to the text.

2. Comment on Keats's use of sound effects throughout the sonnet in describing the natural world.

3. In your opinion, how relevant is this poem to modern life? Briefly explain your response.

STUDY NOTES

Written in the summer of 1816 when Keats was twenty-one and a medical student in London, this poem follows the Petrarchan (or Italian) sonnet structure. The octave (first eight lines) describes the delights of the English countryside while the sestet (last six lines) reflects poignantly on the passing day.

The opening section of the **octave** immediately reveals Keats's preference for nature over city life. **Line 1** is marked by an insistent rhythm and a series of heavy monosyllables which echo the dull monotony of urban routine: 'To one who has been long in city pent'. The emphatic verb 'pent' is particularly effective in highlighting Keats's <u>frustrated sense of confinement</u>. But we soon see his obvious excitement as he considers the 'fair' countryside, personifying its natural beauty as the 'open face of heaven' (**line 3**). The energetic run-on lines and celebratory tone (''Tis very sweet') add to the upbeat mood. For Keats, however, there is more to the unspoilt country than just its beauty and sense of release. He also finds a reverential kind of spiritual peace when he is able to 'breathe a prayer' and reaffirm the joys of existence in such a natural setting. This worshipful tone is reinforced in various religious references to 'heaven' and the 'firmament', a Biblical term often used to describe the sky.

Keats continues to commend nature's virtues in **lines 5–8** by appealing directly to the reader's likely sympathy for 'happy' country living and the joy of relaxing to one's 'heart's content'. He illustrates this with the image of finding a 'pleasant lair' and sinking into the 'wavy grass' to read a 'gentle tale of love and languishment'. Characteristically, **Keats's musical language is filled with rich onomatopoeic effects, interweaving sibilant, assonant and alliterative sounds**. At ease in this tranquil rural landscape, he can enjoy reading a favourite 'tale of love'. This defines his notion of perfect contentment. As always, the most important Romantic qualities of Keats's poetry are the imagination, a love of nature, and the sense of beauty to which a strangeness has been added.

The **sestet**, however, is largely dominated by a **tender sense of loss**. As in so many of his poems, Keats can only escape from the real world for a limited time. Returning home in the evening, he hears the nightingale singing ('the notes of Philomel'). This elevated reference to a tragic mythical figure who was turned into a bird reflects the pervading atmosphere of serenity. The imagery Keats uses is equally mellow. He observes 'the cloudlet's bright career' and 'mourns that day so soon has glided by'. Again, broad assonant vowels enhance the sense of melancholy. Does his brief visit to the countryside symbolise the transience of all human life? **Lines 13–14**, comparing the onset of evening to the falling of 'an angel's tear' are particularly evocative. There is a clear suggestion of some underlying sense of a divine presence existing within nature's mysterious beauty.

Keats's journey from confinement in the city to finding peace in the quiet meadows and finally to **reflective nostalgia** all takes place over a single day. The concise sonnet form is ideally suited to the poet's meditative subject matter. Readers are left with a thought-provoking and cohesive poem whose deft use of metaphorical language illustrate the poet's heartfelt views on nature's restorative power and the realities of human mortality.

ANALYSIS

'The rejuvenating force of nature is a central theme in many of Keats's poems.' Discuss this statement in relation to 'To one who has been long in city pent', using suitable reference to the text.

Sample Paragraph

In his short poem, 'To one who has been long in city pent', the poet describes the experience of a city-dweller who visits the countryside. He is cheered up at once as he breathes in the open atmosphere. Keats uses simple child-like language – 'Tis very sweet'. The sight of the clear blue sky fills his heart with joy. He prays to God in gratitude. I felt that he almost discovered God in nature which he personifies – 'face of heaven'. This image suggests a personal relationship between Keats and nature. I liked the contrast between his lack of freedom in the city where he felt 'pent' and his happiness in the country – 'some pleasant lair'. His mood is so much brighter under the 'blue firmament' where he can lie on a bed of soft 'wavy grass' and reads a sweet romantic story. At that moment he feels as if he is the happiest man on earth. Keats's language is much more positive when he describes the rejuvenating force of nature – 'more happy', 'gentle tale of love'. In the end, he must face reality again. But thanks to nature, he is prepared for city life. He has happy memories of a day that has 'glided by'. The mood at the end is not nearly as upbeat as before. Yet Keats has enjoyed the freedom of day, although I believe that part of him still feels sad that it has passed by too soon.

Examiner's Comment

This is a competent response which includes some worthwhile discussion of the poet's themes and language use. Comments on stylistic features, such as contrast and mood, are well supported by apt reference: 'Keats's language is much more positive when he describes the rejuvenating force of nature'. There is evidence of genuine engagement with the poem, for example in the last sentence. However, the expression is awkward at times: 'His mood is so much brighter under the "blue firmament" where he can lie on a bed of soft "wavy grass" and reads a sweet romantic story'. This also prevents the paragraph from achieving the top grade.

CLASS/HOMEWORK EXERCISES

1. 'John Keats's poetry focuses some of life's mysterious elements.' Discuss this view, with particular reference to the poem, 'To one who has been long in city pent'.

2. 'Keats often makes effective use of metaphors and personification in his poems.' To what extent is this true of 'To one who has been long in city pent'? Support your answer with suitable reference to the poem.

SUMMARY POINTS

- Nature's power to delight, life's transience, the joy of literature.
- Varying moods and atmospheres.
- Effective personification, vivid images and metaphors.
- Musical sound effects, alliteration, broad assonant vowels.
- Complementary use of octave and sestet creates unity.

ODE TO A NIGHTINGALE

I

My heart aches, and a drowsy numbness pains
   My sense, as though of hemlock I had drunk,
Or emptied some dull opiate to the drains
   One minute past, and Lethe-wards had sunk:
'Tis not through envy of thy happy lot,   5
   But being too happy in thine happiness, –
      That thou, light-winged Dryad of the trees,
         In some melodious plot
Of beechen green, and shadows numberless,
   Singest of summer in full-throated ease.   10

II

O, for a draught of vintage! that hath been
   Cooled a long age in the deep-delved earth,
Tasting of Flora and the country green,
   Dance, and Provençal song, and sunburnt mirth!
O for a beaker full of the warm South,   15
   Full of the true, the blushful Hippocrene,
      With beaded bubbles winking at the brim,
         And purple-stained mouth;
That I might drink, and leave the world unseen,
   And with thee fade away into the forest dim: 20

III

Fade far away, dissolve, and quite forget
   What thou among the leaves hast never known,
The weariness, the fever, and the fret
   Here, where men sit and hear each other groan;
Where palsy shakes a few, sad, last gray hairs,   25
   Where youth grows pale, and spectre-thin, and dies;
      Where but to think is to be full of sorrow
         And leaden-eyed despairs,
Where Beauty cannot keep her lustrous eyes,
   Or new Love pine at them beyond tomorrow.   30

IV

Away! away! for I will fly to thee,
   Not charioted by Bacchus and his pards,

But on the viewless wings of Poesy,
    Though the dull brain perplexes and retards:
Already with thee! tender is the night,   35
    And haply the Queen-Moon is on her throne,
        Clustered around by all her starry Fays;
            But here there is no light,
    Save what from heaven is with the breezes blown
        Through verdurous glooms and winding mossy ways.   40

            V
I cannot see what flowers are at my feet,
    Nor what soft incense hangs upon the boughs,
But, in embalmed darkness, guess each sweet
    Wherewith the seasonable month endows
The grass, the thicket, and the fruit-tree wild;   45
    White hawthorn, and the pastoral eglantine;
        Fast fading violets covered up in leaves;
            And mid-May's eldest child,
The coming musk-rose, full of dewy wine,
    The murmurous haunt of flies on summer eves.   50

            VI
Darkling I listen; and, for many a time
    I have been half in love with easeful Death,
Called him soft names in many a mused rhyme,
    To take into the air my quiet breath;
    Now more than ever seems it rich to die,   55
    To cease upon the midnight with no pain,
        While thou art pouring forth thy soul abroad
            In such an ecstasy!
        Still wouldst thou sing, and I have ears in vain –
            To thy high requiem become a sod.   60

            VII
Thou wast not born for death, immortal Bird!
    No hungry generations tread thee down;
The voice I hear this passing night was heard
    In ancient days by emperor and clown:
Perhaps the self-same song that found a path   65
    Through the sad heart of Ruth, when, sick for home,
        She stood in tears amid the alien corn;

        The same that oft-times hath
    Charmed magic casements, opening on the foam
      Of perilous seas, in faery lands forlorn.   70

          VIII
Forlorn! the very word is like a bell
  To toll me back from thee to my sole self!
Adieu! the fancy cannot cheat so well
  As she is fam'd to do, deceiving elf.
Adieu! adieu! thy plaintive anthem fades   75
  Past the near meadows, over the still stream,
    Up the hillside; and now 'tis buried deep
      In the next valley-glades:
  Was it a vision, or a waking dream?
    Fled is that music: – Do I wake or sleep?   80

'in faery lands forlorn'

Glossary

The nightingale has always been considered a secretive bird known for singing very beautifully. It is also associated with romantic love.

2 *hemlock*: poisonous plant.
3 *opiate*: sleep-inducing drug.
4 *Lethe-wards*: forgetfulness. (In Greek mythology, the dead drank from the River Lethe to forget their human lives.)
7 *Dryad*: beautiful woodland maiden; tree nymph.
11 *draught of vintage*: drink of good wine.
13 *Flora*: Roman goddess of flowers.
14 *Provençal*: South-eastern France.
15 *South*: the warm Mediterranean.
16 *blushful Hippocrene*: red wine of the Greek gods, associated with inspiration.
25 *palsy*: wasting disease.
26 *spectre-thin*: ghostly.
29 *lustrous*: radiant, bright.
30 *pine*: yearn for.
32 *Bacchus*: god of wine in Roman legend.
32 *pards*: leopards were used to draw Bacchus's chariot.
33 *Poesy*: poetry
36 *Queen-Moon*: Diana, the Roman moon-goddess.
37 *Fays*: fairy attendants.
40 *verdurous*: grassy green.
42 *incense*: pleasant fragrance.
43 *embalmed*: heavy-scented
44 *endows*: enriches.
46 *eglantine*: sweet briar, a beautiful wild rose.
51 *Darkling*: in the darkness.
53 *mused*: bemused, uncertain.
60 *requiem*: liturgical funeral song.
60 *sod*: clump of earth; grassy soil.
64 *emperor and clown*: the highest and lowest in society.
66 *Ruth*: Biblical character who was exiled.
69 *casements*: windows.
70 *faery*: fairy (early spelling).
70 *forlorn*: abandoned, despondent.
72 *toll*: call.
72 *sole self*: personal loneliness.
73 *fancy*: imagination.
75 *plaintive anthem*: bittersweet song.

INITIAL RESPONSE

1. Comment on the effectiveness of Keats's language throughout the second stanza in conveying his longing to escape from reality.

2. Select two memorable images from the poem that you find particularly effective. Explain your choice in each case.

3. Describe Keats's mood in the poem's final stanza.

STUDY NOTES

'Ode to a Nightingale' is considered one of the finest poems in English literature and reveals John Keats's highest imaginative powers. The beautiful song of the nightingale fills him with a desire to escape from the cares of life. This highly passionate and personal ode illustrates Keats's intense perception of human experience. Written in a single day in May 1819, the poem explores themes of transience, mortality

and nature. It is a typical Romantic ode which emphasises powerful emotions and the importance of imagination. Keats also makes effective use of synaesthesia (the mixing of sense impressions) which is a characteristic of his rich imagery.

The ode begins with an expression of the poet's acute self-awareness and his deep desire to escape. The initial mood of the **opening stanza** combines ecstatic joy and pain – almost to the point of completely dulling the senses. Keats declares his own brooding heartache. He feels 'a drowsy numbness' that he associates with hemlock or opium. Sibilant sounds echo this wistful trancelike feeling. Overwhelmed by the rich music of the nightingale's song, **he appears to be in a meditative dream**, attempting to identify himself with the bird. Heavy alliterative 'd' and 'n' sounds add to the weary tone. Monosyllables ('pains', 'drunk', 'drains') create a slow, deliberate rhythm, reflecting the poet's dejected mood. **Lines 9–10** focus directly on the nightingale and are less lethargic. The mood lightens here, in contrast to the earlier exhausted atmosphere. Vowel sounds sharpen and the sibilance becomes noticeably more energetic ('Singest of summer', 'full-throated ease').

In **stanza two**, Keats longs for the oblivion of alcohol, calling for 'a draught of vintage' that tastes of 'the country-green'. The exclamatory 'O' emphasises his sense of yearning. In his wildly imaginative state, the wine tastes of the French Mediterranean 'Dance, and Provençal song'. But the poet longs for more than just being carefree. He also wishes the wine to inspire him when he refers to the 'Hippocrene', a sacred fountain that was said to bring poetic inspiration to those who drank from it. There is **an abundance of vigorous imagery** throughout these lines and an atmosphere of warmth predominates. The phrase 'sunburnt mirth' combines the idea of sunshine with the joy of young people celebrating. Repeated references to dancing and the 'blushful' wine with its 'beaded bubbles winking at the brim' are enriched by vibrant onomatopoeic sounds. Keats's compressed images often overlap. The senses of sight, hearing and touch are closely associated with tasting the wine as a pleasurable escape from harsh reality.

Ironically, the poet's awareness of the real world makes it impossible for him to 'Fade far away'. Much of the **third stanza** is preoccupied with the human condition at its worst: the 'weariness, the fever, and the fret' of everyday life is illustrated with **a graphic image of physical suffering** where 'youth grows pale, and spectre-thin, and dies'. Assonance emphasises this tragic view of illness and decay. Keats sees time itself as the greatest of all sorrows, worse than any terrible disease. Everything decays and 'Beauty cannot keep her lustrous eyes'. Only the nightingale's singing transcends mortality.

In **stanza four**, the poet orders the nightingale to fly away, and he will follow, not through being intoxicated ('Not charioted by Bacchus'), but through poetry, which will give him 'viewless wings'. As Keats imagines himself joining the nightingale's magical world, the **atmosphere becomes dream-like**: 'tender is the night'. The personified 'Queen-Moon' is surrounded by 'her starry Fays'. This majestic image is typical of the exaggerated senses which heighten the poet's fantasy. An underlying air of excitement pervades the darkness. The imaginary woodland setting is mysterious with the heavenly breeze blowing through 'verdurous glooms and winding mossy ways'. Soft sibilance and consonant 'm' sound effects are used here to further invigorate the poet's ecstatic mood.

Stanza five consists of a single flowing sentence describing Keats's increasingly close union with the nightingale. A vivid sensory impression of smell is created to serve his exuberant imagination. The poet becomes acutely aware of the sweet fragrances around him. Yet even here, it is impossible to avoid the presence of death within the 'embalmed darkness'. He lists the intoxicating forest smells of fresh grass, fruit-trees and flowers. Aural imagery enhances the magical quality of the visual details. Recurring sibilant effects emphasise the beauty of 'White hawthorn', 'pastoral eglantine' and 'Fast fading violets'. In his visionary journey, Keats makes remarkable use of sensory language – and particularly elegant assonance – to create a truly languid atmosphere: 'The murmurous haunt of flies on summer eves.'

Much of the focus in the **sixth stanza** is on escaping painful reality through death. Keats again addresses the nightingale directly: 'Darkling I listen'. He then makes a somewhat unsettling revelation that he has often been 'half in love' with the idea of dying. His use of personification ('Called him soft names') implies that death has seemed like a friend, offering comfort to the poet. He feels that the present moment would be the ideal time to ease into a new spiritual life now that the bird is singing in 'such an ecstasy'. The enthusiastic tone suddenly changes, however, as Keats realises the irony that the bird would continue singing while the poet's lifeless body lies buried in the earth.

Throughout **stanza seven**, he continues to contrast the nightingale (as a symbol of immortality) with his own mortal self. The forceful tone seems almost celebratory: 'Thou wast not born for death'. Indeed, the bird's stirring voice has always been heard, by ancient 'emperor and clown'. He considers how such birdsong once consoled the lonely Biblical figure of Ruth when she 'stood in tears amid the alien corn'. Always the Romantic poet, Keats traces the nightingale's comforting song back to 'faery lands', both magical and tragic. For him, the beauty of nature has fascinated (and sometimes bewitched) humanity throughout generations.

At the start of **stanza eight**, the emphatic word 'Forlorn' rings like a bell to wake Keats from his deep preoccupation back to his 'sole self'. The nightingale has ceased to be a symbol and is again the actual bird the poet heard at the outset. As Keats emerges from his hypnotic state to say farewell, he realises that the bird's song (even if it is immortal) will not always be within his range of hearing: 'thy plaintive anthem fades/Past the near meadows, over the still stream'. This marks a crucial development for the poet, who until now has yearned to leave the physical world and follow the nightingale into a higher realm. The bird flies farther away from him, however, becoming a faint memory and Keats laments that his imagination has failed him. In the **last two lines**, he wonders whether he has had a true insight or whether he has been daydreaming: 'Was it a vision, or a waking dream?'

Throughout the ode, Keats has been caught between a yearning to escape into a permanent ideal world and an acceptance of transient reality. But has he been changed by his visionary experience? Critics have disagreed about the poem's ending, so readers are left to interpret the final tone for themselves. Is it happy, hopeful, sad, excited, despairing or resigned? Only the individual reader can decide.

ANALYSIS

'Tensions and contrasts are central elements of Keats's poetry.' To what extent is this true of 'Ode to a Nightingale'? Support your answer with reference to the text of the poem.

Sample Paragraph

'Ode to a Nightingale' is almost entirely structured around the poet himself, who is aware of his own mortality here on earth, and the bird, which is free. Keats's mood is of longing, but 'not through envy'. The tension is within the poet himself. He is caught between celebrating the nightingale's 'happy lot' and wishing to be part of this ideal existence. His desperate tone reflects this yearning – 'That I might drink … And with thee fade away'. Keats even desires dying as an escape from the pain of this world and admits to being 'half in love with easeful Death'. The mood keeps changing throughout, at times deliriously joyful when enjoying the bird singing 'In such an ecstasy'. But the poet is often downbeat – 'to think is to be full of sorrows'. While Keats reluctantly returns to reality at the end of the poem and accepts that his imagination will not provide a lasting escape from life's suffering, he never seems truly at ease as the nightingale's 'plaintive anthem fades'. For me, this was the most heartbreaking moment in the poem. The last two lines summed up Keats's personal dilemma, as if he was stranded between longing and disappointment, not even sure if the nightingale was part of 'a vision or a waking dream'.

Examiner's Comment

A very assured and controlled answer that addressed both elements of the task, 'tensions' and 'contrasts'. Supportive points made excellent use of accurate quotation and reference ranging over the poem. Expression was also very impressive – fluent and varied: 'The mood keeps changing throughout, at times deliriously joyful'. The brief personal engagement, 'For me this was the most heartbreaking moment in the poem', also enhanced this very successful top grade answer.

CLASS/HOMEWORK EXERCISES

1. 'A deep and disturbing sense of unhappiness often pervades Keats's poetry.' To what extent do you agree with this view of 'Ode to a Nightingale'? Support your answer with reference to the poem.

2. 'Sensuous imagery is a key feature of Keats's distinctive language use.' Discuss this statement with close reference to 'Ode to a Nightingale'.

SUMMARY POINTS

- Themes include the conflicted nature of human life, imagination, the natural world and escapism.
- Contrasting tones and moods: sorrow and joy, the real and ideal.
- Keats's sensuous language and symbols are characteristic of the ode.
- Dense concentration of sense impressions and use of synaesthesia.
- Memorable sound effects – alliteration, assonance, siblance.

3 ON FIRST LOOKING INTO CHAPMAN'S HOMER

Much have I travell'd in the realms of gold,
   And many goodly states and kingdoms seen;
   Round many western islands have I been
Which bards in fealty to Apollo hold.
Oft of one wide expanse had I been told   5
   That deep-brow'd Homer ruled as his demesne;
   Yet did I never breathe its pure serene
Till I heard Chapman speak out loud and bold:
Then felt I like some watcher of the skies
   When a new planet swims into his ken;   10
Or like stout Cortez when with eagle eyes
   He star'd at the Pacific – and all his men
Looked at each other with a wild surmise –
   Silent upon a peak in Darien.

'He stared at the Pacific'

Glossary

Title: Chapman: The writer George Chapman (1559–1634) who translated Homer's epic poems into English.
Homer: Greek epic poet (circa 9th century BC); author of *The Iliad* and *The Odyssey*.
1 *realms of gold*: majestic worlds of the imagination and poetry.
2 *goodly states*: wonderful works of literature.
3 *western islands*: poems from the British Isles and Ireland.
4 *bards in fealty to Apollo*: poets dedicate their work to the Greek god of the arts.
5 *wide expanse*: undiscovered world of great literature.
6 *deep-browed*: wise; scholarly.
6 *demesne*: private kingdom.
7 *serene*: clear air.
9 *watcher of the skies*: astronomer.
10 *ken*: knowledge; understanding.
11 *stout*: fearless.
11 *Cortez*: The explorer Cortez reached Mexico in 1518. Another Spaniard, Balboa, was the first European to glimpse the Pacific Ocean in 1513.
13 *surmise*: surprise; wonder.
14 *Darien*: old name for the narrow stretch of land (now called Panama).

INITIAL RESPONSE

1. In your opinion, what is the central theme of this poem? Support your response with reference to the text.

2. There are several striking metaphors in the octave (first eight lines) of the poem. Choose one that you consider particularly interesting and comment on its effectiveness.

3. Explain how Keats uses language to convey his feelings in the sestet (final six lines).

STUDY NOTES

Written in October 1816, this famous sonnet expresses the intensity of John Keats's experience while reading the translated works of Homer. For the twenty-year-old Keats, there was nothing to equal the excitement of Greek epic rendered into poetry. To show how deeply Homer's genius affected him, Keats uses dramatic images of exploration and discovery. In a sense, the reading experience itself becomes a great voyage, leading to creative writing both for the poet and the reader.

John Keats's intense love of poetry is evident from the start. He addresses the reader directly, comparing himself to a traveller who enjoys visiting exotic places. For him, reading is an adventure. The exclamatory **opening lines** establish his enthusiasm for literature. **Keats makes effective use of vivid comparisons, travel imagery and a vigorous tone to express his feelings.** The vivid phrase 'realms of gold' implies world riches – the power of creativity and the imagination.

Keats develops the metaphor of exploration, reflecting on the many wonderful poems ('goodly states' and 'western islands') that he has already read. In the **second quatrain**, he identifies the 'wide expanse' of Homer's epic works with a vast ocean. Throughout the octave, there is an unmistakable impression of restlessness and eager anticipation. The poet is heartfelt in his praise of Chapman whose 'loud and bold' translation of Homer's poetry allows him to enjoy its invigorating atmosphere ('pure serene').

The sense of fresh discovery brings the reader to the sonnet's volta (or change in the train of thought): 'Then felt I …' (**line 9**). Keats uses two similes that are both beautiful and appropriate to convey the astonishment of finally reading Homer: 'Then felt I like some watcher of the skies/ When a new planet swims into his ken'. Just as the astronomer is excited to discover a newly found world among the stars, Keats is similarly thrilled to finally read the poems of Homer. The swimming metaphor is part of the many recurring water images which add to the poem's cohesive structure.

The second comparison used by Keats is also in keeping with the language of travel and gives the sonnet a unity of imagery that intensifies the poet's experience. He likens his reading of Chapman's translation to the Spanish conquistador Cortez and his crew first setting eyes on the Pacific Ocean. Keats emphasises Cortez's 'eagle eyes' (**line 11**). This alliterative phrase emphasises the visual experience, reflecting the wonder felt by the explorer who is stunned by a vast landscape of beauty.

Cortez's men stand in silent amazement, looking 'at each other with a wild surmise'. The emotion is carefully controlled, with a sureness of diction and sound. The sense of openness to a wide sea of wonder is suggested by long vowels ('wild', 'surmise', 'silent'), tapering off to hushed astonishment in the weak syllables of the final words, 'upon a peak in Darien'. There is no need for overstatement as Keats's restrained ending leaves the reader with a lingering sense of breath-taking exhilaration.

All through the sestet, run-on lines intensify the rhythm to convey a wide-sweeping sense of movement – of planets circling the heavens, and ships circumnavigating the earth. In this way, Keats makes the subtle point that discovery is part of what makes us all human. The poem typifies much of his Romantic style. Internal rhymes and sibilant sound effects give it a rich, sensuous, musical quality. But primarily, this dramatic sonnet expresses the power of Keats's experience and reveals his passion for poetry.

ANALYSIS

'Keats makes effective use of the Petrarchan sonnet form in "On First Looking into Chapman's Homer"'. Discuss this view, using suitable reference to the poem.

Sample Paragraph

'On First Looking into Chapman's Homer' is a Petrarchan or Italian sonnet, clearly divided into an octave and a sestet, with a tightly-controlled rhyme scheme. In the first eight lines, Keats presents the idea of his lifelong desire to read the poetry of 'deep-brow'd Homer'. The opening tone is emphatic: 'Much have I travelled in the realms of gold'. He uses various travel images to explain his great love of books, such as 'Round many western islands have I been'. In line nine, the word 'Then' marks the break or turn in his thought and the sestet records his delight after discovering George Chapman's English version of Homer's epic poems. This is a characteristic of Italian sonnets and Keats develops the subject of his response to Homer through the use of vibrant imagery and similes which convey his sense of surprise. Comparing himself to a successful astronomer who finds 'a new planet' and the famous Spanish explorer Cortez adds energy to the poem. The sensation of shock and incredible joy is evident in the final image, 'Silent, upon a peak in Darien'. There is a sense of unity throughout the poem. Keats uses the condensed sonnet form very effectively to convey the intensity of his feelings – and I could immediately relate to this.

Examiner's Comment

An informative and well-focused response which addresses the question directly throughout. Suitable – and accurate – quotations are integrated successfully, offering valuable support: 'In line nine, the word "Then" marks the break or turn in his thought and the sestet records his delight.' Key points are expressed with confidence in a clear, fluent style: 'This is a characteristic of Italian sonnets and Keats develops the subject of his response to Homer through the use of vibrant imagery and similes'. A top grade paragraph.

CLASS/HOMEWORK EXERCISES

1. Trace the progress of thought in 'On First Looking into Chapman's Homer', using suitable reference to the poem.

2. Comment on the changes of tone between the octave and sestet, supporting your points with apt reference to the text.

> **SUMMARY POINTS**

- Central themes include the excitement of new poetry and the power of imagination.
- Superbly sustained metaphors of exploration.
- Petrarchan or Italian sonnet form (octave and sestet).
- Sensuous language, vivid imagery patterns, contrasting tones.
- Powerful sound effects, run-on lines, contrasting rhythms and moods.

ODE ON A GRECIAN URN

I

Thou still unravish'd bride of quietness,
    Thou foster-child of silence and slow time,
Sylvan historian, who canst thus express
    A flowery tale more sweetly than our rhyme:
What leaf-fring'd legend haunts about thy shape   5
    Of deities or mortals, or of both,
        In Tempe or the dales of Arcady?
    What men or gods are these? What maidens loth?
What mad pursuit? What struggle to escape?
    What pipes and timbrels? What wild ecstasy?   10

II

Heard melodies are sweet, but those unheard
    Are sweeter; therefore, ye soft pipes, play on;
Not to the sensual ear, but, more endear'd,
    Pipe to the spirit ditties of no tone:
Fair youth, beneath the trees, thou canst not leave   15
    Thy song, nor ever can those trees be bare;
        Bold Lover, never, never canst thou kiss,
Though winning near the goal - yet, do not grieve;
    She cannot fade, though thou hast not thy bliss,
        For ever wilt thou love, and she be fair!   20

III

Ah, happy, happy boughs! that cannot shed
    Your leaves, nor ever bid the Spring adieu;
And, happy melodist, unwearied,
    For ever piping songs for ever new;
More happy love! more happy, happy love!   25
    For ever warm and still to be enjoyed,
        For ever panting, and for ever young;
All breathing human passion far above,
    That leaves a heart high-sorrowful and cloyed,
        A burning forehead, and a parching tongue.   30

IV

Who are these coming to the sacrifice?
    To what green altar, O mysterious priest,
Lead'st thou that heifer lowing at the skies,
    And all her silken flanks with garlands dresst?
What little town by river or sea shore,   35

Or mountain-built with peaceful citadel,
   Is emptied of this folk, this pious morn?
And, little town, thy streets for evermore
   Will silent be; and not a soul to tell
     Why thou art desolate, can e'er return.   40

V

O Attic shape! Fair attitude! with brede
   Of marble men and maidens overwrought,
With forest branches and the trodden weed;
   Thou, silent form, dost tease us out of thought
As doth eternity: Cold Pastoral!   45
   When old age shall this generation waste,
     Thou shalt remain, in midst of other woe
Than ours, a friend to man, to whom thou say'st,
   'Beauty is truth, truth beauty' – that is all
     Ye know on earth, and all ye need to know.   50

'Cold Pastoral'

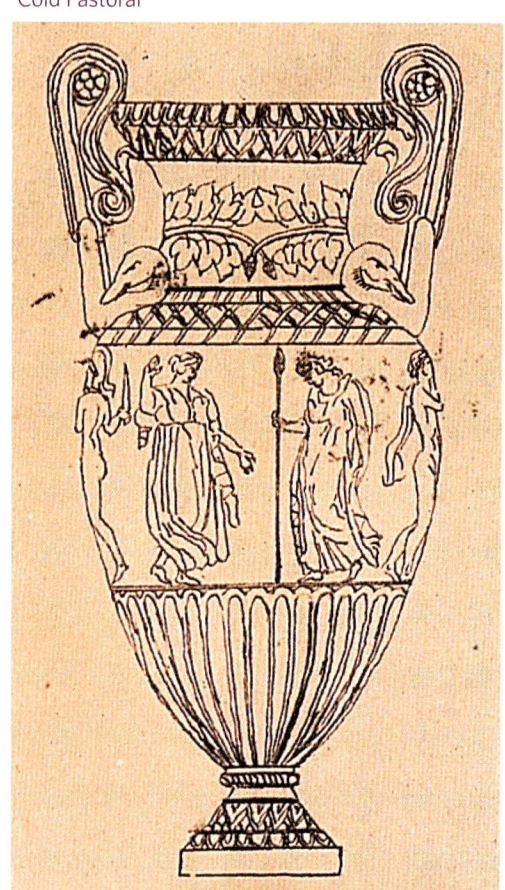

Glossary

Title: **Ode:** celebratory poem addressed to a person or a thing.
Urn: tall vase with stem and base used for storing a person's cremated ashes.
1 **still:** as yet, unmoving.
1 **unravished:** untouched.
3 **Sylvan historian:** storyteller from the woods.
5 **legend:** myth, tale.
7 **Tempe:** Greek valley.
7 **Arcady:** rural district in Greece.
8 **loth:** unwilling.
10 **timbrels:** tambourines.
13 **sensual:** physical.
14 **spirit ditties of no tone:** poems from another dimension which have no earthly sound.
17 **Bold:** confident, fearless.
29 **cloyed:** overfull.
30 **parching:** dried up, thirsty.
33 **heifer:** young cow.
36 **citadel:** stronghold protecting a city.
37 **pious:** God-fearing.
40 **desolate:** deserted.
41 **Attic:** from Athens.
41 **brede:** decoration, embroidery.
42 **overwrought:** frantic, overworked.
44 **tease:** provoke, tantalise.
45 **Cold Pastoral:** passionless story of idealised rural life.

INITIAL RESPONSE

1. In your opinion, what is the main theme of this poem?

2. Select one image from the poem that you found particularly effective. Briefly explain your choice.

3. Comment on the final two lines of the poem.

STUDY NOTES

Keats's famous ode explores the paradoxical relationship between the permanent world of art and transient reality. The poet believed that despite being mortal, human beings must strive to make themselves immortal. The mysterious Grecian urn enables the imagination to operate. It is a symbol of timeless perfection which provokes by silently posing questions. This symbol of eternal beauty is in eternal repose.

The poet stands before an ancient Grecian vase and addresses it in a series of vivid metaphors – 'bride of quietness … foster-child of silence'. Keats is immediately engrossed in the artistic images which are frozen in time. Respectfully, he considers the **meaning of the urn**. The word 'still' establishes an atmosphere of ambiguity ('as yet' or 'not moving'). This 'unravished' urn has not been affected by the destructive power of time. Although it does not speak, this 'Sylvan historian' clearly tells a story. Indeed, it can relate a tale from the countryside much better than the poet – 'thus express/A flowery tale more sweetly than our rhyme'. Keats wonders about the scene that is depicted on the side of the vase: 'What leaf-fringed legend haunts about thy shape?' He speculates that it is an ancient saga about groups of men – or possibly gods – enjoying themselves in the scenic Greek countryside. Several rapid questions close the **first stanza** capturing all the frenzied excitement associated with lovers. The 'mad pursuit' involves unwilling maidens who 'struggle to escape'. This headlong dash is accompanied by wild music on 'pipes and timbrels' and concludes with the climactic phrase, 'wild ecstasy'. In this stanza, Keats has drawn a sharp contrast between the dynamic pursuit portrayed on the urn and the stillness of its own form.

Stanza two opens quietly. The poet makes effective use of a memorable paradox to argue that music heard on earth is 'sweet' but that the music of the imagination is 'sweeter'. He urges the musicians on the urn to 'play on' – even though their other-worldly music cannot be experienced in the mortal world: 'Pipe to the spirit ditties of no tone'. Keats directly addresses one particular young man, 'Fair youth, beneath the trees, thou canst not leave/Thy song'. The breathless run-on lines suggest suspended time – the immediacy of being preserved at a precise moment, forever singing to his beloved. In this idyllic place, the trees will never shed their leaves. **Keats has become deeply engrossed in the urn's images**. Paradoxically, all the characters are immortal, but not living. Although the young lover is very near to the girl he loves, she is just out of reach: 'never, never canst thou kiss'. The double negative reinforces the poignant reality. Nonetheless, the poet offers a consoling insight. Even though the youth cannot embrace his beloved, she can never grow old. Within the permanent reality of art, their love and beauty will live on: 'For ever wilt thou love, and she be fair'.

In the **third stanza**, Keats focuses on the sublime joy of the pastoral scene pictured on the urn where nothing is subject to transience. The poet's mood is ecstatic and he evidently delights in the 'happy, happy boughs' that will not lose their leaves with the passing seasons. Repetition and vibrant rhythm echo his enjoyment. Within the ideal artistic world, it will always be springtime. The 'unwearied' musician will constantly play songs which will stay 'for ever new'. **Time does not exist here.** The pace of the stanza becomes more urgent as the poet immerses himself in the urn's narrative. Emphatic alliteration conveys the joy of escaping the tyranny of ageing: 'More happy love! more happy, happy love!' In contrast to this blissful state of endless 'warm' and 'panting' emotion on the beautiful vase, Keats acknowledges the stark truth of everyday human feeling with its 'burning forehead' and 'parching tongue'. In the real world, people suffer the pain of unreturned love which leaves them with 'a heart high-sorrowful and cloyed'. Is the poet suggesting that idealised love is superior to human love?

Stanza four describes another of the urn's dramatic images – the ritual sacrifice of an animal. Keats inquires about the images of people approaching a 'green altar': 'Who are these coming to the sacrifice?' Readers are also drawn into the scene by the poet's obvious fascination with the festivities recorded on the urn. Keats's **imagery is characteristically sensuous**. A 'mysterious priest' leads in a ceremonial heifer – 'her silken flanks with garlands dresst'. Meanwhile, the nearby village remains strangely deserted, its silent streets desolate 'for evermore'. Like everything else on the urn, its inhabitants are frozen in time and will never return home.

In the **final stanza** the poet steps back from his close observation and looks at the vase in its entirety, 'O Attic shape'. He is completely in awe at its beauty, 'Fair attitude'. Keats acknowledges that the urn confuses mere mortals with its intriguing narrative – 'tease us out of thought'. Human beings cannot ever comprehend the concept of 'eternity'. He refers to the urn as a 'Cold Pastoral' which tells its inanimate story of romance and religious rites. It is eternal and far removed from the living, breathing, imperfect world of those on earth. The urn remains 'in midst of other woe/Than ours'. Others will look at it. It is a 'friend to man' showing beautiful images on its exquisite form which contains the ashes of the dead.

The concluding two lines have long been debated. The urn seems to be addressing man, 'Beauty is truth, truth beauty'. What is beautiful is real and genuine. Keats clearly seems to be celebrating the transcendent powers of art which can offer a glimpse of the unchanging happiness to be realised in eternity. Like all great works of art, the Greek vase will always be 'a friend to man'. Does the urn recognise the limited capabilities of humans to comprehend the mysteries of life and death? While we must make up our own minds about the poet's meaning, at the very least, John Keats has made us consider these important questions through his reflections on the beautiful urn and its enigmatic images.

ANALYSIS

'Keats explores the transient and immortal through striking and sensual imagery.' Discuss this view, with reference to 'Ode on a Grecian Urn'.

Sample Paragraph

The poem, 'Ode on a Grecian Urn', does indeed 'tease' the reader 'out of thought'. The cold marble of this 'Attic shape' was originally used to store ashes. Yet it is decorated with dynamic images of a 'mad pursuit' of maidens by 'men or gods'. Rapid-fire questions mimic the frantic chase, 'What pipes and timbrels? What wild ecstasy?' Keats captures the essence of young love, 'For ever panting', 'For ever warm'. The sensuality and passion of young love is effectively conveyed through the assonance of the long 'a', almost like a young lover's sigh. Yet this is not human love, there is no 'For ever'. It is vividly described in the alliterative phrase, 'heart high-sorrowful and cloyed'. The deep disappointment of human love is suggested with the tangible description of the over-burdened heart. Human love is subject to change, whereas the urn shows a love yet to be enjoyed where the 'Bold lover' will always love and his beloved will always be fair, 'She cannot fade'. The immortality of the images on the urn is quietly drawn by the 'desolate' image of the little town which will never know where its inhabitants have gone because they will never return and the town will remain 'silent'. The 'Cold Pastoral' of the urn will tantalise its viewers through the ages with its idealised pictures of rural life as it silently relates its never-ending tale that 'Beauty is truth, truth beauty'. Through the use of sensuous imagery, Keats has provided an interesting exploration of the transience of the human condition which he contrasts with the permanence of art.

Examiner's Comment
This is a very assured response engaging closely with the poem's main themes of mortality and immortality. Quotations are effectively interwoven to support discussion points: 'Rapid-fire questions mimic the frantic chase, "What pipes and timbrels? What wild ecstasy?"' The expression throughout is both varied and controlled, ensuring the top grade.

CLASS/HOMEWORK EXERCISES

1. Keats becomes deeply involved in the story told on the urn. What questions does he consider? Support your response with close reference to the poem.

2. How does Keats create a mood of excitement in 'Ode on a Grecian Urn'? Comment on his use of questions, the exclamation marks, sentence length and use of repetition in your answer.

SUMMARY POINTS

- Key themes include transience, immortality, art, reality and the desire to escape.
- Innovative use of the ode enables readers to reflect on the subject matter.
- Distinctive moods – contrasting images of the lovers and little town.
- Sensuous language, metaphors, paradoxes, recurring questions, emphatic repetition.
- Variety of tones; effective use of assonance, alliteration, sibilance.

5 WHEN I HAVE FEARS THAT I MAY CEASE TO BE

When I have fears that I may cease to be
Before my pen has gleaned my teeming brain,
Before high-piled books, in charactery,
Hold like rich garners the full ripen'd grain;
When I behold, upon the night's starr'd face,   5
Huge cloudy symbols of a high romance,
And think that I may never live to trace
Their shadows, with the magic hand of chance;
And when I feel, fair creature of an hour,
That I shall never look upon thee more,   10
Never have relish in the faery power
Of unreflecting love; – then on the shore
Of the wide world I stand alone, and think
Till love and fame to nothingness do sink.

'the wide world'

Glossary

2 *gleaned*: gathered; made use of.
2 *teeming*: full (of ideas).
3 *charactery*: print; writing.
4 *garners*: granaries; stores.
6 *high romance*: noble poetic themes.
11 *relish*: pleasure.
11 *faery*: magical.
12 *unreflecting*: spontaneous, natural.

INITIAL RESPONSE

1. In your opinion, what are the main fears expressed by Keats in the poem?

2. Choose one image from the poem that you found particularly interesting. Briefly explain your choice.

3. Comment on the change of tone and mood in lines 12–14.

STUDY NOTES

In this carefully crafted Shakespearean sonnet, consisting of a long single sentence, Keats describes his fear of dying young before he has time to fulfil his artistic potential. He is also fearful of never experiencing the joy of being truly in love. This makes him feel that he is utterly alone in the world. However, he finally resolves his anxiety in the poem's concluding lines by asserting the unimportance of romance and literary fame.

The sombre tone reflecting Keats's fear of failure is evident from the start. Striking images convey the poet's very personal confession about his deepest concerns. Throughout the **first quatrain**, he emphasises the dreadful possibility that he may never achieve his full creative potential. His anxiety is typical of dissatisfied artists throughout time. The **extended autumn harvest imagery** – 'gleaned', 'garners', 'full ripen'd grain'– suggests the fertility of Keats's youthful mind and reinforces his heightened sense of frustration. The adjectives, 'high-piled' and 'rich', clearly indicate how acutely aware he is of his own poetic power ('teeming brain').

In the **second quatrain**, Keats reveals that he is also anxious about not having sufficient time to explore more of life's great mysteries. The strange beauty of creation is symbolised by his **dramatic personification** of the sky – 'night's starred face'. Sadly, there is a suggestion of the unattainable in the poet's dreamlike desire to sit under the stars hoping for inspiration. He recognises the wonders of the natural world and its countless mysteries ('Huge cloudy symbols') masking undiscovered delights. If he is fortunate enough, then such 'shadows' might well prompt him to be creative – depending on the 'magic hand of chance'.

The focus throughout the poem, however, is on **the unstoppable passing of time**, emphasised by Keats's repetitive use of 'When' and 'never'. Its corrosive effects are further considered in the **third quatrain** where the poet is clearly saddened by the thought of losing his lover – 'fair creature of an hour'. Characteristically, he is likely to be using personification here as a poetic technique to highlight the effects of time. For Keats, all of human experience is beautiful but short-lived. Romantic love is also transient, but has 'faery power' or some curious magical quality because it is 'unreflecting' and allows lovers to momentarily escape reality.

As the sonnet builds to a climax in the **rhyming couplet**, Keats achieves some distancing from his own feelings and this enables him to reach a resolution. He considers his own solitary destiny ('I stand alone') and the more general reality of human insignificance. The stark image of being stranded on the shore of 'the wide world' (a traditional image of eternity) signifies an important development of thought from his initial terrors to an acceptance of life's unimportance. **He ceases to fear and yearn**. Some critics have interpreted Keats's view of death as finding freedom from suffering and dread. However, the concluding tone includes both submission and despair – echoed by broad assonant vowels and the final word 'sink'. The slow, deliberate rhythm further reflects the poet's stark realisation that neither love nor poetry can ever challenge mortality.

Overall, this sonnet offers readers **an interesting insight into the Keat's personal perspective on transience and death**. There is a remarkable contrast between the poet's early energetic mood and his eventual acknowledgment of life's brevity. The poem is distinguished by Keats's characteristic archaic language and by his distinctive style, which is marked by melodious sound effects.

ANALYSIS

'John Keats's poems often portray the conflict between the poet's personal feelings and the stark realities of life.' Discuss this view, with reference to 'When I Have Fears That I May Cease to Be'.

Sample Paragraph

The title of 'When I Have Fears That I May Cease to Be' immediately brings us into Keats's private world which is filled with anxiety and uncertainty. Time is seen as the great enemy of his 'teeming brain'. The poet's urgent tone reflects his sense of panic about the certainty of death. The disturbing awareness of his own mortality is seen in the repetition of key words, such as 'When', 'before' and 'never'. Keats compares his creative potential for producing new poems to a farmer harvesting 'the full-ripen'd grain'. He also uses metaphorical language to describe the mysterious universe – 'the night's starred face' which he 'may never live to trace'. This sense of inner conflict and frustration is expressed in the final lines in a memorable image where Keats imagines himself alienated between the land and the sea in transition from this life to the next. He is on the edge 'of the wide world'. The poet's troubled self-analysis has been resolved as he now sees himself as insignificant – 'I stand alone'. In accepting the truth about how short human life is, Keats has come to terms with the fact that his fears about missing out on 'love and fame' are unimportant. In relief and dismay, he faces the reality that his fears 'to nothingness do sink'.

Examiner's Comment
This impressive top grade response makes effective use of apt quotations to address the question directly. The conflict between Keats's feelings and the growing awareness of his mortality is central to the answer. There is also some very good discussion of the poet's language use in developing key themes: 'The poet's troubled self-analysis has been resolved as he now sees himself as insignificant – "I stand alone"'. Controlled fluent expression confirms the high standard.

CLASS/HOMEWORK EXERCISES

1. Outline the central themes in 'When I Have Fears', carefully tracing the progress of thought in the poem.

2. Comment on the effectiveness of Keats's vibrant language in this sonnet. Refer to the text in your answer.

SUMMARY POINTS

- Transience, immortality, poetry and love are central themes.
- Concise Shakespearean sonnet form intensifies Keats's feelings.
- Effective use of language – extended harvest metaphor.
- Vivid imagery, recurring personification, contrasting tones.

6 LA BELLE DAME SANS MERCI

I
O what can ail thee, knight-at-arms,
    Alone and palely loitering?
The sedge has withered from the lake
    And no birds sing.

II
O what can ail thee, knight-at-arms,   5
    So haggard and so woe-begone?
The squirrel's granary is full,
    And the harvest's done.

III
I see a lily on thy brow,
    With anguish moist and fever-dew,   10
And on thy cheeks a fading rose
    Fast withereth too.

IV
I met a lady in the meads,
    Full beautiful – a faery's child,
Her hair was long, her foot was light,   15
    And her eyes were wild.

V
I made a garland for her head,
    And bracelets too, and fragrant zone;
She looked at me as she did love,
    And made sweet moan.   20

VI
I set her on my pacing steed
    And nothing else saw all day long.
For sidelong would she bend, and sing
    A faery's song.

VII
She found me roots of relish sweet,   25
    And honey wild, and manna-dew,
And sure in language strange she said –
    'I love thee true.'

VIII
She took me to her elfin grot,
    And there she wept and sighed full sore,   30
And there I shut her wild wild eyes
    With kisses four.

IX

And there she lulled me asleep,
    And there I dreamed – Ah! woe betide!
The latest dream I ever dreamt   35
    On the cold hill side.

X

I saw pale kings and princes too,
    Pale warriors, death-pale were they all;
They cried – 'La Belle Dame sans Merci
    Hath thee in thrall!'   40

XI

I saw their starved lips in the gloam,
    With horrid warning gaped wide,
And I awoke and found me here,
    On the cold hill's side.

XII

And this is why I sojourn here,   45
    Alone and palely loitering,
Though the sedge is withered from the lake,
    And no birds sing.

'And there I dreamed'

Glossary

Title: The lovely lady without mercy (translated from a medieval ballad).
1 *ail*: make you unwell.
3 *sedge*: marsh plant (resembling coarse grass).
6 *haggard*: looking exhausted and unwell.
6 *woe-begone*: miserable in appearance.
7 *granary*: storehouse for grain.
13 *meads*: flat grassland meadows.
18 *fragrant zone*: flower-filled belt.
21 *steed*: horse.
25 *relish*: delight.
26 *manna*: food (God's food to the Israelites in the wilderness).
29 *elfin*: small and delicate.
29 *grot*: cave, grotto.
40 *in thrall*: in another's power, enslaved.
42 *gaped*: open-mouthed.
45 *sojourn*: remain.

INITIAL RESPONSE

1. How does Keats establish a dreamlike or eerie atmosphere in this poem? In your response consider the effect of medieval allusions, the use of archaic words and the supernatural elements.

2. How effective is the ballad form in conveying Keats's message of doomed love? Support your answer with suitable reference to the poem.

3. In your opinion, what moral lesson can be learned from this poem? Briefly explain your answer.

STUDY NOTES

Keats has set his dramatic ballad in the medieval era. This mysterious poem can be interpreted in several ways. Is it a tale of human yearning for eternal, imperishable love? Is Keats warning against the seductive physical attractions of the deadly femme fatale who loves only to destroy? Does the storyline speak of the loss of freedom that comes with falling in love? The Romantic poets, such as Keats, were interested in nature, art, freedom, love and equality. They usually wrote about these themes in lyrical, descriptive language.

This ballad plunges the reader into a conversation between an unidentified speaker and a dying knight. The first three stanzas contain the sequence of questions which the speaker puts to the knight. The next nine stanzas are the knight's reply. He is unlike the stereotypical heroic figures who appear in legends. Here is no strong, chivalrous warrior intent on overcoming enormous challenges to win his fair lady. Instead, the knight is 'alone and palely loitering'. From the start, he is portrayed as vulnerable and lacking direction, 'O what can ail thee, knight-at-arms'? **The desolate autumn setting is sketched** in a few well-chosen details. The land is arid and the birds have already flown away: 'The sedge has withered from the lake'. The emphatic monosyllables of 'And no birds sing' reinforce the dismal scene. Throughout **stanza one**, Keats makes effective use of pathetic fallacy – almost personifying the bleak landscape – to underline the plight of the unfortunate knight.

Stanza two focuses on the knight's bedraggled appearance: 'So haggard and so woe-begone'. Nature has completed its annual cycle, 'The squirrel's granary is full,/ And the harvest's done'. This natural world is in order, and is one of plenty and ease, unlike the disordered predicament of the distraught knight. In **stanza three**, Keats continues to use descriptive imagery to paint a vivid picture of the lonely, listless knight. Broad vowel sounds ('brow', 'anguish moist') echo his despondent mood. The lily is a flower which is traditionally associated with death and even the rose – usually a symbol of beauty and passion – is 'fading'. The onomatopoeic verb 'withereth' also suggests that the helpless knight is trembling in his death throes.

In **stanza four**, the knight remembers how he met a beautiful and enchanting lady: 'a faery's child'. He describes her alluring appeal: 'Her hair was long, her foot was light'. But this mysterious woman's 'wild' eyes suggest a creature not of this world. The knight courts her in the time-honoured tradition festooning her with flowery garlands and she appears to return his ardour: 'She looked at me as she did love'. The knight is completely obsessed and 'nothing else saw all day long' (**stanza six**). He helps her onto his 'pacing steed', seemingly placing her on a pedestal as an icon to be worshipped while she holds him spellbound by her 'faery's song'.

Almost immediately, this enigmatic lady seduces him with exotic food: 'relish sweet', 'honey wild' and 'manna-dew'. The focus is on the intense physical attraction between the couple and she cannot hide her feelings – 'I love thee true'. But once again, a note of disquiet appears when she begins to speak in 'language strange' – another suggestion of her otherworldliness. The suspense increases further in **stanza eight** when the couple arrive at her 'elfin grot'. Suddenly the lady indulges in an uncontrolled outburst of emotion: 'there she wept and sighed full sore'. Was this because she knew what she was about to do, but was unable to reverse it? The knight attempts to calm her: 'I shut her wild wild eyes/With kisses four'. Repetition and the run-on line give emphasis to the turbulent scene.

However, the romantic mood seems dimmed by her weeping and the knight is 'lulled' to sleep in **stanza nine**. His dreams instantly descend into nightmares as a haunting procession of 'pale kings, and princes too' utter dire warnings: 'La Belle Dame sans Merci/Hath thee in thrall'. The horrific state of these unfortunates is emphasised by the compound word, 'death-pale'. Their grotesque appearance of 'starved lips' which 'gaped wide' show the consequences of becoming involved with this merciless creature.

The poem concludes as it began beside the remote lake. Keats's use of the present tense raises interesting questions. Can the knight ever really escape the dire consequences of his passionate romance with 'La Belle Dame'? The repetition of details from the opening lines give a sense of finality. **An ominous aura of mystery lingers**. Keats has composed a thought-provoking poem which cautions against the risks of being carried away by impulsive desire.

The Romantic poets revived the medieval ballad genre, a form of poetry which simply tells its tale largely through dialogue. The hypnotic alternating rhythm of four and three beats to a line weaves its spell on readers. This unsettling story slowly and deliberately moves to its inevitable tragic ending. The deluded knight who invested so much in pursuing ideal love is left trapped on the 'cold hill's side' (**stanza eleven**). Is Keats issuing a stark warning about the dangers of obsessive lost love?

ANALYSIS

Keats explores themes of transience and death in richly emotional and symbolic poetry. Discuss this statement in relation to 'La Belle Dame Sans Merci', supporting your points with suitable reference to the poem.

Sample Paragraph

The poet explores the divide between human mortality and eternity which can never be bridged in the mysterious medieval ballad, 'La Belle Dame Sans Merci'. In this puzzling narrative of the knight and his lady, Keats examines the difficulties of seeking never-ending romantic love. Various voices are heard in the story, the unidentified speaker, 'O what can ail thee knight-at-arms', the lovesick knight, 'I met a lady in the meads', and the bewitching woman, 'I love thee true'. The timeless landscape is richly dramatised with a few well-chosen details, 'The sedge has withered' and 'no birds sing'. I thought this was symbolic of the knight's predicament, facing up to a life without hope. The description of his physical and mental state was caught very effectively through the image of flowers, the lily a symbol of death and the decaying rose. How different this was to the lovely garlands he had given to his love when he first fell for her. The nightmarish consequences of his doomed affair is explicitly detailed in the procession of former lovers of this bewitching creature, 'pale warriors, death-pale were they all'. The repetition of the adjective, 'Pale' suggests how they were tricked and overwhelmed by this enchantress. Readers are left wondering if this strange lady will continue to captivate other unsuspecting men with her dangerous promise of perfect love. Keats's highly-charged enigmatic poem continues to weave its magic.

Examiner's Comment

A mature and insightful reaction to a challenging question, addressing both the poet's subject matter and language use. Quotations are used to effectively support key discussion points: 'The nightmarish consequences of his doomed affair is explicitly detailed in the procession of former lovers of this bewitching creature, "pale warriors, death-pale were they all"'. Worthwhile personal engagement and fluently expressed ideas contribute to this highly successful top grade paragraph.

CLASS/HOMEWORK EXERCISES

1. Comment on the effectiveness of Keats's imagery in this ballad. Refer closely to the text in your answer.

2. 'Keats's use of contrast in "La Belle Dame Sans Merci" is an important part of the poem's fascination.' Discuss this view, supporting your points with suitable reference to the text.

SUMMARY POINTS

- Reality, the supernatural, and romantic love are key themes.
- Archaic language adds to the mysterious world of the poem.
- Evocative imagery intensifies the timeless scene.
- The ballad form is effectively used to relate the story of the knight and his lady.
- Effective use of setting, contrasting atmospheres, onomatopoeia and repetition.

'Season of mists'

7 TO AUTUMN

I

Season of mists and mellow fruitfulness,
    Close bosom-friend of the maturing sun;
Conspiring with him how to load and bless
    With fruit the vines that round the thatch-eaves run;
To bend with apples the moss'd cottage-trees,   5
    And fill all fruit with ripeness to the core;
        To swell the gourd, and plump the hazel shells
    With a sweet kernel; to set budding more,
And still more, later flowers for the bees,
Until they think warm days will never cease,   10
    For Summer has o'er-brimm'd their clammy cells.

II

Who hath not seen thee oft amid thy store?
    Sometimes whoever seeks abroad may find
Thee sitting careless on a granary floor,
    Thy hair soft-lifted by the winnowing wind;   15
Or on a half-reaped furrow sound asleep,
    Drowsed with the fume of poppies, while thy hook
        Spares the next swath and all its twined flowers:
And sometimes like a gleaner thou dost keep
    Steady thy laden head across a brook;   20
    Or by a cider-press, with patient look,
        Thou watchest the last oozings, hours by hours.

III

Where are the songs of Spring? Ay, where are they?
    Think not of them, thou hast thy music too, –
While barred clouds bloom the soft-dying day,   25
    And touch the stubble-plains with rosy hue;
Then in a wailful choir the small gnats mourn
    Among the river sallows, borne aloft
        Or sinking as the light wind lives or dies;
And full-grown lambs loud bleat from hilly bourn;   30
    Hedge-crickets sing, and now with treble soft
    The red-breast whistles from a garden-croft;
        And gathering swallows twitter in the skies.

Glossary

1. *mellow*: pleasantly smooth, soft to taste and in colour.
3. *Conspiring*: making secret plans.
4. *thatch-eaves*: overhanging roof of straw.
6. *core*: centre.
7. *gourd*: large fleshy fruit.
8. *kernel*: soft part of nut.
11. *clammy*: unpleasantly damp.
13. *abroad*: over a large expanse.
14. *sitting careless*: seated unconcerned.
15. *winnowing*: removing chaff (the dry outer covering of grain).
17. *poppies*: flower, cutter.
18. *swath*: strip of corn cut by scythe.
18. *twined*: twisted around.
19. *gleaner*: gatherer of leftover grain after harvest has been cut.
25. *bloom*: give a glow to.
26. *stubble-plains*: field after harvest is cut.
27. *gnats*: small flies.
28. *sallows*: young willows.
30. *bourn*: small stream.
31. *Hedge-crickets*: shrill, chirping insect.
32. *garden-croft*: cultivated area near to country cottage.

INITIAL RESPONSE

1. In your opinion, what is the main theme of the poem?

2. Choose one image from the poem which appealed to you and comment on its effectiveness.

3. How does Keats create a mood of serenity in this poem? Refer to aspects of his content and style in your response.

STUDY NOTES

In a letter written in September 1819, Keats says: 'How beautiful the season is now – How fine the air ... I never liked stubble-fields so much as now – Aye better than the chilly green of the spring. Somehow, a stubble-field looks warm – in the same way that some pictures look warm. This struck me so much in my Sunday's walk that I composed upon it.' What he composed was the ode, 'To Autumn'. This was written at a time when Keats knew he was seriously ill. Yet, in this poem, he achieves a great serenity. Acutely aware that moments of intense pleasure do not last, he sets his love of the beautiful against the uncontrollable reality of suffering and death.

This is Keats's final ode in his celebrated sequence of 'Great Odes'. It is a valediction, a farewell to the season of abundance and fruition. The poet absents himself from this poem, unlike his very obvious presence in his other two odes. There is no use of the personal pronoun, 'I'. Nonetheless, the reader is very much aware of the presence of the poet who is delighting in this rich 'Season of mists and mellow fruitfulness'. Keats does not even include the term 'ode' in the title. Indeed, a low-key invocation begins the poem. He is enabling us to enter into the season itself' thanks to his rich evocation of its pleasures.

Stanza one concentrates on the imagery of touch. In **stanza two**, he focuses on the visual while the **third stanza** appeals to the ear. Over the course of the poem, Keats examines various aspects of the season – including vegetation, human activity, animals, birds and insects. The ode moves slowly from the ripeness just before the harvest to the activities associated with harvest-time and its aftermath. In its broad structure, the poem follows the pattern of a typical autumn day, progressing from the 'maturing sun' to the actual harvesting to the evening's 'soft-dying day'.

Lines 1–11 invite us to experience the season directly, through concrete images of ripeness and fulfilment, 'fruit the vines', 'bend with apples'. The **wonderful excess** of the season is represented through repetition – 'budding more,/And still more'. The endless pleasure of the season is vividly conveyed by the soft alliterative 'm', 'For summer has o'er-brimmed their clammy cells'. Even the bees are deceived into thinking this warm atmosphere will last. Personification of autumn as a co-conspirator with the sun adds to the season's enigmatic image. Precise and onomatopoeic verbs ('load', 'bend', 'fill', 'swell', 'plump', 'o'er-brimm'd') trace the ongoing quiet activity of growth and maturity. There is even a sacred quality (implied by the word 'bless') to this creative world of nature. Keats's tactile imagery focuses on this seemingly endless abundance, 'swell'. The essence of the season is conveyed in one long sentence and there is no suggestion that this season is going to end.

Stanza two personifies the season as several youthful workers engaged in bringing in the harvest. A beautiful picture of a young girl with her hair blowing softly in the autumn breeze is portrayed in the phrase 'soft-lifted by the winnowing wind'. Even the breeze is busy harvesting. The image of the exhausted granary labourer is suggestive of a lingering season, work as yet incomplete, 'half-reaped furrow sound asleep'. Keats skilfully conjures up an air of lethargy in the deep peace of this rich time of year. The gleaner is described as balancing a load on her head as she crosses the brook unhurried. Finally, autumn is portrayed as the patient watcher, the cider-maker who ensures that he gets the 'last oozings' of the apples. The slow movement is caught in the sibilant 's' sounds, reminding us that autumn is indeed a season of **sensuous profusion**.

Somewhat surprisingly, **stanza three** does not proceed directly to winter, but instead returns to spring: 'Where are the songs of spring?' The poet is untroubled by that and listens to the mournful sounds of autumn. Its **melancholic music** is wistfully relayed in the 'wailful choir' of gnats who 'mourn', as they rise and fall on the 'light wind'. We can imagine hearing the grown lambs in the onomatopoeic 'bleat', adding to the mood of nostalgia. The chirping of the hedge-crickets joins the melodic ensemble. Finally, the robin 'whistles', contributing its distinctively shrill tone to the choir – and suddenly the reality of autumn is upon us. Robins are usually associated with winter. The migrating swallows 'twitter' but will soon be heard no more – it is a 'soft-dying day'. This **final stanza** – with its many suggestions of death contrasts sharply with the vitality and excess of the first. But even the poem's open and closing rhyme scheme reinforces the natural symmetry and sense of finality. In his mature ode, Keats has succeeded in blending 'beauty' and 'truth'. This magnificent season must end because the world is governed by time and mortality. Having experienced the delights of autumn, the poet is now quietly resigned to the cycle of nature.

ANALYSIS

'Keats explores the beauty of the world with sensuous passion, but he also views it honestly.' Discuss this view, with reference to the subject matter and style of 'To Autumn'.

Sample Paragraph

I found the poet, Keats, assailed my senses with a dazzling display of imagery in the poem 'To Autumn'. He allowed me to experience this season almost in 3D because he fused a picture into both tactile and visual imagery, 'touch the stubble-plains with rosy hue'. I could see the rich reddish colour of the setting sun and feel the sharp bristles of the cut corn in the harvested field. The visual image of a girl's hair softly lifted by a light breeze, 'Thy hair soft-lifted by the winnowing wind' is portrayed in sensuous detail. Again I could almost feel the smoothness. But it is not just poetic imagery, there is the reality of the actual harvesting operations, the heavy lifting, 'laden head', the exhaustion of cutting, 'on a half-reaped furrow sound asleep' and the sheer grind, 'last oozings'. Similarly, Keats does not shy away from the reality of the dying year. In the last stanza, he faces the transience of the season unlike the bees who 'think warm days will never cease'. There are many melancholy words and phrases, 'wailful', 'mourn', 'soft-dying', 'sinking', all contributing to the truth that winter inevitably follows autumn. There is also an inherent sadness which cannot be denied in the long vowel sounds of 'mourn', 'borne' and 'bourn'. The lavish sumptuousness of autumn, its 'mellow fruitfulness', is slowly receding into the mists. Keats has examined the beauty of this season, but truthfully.

Examiner's Comment

An assured personal response engaging closely with the question. Quotations are well integrated into the commentary to support discussion points. A highly commendable detailed analysis of aural effects and tone: 'There is also an inherent sadness which cannot be denied in the long vowel sounds of "mourn", "borne" and "bourn"'. Expression throughout is varied, fluent and controlled: 'the lavish sumptuousness of autumn, its "mellow fruitfulness" is slowly receding into the mists'. An excellent top grade paragraph.

CLASS/HOMEWORK EXERCISES

1. The first eight lines deal with the process of watching and contemplating. How do you think Keats watches and contemplates the season in this poem? Support your response with close reference to the poem, 'To Autumn'.

2. How does Keats create a mood of serenity in the poem? Refer to his use of imagery and sound effects in your answer.

SUMMARY POINTS

- Key themes of this great ode include rich abundance of the season, the reality of transience.
- Sensuous visual, tactile and aural imagery.
- Sound effects – alliteration, assonance, sibilance, repetition, rhyme.
- Distinctive moods – elation, melancholy.

8 BRIGHT STAR, WOULD I WERE STEADFAST AS THOU ART

Bright star, would I were steadfast as thou art –
   Not in lone splendour hung aloft the night
And watching, with eternal lids apart,
   Like nature's patient, sleepless Eremite,
The moving waters at their priestlike task   5
   Of pure ablution round earth's human shores,
Or gazing on the new soft-fallen mask
   Of snow upon the mountains and the moors –
No – yet still steadfast, still unchangeable,
   Pillow'd upon my fair love's ripening breast,   10
To feel for ever its soft fall and swell,
   Awake for ever in a sweet unrest,
Still, still to hear her tender-taken breath,
And so live ever – or else swoon to death.

'still steadfast, still unchangeable'

Glossary

1. *steadfast*: steady, unswerving, resolute.
2. *aloft*: above.
3. *lids*: eyelids.
4. *Eremite*: hermit, recluse.
6. *ablution*: the act of cleansing.
10. *Pillowed*: cushioned.
13. *tender*: youthful, warm, romantic.
14. *swoon*: faint, pass out.

INITIAL RESPONSE

1. Outline the contrasts which Keats draws between himself and the star. Illustrate your answer with close reference to the poem.

2. Keats uses repetition extensively throughout this poem. In your opinion, what is its effect on the reader? Support your answer with reference to the text.

3. Choose one image from the poem that you found particularly effective. Briefly explain your choice.

STUDY NOTES

In 1820 when Keats was setting sail to Italy to find a cure for his worsening ill-health, he inscribed this sonnet into a book of Shakespearean poetry belonging to a friend. It is thought to be one of the last poems he ever composed. The poet focuses primarily on the differences between eternity and mortality.

This well-known poem consists of a single sentence and is divided into an octet and sestet from the Italian sonnet form. **Line 1** begins with the arresting exclamation, 'Bright star'. Keats is startled by the brilliance of a distant star's 'splendour'. A heartfelt wish swiftly follows and he desires to be as dependable as the faraway star, 'hung aloft the night'. But in **line 2**, the emphatic 'Not' conveys his misgivings about the star's detached situation. Its isolation is implicit in its solitary occupation which consists of 'watching', 'gazing' on the earth. But the poet does not wish to be 'lone'. Personification emphasises the star's solitary existence. It observes, but does not participate. Existing on the periphery, there is no rest for this star because it continually views the ocean 'with eternal lids apart'. However, its sleeplessness is non-human, so the poet's goal seems already to be futile.

Line 4 adds to the reclusive image of the star which the poet likens to 'nature's patient, sleepless Eremite'. The sea's restless stirrings are presented as a stately religious ceremony, a 'priestlike' ritual. It cleanses 'earth's human shores'. The poet's focus has now changed from contemplating the permanence of the star to the flux and flow of life here on earth. The rise and fall of the sea is beautifully expressed in the gentle run-on **lines 5–6**. Broad 'u' and 'o' vowels create a serene, flowing movement which is in stark contrast to the still star. **Line 7** reveals another transient image of life on earth. The blanket of snow covering all in its white purity is regarded as a temporary 'mask'. It conceals – but only for a time. Keats uses the compound word, 'soft-fallen' to mimic the snowfall's silent arrival. The tranquillity of the newly-transformed landscape is suggested by the alliterative phrase, 'the mountains and the moors', diverse places encased in a harmonious covering. The octet concludes with positive suggestions of life on earth – 'pure', 'new' and 'soft'.

However, the sharp monosyllabic negative, 'No', marks the turning-point of this sonnet. Is Keats rejecting the cold, eternal life of the star? Or is he refusing to accept the transience of human life? The adverb 'still' is repeated, announcing his desire to spend eternity frozen in a special moment, 'Pillowed upon my fair love's ripening breast'. **He clearly desires the permanence of the star's life, but not its cold, isolated existence. He also wants the warmth of a human relationship.** This is evocatively conveyed in the rich imagery and sound effects of **line 11**. The intimate sensuality of human love is shown in the rise and fall of his lover's breath: 'To feel for ever its soft fall and swell'. This is reminiscent of an incoming, outgoing tide. A sharp contrast with the passive star is evident with the poet's wish to be 'Awake for ever in a sweet unrest'. More than anything, he wants to be constantly aware of his blessed state.

Unfortunately what he desires is impossible. All moments on this earth end. They will not last 'for ever' (**line 12**). His lover's mortality is conveyed in her even breathing which resonates in the compound word 'tender-taken'. This personal search for an ideal ('And so live ever') cannot be achieved by a human being whose world is one of change and ending. The poem's final phrase accepts this inescapable inevitability. **If Keats cannot live forever, he will have to 'swoon to death'** and pass into another kind of eternity. The Shakespearean sonnet's couplet provides a conclusive finish to the poem: 'breath' ceases on 'death'.

ANALYSIS

'John Keats often expresses profound concern for life's deepest questions in poetry of rich description and sensual language.' Discuss this view, with reference to 'Bright Star'.

Sample Paragraph

In 'Bright Star', Keats travels from the high heavens to blackest death as he explores the unobtainable, but much sought-after goal of enjoying the pleasures of this life forever. The permanence of the star is much admired by Keats as he addresses some important questions about life. He quickly rejects the star's solitary existence, not once but twice, 'Not', 'No'. The poet does not wish for its 'lone splendour' nor its 'Eremite' life. Instead, Keats paints dynamic pictures of life on earth, 'the moving waters, 'the mask/Of snow'. Although these are temporary, the poet glorifies the tides which cleanse 'round earth's human shores'. The broad vowels, 'u' and 'o', create a mood of calmness. The snow is a unifying influence on 'mountains and the moors'. The scene is caught in the gentle phrase 'new soft-fallen'. Keats also presents us with the significance of human intimacy where the lovers embrace: 'Pillow'd upon my fair love's ripening breast'. The explosive 'p' and 'b' together with the lyrical 'l' sounds suggest a sensual picture of warmth. How different from the reclusive, distant star! The soft rise and fall of his beloved's breathing is heard in the alliterative word, 'tender-taken'. Keats desperately wishes to remain in this moment endlessly. But that is not mankind's destiny. So he accepts reality and death, but even here he conveys a graceful, sensual action – he will 'swoon' to death.

Examiner's Comment
This is an excellent response to a challenging question. There is close engagement with the viewpoint and language in the poem: 'The snow is a unifying influence on "mountains and the moors"'. Points are clearly expressed and supported by useful and accurate quotation. The analysis of the poet's technique in using aural imagery is particularly impressive: 'The explosive "p" and "b" together with the lyrical "l" sounds suggest a sensual picture of warmth'. A top grade answer.

CLASS/HOMEWORK EXERCISES

1. 'Tensions between the transient and the immortal are often found in Keats's poetry.' Discuss this view, using suitable reference to 'Bright Star, Would I were Steadfast as Thou Art'.

2. Keats led a 'life of sensation' and also a 'life of thoughts'. Discuss this statement in relation to the poem. Support your points with close reference to the text in your answer.

SUMMARY POINTS

- Eternity and mortality are central themes.
- Precise descriptions convey contrasts between the star and transient human life.
- Distinctive imagery patterns reinforce the tensions within the poem.
- Sonnet forms frame Keats's intense feelings.
- Repetition, musical language and personification enhance the sensual experience.

LEAVING CERT SAMPLE ESSAY

'Keats's distinctive writing style reflects his deeply-felt belief in the importance of imagination.' To what extent do you agree or disagree with the above statement? Support your answer with reference to both the themes and language found in the poetry of John Keats on your course.

Marking Scheme Guidelines
Candidates are free to agree and/or disagree with the statement. However, the key terms, 'distinctive writing style' and 'belief in the value of the imagination' should be addressed implicitly or explicitly. Reward responses that show clear evidence of personal engagement with the poems.

Indicative Material:
- Intense exploration of the reality of life and a quest for perfection.
- Heightened sensitivity.
- Poet's powerful sense of the natural world, time, mortality, death.
- Freshness of the poet's vision; wide-ranging atmospheres, tones and moods.
- Sensuous language, onomatopoeic/musical effects, varied poetic forms, etc.

Sample Essay
(A distinctive writing style reflects Keats's deeply-felt belief in the importance of the imagination.)

1. From reading the poems of John Keats, it is clear that he was a typical Romantic poet who was almost obsessed with the imagination. The great odes show a deep desire to avoid the harsh experiences of real life and find some kind of perfect happiness. The conflict between the world of imagination and reality is obviously important to the poet because without imagination, the real world is one of disappointment, pain and ugliness. For Keats, imagination provided an escape – at least a temporary one – from suffering.

2. In his famous poem, 'Ode on a Grecian Urn', Keats is fascinated by the artistic story painted on the mysterious vase. He believes that the creations within the imagined world are just as true as everyday reality. There is a sense of intimacy in the way he addresses the urn: 'Thou still unravished bride of quietness'. His hushed tone shows his respect for the timeless scene and for the work of art itself. He compares the urn to a young bride and to his foster child. This closeness with the urn is created by Keats's imagination – which has the power to transform the usual rules we experience in the real world by heightening joys and extending the experience forever.

3. Keats constantly contrasts the imaginary and real worlds: 'Heard melodies are sweet, but those unheard/ Are sweeter'. As a music lover, I could easily relate to this as it is quite possible to experience any song just by imagining it and 'singing' it in one's mind. To Keats, the unheard tones are 'more endeared' and sweeter. He even suggests that it may be a spiritual experience – 'spirit ditties of no tone'. What makes the experience in the mind even more enjoyable, is that it will last forever – 'Fair youth, beneath the trees, thou canst not leave thy song'. Keats loved the world of his imagination so much because he saw it as just as valid as the real world. He says: 'Beauty is truth, truth beauty'. Such powerful admissions of his own personal beliefs are characteristic of the poet. For Keats, as long as what he experienced was beautiful, even if it didn't exist to the five senses, it was true.

4. In both 'On First Looking into Chapman's Homer' and 'La Belle Dame Sans Merci', the narratives Keats creates are imaginative in themselves and they also invite the reader to enter new realities. The tragic story of the 'palely loitering' knight who is beguiled by 'the lady in the meads', is a warning to dreamers who imagine perfect love. Keats recreates a haunting medieval atmosphere through a hypnotic rhythm and evocative images – 'The sedge is withered', 'a faery's child', 'starved lips in the gloam'. The love-sick knight's joy ends abruptly in tragic disappointment and he is left 'in thrall', enslaved by unrequited love. The ideal romance he imagined is nothing more than a dream.

5. The power of great literature to excite imagination and inspire the poet is seen much more positively in 'Chapman's Homer'. Keats uses a series of geographical metaphors for the classics – 'realms of gold', 'goodly states', 'western islands' – and compares himself to an explorer who is thrilled to discover a new 'expanse' of land. The power of imagination is central to both travel and reading. It is easy to sense the wonder and delight of Cortez and his men who first gazed at the great Pacific and 'Looked at each other with a wild surmise'.

6. 'Ode to a Nightingale' is a very good example of Keats's obsessive interest in escaping into a perfect world by means of his imagination. It is a typical Romantic poem highlighting powerful feelings and the value of imagination. The poet repeatedly uses synaesthesia, expertly blending different sense impressions, a typical feature of his rich language. The nightingale's mesmerising song is filled with sensuous appeal drawing Keats from his 'drowsy numbness' into a warm Mediterranean world of 'Provencal song and sunburnt mirth'. Vivid visual images and suggestive sound effects illustrate his dreamlike state of sheer luxury as he drinks a glass of wine 'With beaded bubbles winking at the brim'. Unfortunately, the experience is transitory and the poet is brought back to reality. The tone changes in line with Keats's disappointment. The bird nightingale's song fades to a 'plaintive anthem' and he is forced to accept that his imagination only offers a temporary relief from this world. In the poem's final lines, he still wonders about the great mystery of consciousness: 'Do I wake or sleep?'

7. For me, Keats is a unique poetic voice. At times he seems confused and frustrated about finding meaning in life. His passion and energy interest me as a young person, and I can understand how his poetic language continues to appeal. What is without doubt, however, is his belief that sensations and feelings – especially passionate love – inspired the imagination into the creation of genuine beauty. For an artist or poet, this is the truest and most important part of life.

(approx. 830 words)

Examiner's Comment

This is an impressive and sustained personal response, showing good engagement with Keats's poetry. The discussion is informative and well-focused on addressing the question directly. Apt – and accurate – quotations are integrated successfully, offering valuable support. Overall, incisive key points are expressed succinctly.

MARKING SCHEME
P = 15/15
C = 15/15
L = 15/15
M = 5/5
Total = 50/50

SAMPLE LEAVING CERT QUESTIONS ON KEATS' POETRY

(45/50 MINUTES)

1. 'John Keats conveys philosophical ideas in honest, vibrant language.' To what extent do you agree or disagree with this view of his poetry? Support your points with reference to the poetry of Keats on your course.

2. 'Keats's mastery of sensuous language conveys the conflicts of mortality and desire.' Discuss this statement with reference to both the content and style of the poems by John Keats on your course.

3. 'Keats' evocative poetry often balances moments of pain and anguish with glimpses of intense beauty and joy.' Discuss this statement with reference to both the subject matter and language use in the poems by Keats on your course.

Sample Essay Plan (Q2)

'Keats's mastery of sensuous language conveys the conflicts of mortality and desire.' Discuss this statement with reference to both the content and style of the poems by John Keats on your course.

- Intro: Keats's belief in poets bringing 'healing' to the suffering world by evoking a world of escape and timeless myth. Does his skill as poet enable the reader to transcend mortality by focusing on beauty?

- Point 1: 'When I have fears' – Fear of dying before achieving. Rich imagery conveys the mortal state, ('on the shore/Of the wide world I stand alone') and the overflowing poetic imagination, ('Hold like rich garners the full ripened grain'). Despondent conclusion – life's transience cannot be avoided ('Till love and fame to nothingness do sink').

- Point 2: 'On First Looking' – Unlike previous poem, escape through poetic imagination is possible. Splendid imagery, ('realms of gold'). Discoverer of new lands ('stout Cortez when with eagle eyes/ He stared at the Pacific').

- Point 4: Conflict of mortality and desire in 'Ode to a Nightingale' – attempt to resolve conflict between sad world ('My heart aches… as though of hemlock I had drunk') and perfect eternal world of nightingale's song ('for I will fly to thee'). Luxuriant imagery paints the natural world. Escape fails.

- Point 5: Attempt to resolve transience and immortality also in 'Ode on a Grecian Urn'. Sensuous images depict the frozen moment ('Fair youth', 'She cannot fade'). But the urn is lifeless ('Cold Pastoral'). Conflict remains unresolved.

- Conclusion: Rich, powerful poetry fuses two conflicting perspectives – warm, pulsing natural world and cold vastness of eternity. Attempts to escape harsh human reality… but finds eternity wanting.

Sample Essay Plan (Q2)
Develop one of the above points into a paragraph.

Sample Paragraph: Point 4
Keats is torn between wanting to escape the suffering of this world, graphically conveyed in the image of youth, 'pale, and spectre-thin' and the loss of beauty, 'Where beauty cannot keep her lustrous eyes'. Despite the difficulties of this mortal world, it is its pleasures which are memorably portrayed and which linger in the imagination of the reader. Who can forget the 'beaker full of the warm South …/With beaded bubbles winking at the brim'? Who would not want to listen to an evening full of 'The murmurous haunt of flies'? The use of evocative sounds here really echo the sense of summer. Yet Keats is in despair, 'My heart aches', and he yearns to join the nightingale in eternity, 'Thou wast not born for death, immortal Bird'. However, the limitations of eternity are all too soon discovered, 'His human senses would fail there' – because they are of this earthly world. He could not see the flowers, he could not even hear the song of the bird, 'Still wouldst thou sing, and I have ears in vain'. The poem's tone and meaning change dramatically with the word 'forlorn'. Keats has to accept reality, imagination is a 'deceiving elf'. He is left perplexed wondering if the nightingale's song was just a dream. 'Do I wake or sleep?' Does reality even exist? Or was the vision authentic? The poet's struggle is unresolved.

Examiner's Comment

As part of a full essay, this is an assured response which includes some insightful discussion of the poet's inner struggle: 'Yet Keats is in despair, "My heart aches", and he yearns to join the nightingale in eternity, "Thou wast not born for death, immortal Bird"'. Effective use is made of relevant quotations to support points. Expression is mature and very well controlled. Use of rhetorical questions convey personal engagement: 'Who can forget the "beaker full of the warm South…/ With beaded bubbles winking at the brim"?' An excellent top grade answer.

LAST WORDS

'I am certain of nothing, but of the holiness of the Heart's affections and the truth of Imagination.'

John Keats

Keats's poetry is 'an ark of the covenant between language and sensation'.

Seamus Heaney

'Poetry should please by a fine excess … It should strike the reader as a wording of his highest thought'.

John Keats

PHILIP LARKIN

1922–85

'An event provides a lead into a poem.'

Philip Larkin was born in 1922 in Coventry, England. He did not enjoy his childhood: 'Get out as early as you can/And don't have any kids yourself'. Nor did he like school. He had a stammer and was short-sighted, although he read widely and contributed to the school magazine. After graduating from Oxford, he went on to become a librarian. Larkin became a great admirer of Thomas Hardy's poetry, learning from Hardy how to make the commonplace and often dreary details of his life the basis for extremely tough, unsparing and memorable poems. He published several collections of poetry, much of which reflect ordinary English life. His searing, often mocking wit rarely concealed the poet's dark vision and underlying obsession with universal themes of mortality, love and human solitude. Yet Larkin's poems face the trials of living and dying with an orderly elegance that always moves the reader. Philip Larkin believed poetry should come from personal experience: 'I write about experiences … simple everyday experiences … I hope other people will come upon this … pickled in verse … and it will mean something to them.'

INVESTIGATE FURTHER

To find out more about Philip Larkin, or to hear a reading of his poems, you could do a search of the useful websites such as YouTube, bbc.co.uk and poetryarchive.org or access additional material on this page of your eBook.

Prescribed Poems

HIGHER LEVEL

① 'Wedding-Wind'
A celebration of the healing power of love and marriage. The speaker is a young bride who is looking forward to a life of happiness. — **298**

② 'At Grass'
A nostalgic narrative poem describing retired racehorses, in which the poet reflects on the changes brought about by time and the contentment of old age. — **302**

③ 'Church Going'
Conversational and self-mocking, Larkin meditates on the role and significance of churches and religious practice in people's lives. — **307**

④ 'An Arundel Tomb'
This bittersweet exploration of the power of love to transcend time was written after the poet visited the tomb of the medieval Earl and Countess of Arundel. — **313**

⑤ 'The Whitsun Weddings'
The central theme is marriage in all its complexity and its importance within an increasingly urbanised society. — **319**

⑥ 'MCMXIV'
The Roman numeral title stands for 1914, the start of World War I. For Larkin, the date marked the end of innocence for the young soldiers and their families. — **326**

⑦ 'Ambulances'*
This poem uses the symbol of an ambulance to outline Larkin's views on the futility of life and the inevitable reality of death. **331**

⑧ 'The Trees'
This short poem, contrasting nature (the trees) and the lives of human beings, is another review of the theme of transience. **336**

⑨ 'The Explosion'*
An affirmative poem based on a tragic coal mine accident. There were reports that at the time of the explosion, some of the miners' wives saw visions of their husbands. **340**

⑩ 'Cut Grass'
Another short lyric about the cycle of life and death. The poem's title image suggests how life and natural growth can be abruptly ended. **345**

1 WEDDING-WIND

The wind blew all my wedding-day,
And my wedding-night was the night of the high wind;
And a stable door was banging, again and again,
That he must go and shut it, leaving me
Stupid in candlelight, hearing rain, 5
Seeing my face in the twisted candlestick,
Yet seeing nothing. When he came back
He said the horses were restless, and I was sad
That any man or beast that night should lack
The happiness I had. 10

    Now in the day
All's ravelled under the sun by the wind's blowing.
He has gone to look at the floods, and I
Carry a chipped pail to the chicken-run,
Set it down, and stare. All is the wind 15
Hunting through clouds and forests, thrashing
My apron and the hanging cloths on the line.
Can it be borne, this bodying-forth by wind
Of joy my actions turn on, like a thread
Carrying beads? Shall I be let to sleep 20
Now this perpetual morning shares my bed?
Can even death dry up
These new delighted lakes, conclude
Our kneeling as cattle by all-generous waters?

'and the hanging cloths on the line'

Glossary

12 *ravelled*: pulled apart and untangled.
16 *thrashing*: moving; beating violently.
18 *borne*: carried by, endured.

INITIAL RESPONSE

1. How realistic do you think Larkin's portrayal of marriage is? Support your views with reference to the text.

2. Trace the tone in this poem. Does it change? What is different in the attitude of the speaker in the second section?

3. In your opinion, why does the poem end with three questions?

STUDY NOTES

'Wedding-Wind' was published in 1946. This narrative poem (Larkin was also a novelist) records details of a wedding day, night and the morning after. Larkin adopts the persona of a young bride to tell the story. He said, 'I can imagine … the emotions of a bride … without ever having been a woman or married.' This poem is a celebration of the joy of passionate love.

This direct, personal poem's **opening section** begins with the young bride stating that 'The wind blew all my wedding-day'. This 'high wind' blew throughout her day and the wedding night. Is it a symbol for passion and change? Is the poem linking the energy of the natural world with the force of human love? The adjective 'high' for Larkin meant elevated and elevating experiences. People rise above the ordinary to experience a spiritual feeling. The restless atmosphere of the day and night is caught in the description of the stable door 'banging, again and again'. This mundane detail shows Larkin's ear for the ordinary. The young woman relates how her husband has to 'go and shut' the banging door. Larkin believed that life as it was lived by ordinary people should and could provide the subject for poetry. The young bride feels inadequate, 'Stupid in candlelight', 'seeing nothing'. Her new husband returns, saying 'the horses were restless'. She feels compassion for all living things that are not experiencing the happiness 'I had'.

The **second section** of the poem is an *interior monologue* by the bride as she observes the destruction caused by the 'wind's blowing'. 'All's ravelled under the sun': the debris of the storm is clear for everyone to see. Both the world and the bride have been changed by some huge elemental force. She is now a woman of responsibilities. She recognises the practicalities of farming. There is no honeymoon. 'He has gone to look at the floods' and she has gone to feed the chickens. The detail of her 'chipped pail' lends a human, imperfect note to the scene. She sets the pail down and begins to reflect ('stare').

Now, unlike last night, she is seeing. The wind, this powerful force of nature, was a predator, 'Hunting through clouds and forests' (**line 16**). The violent force of the wind is contained in the verb 'thrashing'. Does this have connotations of the violent passion of love? Again, an ordinary sight, clothes hanging on a washing line ('My apron and the hanging cloths on the line'), makes the poem accessible to all, academic and non-academic. There is no exclusive reference to classical mythology, but the common stuff of life. The **poem concludes with three questions**. The young woman wonders if she will survive the 'joy my actions turn on'. The compound word 'bodying-forth' and the verb 'borne' suggest pregnancy. The simile 'like a thread/Carrying beads' implies praying and the sacredness of the holy state of matrimony. Or this thread could refer to a necklace, a gift or symbol of love given between the young couple.

The second question poses the problem of sleep: 'Shall I be let to sleep' (**line 20**). The bride now feels that every day is 'perpetual morning', as life seems full of exciting possibilities, so it is impossible to rest. She feels so blessed by love that she has almost been made immortal: 'Can even death dry up' her joy? She believes that these 'new delighted lakes' can never be 'dry', even though the wind dries water from the land. She is compelled to make a sign, 'conclude/Our kneeling as cattle'. The **biblical tones** of the compound word 'all-generous' show an optimistic view that joy can outlive death.

Larkin wanted his readers to experience his poetry and say, 'I've never thought of it that way before, but that's how it is.' He believed poetry should come from personal experience. Larkin disliked the idea that poetry should come from other poems. He was opposed to Modernism, a poetry movement that is allusory and inaccessible to the ordinary person. It is interesting to note that this poem takes **a private, human experience and links it with nature**. Does this lend a note of danger to the experience of young, passionate love? Parallel to the poem, dramatic changes were taking place in English society. The Second World War had just ended, followed by the depression of the 1950s, the affluence and student unrest of the 1960s and the emergence of socialism and multiculturalism. This rural English experience of young love is preserved by Larkin, 'pickled as it were in verse', despite all the changes taking place.

ANALYSIS

Larkin believed that poetry should help us 'enjoy and endure'. Do you agree or disagree with this statement? Support your view with references from the poem.

Sample Paragraph

I believe that this poem helps us enjoy life, thanks to the beautiful, passionate narrative of this young bride. The wind represents change and dynamism in the natural world, as well as in the world of the young woman. It is 'sacred', a 'high wind', which both scatters and cleans, 'All's ravelled under the sun by the wind's blowing'. The human details of ordinary life shine under the craftsmanship of Larkin, 'chipped pail', 'stable door … banging, again and again', 'hanging cloths on the line'. The ordinary, somewhat irksome chores which we all must endure become the basis of passionate poetry as the young bride wonders whether all this 'joy of action' can be 'borne'. We are elevated, as the woman is, by the optimistic, mystical vision that love cannot be dimmed by death. We kneel at the 'all-generous waters'. Larkin has helped us to enjoy and endure.

Examiner's Comment

This short paragraph addresses both aspects of the question (enjoy and endure). The response shows a real appreciation of Larkin's poetic beliefs. More detailed analysis and comment on the key quotations would have resulted in a higher grade. However, the style throughout is assured and vocabulary and expression are very good. Falls just below the top grade.

CLASS/HOMEWORK EXERCISES

1. Write a paragraph on how effectively Larkin uses metaphors to communicate his message in this poem. Support your answer with reference to the text.

2. 'In his poem, "Wedding-Wind", Larkin conveys an entirely positive view of married life.' Discuss this statement, supporting your answer with reference to the text.

SUMMARY POINTS

- Key themes include the joy of romantic love and the frailty of happiness in life.
- Narrative, conversational style expressed through the voice of a young bride.
- Recurring images of the countryside reflect the pleasures of marriage.
- Rhythm and sound effects are important throughout the poem.

AT GRASS

The eye can hardly pick them out
From the cold shade they shelter in,
Till wind distresses tail and mane;
Then one crops grass, and moves about
– The other seeming to look on – 5
And stands anonymous again.

Yet fifteen years ago, perhaps
Two dozen distances sufficed
To fable them: faint afternoons
Of Cups and Stakes and Handicaps, 10
Whereby their names were artificed
To inlay faded, classic Junes –

Silks at the start: against the sky
Numbers and parasols: outside,
Squadrons of empty cars, and heat, 15
And littered grass: then the long cry
Hanging unhushed till it subside
To stop-press columns on the street.

Do memories plague their ears like flies?
They shake their heads. Dusk brims the shadows. 20
Summer by summer all stole away,
The starting-gates, the crowds and cries –
All but the unmolesting meadows.
Almanacked, their names live; they

Have slipped their names, and stand at ease, 25
Or gallop for what must be joy,
And not a fieldglass sees them home,
Or curious stop-watch prophesies:
Only the groom, and the groom's boy,
With bridles in the evening come. 30

'The starting-gates, the crowds and cries'

Glossary

At Grass: a reference to the retirement of old racehorses.
3   *mane*: the hair on the back of a horse's neck.
4   *crops*: eats, chews.
8   *Two dozen distances sufficed*: 24 races were enough.
9   *To fable*: to make famous.
10 *Cups and Stakes and Handicaps*: various types of horse races.
11 *artificed*: displayed (on trophies, etc.).
12 *inlay*: ornamental fabric.
12 *classic*: traditional, important June races.
13 *Silks*: shirts ('colours') worn by jockeys.
14 *Numbers*: betting numbers displayed by bookies.
14 *parasols*: ladies' umbrellas.
15 *Squadrons*: long lines (of parked cars).
18 *stop-press*: news update (latest racing results).
19 *plague*: irritate.
23 *unmolesting*: harmless, gentle.
24 *Almanacked*: listed in the racing records.
29 *groom*: worker who looks after the horses.
30 *bridles*: restraints placed on the heads of horses.

INITIAL RESPONSE

1. Using close reference to the text, describe the atmosphere/mood in the opening stanza.

2. How does Larkin convey the excitement of the racecourse in stanza three? Refer to the text in your answer.

3. Choose two memorable images from the poem and briefly explain their effectiveness.

STUDY NOTES

'At Grass' was written in 1950 after the poet had seen a documentary film about a retired racehorse. Larkin, himself a lover of horses, saw them as exploited during their racing careers. This strikingly reflective poem, exploring the changes brought about by the passage of time, has been interpreted as a criticism of the passing fashion of celebrity and as a requiem for a bygone age.

Stanza one begins with a short description of two horses sheltering in the distance. Larkin remarks that 'The eye can hardly pick them out' before he has even explained what there is to pick out. It is only when a slight breeze 'distresses tail and mane' that the horses come to life. Even then, the 'cold shade' setting has a vague suggestion that these forgotten ('anonymous') animals are close to death. There is an **evocative visual quality** within these early lines and a mood of wistful sadness dominates.

In contrast to this feeling of stillness, Larkin begins to imagine the racehorses in their prime 'fifteen years ago'. The nostalgic flashback in the **second and third stanzas** recalls their triumphs in 'Cups and Stakes and Handicaps', enough 'To fable them' and ensure their reputation in racing history. The thrill and glamour of 'classic Junes' is recreated through vibrant images of the jockeys' colours ('Silks') and the 'Numbers and parasols'. **Cinematic details** ('empty cars', 'littered grass') and the excited cheering ('the long cry') of the crowds all convey the joy of unforgettable race meetings.

Stanza four returns to the present as Larkin considers the conscious experiences of the horses themselves. The line 'They shake their heads' is playfully ambiguous, both a negative response to the earlier question ('Do memories plague their ears like flies?') and an actual movement which horses carry out naturally. Larkin's **elegant imagery** communicates the subtle advance of time: 'Summer by summer' as 'Dusk brims the shadows'. There is a strong sense that at the end of their lives, these once-famous horses deserve to take their ease in 'unmolesting meadows'. Interestingly, the most remarkable verbs in the poem – 'fabled', 'artificed', 'inlay', 'Almanacked' – are all concerned with the way people have seen and recorded these horses. They have become racecourse stories, names engraved into trophies and recorded in official histories.

The dignified language and slow rhythm of **stanza five** suggest both the tranquil freedom of these retired horses and the reality that they are nearing the end of their long lives. For the moment, though, they 'gallop for what must be joy' – a typical Larkin comment which throws doubt onto an assertion even while in the process of making it. The poem ends on a consolatory note. Now that the horses have 'slipped their names' and are no longer chasing fame or glory, they can 'stand at ease', enjoying the peace and quiet. Broad assonant effects emphasise their sense of quiet fulfilment: 'Only the groom, and the groom's boy,/With bridles in the evening come'. The inverted syntax and mellow tone add to the sense of finality. In completing the natural cycle of their lives, Larkin's racehorses offer a model for the human condition of youth, achievement and old age. Characteristically, the development of thought in the poem moves from observation to reflection, leaving us to appreciate the **blend of celebration and sadness** that mark this beautiful poem.

ANALYSIS

Using close reference to the text, comment on the poet's use of contrast in 'At Grass'.

Sample Paragraph

Philip Larkin uses two distinct settings in 'At Grass'. This is a very effective device to highlight the past and present lives of the racehorses. At the start of the poem, he describes two horses grazing – but they are 'anonymous'. There is a dreamy, timeless feeling to the picture Larkin paints. I thought that even the title of the poem was similar to the title used of a painting of racehorses. There is very little movement involved in the description of the retired horses – in complete contrast with the middle section of the poem, where Larkin brings us back to their glory days, winning 'Cups, Stakes and Handicaps'. The hustle and bustle of the busy racetracks is seen in the colourful images and lively rhythms – 'Silks at the start against the blue sky'. The scene is noisy, with race goers shouting and reporters rushing to write their 'stop-press columns' after the winners are announced. The two contrasting atmospheres are very different. At the end of the poem, we see the two old horses 'stand at ease' – even the gentle sibilant sounds are in contrast with the hectic description of 'littered grass' at the race meetings. The tone in the last lines of the poem as the grooms 'in the late evening come' is gentle and subdued, highlighting the final days of these champion horses. Overall, Larkin uses contrasts very effectively to show the dramatic changes in the lives of these great horses, who have swapped their past glory for a well-earned rest.

Examiner's Comment

This is a well-sustained and focused response that examines the poet's use of contrasting settings, moods and sound effects in some detail. The commentary is informed and interesting. However, the answer is less successful due to the inaccurate quotations. This solid response just falls below the top grade.

CLASS/HOMEWORK EXERCISES

1. Describe the tone of the poem. Is it celebratory, sorrowful, resigned or realistic, or a combination of these? Refer to the text in your answer.

2. "Larkin is able to to address the sensitive issues of human life without ever becoming sentimental.' To what extent is this true of 'At Grass'? Support your answer with reference to the poem.

SUMMARY POINTS

- Transience, ageing, and the natural cycle of life and death are central themes.
- Contrasting patterns of imagery – subdued, vibrant.
- Variety of tones – nostalgic, celebratory, reflective, realistic, resigned.
- Effective use of evocative imagery, sound, contrast and flashback.

❸ CHURCH GOING

Once I am sure there's nothing going on
I step inside, letting the door thud shut.
Another church: matting, seats, and stone,
And little books; sprawlings of flowers, cut
For Sunday, brownish now; some brass and stuff   5
Up at the holy end; the small neat organ;
And a tense, musty, unignorable silence,
Brewed God knows how long. Hatless, I take off
My cycle-clips in awkward reverence,

Move forward, run my hand around the font.   10
From where I stand, the roof looks almost new –
Cleaned, or restored? Someone would know: I don't.
Mounting the lectern, I peruse a few
Hectoring large-scale verses, and pronounce
'Here endeth' much more loudly than I'd meant.   15
The echoes snigger briefly. Back at the door
I sign the book, donate an Irish sixpence,
Reflect the place was not worth stopping for.

Yet stop I did: in fact I often do,
And always end much at a loss like this,   20
Wondering what to look for; wondering, too,
When churches fall completely out of use
What we shall turn them into, if we shall keep
A few cathedrals chronically on show,
Their parchment, plate and pyx in locked cases,   25
And let the rest rent-free to rain and sheep.
Shall we avoid them as unlucky places?

Or, after dark, will dubious women come
To make their children touch a particular stone;
Pick simples for a cancer; or on some   30
Advised night see walking a dead one?
Power of some sort or other will go on
In games, in riddles, seemingly at random;
But superstition, like belief, must die,
And what remains when disbelief has gone?   35

Grass, weedy pavement, brambles, buttress, sky,
A shape less recognisable each week,
A purpose more obscure. I wonder who
Will be the last, the very last, to seek
This place for what it was; one of the crew   40
That tap and jot and know what rood-lofts were?
Some ruin-bibber, randy for antique,
Or Christmas-addict, counting on a whiff
Of gowns-and-bands and organ-pipes and myrrh?
Or will he be my representative,   45

Bored, uninformed, knowing the ghostly silt
Dispersed, yet tending to this cross of ground
Through suburb scrub because it held unspilt
So long and equably what since is found
Only in separation – marriage, and birth,   50
And death, and thoughts of these – for which was built
This special shell? For, though I've no idea
What this accoutred frowsty barn is worth,
It pleases me to stand in silence here;

A serious house on serious earth it is,   55
In whose blent air all our compulsions meet,
Are recognised, and robed as destinies.
And that much never can be obsolete,
Since someone will forever be surprising
A hunger in himself to be more serious,   60
And gravitating with it to this ground,
Which, he once heard, was proper to grow wise in,
If only that so many dead lie round.

'Which, he once heard, was proper to grow wise in,/If only that so many dead lie round'

Glossary

9 **cycle-clips**: old-fashioned clips that fasten a cyclist's trouser leg.
10 **font**: stone bowl in a church used to store holy water.
13 **lectern**: a tall stand from which a speaker can read.
13 **peruse**: read carefully.
14 **Hectoring**: bullying, blustering.
15 **'Here endeth'**: Church of England services end each reading with the phrase 'Here endeth the lesson'.
24 **chronically**: lasting a long time; very badly.
25 **parchment**: animal skin formerly used for writing on.
25 **plate**: bowls, cups, etc. made of gold or silver and used for religious ceremonies.
25 **pyx**: container in which the blessed bread of the Eucharist is kept.
28 **dubious**: doubtful.
30 **simples**: medicinal herbs.
30 **cancer**: malignant growth.
31 **Advised**: recommended.
36 **buttress**: support for a wall.
41 **rood-lofts**: galleries in the shape of a cross.
42 **ruin-bibber**: someone fond of old buildings.
42 **randy**: excited.
44 **gowns-and-bands**: clerical dress.
44 **myrrh**: sweet-smelling resin used in incense at a religious ceremony.
46 **silt**: deposit left behind.
49 **equably**: calm and even-tempered.
53 **accoutred**: dressed; equipped.
53 **frowsty**: stale smelling; musty.
56 **blent**: blended, mixed.
56 **compulsions**: irresistible urges to do something.
58 **obsolete**: out of date.
61 **gravitating**: attracted towards.

INITIAL RESPONSE

1. What impression do you have of the speaker in the first two stanzas of this poem? Support your answer with reference to the text.

2. List two images that you consider to be spiritual in 'Church Going'. Comment on their effectiveness.

3. How does this poem change after the first two stanzas? What are the main considerations of the poet? Refer closely to the poem in your response.

STUDY NOTES

'Church Going' was written in 1954 as part of Larkin's poetry collection The Less Deceived. *He adopts his famous persona of the self-deprecating, observant, conversational outsider. Larkin said he felt the need to be on 'the periphery of things'. The title is a pun, suggesting both the attendance of religious ceremonies (church-going) and also suggesting that religious practice/religion itself was on the way out, passé. The inspiration for the poem came from an actual event experienced by Larkin when he stopped to look at a church while on a cycling trip.*

In the **first stanza**, Larkin is an interloper/intruder who only enters the church when he's sure it's empty ('nothing going on'). The run-on line movement mirrors the poet popping inside ('I step inside'). The onomatopoeic closing of the door echoes in 'thud shut'. We hear what is happening. A **jaded tone** of one who has seen and done it all before sounds from the phrase 'Another church'. He now gives us a general view of the church from floor to wall: matting, wooden seats, stone walls. He then closes in for a detailed view: 'little books', flowers that are 'brownish now'. This telling detail suggests something is not fresh; it's dying. Is this similar to church-going? Larkin felt strongly that when you go into church, you get a feeling that something is over, derelict.

He now becomes dismissive as he describes the sacred objects as 'some brass and stuff'. He says it is 'Up at the holy end'. He is indifferent rather than ignorant: 'I don't bother about that kind of thing,' he once declared. The atmosphere is 'tense', not serene; the church is 'musty', stale smelling. The **silence is all pervasive**, 'unignorable'. The atmosphere has been stewing or fermenting a long time, like tea or beer – only 'God knows how long'. This fact makes him anxious to show respect. He had already removed his hat, but now he cuts a slightly ridiculous figure as he removes his cycle-clips 'in awkward reverence'.

He moves around in the **second stanza**, like an uninformed tourist, randomly touching things ('run my hand around the font'). The use of the present tense in the first two stanzas gives an immediacy to the description. A telling question, 'Cleaned, or restored?', shows the poet's mind at work. It also shows that there is a community at work, and therefore continuity. The roof is being preserved, just as Larkin is preserving the church in his poem. Yet the dismissive, casual, **conversational tone** returns when he says that he thinks 'the place was not worth stopping for'.

A more formal, serious voice now is heard as the poet's inner self comes into focus. He begins to meditate in **stanza three** on the importance of churches ('wondering, too,/When churches fall completely out of use/What we shall turn them into'). This knowledgeable voice knows the ecclesiastical vocabulary: 'parchment', 'pyx'. In the future, these will no longer be used for ceremonies, but stored 'in locked cases'. Larkin was fond of the traditions of the Anglican Church, but now the old world is fading. He imagines the future of these churches as 'rent-free', worth nothing, housing only 'rain and sheep'. Here is a **desolate outlook**. The use of the plural first person pronoun 'we' suggests that Larkin thinks we will all be confronted with what to do with these large empty buildings. The negative view continues as the churches are described as 'unlucky places'.

In **stanza four**, superstition is overtaking belief. This is 'dark', 'dubious'; Larkin doesn't approve. However, he feels the power will remain ('Power of some sort'), and eventually, as always happens, nature will reclaim it: 'Grass … brambles … sky'. This landscape recalls the opening view of the interior of the church. Now, in Larkin's imaginings, it lies open to the elements. The long sentence shows the **ruminative mood** of the poet, as he wonders, in **stanza five**, who will be the last to seek out this place for what it once was, a dynamic church. He dismisses the learned academics ('ruin-bibber'), someone mad for old buildings.

In **stanza six**, Larkin wonders if his 'representative', 'Bored', will be one who understood the church's role in marking the great human landmarks of a life: birth, marriage and death. The poet is happy to be part of this space: 'It pleases me to stand in silence here'. In the **seventh stanza**, the **contemplative voice** states, 'A serious house on serious earth it is'. He realises he will be someone who is drawn to this place, as it is a place 'to grow wise in' as he experiences the essence of life, being alone ('dead lie around').

Larkin uses a traditional form of English poetry, a formal stanza pattern of seven nine-line stanzas. The rhythm is iambic pentameter, the traditional rhythm of English verse. The large, spacious form of the poem echoes the cavernous space of the church. The **regular rhyme scheme** punctuates this ordered but disappearing world. This poem is reminiscent of Shakespeare's sonnet recording the ruins of England's monasteries: 'Bare ruined choirs, where late the sweet birds sang'. Both poems are shot through with melancholy for a disappeared world.

ANALYSIS

From your reading of 'Church Going', what insights have you gained about Larkin's views on religion and spirituality? Support your answer with reference to the poem.

Sample Paragraph

I feel I have gained insight about religious belief from this poem, although the poet is dismissive of yet 'Another church'; in the opening stanza. Larkin offhandedly remarks that 'the place was not worth stopping for'. Nevertheless, he also admits that this empty church deserves reverence, however 'awkward'. This place has a 'Power of some sort'. When Larkin's more serious side emerges, at the end of the poem, he acknowledges that people need religion – it is a kind of 'hunger'. We cannot exist totally on the level of animals, or in the shallow state of the arch, cynical, critical sneer. He uses the word, 'gravitating', as if church-goers are pulled by an irresistible force 'to this sacred ground'. I believe that Larkin is distinguishing organized religion from human spirituality. He obviously has respect for the spiritual yearning that makes people look for a deeper purpose to their lives. In this sense, 'Church Going' is a positive poem and the church itself is a 'proper' place to grow 'wise in'. The final line of the poem, 'If only that so many dead lie round', shows us that this place marks the real and final stage of life. We live our lives in the shadow of our death, our loved ones' deaths, and the death of all living things. This might not be optimistic, but it does emphasize a basic truth which has given me an important insight into reality.

Examiner's Comment

This top grade paragraph directly responds to the question in a focused way. The answer traces the development of thought in the poem and integrates precise quotation to lend weight to the discussion points. Vocabulary and syntax are excellent throughout. Some of the expression is particularly impressive, e.g. 'Larkin is distinguishing organized religion from human spirituality'. Overall, a competent and assured standard.

CLASS/HOMEWORK EXERCISES

1. Larkin stated that the 'impulse to preserve lies at the bottom of all art'. What is Larkin trying to preserve in the poem 'Church Going'? In your opinion, does he succeed or fail? Support your answer with reference to the text.

2. Choose three contrasting tones which Larkin uses in this poem. Which two of the tones do you identify with most? Explain your answer.

SUMMARY POINTS

- The significance of religion and the search for meaning in life are key themes.
- Interesting images and metaphors create atmosphere and reflect meaning.
- Contrasting tones – disappointed, critical, casual, sad, reflective, humorous.
- Effective use of rhetorical questions, alliteration, assonance, rhyme.

4 AN ARUNDEL TOMB

Side by side, their faces blurred,
The earl and countess lie in stone,
Their proper habits vaguely shown
As jointed armour, stiffened pleat,
And that faint hint of the absurd –   5
The little dogs under their feet.

Such plainness of the pre-baroque
Hardly involves the eye, until
It meets his left-hand gauntlet, still
Clasped empty in the other; and   10
One sees, with a sharp tender shock,
His hand withdrawn, holding her hand.

They would not think to lie so long.
Such faithfulness in effigy
Was just a detail friends would see: 15
A sculptor's sweet commissioned grace
Thrown off in helping to prolong
The Latin names around the base.

They would not guess how early in
Their supine stationary voyage   20
The air would change to soundless damage,
Turn the old tenantry away;
How soon succeeding eyes begin
To look, not read. Rigidly they

Persisted, linked, through lengths and breadths   25
Of time. Snow fell, undated. Light
Each summer thronged the glass. A bright
Litter of birdcalls strewed the same
Bone-riddled ground. And up the paths
The endless altered people came,   30

Washing at their identity.
Now, helpless in the hollow of
An unarmorial age, a trough

Of smoke in slow suspended skeins
Above their scrap of history, 35
Only an attitude remains:

Time has transfigured them into
Untruth. The stone fidelity
They hardly meant has come to be
Their final blazon, and to prove 40
Our almost-instinct almost true:
What will survive of us is love.

'What will survive of us is love'

Glossary

Title: The title refers to a 14th-century monument of the Earl of Arundel and his wife in Chichester Cathedral, West Sussex, England.

3 *proper habits*: appropriate burial clothes.
4 *pleat*: fold.
7 *pre-baroque*: plain, simple design (before the elaborate 17th-century baroque style).
9 *gauntlet*: glove.
14 *effigy*: figure, sculpted likeness.
20 *supine*: lying down.
22 *tenantry*: tenants living on a landlord's estate.
27 *thronged*: crowded.
28 *strewed*: spread across.
29 *Bone-riddled ground*: buried human remains.
33 *unarmorial*: unheroic.
33 *trough*: channel.
34 *skeins*: threads or coils (of smoke).
37 *transfigured*: transformed.
40 *blazon*: sign, symbol.

INITIAL RESPONSE

1. How would you describe the tone in the first stanza? Reverential? Intrigued? Superior?

2. Select two illustrations from the poem to show Larkin's keen eye for detail. Comment briefly on the effectiveness of each example.

3. Write a short personal response to this poem, highlighting the impact it made on you.

STUDY NOTES

'An Arundel Tomb' was written in 1956 after Larkin had visited Chichester Cathedral. He said that the effigies were unlike any he had ever seen before and that he found them 'extremely affecting'. The poem can be viewed in many ways – as a meditation on love and death, as a tribute to the power of art or even as a celebration of English history. Despite differences of interpretation, 'An Arundel Tomb' has always been a favourite of Larkin readers. It was read aloud at his memorial service held in London's Westminster Abbey in 1986.

In **stanza one**, we are immediately located before the stone statue of the Earl and Countess of Arundel. Larkin's description of the couple seems detached, the tone one of **ironic hesitation**. The couple's 'blurred' faces (eroded by time) are indistinct. Indeed, the earl's outdated armour and the 'little dogs under their feet' add a ludicrous dimension (a 'faint hint of the absurd') to the commemorative monument.

The poet continues to criticise the 'plainness' of the lifeless sculpture in **stanza two**. It is etched in an unappealingly dull 'pre-baroque' style. But he is suddenly taken by one particular detail. The earl's left hand has been withdrawn from its 'gauntlet' and is 'holding her hand'. This affectionate gesture between husband and wife has an immediate impact on Larkin – 'a sharp tender shock'. The image of 'His hand withdrawn, holding her hand' stops the poet in his tracks. We can sense Larkin's concentration in the **slow rhythm** and emphatic 'h' alliteration of **line 12**. Do the joined hands represent the triumph of love over time, or is that just wishful thinking?

In **stanza three**, Larkin reflects on the relationship between the earl and countess. **Line 13** is puzzling: 'They would not think to lie so long'. Is this an obvious reference to the couple's long rest in the tomb? Or have they failed to find a heavenly afterlife? Might there be a **pun on the word 'lie'**? Perhaps the loving hand-holding is an untrue representation? Larkin wonders if the sculptor invented this demonstrative touch to make the statue more interesting to the general public and to 'prolong' the earl's family name long after the Latin inscription would be understood.

Stanzas four and five focus particularly on the passing of time, a central theme in the poem. The earl and countess could not have imagined the effects of the damp cathedral air ('soundless damage') eroding their tomb. Great social change has also happened over the centuries; 'the old tenantry' and the use of Latin – and the importance of Christianity, presumably – have disappeared. Larkin's strikingly **sensory images** evoke the changing seasons: 'Snow fell, undated. Light/Each summer thronged the glass'. The signs of natural vitality and rejuvenation are in stark contrast to the 'Bone-riddled ground' over which modern-day visitors to the cathedral ('endless altered people') arrive to view the monument.

The countless tourists to the medieval couple's tomb have long been 'Washing at their identity' (**stanza six**). There is a suggestion of erosion (the earl and countess are no longer understood as they once were) and purification (the couple are idealised as romantic and artistic symbols). Larkin asserts that the effigies are 'helpless' in this 'unarmorial age'. The poet's **cynical tone** reflects his distaste for the vulgarity and ignorance around him. Today's generation has a shallow appreciation of love – 'Only an attitude remains'.

This idea is developed in **stanza seven**, where Larkin questions the public's misguided response to the statue. For him, the sentimental yearning to see the couple's 'fidelity' as a triumph of love over death is an 'Untruth', and something the earl and countess probably never intended. Nonetheless, the instinctual desire for enduring love may well be another admirable aspect of human behaviour. Many commentators view the final lines ('Our almost-instinct almost true:/What will survive of us is love') as a positive affirmation by Larkin. Others see in it a typically despondent statement of the opposite (namely, self-deluding hope in the face of reality). Like the rest of the poem, the ending is **typically paradoxical** and thought provoking, allowing us to decide for ourselves about Larkin's attitude concerning the power of love to transcend time.

ANALYSIS

'In addressing universal themes of love and death, Philip Larkin often uses ambiguous language.' Discuss this statement, with particular reference to 'An Arundel Tomb'.

Sample Paragraph

Larkin's poetry is noted for its ambiguity. The opening description of the rigid figures carved in stone is both sympathetic and satirical. The adjective 'blurred', used to describe their faces, suggests they are anonymous and unreal. Inactivity and action are described in contrasting imagery, 'their supine stationary voyage'. What is real? Larkin finds the detail of the 'little dogs under their feet' ridiculous and the patronising tone suggests the spoiled and privileged former existence of the earl and the countess. However, this detail could be viewed as a humanising touch on the part of the sculptor. Suddenly another detail catches his attention and he is stopped with a 'sharp gentle shock'. The earl's hand is depicted as withdrawn from his gauntlet and 'holding' his countess's hand. Is this suggesting a sentimental attitude or the universal triumph of love over death? Larkin continues to tease us through the word 'lie'. The couple 'lie in stone'. This could refer to the position of their bodies, but it could also mean they are sending out a false message that they are a loving couple whose love has vanquished death. But the earl and countess 'would not think to lie so long', they never planned to give this false impression. The typically paradoxical ending challenges us to consider the truth of the poet's final enigmatic statement: 'What will survive of us is love'.

Examiner's Comment

A well-illustrated personal response that examines Larkin's subtle use of language: 'This could refer to the position of their bodies, but it could also mean they are sending out a false message that they are a loving couple whose love has vanquished death.' Expression throughout the paragraph is excellent: 'The opening description of the rigid figures carved in stone is both sympathetic and satirical'. A successful top grade answer.

CLASS/HOMEWORK EXERCISES

1. Outline the main theme presented in 'An Arundel Tomb'. In your answer, trace the way the poet develops his ideas during the course of the poem.

2. 'Philip Larkin has often been criticized for the gloom and moroseness of his poems.' Discuss this statement, with particular reference to 'An Arundel Tomb'.

SUMMARY POINTS

- Central themes include love, mortality and the endurance of art.
- Descriptive/narrative opening leads to wonder and reflection.
- Effective use of vivid imagery, onomatopoeia, steady rhythm and set rhyme.
- Tone varies from the ironic and cynical to the ambivalent and positive.

THE WHITSUN WEDDINGS

That Whitsun, I was late getting away:
    Not till about
One-twenty on the sunlit Saturday
Did my three-quarters-empty train pull out,
All windows down, all cushions hot, all sense   5
Of being in a hurry gone. We ran
Behind the backs of houses, crossed a street
Of blinding windscreens, smelt the fish-dock; thence
The river's level drifting breadth began,
Where sky and Lincolnshire and water meet.   10

All afternoon, through the tall heat that slept
    For miles inland,
A slow and stopping curve southwards we kept.
Wide farms went by, short-shadowed cattle, and
Canals with floatings of industrial froth;   15
A hothouse flashed uniquely: hedges dipped
And rose: and now and then a smell of grass
Displaced the reek of buttoned carriage-cloth
Until the next town, new and nondescript,
Approached with acres of dismantled cars.   20

At first, I didn't notice what a noise
    The weddings made
Each station that we stopped at: sun destroys
The interest of what's happening in the shade,
And down the long cool platforms whoops and skirls   25
I took for porters larking with the mails,
And went on reading. Once we started, though,
We passed them, grinning and pomaded, girls
In parodies of fashion, heels and veils,
All posed irresolutely, watching us go,   30

As if out on the end of an event
    Waving goodbye
To something that survived it. Struck, I leant
More promptly out next time, more curiously,
And saw it all again in different terms: 35

The fathers with broad belts under their suits
And seamy foreheads; mothers loud and fat;
An uncle shouting smut; and then the perms,
The nylon gloves and jewellery-substitutes,
The lemons, mauves, and olive-ochres that   40

Marked off the girls unreally from the rest.
    Yes, from cafés
And banquet-halls up yards, and bunting-dressed
Coach-party annexes, the wedding-days
Were coming to an end. All down the line   45
Fresh couples climbed aboard: the rest stood round;
The last confetti and advice were thrown,
And, as we moved, each face seemed to define
Just what it saw departing: children frowned
At something dull; fathers had never known   50

Success so huge and wholly farcical;
    The women shared
The secret like a happy funeral;
While girls, gripping their handbags tighter, stared
At a religious wounding. Free at last,   55
And loaded with the sum of all they saw,
We hurried towards London, shuffling gouts of steam.
Now fields were building-plots, and poplars cast
Long shadows over major roads, and for
Some fifty minutes, that in time would seem   60

Just long enough to settle hats and say
    I nearly died,
A dozen marriages got under way.
They watched the landscape, sitting side by side
– An Odeon went past, a cooling tower,   65
And someone running up to bowl – and none
Thought of the others they would never meet
Or how their lives would all contain this hour.
I thought of London spread out in the sun,
Its postal districts packed like squares of wheat: 70

There we were aimed. And as we raced across
    Bright knots of rail
Past standing Pullmans, walls of blackened moss
Came close, and it was nearly done, this frail
Travelling coincidence; and what it held 75
Stood ready to be loosed with all the power
That being changed can give. We slowed again,
And as the tightened brakes took hold, there swelled
A sense of falling, like an arrow-shower
Sent out of sight, somewhere becoming rain. 80

'now and then a smell of grass'

Glossary

Title: Whit (Pentecost) Sunday, the seventh after Easter, was a popular time for weddings.
19 *nondescript*: ordinary.
25 *skirls*: high-pitched cries.
26 *larking*: joking, carrying on.
28 *pomaded*: perfumed.
29 *parodies*: imitations.
30 *irresolutely*: hesitantly.
37 *seamy*: lined.
38 *smut*: rude or suggestive comments.
38 *perms*: waved hairstyles popular at the time.
40 *olive-ochres*: green and gold colours.
41 *unreally*: falsely.
44 *annexes*: reserved areas.
57 *gouts*: great spurts.
65 *Odeon*: popular cinema name.
73 *Pullmans*: luxury rail carriages (sleeping cars).
79 *arrow-shower*: short outburst of rain.

INITIAL RESPONSE

1. What is Larkin's attitude to the wedding parties that he describes in stanzas three and four? Refer to the text in your answer.

2. Select two visual images from the poem to show Larkin's eye for observational detail. Comment briefly on the effectiveness of each example.

3. Write a short personal response to 'The Whitsun Weddings', highlighting the impact it made on you.

STUDY NOTES

Larkin began writing 'The Whitsun Weddings' in 1957, and spent over a year drafting it. He said, 'You couldn't be on that train without feeling the young lives all starting off, and that just for a moment you were touching them. Doncaster, Retford, Grantham, Newark, Peterborough, and at every station more wedding parties. It was wonderful, a marvellous afternoon.' While the poem is lengthy by Larkin's standards, it moves typically from specific observation to an insightful reflection of love and marriage.

The poem's positive **title** immediately suggests celebration. Larkin's personal narrative makes use of everyday colloquial speech ('I was late getting away') to introduce this seemingly ordinary account of his afternoon journey from Hull to London. The **opening lines** of **stanza one** build to a steady rhythm, like a train leaving a railway station. At first, the poet's senses are engaged but not fully absorbed in his surroundings. However, his language ('The river's level drifting breadth') conveys the numbing drowsiness of a warm summer day. Larkin's characteristic eye for detail evokes the **claustrophobic atmosphere** inside the carriage: 'All windows down, all cushions hot'. The panoramic picture of the outside view 'Where sky and Lincolnshire and water meet' reveals his appreciation of nature and an enthusiasm for the English landscape.

Although the poet seems somewhat removed from the rest of society, his sense of place and expressive description continue into **stanza two**: 'Wide farms went by, short-shadowed cattle'. The June weather is personified ('the tall heat that slept'), adding to an already oppressive mood. Occasional run-through phrasing ('hedges dipped/And rose') echoes the movement of the train on its 'curve southwards'. Always a realist, Larkin includes a number of unappealing images associated with the industrial age: 'floatings of industrial froth' and 'acres of dismantled cars'. This convincing sense of the familiar is characteristic of a poet who is known for vividly recording life in post-war England.

Stanza three focuses on the various wedding groups arriving on the station platforms. Larkin gradually realises that the 'whoops and skirls' he hears on the platforms are the animated voices of 'grinning and pomaded' girls who are seeing off the honeymooners. The poet's tone wavers between derision of the guests' style ('parodies of fashion') and admiration of their glamorous 'heels and veils'.

Despite his ironic detachment, Larkin cannot help but be increasingly attracted ('more curiously') to the small dramas taking place around him. He observes the various groups – 'fathers with broad belts under their suits', 'mothers loud and fat'. For much of **stanza four**, his attitude is condescending, referring to one vulgar uncle 'shouting smut'. He is equally disdainful of the clothes on show ('lemons, mauves and olive-ochres') and the cheap 'jewellery-substitutes'.

The poet's apparent class superiority is also evident in **stanza five** as he begins to wonder about the tawdry wedding receptions that have been taking place in 'cafés' and 'banquet-halls up yards'. Despite all this derision, Larkin detects a more important undertone beneath the brash celebrations. All the newlywed couples are about to leave their familiar lives behind. The inherent sadness and inevitability of the moment are summed up as 'The last confetti and advice were thrown'. Meanwhile, real life resumes for the children after the enjoyment of the day, while proud fathers feel relieved that all the fuss is over. For Larkin himself, however, the occasion has brought him closer to the people he has been observing and criticising.

Stanza six marks a change in the poet's outlook. More sensitive than before, he imagines how the older, more realistic wives view married life pragmatically as 'a happy funeral', likely to bring both joy and sorrow. This 'secret' is not yet understood by the impressionable younger girls carefully 'gripping their handbags tighter' and who presumably have more romantic notions about marriage. Larkin sees them as facing 'a religious wounding', a typically ambiguous comment, suggesting both the wedding ritual and the likely hurt that lies ahead. From this moment, the poet associates himself more closely with the newlywed couples aboard the train ('Free at last'). He is no longer merely a detached observer as 'We hurried towards London'. The poem's rhythm gathers pace, perhaps reflecting his growing mood of optimism.

The lines maintain their momentum in **stanza seven** as Larkin's fellow-passengers relive the excitement of the day ('I nearly died'). The train journey has let the poet realise that the people he has seen are all interconnected ('their lives would all contain this hour'). This is coupled with the poignant understanding that it is only Larkin himself who is conscious of this fact ('none/Thought of the others they would never meet'). This overview of how the random lives of individuals form a greater pattern is teased out further as he uses an **inventive rural simile** to describe London's numerous 'postal districts packed like squares of wheat'.

At the start of **stanza eight**, there is little doubt that Larkin is aware of the full significance of this weekend outing. The 'dozen marriages' have made a lasting impact on the poet. As the train arrives at its destination, he reflects on 'this frail/Travelling coincidence'. Is he simply saying that all of life can be viewed as a journey where we meet people by chance, and that some of these encounters have the power to change us? The **last lines** reach a high point 'as the tightened brakes took hold' and the poem ends on a **dramatic note** ('A sense of falling'), suggesting both danger and adventure. The final image of the distant 'arrow-shower … becoming rain' is an exciting one, hinting at romance, beauty and even sadness. Elusive to the end, Larkin's poem invites us to consider the wonderful experience of life in all its richness.

ANALYSIS

It has been said that Philip Larkin's poetry is gloomy and pessimistic. In your opinion, is this true of 'The Whitsun Weddings'? Refer to the poem in your answer.

Sample Paragraph

Larkin is more of a realistic poet than a pessimistic one. In my opinion, he celebrated traditional English life in 'The Whitsun Weddings'. He has a love for the English landscape. Even the fish-dock in Hull get his attention. His description of the horizon 'where the sky over Lincolnshire and the water meet' is evidence of his love of his native land. He seems obsessed by the young wedding couples and their families when he sees them at the rail stations. He might be poking fun at them here and there, but it is all good-natured, never mean. Larkin laughs at the 'nylon gloves and the jewellery substitutes' and at the 'uncle shouting out smut' at the honeymooners. This is all very good-natured. And certainly not gloomy. I think the speaking tone he uses shows that he admires these happy wedding guests. He's almost envious of their enjoyment. Philip hears the 'whoops' of the 'mothers loud and very fat', but he seems to be just smiling at their sense of fun. Not that Larkin is a complete bundle of laughs. There are some serious bits, of course. However, he is just being real when he describes the secret comments of the experienced wives who see married life as 'a happy funeral'. Overall, I think Philip is upbeat and celebrates working-class life.

Examiner's Comment

A fairly solid response that makes a good attempt at tackling the question of Larkin's tone. There are apt references to how the poet 'celebrated' traditional English life and how its overall attitude is 'good-natured'. Expression is note-like and lacks control at times. The answer is further weakened by occasional slang, slightly inaccurate quotes, and overly familiar mention of 'Philip'. Overall, an average middle grade standard.

CLASS/HOMEWORK EXERCISES

1. It has been said of Larkin that he observes 'ordinary people doing ordinary things'. To what extent do you agree with this statement in light of your reading of 'The Whitsun Weddings'?

2. 'Larkin's poems are memorable for their sharp wit and irreverence.' Discuss this view, with particular reference to 'The Whitsun Weddings'.

SUMMARY POINTS

- Key themes include marriage, class and culture in England during the 1950s.
- Contrasting atmospheres – the claustrophobic carriage, noisy stations, open countryside.
- Effective use of sensual imagery, sound, regular rhyme and rhythm.
- The final metaphor is startling and dramatic – and layered with meaning.

6 MCMXIV

Those long uneven lines
Standing as patiently
As if they were stretched outside
The Oval or Villa Park,
The crowns of hats, the sun   5
On moustached archaic faces
Grinning as if it were all
An August Bank Holiday lark;

And the shut shops, the bleached
Established names on the sunblinds,   10
The farthings and sovereigns,
And dark-clothed children at play
Called after kings and queens,
The tin advertisements
For cocoa and twist, and the pubs   15
Wide open all day;

And the countryside not caring:
The place names all hazed over
With flowering grasses, and fields
Shadowing Domesday lines   20
Under wheat's restless silence;
The differently-dressed servants
With tiny rooms in huge houses,
The dust behind limousines;

Never such innocence,   25
Never before or since,
As changed itself to past
Without a word – the men
Leaving the gardens tidy,
The thousands of marriages   30
Lasting a little while longer:
Never such innocence again.

'Those long uneven lines'

Glossary

Title: The title refers to the Roman numerals for 1914, the year that World War I began. It became known as the Great War, a landmark event in the 20th century.

4 *The Oval*: famous cricket ground near London.
4 *Villa Park*: Birmingham home ground of Aston Villa football club.
6 *archaic*: dated, old-fashioned.
8 *lark*: celebration, spree.
11 *farthings and sovereigns*: currency used at the time. The copper farthing was just a quarter of a penny, while the gold sovereign coin was worth £1.
15 *twist*: probably refers to a small piece of tobacco.
20 *Domesday*: medieval spelling of Doomsday (or Judgement Day); in 1086, William the Conqueror compiled a record of English land ownership in the Domesday Book.
24 *limousines*: luxury cars.

INITIAL RESPONSE

1. Suggest a reason to explain why the poet chose to write the title in Roman numerals. (Where else might the letters MCMXIV be seen?)

2. In your opinion, is Larkin's view of the past accurate and realistic or is it sentimental and idealised? Refer to the text in your answer.

3. What do you think is meant by the final line, 'Never such innocence again'? Briefly explain your answer.

> **STUDY NOTES**
>
> *This elegiac poem, written in 1960, has often been read as a nostalgic account of a vanished English way of life. The Roman numerals of the title evoke war memorials and the detailed descriptions seem to suggest old photographs. The whole poem consists of one long sentence, giving a sense of timelessness and connecting readers with the men lining up for army service.*
>
> Larkin's meditation begins with a description of an old photograph of 'uneven lines' of British volunteers outside an army recruiting office at the start of World War I. In **stanza one**, the poet observes that the men are queuing happily, as if for a game of cricket or football. The **tragic irony** of their fate is suggested by the image of the sun shining on their 'moustached archaic faces' and their carefree expressions, 'Grinning' as if it was all just a 'lark'. Larkin's tone seems unclear. Does he admire the men's idealism and courage or is there a sense that these raw recruits are naïvely seeking adventure?
>
> The holiday atmosphere continues in **stanza two** with a wistful celebration of pre-war English life. Larkin lists some of the hallmarks of a bygone era: 'farthings and sovereigns', 'children at play', 'cocoa and twist'. Trusted shops ('Established names') and public houses ('Wide open all day') add to this **relaxed feeling** of security. Overall, this idealised image of a long-lost England is one of innocence, freedom and stability.
>
> The poet swaps the familiar town setting for the open countryside in **stanza three**. At first, the mood seems untroubled ('not caring'). The alliterative effect and soft sibilant sounds of 'flowering grasses, and fields' evoke England's green and pleasant land. But the positive mood is suddenly overshadowed by the reference to 'Domesday lines' – a chilling echo of the earlier 'uneven lines' of men whose lives are likely to end on the battlefield. The reality of mass war graves is further stressed by the unsettling image of the 'wheat's restless silence'. Larkin's **tone becomes increasingly critical** as he focuses on the class divisions ('differently-dressed servants') prevalent within English society. Images of 'tiny rooms in huge houses' and 'dust behind limousines' suggest that social inequality was hidden away hypocritically.
>
> The powerfully emotive force of **stanza four** emphasises the passing of an innocent age: 'Never before or since'. Purposeful rhythm and repetition ('never' is used three times) reflect Larkin's shocking realisation that the war would mark a turning point in our understanding of man's inhumanity to man. The compelling image of countless naïve volunteers leaving their homes, unaware that their marriages would only last 'a little while longer', is undeniably poignant. Rather than being a hymn of sentimental nostalgia, the **poem is dark** with the shadow of unexpected death and we are left with an enduring sense of the human tragedy involved.

ANALYSIS

'Philip Larkin powerfully evokes a lost land of innocence.' Discuss this statement, with reference to 'MCMXIV'.

Sample Paragraph

Many of Philip Larkin's poems on our course, e.g. 'Ambulances' and 'The Whitsun Weddings', give me a good insight into the past and ordinary English life. This is certainly true of his war poem 'MCMXIV'. The poem begins with a series of images showing long lines of young men signing up to enlist in the war. They are 'Grinning' and have no notion of the horrors before them. Their innocence is very well seen in the way Larkin shows them standing 'patiently' as though they were waiting to enter a football stadium. There is a photographic quality to his descriptions. Life seems simple, carefree. The poet suggests this with images of bank holidays, familiar shop advertisements, young children playing and the pubs 'Wide open all day'. But there is another, darker side to pre-war society – social division. Larkin reminds us of the 'differently-dressed servants' who are slaving away in 'tiny rooms' for the upper classes. By the end of the poem, he suggests that the innocent pre-war years were about to be replaced with a horrifying time of conflict, mass destruction and death. I found the final verse very effective, repeating the awful truth – 'Never such innocence again'. The peace and harmony of the past would be shattered for all time.

Examiner's Comment

An assured personal response, focused throughout and well-illustrated. The opening sentence contains a good example of cross reference. Quotations are integrated effectively and the answer ranges widely over the positive and negative aspects: 'images of bank holidays, familiar shop advertisements' and 'long lines of young men signing up to enlist'. Good personal engagement at the conclusion secures the top grade.

CLASS/HOMEWORK EXERCISES

1. How does Larkin establish the underlying sense of death that pervades the poem? Refer closely to the text in your answer.

2. 'In "MCMXIV", Larkin controls his sense of outrage while offering present readers a searing exposé of modern warfare'. Discuss this statement, supporting your answer with reference to the poem.

SUMMARY POINTS

- The significance of World War I and the passing of innocence are central themes.
- Tone varies – nostalgic, celebratory, ironic, sympathetic, critical, tragic.
- Descriptive details, evocative visual images and sound effects.
- Good use of powerfully emotive language and emphatic repetition.

7 AMBULANCES

Closed like confessionals, they thread
Loud noons of cities, giving back
None of the glances they absorb.
Light glossy grey, arms on a plaque,
They come to rest at any kerb:　　　　　　　　5
All streets in time are visited.

Then children strewn on steps or road,
Or women coming from the shops
Past smells of different dinners, see
A wild white face that overtops　　　　　　　　10
Red stretcher-blankets momently
As it is carried in and stowed,

And sense the solving emptiness
That lies just under all we do,
And for a second get it whole,　　　　　　　　15
So permanent and blank and true.
The fastened doors recede. *Poor soul*,
They whisper at their own distress;

For borne away in deadened air
May go the sudden shut of loss　　　　　　　　20
Round something nearly at an end,
And what cohered in it across
The years, the unique random blend
Of families and fashions, there

At last begin to loosen. Far　　　　　　　　　　25
From the exchange of love to lie
Unreachable inside a room
The traffic parts to let go by
Brings closer what is left to come,
And dulls to distance all we are.　　　　　　　　30

'They come to rest at any kerb'

Glossary

1 *confessionals*: small, box-like rooms used by Catholic priests to hear confessions.
4 *plaque*: shiny metal sign on the side of the ambulance.
7 *strewn*: scattered around.
12 *stowed*: stored.
17 *recede*: move away.
22 *cohered*: brought together.

INITIAL RESPONSE

1. How does Larkin present the ambulances in stanza one? Are they mysterious? Comforting? Disturbing? Refer to the text in your answer.

2. From your reading of the second stanza, what evidence can you find of the poet's superb eye for interesting detail?

3. Critics have said that Philip Larkin's poems are more realistic than pessimistic. In your opinion, is this the case in 'Ambulances'? Give reasons for your answer.

STUDY NOTES

'Ambulances' is a reflection on life and mortality, written in the early 1960s when an ambulance was usually associated with bad news. Larkin once remarked that everything he wrote had 'the consciousness of approaching death in the background'.

What do you think of when you see an ambulance? A serious road accident or some other emergency? Do you feel a sense of fear or of hope? People usually become apprehensive when they hear an ambulance siren. Are they genuinely concerned or are they just being inquisitive and voyeuristic?

From the outset of 'Ambulances', the **tone is uneasy**. There is an immediate sense of threat from these anonymous 'grey' vans that prowl around 'Loud noons of cities'. Even in the hustle and bustle of urban life, nobody escapes. Larkin sees these vehicles as symbols of death. An ambulance can take anyone away at any time. The patient is confined and vulnerable in much the same way as everyone is unable to escape dying: 'All streets in times are visited'. The dramatic **opening line** of the **first stanza** compares the ambulance van to a confessional – a place where people experience spiritual rebirth and make their peace with God. This religious image forces readers to face up to the inevitability of death. The poet personifies the vehicles, but they are as unresponsive as a corpse, 'giving back/None of the glances they absorb'. Bystanders glance nervously at passing ambulances, perhaps hoping deep down that their time has not yet come. However, the randomness of death is starkly emphasised by the line 'They come to rest at any kerb'. We are all powerless against the stark reality of our mortality.

Stanza two demonstrates Larkin's **keen eye for vivid detail** as he describes the reaction of onlookers when an ambulance arrives and disturbs a quiet neighbourhood. The street is suddenly transformed. Normal life stops for a moment as people consider the significance of what is happening. Simple, colloquial language illustrates the sharp contrast between everyday life ('children strewn on steps or road') and the hidden terror of death as the patient (now an unknown body described as 'it') is carried out to the ambulance. The colour images highlight the anguish of life-threatening illness ('A wild white face') and danger ('Red stretcher-blankets').

Larkin's tone is much more reflective in **stanza three**. This is typical of his writing. The crowd of spectators watching the small drama taking place 'sense the solving emptiness/That lies just under all we do'. They have been forced to confront the one underlying truth that all life ends with the mystery of dying. The poet himself was an atheist who could only believe in the 'emptiness' of oblivion after death. Unlike the earlier third-person description in the opening stanzas, the introduction of the pronoun 'we' gives the poem a universal significance. Death is our common fate and, in Larkin's belief, makes life meaningless. This seems to be the central moment of truth, or **epiphany**, in the poem – the morbid discovery that human existence is futile. Modern secular society avoids death. It is a taboo subject that we only think about when we are forced to.

For Larkin, all of our daily concerns – cooking, playing, etc. – are merely ways of filling time until death transports us to a state of 'permanent and blank' nothingness. As the ambulance pulls away, the poet suggests that people's whispered sympathy ('Poor soul') for the patient is really a selfish expression of 'their own distress'. Such irony is a common feature of Larkin's cynical observations of everyday life.

In the **final two stanzas**, the mood of depression deepens as Larkin considers the dying patient experiencing 'the sudden shut of loss'. **Stark imagery** and a deliberate rhythm combine to suggest the great change that death will bring, separating the individual from family and identity. The sensation of being isolated inside the ambulance ('Unreachable inside a room') echoes the earlier alienation of the confessional and adds to the growing sense of panic. Death will eventually alter ('loosen') everything.

Although the syntax (order of words) is complex at the end, Larkin manages to give a clear impression of his own sombre philosophy. As with much of his work, he is able to take a particular circumstance and find a general truth in it. The poem ends on a sweetly serene note of disillusion. Although ambulances try to save lives, they are actually the messengers of unavoidable death. The final disarming image leaves a **lingering sense of bleakness**. As the traffic parts and the ambulance siren quickly fades away, death also 'dulls to distance all we are'. For Larkin, there is no higher purpose to human existence, no comforting afterlife.

ANALYSIS

'Vivid details illustrate Larkin's reflections on life and mortality.' Discuss this statement, with particular reference to 'Ambulances'.

Sample Paragraph

The opening lines of 'Ambulances' contain many authentic images of the vans weaving in and out of traffic as they 'thread' their way through a busy city. We are given an immediate sense of the everyday setting and the noisy street: 'Loud noons of cities'. This condensed image effectively conveys a realistic impression of the city-centre sounds at midday. Larkin adds drama to the scene by describing one 'Light glossy grey' ambulance suddenly coming to a 'rest at any kerb'. It is the immediate focus of attention. The poet fills in the dramatic scene with precise pictures of the various spectators. Women coming from the shops stop and stare. There is realistic detailed description of the 'smells of different dinners' and of the children who are innocently playing, 'strewn on steps or road'. However, Larkin's picture of the sick patient is the most convincing of all. 'A wild white face' staring up from the 'Red stretcher-blankets' suggests pain and fear. The vivid images create a compelling sense of the seriousness of what is happening.

Examiner's Comment

As part of a full answer, this strong paragraph is firmly focused on how Larkin selects vibrant and energetic images to convey meaning and reinforce themes: 'many authentic images of the vans weaving in and out of traffic as they "thread their way through a busy city"'. The quotations are effectively used to illustrate the poet's skill in creating key moments of drama surrounding the sudden arrival of the ambulance: '"A wild white face" staring up from the "Red stretcher-blankets" suggests pain and fear'. A well-written top grade answer.

CLASS/HOMEWORK EXERCISES

1. How would you describe the dominant mood of 'Ambulances'? Using evidence from the poem, write a paragraph showing how Larkin creates this mood. (Model your answer on the sample paragraph above.)

2. 'Philip Larkin uses a variety of poetic techniques to express the deeper significance of ordinary everyday scenes.' Discuss this statement, supporting your answer with reference to the poem 'Ambulances'.

SUMMARY POINTS

- The universal experience of mortality is central to the poem.
- Larkin uses the extended metaphor of the ambulance throughout.
- Characteristic use of colloquial language and closely observed details.
- Vivid, realistic imagery, bleak atmosphere and a dark, depressing tone.

8 THE TREES

The trees are coming into leaf
Like something almost being said;
The recent buds relax and spread,
Their greennesss is a kind of grief.

Is it they are born again   5
And we grow old? No, they die too.
Their yearly trick of looking new
Is written down in rings of grain.

Yet still the unresting castles thresh
In fullgrown thickness every May.   10
Last year is dead, they seem to say,
Begin afresh, afresh, afresh.

'The recent buds relax and spread'

INITIAL RESPONSE

1. Larkin compares and contrasts the world of nature in 'The Trees' with the world of man. List one similarity and one contrast and comment on their effectiveness. Support your views with reference to the poem.

2. 'Like something almost being said'. In your opinion, what is almost being said? To whom and by whom is it being said?

3. 'Begin afresh, afresh, afresh.' Do you think this line is optimistic or full of false hope?

STUDY NOTES

'The Trees' was written in 1967 and forms part of the High Windows *collection. At this point, Larkin's personal life had become complicated. His mother was suffering from the early stages of Alzheimer's. This adds a special resonance to the last line of the poem. Do you think that people often long to 'Begin afresh, afresh, afresh'?*

Larkin deals with the classic theme of transience (passing time) in this lyric poem. The language in the **opening stanza** is harmonious and sombre, as long vowel sounds ('a', 'o' and 'u') announce the arrival of spring. The event is seen as inevitable; Larkin conveys the feeling that this has happened so often before. The mystery of the leaves' tentative arrival is suggested in the simile 'Like something almost being said'. We know it's going to happen, but we don't know how or why. It just does. Note the use of 'we' – this is a message for all of us. The verbs 'relax and spread' vividly convey the abundant covering of leaves on the former bare branches. But this **rejuvenation of nature** is not greeted warmly by the poet, who states that it is 'a kind of grief'. For whom is there sorrow? Man is unable to renew himself. Is the poet perhaps thinking of lost opportunities, what might have been? Or perhaps he is thinking of loved ones who are sick. The slow three-beat rhythm (iambic tetrameter) perfectly suits this lyrical meditation on the theme of decay and death.

In the **second stanza**, Larkin asks a **rhetorical question** to explore this thought further: 'Is it that they are born again/And we grow old?' The stark answer comes in the broken line 'No, they die too'. He does not flinch from the unpalatable reality of the finality of all living things. Time passes relentlessly and mercilessly, and the passage through time is recorded 'in rings of grain' in the tree trunks. The trees' appearance of renewal is just that – appearance, a 'trick'. The rhyme here (*cddc*) is pertinent: 'born again' rhymes with 'rings of grain', emphasising that their trick of renewal is exposed in the tree trunk.

Larkin's tone changes abruptly in the **third stanza**. The energy and life of the blossoming trees is celebrated in the metaphor 'unresting castles'. Spring's dynamic growth is shown in the compound word 'fullgrown' and in the assonance of 'unresting' and 'thresh'. Life springs back 'every May'. The trees, symbols of courage, are giving a message of hope to mankind as they seem to say, 'Last year is dead'. There is no use grieving over what is gone; concentrate on the future. The trees' exhortation is charged with urgency in the appeal 'Begin afresh, afresh, afresh'. Is this what was hinted at in the earlier phrase, 'Like something almost being said'? The **vibrant rhetoric** of spring demands that we seize the day. The life-force of the trees is sending out the hope-filled message: don't give up. Is this longing for life attractive but false? Which is the abiding message of the poem: the vitality of life or the inevitability of death? Could it be both?

ANALYSIS

'Larkin was a self-deprecating poet who often dismissed his own insightful reflections.' Discuss this statement in relation to 'The Trees', using close reference to the text.

Sample Paragraph

Larkin mocked his poem 'The Trees' as 'awful tripe'. It was here he wrote of his 'astounded delight at the renewal of the natural world'. This lyric, with its theme of transience, emphasises this view, but also brings it a step further. Here is no attractive, false idea of renewal. The poet realises that the trees will – after renewing themselves year after year (unlike humans) – eventually die. The abrupt broken line, 'No, they die too', baldly states this fact. He calls their rejuvenation a 'trick', as if there is something false or deceitful in what they do. The passage of inexorable time is marked in the material, decaying world in 'rings of grain'. This is definitely not 'tripe', but genuine insight into the nature of things, however unsavoury. I feel that his imagination is caught by the vitality and dynamism of the growing trees, which he describes as 'unresting castles'. The onomatopoeic 'thresh' captures this swaying movement and sense of being vibrantly alive. The concluding line, with its repetitive appeal, to 'Begin afresh. afresh, afresh', seems to me to be a plea for hope. Life should be lived to the brim. So the voice of the trees/the voice of the poet is telling us to seize the day. I believe that Larkin was very wrong to be so dismissive of this lyric. It reminds us that each new day brings with it the possibility of wonder.

Examiner's Comment

This focused paragraph eloquently argues the merits of Larkin's poem. A clear viewpoint is established, detailing a range of points. Expression and vocabulary are impressive: 'The passage of inexorable time is marked in the material, decaying world in "rings of grain".' The judicious use of quotation adds weight to this successful top grade response.

CLASS/HOMEWORK EXERCISES

1. Larkin said, 'When you've read a poem, that's it, it's all quite clear what it means.' Having read 'The Trees', would you agree or disagree with this view? Support your answer with reference to the text.

2. 'Larkin's poems often convey a strong sense of place which adds authenticity to the poet's observations.' To what extent is this true of 'The Trees'? Support your answer with reference to the poem.

SUMMARY POINTS

- Larkin contrasts human transience with the renewal of nature.
- Tone varies – downbeat, calm, reflective, hopeful.
- Compact structure, vivid images, rich sounds.
- Effective use of metaphor, personification, repetition and rhetorical language.

9. THE EXPLOSION

On the day of the explosion
Shadows pointed towards the pithead:
In the sun the slagheap slept.

Down the lane came men in pitboots
Coughing oath-edged talk and pipe-smoke, 5
Shouldering off the freshened silence.

One chased after rabbits; lost them;
Came back with a nest of lark's eggs;
Showed them; lodged them in the grasses.

So they passed in beards and moleskins, 10
Fathers, brothers, nicknames, laughter,
Through the tall gates standing open.

At noon there came a tremor; cows
Stopped chewing for a second; sun,
Scarfed as in a heat-haze, dimmed. 15

The dead go on before us, they
Are sitting in God's house in comfort,
We shall see them face to face –

Plain as lettering in the chapels
It was said, and for a second 20
Wives saw men of the explosion

Larger than in life they managed –
Gold as on a coin, or walking
Somehow from the sun towards them,

One showing the eggs unbroken. 25

'Fathers, brothers, nicknames, laughter'

Glossary

2 *pithead*: the top part of a mine.
3 *slagheap*: man-made hill formed from the waste of coal mining.
4 *pitboots*: heavy boots worn by miners.
8 *lark's eggs*: the eggs of the skylark, a native bird of England and Ireland.
10 *moleskins*: heavy material worn by working men.
15 *Scarfed*: wrapped up.

INITIAL RESPONSE

1. Does Larkin give a realistic picture of the working men? Choose two realistic details (images) that you found effective.

2. In your opinion, is this a sentimental poem? Give reasons for your answer.

3. Comment on the concluding image as a symbol of redemption.

STUDY NOTES

'The Explosion' documents a tragedy that can randomly happen to a community, but it offers a consolation that is not present in Larkin's other poems. The word 'explosion' brings to mind a loud bang, destruction, dead bodies. What other words do you associate with the word 'explosion'?

The source of this poem was a documentary Larkin watched on the coal-mining industry. The poem gives an account of an underground accident in which a number of miners lost their lives. Many of the miners' wives were supposed to have seen visions of their husbands at the moment of the explosion. Larkin also said, 'I heard a song about a mine disaster … it made me want to write the same thing, a mine disaster with a vision of immortality at the end … that's the point of the eggs.'

The poem opens quietly as the scene is observed in **stanza one** and we are gently led into the drama: 'On the day of the explosion'. Notice the word 'the'. This is a specific event that will affect specific people. The details give a premonition of disaster: 'Shadows pointed towards the pithead'. The alliteration of the explosive letter 'p' adds to the menace, as does the personification: 'slagheap slept'. The image of a sleeping monster that will wreak havoc if awoken is suggested. The alliteration of 's' emphasises the **uneasy peace**.

In contrast, along come the noisy miners, swearing and coughing in **stanza two**. An impression of proud, ordinary, strong young men from the tough world of the mines is given in a few well-chosen details: 'pitboots', 'Coughing oath-edged talk and pipe-smoke'. The **onomatopoeia** in the line 'Shouldering off the freshened silence' gives an idea of their rough strength. They walk unknowing, but we know and this adds to the growing tension and suspense in the poem. We are brought closer to the miners in **stanza three** as we observe them playing about. One chases rabbits, but comes back with a 'nest of lark's eggs'. He 'shows' the eggs. These are men who are interested in and deeply respectful of nature. He 'lodged' the eggs in the grasses, where the mother bird could find them. We see the sensitivity in these tough men.

The miners are part of a close-knit community, as we learn in **stanza four**: 'Fathers, brothers, nicknames, laughter'. The poignancy is becoming unbearable for the reader as we realise all will be blown apart by the event that is about to occur. The 'tall gates' are waiting, 'standing open', almost like the gates of the underworld, inescapable. These men meet their fate in **stanza five** ('So they passed'). The **language is almost biblical**. The ending is becoming inevitable. Larkin records the accident calmly, without melodrama. Instead we are presented with the ripple effects of the explosion on nature: 'cows/Stopped chewing' and the sun 'dimmed' as it was supposed to have done at the crucifixion of Christ. Time stands still. The explosion only registered for a 'second'. This is in contrast with the world of the men, where nothing will ever be the same again. But the rescue and the grief are unmentioned. We are left to imagine the horror.

In the final part of the poem (**stanzas six to nine**), the focus is changed. Now we are looking at the wives and their reactions to the deaths. The passage from the Bible is in italics, words of comfort, a certainty of resurrection: 'We shall see them face to face'. The wives believe this so strongly that they have a glimpse of their husbands and sons 'for a second'. Notice the difference of the reaction of the wives and the animals. The women's lives are irrevocably changed, but the animals resume their grazing. This terrible tragedy is of no consequence to the world of nature. They are unable to explain this vision 'Somehow'. These men are as they were and also are now transformed, 'Larger than in life'. They are walking in brilliant light. The sun is now the blazing sun of eternity. They are 'Gold as on a coin', a pure and enduring metal. The **rhythm is stately and formal**, which suits the religious viewpoint.

The poem ends on a note of affirmation, with the **potent image** of the unbroken eggs suggesting the hope of resurrection, the continuity of life and the strength of the ties of love. The **last line** stands alone, separated from the eight other three-line stanzas. Larkin's scepticism is absent. He is moved by sympathy for these men and their families. As the poet has said (in 'An Arundel Tomb'), 'What will survive of us is love'. This is the last poem in his last collection of poetry. Is it being suggested that love triumphs over death? Is this a modern religious poem?

ANALYSIS

'Memorable imagery illustrates the beautiful, consoling poetry of Philip Larkin.' Discuss this statement with reference to 'The Explosion'.

Sample Paragraph

Larkin captures the scene on the day of the explosion with a few well-chosen visual details. He alerts the reader to the possibility of disaster with the sinister image of the 'shadows' which 'pointed towards the pithead', almost as if they were arrows of destiny marking the target of the miners. The air of menace is further emphasised with the memorable image of the slagheap as it 'slept' in the sun. The personification suggests a sleeping monster that will cause chaos if woken up. The image of the 'tall gates standing open' appealed to me, as it suggested the entry of the men into death's kingdom. The long vowel sounds slow the line. Death does not know time. These vowels, 'a' and 'o', lend a stately, solemn rhythm to the phrase, which reminds me of a ceremonial funeral march. The final image, contained in the floating last line, 'One showing the eggs unbroken', is full of optimism and hope, as it reminds me of Easter and the Resurrection of Christ. The image reflects a rare moment when Larkin has a positive attitude towards a Christian afterlife. The little eggs suggest renewal, the beginning of a new era. Larkin has laid aside his cynicism. The poem ends on this memorable image of transcendence, making the poem a beautiful religious credo.

Examiner's Comment

This is a succinct and well-controlled paragraph showing a close knowledge of the text. Expressive language use: 'These vowels, "a" and "o", lend a stately solemn rhythm to the phrase, which reminds me of a ceremonial funeral march'. Fluent writing throughout and effective use of quotation raise the answer to the highest grade.

CLASS/HOMEWORK EXERCISES

1. Write a paragraph on how the structure of the poem helps Larkin communicate his theme effectively. (Look at the arrangement of the stanzas scene by scene on the page, the use of run-on lines, the placement of key words, the use of italics and the separate last line.)

2. 'Many of Philip Larkin's poems are known for their underlying tension.' To what extent is this true of 'The Explosion'? Support your answer with reference to the poem.

SUMMARY POINTS

- The universality of death, the preciousness of life and the human need for a reassuring afterlife are central themes.
- Narrative/descriptive details portray the miners in all their ordinariness.
- Variety of tones – impersonal, subdued, sympathetic, formal, positive.
- Effective use of sound, contrast, imagery, metaphor and personification.

CUT GRASS

Cut grass lies frail:
Brief is the breath
Mown stalks exhale.
Long, long the death

It dies in the white hours
Of young-leafed June
With chestnut flowers,
With hedges snowlike strewn,

White lilac bowed,
Lost lanes of Queen Anne's lace,
And that high-builded cloud
Moving at summer's pace.

'Lost lanes of Queen Anne's lace'

Glossary

2   *Brief is the breath*: life is short (the Bible says: 'all the glory of man is as flowers of grass').

8   *strewn*: covered untidily.

10   *Queen Anne's lace*: cow parsley, a white wild flower with lace-like blooms.

INITIAL RESPONSE

1. This poem gives a picture of a rural landscape. What colour predominates? List three examples. What is the colour white usually associated with? (Innocence, weddings, funeral flowers, purity, etc.) In your opinion, why does Larkin use this colour?

2. In your opinion, what is the mood of the poem? Does it change or not? Give evidence from the text to support your view.

3. Write a paragraph giving your own personal response to this poem. Refer closely to the text in your answer.

STUDY NOTES

'Cut Grass' is a lyric dealing with a recurring theme in Larkin's poetry: passing time and death. Written in 1971, it appeared in his collection High Windows. *It is a calm poem that Larkin saw as a 'succession of images'. His verdict was, 'I like it all right'. Yet it was written at the end of Larkin's life, when he was very bitter about the state of England ('what an end to a great country'). He was critical of socialism and immigrants: 'I have always been right wing ... I identify with certain virtues (thrift, hard work, reverence, desire to preserve).'*

    The Bible states that 'All flesh is grass'. The title of 'Cut Grass' echoes this classic theme implicitly as we are reminded of the figure of Father Time/Death with his scythe. All living things are mown down. The setting of this poem is a meadow that has been recently mown. 'Cut grass lies frail' suggests the fragility and brevity of life against the relentless approach of inescapable death. The word 'frail' almost seems to expire as its sound drifts away at the end of the **first line** of **stanza one**. The short, unpredictable life of the grass is eloquently captured in the alliterative phrase 'Brief is the breath'. Explosive 'b' sounds reflect the action of breathing in and out. This **personification**, continued in the verb 'exhale', implies the parallel between our tenuous hold on life and that of all living things. The full stop at the end of this line underscores the reality of death and its finality. In contrast to this, the first stanza runs on into the next stanza to emphasise the fact that death is endless; it is not subject to time: 'Long, long the death'.

Stanza two tells us when the grass in the meadow dies, just at the moment when all other things are growing profusely. The trees are beginning to come into leaf and the hedges are covered in foaming whitethorn, like snow ('snowlike strewn'). The alliteration and **run-on lines** suggest the abundance of nature. Nature has the ability to renew itself, as the compound word 'young-leafed' suggests. We wonder: can man renew himself? The assonance ('hours', 'flowers') adds a poignant, melancholy note to this stanza, as in the midst of life is death.

In the **third stanza**, this abundance continues as the succession of beautiful white images mirror each other: 'White lilac bowed' flows into frothy 'lanes of Queen Anne's lace'. This wild flower appears every summer in out-of-the way lanes throughout rural England. Is this poem also an elegy for a disappearing England? The **alliteration** of 'l' suggests the meandering, winding lanes of the countryside. Towering white clouds add to this picture of rural serenity, as they glide effortlessly by, 'Moving at summer's pace'. But all will die in their own time. This elegy is like a lament or requiem, its long vowel sounds suggesting the lingering of the bereaved, unwilling to let the dead go. The poet's tone is sympathetic, resigned to the inevitable.

Here is no Christian consolation, no exhortation to live life passionately. The two-sentence poem is divided into short, abrupt phrases at the start which showcase the harsh finality of death. The poem then moves into the long run-on lines of the second sentence, which is stately and dignified and is suitable for a lament. The **regular rhyme scheme** (*abab, cdcd, efef*) underpins the fact that time passes and death comes; it is unavoidable. Larkin clearly valued traditional English poetry forms, as he valued England.

ANALYSIS

'Larkin said he wrote two kinds of poetry, "the beautiful and the true". Discuss this statement, with reference to 'Cut Grass'.

Sample Paragraph

In my opinion, Larkin has indeed written a poem that resonates with truth. There is no escaping the sad finality of all human existence, 'Brief is the breath'. The poet does not give us any consolation either in this elegy. The real truth of human mortality floats in our consciousness as timeless and as inevitable as the 'high-builded cloud' floats in the sky on a summer's day. I also think this poem is beautiful, as the succession of idyllic images which are truly English are presented to us. The smell of cut grass is suggested in the evocative line 'Mown stalks exhale'. The abundance and generosity of nature is shown in the alliterative phrase 'hedges snowlike strewn'. But for me the real beauty of the poem lies in the musical writing. It reminds me of a song lyric. The assonance of long vowel sounds ('Long, long') and slender vowels ('White lilac') evoke long, lazy summer evenings that are quintessentially English. The melancholic phrase 'Lost lanes' seems to be lamenting a lost way of life, as well as death, as the 'l' sound lingers on the ear. Larkin is a superb craftsman. The gentle fading sounds of the words 'frail' and 'exhale' both disappear, as all individual existence does into the inevitability of death. The finality of death is punctuated sternly by the full stop after 'exhale'. The compound words 'young-leafed', 'high-builded' show the beauty of life. The regular rhyme scheme (*abab*, *cdcd*, *efef*) moves as effortlessly as the clouds 'at summer's pace'. Larkin expresses a classic, true theme in a beautiful way. Like him, I like this poem 'all right'.

Examiner's Comment

This top grade paragraph addresses the two elements of the question ('beautiful' and 'true'). It shows a real appreciation of poetic technique: 'The assonance of long vowel sounds ("Long, long") and slender vowels ("White lilac") evoke long, lazy summer evenings that are quintessentially English'. Fluent expression, particularly the impressive vocabulary, results in a strong, successful answer.

CLASS/HOMEWORK EXERCISES

1. Larkin's poems show 'loneliness, emptiness and mortality'. Do you agree that this is true of 'Cut Grass'? Refer to the text in your answer.

2. Comment on Larkin's use of sound in 'Cut Grass'. Refer closely to the poem in your answer.

SUMMARY POINTS

- Key themes – the cycle of life and death.
- Short lyric form evokes the frailty and brevity of life.
- While the tone is poignant and elegiac, it is not solely negative.
- Effective use of imagery, personification, regular rhyme and onomatopoeia.

LEAVING CERT SAMPLE ESSAY

'Philip Larkin explores the darker side of life, but with a warm, compassionate voice.' Discuss this statement, supporting the points you make with suitable reference to the poems by Larkin on your course.

Marking Scheme Guidelines

Candidates are free to agree and/or disagree with the given statement. However, they should show clear evidence of personal engagement with the poetry of Philip Larkin. The key terms ('darker side of life' and 'warm, compassionate voice') should be addressed either implicitly or explicitly. Allow for a wide range of approaches in the answering.

Indicative material:

- Ambivalent attitude to love, death, religion
- Larkin projects a misleading/enigmatic persona
- Widely varying tones and atmospheres
- Can be seen to celebrate/criticise ordinary English life
- Ambiguous interpretation of his imagery
- Fatalistic/pessimistic attitude, etc.

Sample Essay

(Larkin explores the darker side of life with a warm, compassionate voice)

1. Philip Larkin seems to enjoy adopting a morose persona. His subject matter can be dark and he can be a very critical poetic voice. Larkin often reflects on the futility of life and the inevitability of death e.g. in his poem, 'Ambulances'. Elsewhere, he addresses random tragedy in a sympathetic way ('The Explosion'). His tone is sometimes filled with gloom and melancholy, 'Brief is the breath'. He can be critical, 'differently-dressed servants'. Yet I like Larkin's poetry because he celebrates the healing power of love and marriage ('Wedding Wind'). Many of his poems reveal an affection for English communities and ordinary people. He explores how love transcends time ('An Arundel Tomb'). At times, his imagery is beautiful and affirmative and I enjoy his dry sense of humour.

2. I don't know of a more touchingly tender moment than that described in 'An Arundel Tomb'. At first, the poet seems detached at the sight of the tomb of the Earl of Arundel and his wife. Their faces are 'blurred', worn by time. The 'little dogs under their feet' are that 'faint hint of the absurd'. But the poet draws the reader's attention 'with a sharp tender shock' to this detail of affection. The Earl's 'hand is withdrawn, holding her hand'. The alliteration of 'h' and the stately rhythm emphasise the importance of close human relationships. Can love transcend time in this 'stone fidelity'? The poem's last line states 'What

will survive of us is love'. Even if 'Only an attitude remains', I am comforted that the message is one of lasting love.

3. Love is also the subject of 'Wedding Wind'. Larkin adopts the persona of a young bride, 'I can imagine … the emotions of a bride'. I found it interesting that life lived by ordinary people should be a subject for poetry. The imperfect detail, 'I/Carry a chipped pail to the chicken run' and mundane sight of 'My apron and the hanging cloths on the line' glow due to the skill of the poet. Irritating jobs may have to be endured, but they are transfigured by the joy of the young woman, 'this bodying forth by wind/Of joy my actions turn on'. These actions are 'like a thread carrying beads'. The sacrament of marriage is vividly evoked by this simile. I realised that these ordinary actions form part of the state of holy matrimony. The young woman feels so blessed she wonders 'Can even death dry up/These new delighted lakes'. Larkin has celebrated passionate young love in the English countryside.

4. 'Ambulances' reflect Larkin's view of life's futility. An ambulance arrives, a common experience in modern life. But Larkin adds 'They come to rest at any kerb'. Suddenly the perspective has changed. The reader and the bystanders all hope that their time will not come soon. I found the way the poet allowed the second last stanza rush into the last one very interesting as I now became aware that it was mimicking what was happening. All ties were unravelling for the sick person. All that was familiar was receding, 'the unique random blend/Of families and fashions, there/At last begin to loosen'. Here is a poet who is compassionate, who understands what it means to be human, and how terrifying it must be as sickness 'dulls to distance all we are'.

5. Philip Larkin can also be dryly humorous. In his affectionate account of a summer train journey, 'The Whitsun Weddings', I enjoyed the seaside postcard sketches of 'mothers loud and fat;/An uncle shouting smut; and then the perms,/The nylon gloves and jewellery-substitutes'. But he also made me think about the reality of families parting and changing as children set off on their new lives and parents are left behind, 'The last confetti and advice were thrown'. The sheer richness of the experience of life is described.

6. Larkin explores death, the banal every day, sickness and the vulgarity of ordinary life. In my opinion, the reason Philip Larkin is popular is not because of his exploration of cruelty and fear, but because the warm voice of the poet emerges. The detail of the held hand, the image of the 'thread carrying beads', the compassion for the aloneness of the sick, 'Far from the exchange of love to lie', the heightened exciting distant 'arrow shower … becoming rain' all remain in my memory. For me the sympathetic voice of the poet in the midst of life's traumas is the reason for Larkin's enduring popularity.

(approx. 740 words)

Examiner's Comment

A well-organised essay, confidently written and showing some close personal engagement with Larkin's poetry: 'In my opinion, the reason Philip Larkin is popular is not because of his exploration of cruelty and fear, but because the warm voice of the poet emerges'. Some points deserve fuller discussion, e.g. 'The Whitsun Weddings' is superficially treated in Paragraph 5. However, there is effective use of quotations and the expression throughout is impressive.

MARKING SCHEME
P = 15/15
C = 13/15
L = 15/15
M = 5/5
Total = 48/50

SAMPLE LEAVING CERT QUESTIONS ON LARKIN'S POETRY

1. 'Philip Larkin speaks intimately to the reader about love and loss through visual images, metaphors and sound effects.' Do you agree with this assessment of his poetry? Your answer should focus on his themes and the way he expresses them. Support the points you make with suitable reference to the poems by Larkin on your course.

2. 'A dark ironic wit energises Larkin's realistic reflections on mortality and immortality.' Discuss this statement, supporting your answer with suitable reference to the poetry by Larkin on your course.

3. 'Larkin's poems explore the lives of ordinary people in a poetic style that is elegant and understated.' Discuss this statement, supporting your answer with reference to the poetry of Philip Larkin on your course.

Sample Essay Plan (Q1)

'Philip Larkin speaks intimately to the reader about love and loss through visual images, metaphors and sound effects.' Do you agree with this assessment of his poetry? Your answer should focus on his themes and the way he expresses them. Support the points you make with suitable reference to the poems by Larkin on your course.

- Intro: Identify the elements of the question to be addressed ('intimately', themes of mortality and love, using the techniques of 'visual images, metaphors and sound effects'). The observant eyes of Larkin compassionately view relevant and recurring themes of transience, death and love. He faces up to universal fears honestly while maintaining compassion for the ordinary individual.

- Point 1: 'Wedding Wind' – by adopting the persona of a young bride, Larkin celebrates the joy of passionate love and also its everyday irritants through vivid imagery ('All's ravelled under the sun') and powerful similes ('like a thread/Carrying beads').

- Point 2: 'Cut Grass' – quiet exploration of the fragility and brevity of life through the predominance of the colour white ('hedges snowlike strewn'), explosive sound effects ('Brief is the breath') and effective personification ('Mown stalks exhale').

- Point 3: 'The Explosion' – captures the random nature of disastrous events. Menace of impending doom shown through personification: 'the slagheap slept'. Uplifting, affirming images: 'Gold as on a coin', 'showing the eggs unbroken'.

- Point 4: 'The Trees' – celebration of human resilience and courage in the face of certain death. Use of present continuous tense, sibilance and an even rhyme scheme gently give a positive outlook.

- Point 5: 'Ambulances' – indiscriminate nature of disaster in human affairs graphically described through evocative imagery ('Closed like confessionals') and sound effects ('A wild white face').

- Conclusion: Larkin speaks quietly about the terrifying aspects of life, transience, disaster and death, sometimes offering comfort, sometimes accepting what cannot be changed. He celebrates love by showing ordinary people doing ordinary things.

Sample Essay Plan (Q1)

Develop one of the above points into a paragraph.

Sample Paragraph: Point 2

In the calm elegy 'Cut Grass', Larkin conjures up an idealised image of rural England that was fast disappearing: 'White lilac bowed,/Lost lanes of Queen Anne's lace'. The long vowel sounds 'a' and 'o' convey the reluctance of letting go of something precious. The poet does not offer comfort in this lyrical exploration of the finality of death, starkly stating 'Brief is the breath'. The explosive 'b' sounds mimic the in-and-out motion of inhaling and exhaling, a true sign of life. Through personification, 'Cut grass lies frail', 'Mown stalks exhale', the finality of death is presented. Here the reader comes face to face with the tenuous hold on life and the finality of death. The full stop emphasises the reality from which there is no escape while the run-on line stresses limitless death: 'Long, long the death /It dies'. The dignified tone of the poem brought home clearly to me the chilling message that time cuts down all living things. In the regular rhyme scheme ('frail', 'exhale'; 'breath', 'death'), Larkin effortlessly captures the unavoidable fact that we all disappear into the inevitable unknown after death. Confidentially, as if speaking to a child, this poet allows us to look at the reality of his human existence and experience the still, sad music of humanity.

Examiner's Comment

This engaging personal response focuses on the poet's techniques used to recall the secluded English countryside: sound effects, use of metaphor, personification, vivid verbs and tactile imagery.

'In the regular rhyme scheme ("frail", "exhale"; "breath", "death"), Larkin effortlessly captures the unavoidable fact that we all disappear into the inevitable unknown after death'. Expressive language raises this paragraph to the top grade.

LAST WORDS

'Larkin's poems are melancholy, melodious, disenchanted, bewitching, perfectly written and perfectly approachable.'

Seamus Heaney

'People marvelled that a poet they had never met could have spoken to them so intimately.'

Andrew Motion

'I want readers to feel yes, I've never thought of it that way, but that's how it is.'

Philip Larkin

JOHN MONTAGUE

1929–

'Poetry is a weapon, a prayer before an unknown altar.'

The author of many books of poetry, stories and essays, John Montague has been called 'the greatest Irish poet of his generation' by Derek Mahon. Born to Catholic parents in New York, he returned to Garvaghey, County Tyrone, at the age of four to be raised by his father's sisters. As a schoolboy in St Patrick's College, Armagh, Montague developed an interest in Irish poetry. His first poems were published when he was a student at University College Dublin in the late 1940s. He has since travelled the world as poet, teacher and journalist, but all the while keeping a literary and emotional anchor in Ireland. Family and personal history – as well as Irish history – are central themes in his poetry. The love and legend of Ireland permeate his work; people and places from his own past continually capture his attention. Other recurring themes include nature, isolation, relationships, exile and personal loss. The purposeful use of vowel sounds, line breaks and natural speech rhythms are all notable features of his writing style. Montague has succeeded in recording memories and expressing feelings of a common humanity. It has made him one of the most influential figures in the international evolution of Irish poetry in modern times.

To find out more about John Montague, or to hear readings of his poems, you could do a search of some of the useful websites available such as YouTube, bbc.co.uk and poetryarchive.org or access additional material on this page of your eBook.

Prescribed Poems — HIGHER LEVEL

❶ 'Killing the Pig'
The routine violence of traditional farm life is central to this dramatic memoir from the poet's childhood. Haunting sound effects and vivid details convey the lingering horror of the pig's death. Montague himself remains a compassionate witness throughout the stage-by-stage slaughtering process. **358**

❷ 'The Trout'
Another intense boyhood memory reflecting Montague's closeness to the natural world. In this atmospheric reconstruction, precise imagery and controlled rhythm capture the intimacy and tension of the poet's unforgettable experience when he used his hands to fish in a small stream. **363**

❸ 'The Locket'*
This poignant poem explores the uneasy relationship between Montague and his mother, who had difficulty expressing her feelings openly. The poet finds some comfort and a 'mysterious blessing' in discovering that the oval locket she always wore contained his photograph. **367**

❹ 'The Cage'*
In a characteristically honest reflection, the poet records the unhappy life and death of his father, a 'traditional Irishman' who had left Ireland to find work in New York. The cage is a powerful symbol of 'lost years' of exile, and the distant relationship between father and son. **372**

❺ 'Windharp'
The timeless beauty of Ireland's windswept landscape is caught in this short poem. Within an extended single sentence, Montague combines memorable aural and tactile images with a series of sensuous word pictures to evoke the 'restless whispering' of the distinctive Irish countryside. **378**

❻ 'All Legendary Obstacles'

One of Montague's best-known love poems, it is set against the dramatic landscape of America's vast western plains and a Californian railway station where two lovers are reunited. With honest realism, this tense drama addresses both the hope and uncertainty involved in a romantic relationship. **382**

❼ 'The Same Gesture'

This deeply personal poem explores the realisation that the same gesture can take on a different meaning depending on the setting and circumstances. Using rich imagery and evocative description, Montague celebrates the exclusive relationship between two lovers in their 'secret room'. **387**

❽ 'Like Dolmens Round My Childhood'*

A series of powerful pen portraits vividly showcases some of the eccentric individuals and lonely figures scattered through the harsh rural terrain of County Tyrone where the poet grew up. As always, Montague writes about communities which belong to an older lifestyle with sensitivity and realism. **391**

❾ 'The Wild Dog Rose'

Montague's vivid portrayal of a brutal assault on an elderly spinster is haunting and uncomfortable throughout. While revealing the darker side of Irish rural life, the poet's sympathetic description of human loneliness concludes with the enduring image of the wild flower, 'the only rose without thorns'. **398**

❿ 'A Welcoming Party'

The poem recalls a school visit on that 'dead Sunday in Armagh' to view newsreel films about World War Two. The horrifying conditions of the Nazi camps made a lifelong impact. Characteristically, the poem reflects Montague's emotional honesty in addressing important themes which have universal significance. **405**

1 KILLING THE PIG

The noise.

He was pulled out, squealing,
an iron cleek sunk in the roof
of his mouth.

(Don't say they are not intelligent: 5
they know the hour has come
and they want none of it;
they dig in their little trotters,
will not go dumb or singing
to the slaughter.) 10

That high-pitched final effort,
no single sound could match it –

a big plane roaring off,
a diva soaring towards her last note,
the brain-chilling persistence of an electric saw, 15
scrap being crushed.

Piercing & absolute,
only high heaven ignores it.

Then a full stop.
Mickey Boyle plants 20
a solid thump of the mallet
flat between the ears.

Swiftly the knife seeks the throat;
swiftly the other cleavers work
till the carcass is hung up 25
shining and eviscerated as
a surgeon's coat.

A child is given
the bladder to play with.
But the walls of the farmyard 30
still hold that scream,
are built around it.

'shining and eviscerated'

Glossary

3 *cleek*: metal hook.
8 *trotters*: the pig's feet.
14 *diva*: famous female opera singer.
15 *persistence*: perseverance.
21 *mallet*: wooden hammer.

24 *cleavers*: instruments used for cutting meat.
25 *carcass*: dead body.
26 *eviscerated*: gutted.
29 *bladder*: the pig's inflatable urinary organ.

INITIAL RESPONSE

1. How, in your opinion, does Montague feel about the killing of the pig? Refer to the poem in your answer.

2. Comment on the four images the poet uses to describe the noise of the pig's screeching (lines 10–16). Which image conveyed the pig's squeals most effectively? Briefly explain why.

3. Write your own personal response to the poem. Were you shocked, disgusted, unperturbed…? Explain your answer.

STUDY NOTES

'Killing the Pig' is a powerful dramatisation of an event which is familiar and even routine to some people, but which shocks and disturbs others. Throughout the poem, John Montague is a compassionate witness at a slaughtering and he leaves readers to reflect on profound questions of morality and humanity. In recalling another childhood experience, the poet presents the farmyard killing through typically conversational language.

The fragmented form of the poem's opening creates a suitable subtext for the cruel event that is about to take place. Two terse words ('The noise'), set the scene in motion. The title clarifies the deed: 'Killing the Pig'. Montague chooses to use the definite article ('the') in obvious recognition of the animal's distinctiveness. In **line 2**, the pig is described as 'He', a further acknowledgement of the animal's unique life-force. All the focus is on the violence and indignity being wreaked on the pig as it is 'pulled out'. **The desperate terror of shrill resistance can be heard** in the onomatopoeic verb 'squealing'. Montague's haunting verbal music is dissonant and harsh, with hard 'k' sounds suggesting the brute force with which the pig is being handled. The disturbing image of a sharp iron hook sunk into the pale 'roof/of his mouth' contrasts with the pig's vulnerable pink flesh.

The poet's tone becomes increasingly didactic. Lines **5–10** anticipate the customary claim that animals are unaware of being slaughtered, an argument which is often used to justify their treatment.

In an angry comment placed inside parentheses (brackets), Montague states: 'Don't say they are not intelligent'. Insisting that they know what is to happen 'and they want none of it', he humanises the terrified pigs: 'they dig in their little trotters'. The adjective 'little' underpins the animals' defencelessness. Readers are not given the luxury of imagining the pigs 'singing to the slaughter', happily going unawares to meet their fate. Instead, **the poet does not allow us to ease our consciences** by denying the reality of what is happening. He emphasises the terrible noise – 'That high pitched final effort' as the pig protests in vain. In **line 12**, its unique wail is alliteratively caught, 'no single sound could match it'.

Montague employs four contemporary **metaphors to convey the animal's frantic voice**. Like the ear-splitting noise of a plane 'roaring off', it drowns out all other sound. The onomatopoeic 'roaring' echoes the 'soaring' song of the famous opera singer striving to reach the glass-shattering 'last note'. Will the pig's traumatised scream also be his final note? The animal's relentless squeals are compared to a rasping 'electric saw' in the aptly extended **line 15**. A final aural image ('scrap being crushed') is brusque, perhaps suggesting that the pig is easily disposable and of as little consequence as everyday rubbish. Again, the discordant hard 'c' records the ordeal of the killing indelibly on both poet and reader.

For Montague, **this sound is beyond compare**, 'Piercing & absolute' (**line 17**). The pig's dying high-pitched cry forces its way into our consciousness. But surprisingly, 'high heaven ignores it'. Is the poet suggesting God's indifference to the suffering of his creation? Inevitably, the awful drama ends ('Then a full stop') marking a clear change of mood as Montague's observant eye pans around the farmyard. There is a cinematic quality to his description of the actual slaughtering process. Montague recalls the concentration of 'Mickey Boyle' who carries out the various stages of his task with impassive efficiency. Initially, he 'plants' the wooden mallet with a 'solid thump' to stun the pig before killing it. Like a surgeon, he acts deftly using deliberate movements. The butcher's knife is personified – 'it seeks the throat'. Montague carefully avoids giving any graphic details of blood-letting, but uses antiseptic imagery to depict the hanging carcass, 'shining and eviscerated'.

In the aftermath of the killing, the mood is lifted momentarily in the **last stanza** as a child is given the pig's bladder 'to play with'. **For the farming community, this has been an everyday act.** But the poet chooses to end the poem by singling out the unforgettable horror of what has happened – etched in his memory by 'that scream'. The walls where the animal suffered such a cruel fate reverberate with the alarming sound and Montague himself will forever associate that place with the fearful cry.

'Killing the Pig' typifies John Montague, the compassionate image-maker. Most of his subject matter comes from personal experience. As always, the **poet's tone is open to various interpretations**. Is he criticising people for their cruelty to animals? Or does he accept that suffering is a routine part of traditional farm practice? What is beyond doubt is his own sympathy for the terrified animal. The pig's frightened resistance to its imminent doom continues to echo through the deserted yard. 'The noise' remains.

ANALYSIS

'The harshness of life looms large in Montague's poetry.' Discuss this view with particular reference to 'Killing the Pig'.

Sample Paragraph

John Montague certainly does not shirk from the harsh cruelties of life. He faces them squarely and helps the reader to confront unpleasant realities. In 'Killing the Pig', the distress of the unfortunate animal is seen in the dramatic two-word opening, 'The noise'. The savage treatment of the pig is illustrated by the grim contrast of the brutal 'iron cleek sunk in the roof' of the pig's mouth. This poet spared me none of the brutality. He even dismisses the usual excuses of a 'dumb' animal totally unaware of knowing what is happening to it. Instead I was forced, just as the pig 'was pulled out', to face the awfulness of its cruel fate and his hopeless protest. I found the poem was most powerful in conveying the pig's terror through Montague's focus on the squeals, 'Piercing and relentless', 'no single sound could match it'. Four very powerful images of totally mind-blowing noise push the message home – the ear-shattering sound of the plane as it takes off, the tragic 'last note' of the opera singer, the totally 'brain-chilling' drone of the non-stop 'electric saw', the brutal image of 'scrap being crushed'. The last three lines compel us to recognise the pitiless reality of farm-life. Even though the pig ends up just a 'carcass', 'hung up/shining and eviscerated', its 'scream' still totally dominates the farmyard in the memory of the poet. Similarly in 'The Trout', Montague faces up to the harshness of life. Long after the fish has been caught, Montague can still 'taste' the fish's 'terror' on his hands.

Examiner's Comment

This is a generally focused attempt at addressing the question personally. Suitable references and quotations show very good engagement with the poem. The expression varies at times, but is mostly fluent. 'The savage treatment of the pig is illustrated by the grim contrast of the "brutal cleek sunk in the roof" of the pig's mouth'. The word 'totally' is over-used. This uncertain control of language results in the answer just missing the top grade.

CLASS/HOMEWORK EXERCISES

1. 'Montague's poetry describes the reality of being human.' Discuss this statement in relation to the poems of Montague studied by you on your course. Refer closely to the texts in your response.
2. 'Small dramas define many of John Montague's most memorable poems.' Discuss this statement, with particular reference to 'Killing the Pig'.

SUMMARY POINTS

- Key themes include the violent treatment of animals, memory and coming-of-age.
- Graphic imagery and metaphors convey the drama and cruelty of farm life.
- Varied tones and moods: fear, outrage, confusion, sympathy.
- Powerful aural effects (assonance, echo, alliteration) enhance meaning.

THE TROUT

for Barrie Cooke

Flat on the bank I parted
Rushes to ease my hands
In the water without a ripple
And tilt them slowly downstream
To where he lay, tendril-light,　　　　　　5
In his fluid sensual dream.

Bodiless lord of creation,
I hung briefly above him
Savouring my own absence,
Senses expanding in the slow　　　　　　10
Motion, the photographic calm
That grows before action.

As the curve of my hands
Swung under his body
He surged, with visible pleasure.　　　　15
I was so preternaturally close
I could count every stipple
But still cast no shadow, until

The two palms crossed in a cage
Under the lightly pulsing gills.　　　　　20
Then (entering my own enlarged
Shape, which rode on the water)
I gripped. To this day I can
Taste his terror on my hands.

'In his fluid sensual dream'

Glossary

Dedication: Barrie Cooke, prominent abstract impressionist artist and keen fisherman. Montague shared his fascination with the world of nature.
5   *tendril-light*: delicate, thread-like.
6   *fluid*: flowing, graceful.
6   *sensual*: pleasurable.
15 *surged*: sudden powerful movement.
16 *preternaturally*: beyond what is normal or natural.
17 *stipple*: speckled mark or dot.
20 *gills*: respiratory organs of fish.

INITIAL RESPONSE

1. Trace the poet's feelings as he pursues the fish and catches it. Refer closely to the poem in your response.

2. Choose two images from the poem which you found effective. Briefly explain your choice in each case.

3. Did you find the final two lines of the poem convincing or not? Refer to the text in your response.

STUDY NOTES

John Montague is a poet of place and emotion who is fascinated by the natural world and has great respect for its beauty. This eloquent poem is based on a vivid childhood memory when he used his hands to fish in a small stream. Montague's voice is clear and coherent, expressing an intensity of thought and emotion. The precision of image is characteristic of his work.

    This lyrical memory poem captures two contrasting perspectives, the beauty of nature and the thrill of the hunt. Montague freeze-frames a specific moment from his childhood in compelling detail. He recalls his experience lying 'Flat on the bank', catching fish with his bare hands. **Stanza one** traces the **increasing anticipation and tension** as the boy gently eases his hands into 'the water without a ripple' so that the trout remains undisturbed. The line break, 'I parted/Rushes', mimics the movement of quietly separating the undergrowth to allow the sliding of his hands into position. The boy's concentration is presented through a series of dramatic verbs ('parted', 'ease', 'tilt') which highlight his close knowledge of the natural environment. The tranquil beauty of the trout is beautifully depicted, 'he lay, tendril-light/In his fluid sensual dream'. The compound word emphasises the fragility of this marvellous creature. Montague's understated verbal music (particularly the assonant vowel 'i' and sibilant 's' sounds) showcases the glistening fish as it lies in a secure womb-like state of innocence.

The boy's sense of wonder at this serene creature in its natural idyll gives way to a feeling of control in **stanza two**. Suddenly conscious that he can be considered a 'Bodiless lord of creation' who possesses the power of life or death over the fish, he imagines himself as a kind of divine being ('I hung briefly above him') who can now determine the trout's destiny. This feeling becomes transcendental and the boy is aware of the strangest sense ('Savouring my own absence') in what seems like an out-of-body encounter. The intensity of the boy's focus on the task in hand means that nothing else matters. **Time itself appears to be suspended**, 'Senses expanding in the slow/Motion'. Broad vowels restrain the rhythm of the line as meaning and movement harmonise to catch the shock of the moment.

Three final run-on lines in **stanza three** re-establish the pace as the boy acts swiftly: 'the curve of my hands/Swung under his body'. Momentarily, the fish 'surged', responding to the initial touch. The boy is now so 'preternaturally close' that he sees every mark ('stipple') on the trout's skin. For an instant, he instinctively understands the common life-force they share. Because the fish remains oblivious of its vulnerability, the sense of impending danger continues to intensify in **stanza four** as it is effectively trapped within the boy's 'two palms crossed in a cage'. Montague dramatises the confrontation and the boy's exhilaration as his 'own enlarged/Shape... rode on the water'. In this swiftly executed act, the trout's fate is decided: 'I gripped'. Finally, we hear the adult poet's reflective voice: 'To this day I can/Taste his terror on my hands.' The alliteration of the hard 't' sound suggests the **enduring guilt felt by the poet** at the memory of his attack on the panic-stricken fish. For Montague, the encounter between nature and human nature seems to mark a personal turning point. But what has he learned? Has he violated God's natural world?

ANALYSIS

John Montague has said: 'I think the ultimate function of the poet is to praise.' Discuss this statement in relation to his poem, 'The Trout'. Support the points you make with suitable reference to the text.

Sample Paragraph

Montague has called 'The Trout' his first love poem. He describes the fish – which he personifies throughout – in its natural element with all the tenderness of a lover. A magical, almost idealised figure of the dreaming trout is presented through visual detail and verbal music. The fish 'lay, tendril-light,/In his fluid sensual dream'. The soft 'l' combined with the assonance of the vowels 'i' and 'u' convey the stillness of the innocent creature. The beautiful patterns on the trout are depicted by the graphic word 'stipple' suggesting its glistening dotted markings. I also think the poet is praising the natural childhood activities of the countryside. The skill of the young boy as he slipped his hands into the water without disturbing the trout is evoked in the smooth run-on lines, 'ease my hands/In the water without a ripple/And tilt them slowly downstream/To where he lay'. But Montague is primarily a poet of compassion, especially for nature's creatures. In the alliterative last lines, he admits his guilt, 'To this day I can/Taste his terror on my hands'. The abrupt phrase, 'I gripped', describes the savage attack. He is aware that he disturbed the harmony of nature and killed one of its creatures. So, I think this poem is typical of Montague, the nature-lover. However, it is not only praising the beauty of nature, but it is also a poem of atonement as the poet seeks to remove his guilt over his act of desecration.

Examiner's Comment

This is a well-illustrated response which uses apt references to explore Montague's relationship with nature. Effective use is made of detailed reference: 'The soft "l" combined with the assonance of the vowels "i" and "u" convey the stillness of the innocent creature'. There is some good personal engagement with the poem. Expression throughout is highly impressive – 'A magical, almost idealised figure of the dreaming trout is presented through visual detail and verbal music'. A successful top grade answer.

CLASS/HOMEWORK EXERCISES

1. 'Among the welter of the world's voices… you find your own voice.' In what ways do you think Montague has succeeded in speaking in his own unique voice in poems such as 'The Trout'? Refer to both subject matter and the use of stylistic devices in your response.

2. 'Drama and tension are common features of Montague's poetry.' Discuss this statement, with particular reference to 'The Trout'.

SUMMARY POINTS

- Central themes include childhood, innocence and nature.
- Vivid detail and dramatic verbs capture the tense atmosphere.
- Effective use of evocative sounds – sibilance, alliteration, assonance.
- Contrasting tones/moods – wonder, apprehension, fear, guilt, tenderness.

THE LOCKET

Sing a last song
for the lady who has gone,
fertile source of guilt and pain.
The worst birth in the annals of Brooklyn,
that was my cue to come on,
my first claim to fame.

Naturally she longed for a girl,
and all my infant curls of brown
couldn't excuse my double blunder
coming out, both the wrong sex,
and the wrong way around.
Not readily forgiven,

So you never nursed me
and when my father's songs
couldn't sweeten the lack of money,
'when poverty comes through the door
love flies up the chimney',
your favourite saying.

Then you gave me away,
might never have known me,
if I had not cycled down
to court you like a young man,
teasingly untying your apron,
drinking by the fire, yarning

Of your wild, young days
which didn't last long, for you,
lovely Molly, the belle of your small town,
landed up mournful and chill
as the constant rain that lashes it
wound into your cocoon of pain.

Standing in that same hallway,
'Don't come again', you say, roughly,
'I start to get fond of you, John,

and then you are up and gone';
the harsh logic of a forlorn woman   35
resigned to being alone.

And still, mysterious blessing,
I never knew, until you were gone,
that always around your neck,
you wore an oval locket   40
with an old picture in it,
of a child in Brooklyn.

'mysterious blessing'

Glossary

- 4 *annals*: records, files.
- 4 *Brooklyn*: New York suburb where Montague was born in 1929.
- 5 *cue*: signal.
- 11 *the wrong way round*: difficult breech birth.
- 19 *you gave me away*: when he was four, Montague was sent home to Northern Ireland to be raised by his aunts.
- 24 *yarning*: telling stories.
- 27 *lovely Molly*: the poet's mother.
- 30 *cocoon*: heart, protected core.
- 35 *logic*: consideration, reasoning.
- 35 *forlorn*: lonely, forsaken.

INITIAL RESPONSE

1. In your view, what is the meaning or significance of the locket to the poet? Refer to the text of the poem in your answer.

2. How do your feelings towards Montague's mother change over the course of the poem?

3. Write a short personal response to the poem, highlighting its impact on you.

STUDY NOTES

John Montague has described 'The Locket' as 'a kind of ballad sung at my mother's funeral'. This lyrical lament for 'the lady' recounts the childhood experience of living without a mother's love. He did not fully address his hurt until he became an adult and wrote this autobiographical poem marking her passing. Although there is an underlying sense of loss throughout, the poignant narrative tone, half-rhyme and wry humour lighten the pervading gloom as the locket and its picture ultimately console the poet.

The opening lines of **stanza one** have the lively effect of a nursery rhyme, 'Sing a last song/for the lady who has gone'. Montague reflects on his lonely childhood when there was no mother's rhyme for this little boy. **He recognises the reality of their distant relationship**, the bleak mood highlighted by the repetition of 'a' and 'ai' sounds. Growing up, the poet was made to feel at fault, 'fertile source of guilt and pain'. He remains haunted by his mother's voice, rejecting him: 'The worst birth in the annals of Brooklyn'. This reference to his breech birth is wryly acknowledged as 'my first claim to fame'.

Throughout the **second stanza**, Montague's attitude towards his mother seems to be caught between sympathy and bitterness: 'Naturally she longed for a girl'. Does the poet now understand her desire? Or is he still filled with anger and self-pity over his 'double blunder'? There is little doubt, however, about his mother's initial resentment which left him 'Not readily forgiven'. This blunt statement leads into **stanza three** and points accusingly to the heart of the matter as Montague addresses his mother directly: 'So you never nursed me'. Although apparently unflattering, there is a growing **awareness of the pressures resulting from family poverty and his parents' failing marriage**. The mother's voice is heard again: 'when poverty comes through the door/love flies up the chimney'.

Stanza four opens with another frank accusation: 'Then you gave me away'. The plain language resounds with **the pain of the abandoned child**. Montague's mother returned to Ireland when he was seven, but was unwilling to make contact with him. Later, as a young man, he knew that their relationship would never be salvaged 'if I had not cycled down'. Looking back, he sees himself re-enacting his father's role courting her, 'teasingly untying your apron'. The verb 'yarning', with its broad vowel sound, spills over into **stanza five** mimicking their long conversations about his mother's 'wild, young days'. Compassionately, Montague notes that her carefree youth was short-lived. But while the lively repetition of 'l' highlights the prettiness of 'lovely Molly, the belle of our small town', this is immediately contrasted with the harsh reality of the woman she had become, 'mournful and chill'. Her difficult adult life is further emphasised by 'the constant rain', an effective simile for this sad woman. The final twisting line describes how Molly became wreathed into a claustrophobic state, 'wound into your cocoon of pain'.

Stanza six recalls the traumatic occasion when Montague's mother asked him to stop visiting: 'Don't come again'. Yet even here, there is a suggestion that he could appreciate her deep fear of expressing emotion and the prospect of further disappointment. It is difficult not to be moved by the tentative nature of their feelings. The poet now accepts the 'harsh logic of a forlorn woman' who would prefer to be alone rather than risk being touched by a close relationship. For her own reasons, she appears to be unable to communicate fully with her son. Despite the poem's central bleakness, the mood changes in **stanza seven**. Soft 's' sounds ease the desolate atmosphere as a 'mysterious blessing' occurs. Now that his mother is dead, Montague finds that in 'an oval locket' which she wore 'always', there is 'an old picture in it,/of a child in Brooklyn'. **The poet is both amazed and relieved by this secret gesture of unspoken love.** Significantly, he can come to terms with the past, knowing that she had never forgotten him and she did care for him, in her own way. He has finally been given the opportunity to forgive.

While most of Montague's memories have focused on the damaging influence of an unsatisfactory relationship, this is **essentially an unselfish poem** which explores his mother's life and decisions from her point of view. Moving between past and present, the poet allows us to hear her voice as well as his own. He also gives us an insight into an earlier time in Irish society when emotions were often oppressed. Such an intensely sensitive and honest approach is characteristic of Montague's poetry.

ANALYSIS

'Montague is an autobiographical poet.' In your opinion, does Montague attempt to live in the past? Explore this idea with reference to 'The Locket', supporting the points you make with reference to the poem.

Sample Paragraph

John Montague has written, 'A door closed when I was four, the separation from my mother… is at the centre of my emotional life'. In his poem, 'The Locket', Montague affectionately and openly re-evaluates the difficult relationship he had with his mother. She had endured a miserable life joining his father in New York in 1928 on the eve of the Great Depression. However, the emphasis of this poem is not, I believe, an effort to live or recapture the past. It is a study of the damaging influence of his mother on his own life. Montague makes the skeletons in the family cupboard 'dance' as he roundly accuses her of abandoning him three times, 'So you never nursed me', 'Then you gave me away', 'Don't come again'. But this poet and this poem are not like his mother, 'wound into' a 'cocoon of pain'. He is willing to accept her unspoken gesture, the 'mysterious blessing' of the 'oval locket/ with an old picture in it/of a child in Brooklyn'. He is willing to forgive. There is the astonishment, 'I never knew', of the poet as he realises that she had always secretly cared for him, although she had not articulated this love. In this revealing memoir, the mental anguish of being a displaced, unwanted child dissolves into the 'mysterious blessing' given by the locket his mother 'always' wore. The poem ends happily. We can clearly sense Montague's personal relief at not being rejected.

Examiner's Comment
This focused paragraph succeeds in addressing the central importance of Montague's awkward relationship with his mother: 'he roundly accuses her of abandoning him three times, "So you never nursed me", "Then you gave me away"'. The ideas are interesting throughout and firmly rooted in the accurate quotations from the text. Expression is also mature and well controlled, resulting in a top grade answer.

CLASS/HOMEWORK EXERCISES

1. 'John Montague is a chillingly realistic poet.' Discuss this statement referring closely to the poems on your prescribed course.

2. 'John Montague's quietly powerful language is ideally suited to his emotional subject matter.' Discuss this statement, with particular reference to 'The Locket'.

SUMMARY POINTS

- Key themes – childhood memories, the mother-son relationship, unspoken love.
- Personal narrative, using revealing anecdotes to reflect on the past.
- Contrasting moods of rejection, regret, yearning, happiness.
- Effective use of adjectives, direct speech, contrast and evocative imagery.

4 THE CAGE

My father, the least happy
man I have known. His face
retained the pallor
of those who work underground:
the lost years in Brooklyn 5
listening to a subway
shudder the earth.

But a traditional Irishman
who (released from his grille
in the Clark Street IRT) 10
drank neat whiskey until
he reached the only element
he felt at home in
any longer: brute oblivion.

And yet picked himself 15
up, most mornings,
to march down the street
extending his smile
to all sides of the good,
(all-white) neighbourhood 20
belled by St Teresa's church.

When he came back
we walked together
across fields of Garvaghey
to see hawthorn on the summer 25
hedges, as though
he had never left;
a bend on the road

which still sheltered
primroses. But we 30
did not smile in
the shared complicity
of a dream, for when
weary Odysseus returns
Telemachus should leave. 35

Often as I descend
into subway or underground
I see his bald head behind
the bars of the small booth;
the mark of an old car   40
accident beating on his
ghostly forehead.

'listening to a subway'

Glossary

- 3   *pallor*: pale look, unhealthy appearance.
- 5   *Brooklyn*: district in New York.
- 9   *grille*: screen of iron bars.
- 10 *I.R.T.*: New York subway, the Interborough Rapid Transport rail line.
- 14 *oblivion*: unawareness, unconsciousness.
- 24 *Garvaghey*: Co. Tyrone, birth place of the Montague family.
- 32 *complicity*: close involvement, connivance.
- 34 *Odysseus*: in Greek mythology, when Odysseus returned home from his epic voyage, his son Telemachus was eventually forced to leave.
- 39 *booth*: kiosk, enclosed cubicle.

INITIAL RESPONSE

1. In your opinion, what does the poem's title suggest about John Montague's father and his life? Refer closely to the text in your answer.

2. Identify and comment on the atmosphere or mood created by the poet in lines 21–34.

3. Write your own personal response to the poem, explaining its impact on you.

STUDY NOTES

'The poem on my father, "The Cage", sways between gloom and gaiety. It sways also between the Brooklyn of my birth – an urban background and the secret rural world of Garvaghey in Tyrone, where I grew up, and which in a way, had become my father's dreamscape'. (John Montague) The poet was born into a family of Irish exiles in Brooklyn in 1929, the year of the Great Depression. His parents (James and Molly) struggled to make ends meet as their marriage faltered and failed. Montague was sent home to Northern Ireland to be reared by relatives while his father remained in New York for the next nineteen years.

Stanza one opens with a shocking admission as if Montague is answering the question, 'What was your father like?' His response is both poignant and startling: 'the least happy/man I have known'. This blunt statement suggests someone who was **a prisoner of emigration, work and drink**. James Montague's face held 'the pallor' of the underground worker cut off from fresh air and light in his ticket-kiosk. His time in Brooklyn seems wasted, 'lost years', as if he has been incarcerated or doomed to dwell in Hades (the mythical underworld). There is no other sound except the 'shudder' of reverberating trains. We wonder if the father is also shuddering, trapped in this bleak place, almost buried alive.

The **second stanza** focuses on James Montague's solitary life as an emigrant worker – 'a traditional Irishman'. The poet imagines his father's daily routine, 'released' from his underground ticket-booth to spend his time drinking alone. Far from his family, he relies on 'neat whiskey' to escape from loneliness into 'the only element/he felt at home in'. **The poet's tone – describing his father's drunken state as 'brute oblivion' – seems to combine sympathy and disgust**. The repulsive adjective and explosive 'b' sound suggest a savage animal. However, Montague does not condemn his father directly, but describes his painful existence with an air of intellectual detachment.

In **stanza three**, we see the smiling public face of the functioning alcoholic. Well used to morning hangovers, James Montague 'picked himself/up, most mornings'. **The tone is one of admiration for his father's plucky perseverance.** The alliterative 'm' sounds (in 'most mornings') emphasise the strong-minded nature of the man. His confident stride is captured in the verb 'march' as he charmingly displays 'his smile/to all sides'. Is the poet suggesting that his father could be a house devil and street angel? The carefully-placed brackets aptly illustrate the racism '(all-white)' prevalent in New York's working-class suburbs. This predominantly Irish Catholic neighbourhood is 'belled by St Teresa's church'. The onomatopoeic verb vividly suggests the chapel bell ringing to summon a compliant congregation. Montague powerfully summons up the uneasy atmosphere in urban America during the 1940s. Is this also a prison of sorts?

Stanza four signals a significant change of mood. The poet recalls his father's return in the 1950s to his home-place in Tyrone where he had grown up. Fast-flowing run-on lines convey the ease of life as father and son 'walked together' through the beautiful Northern Ireland countryside, 'to see hawthorn on the summer/hedges'. The long years spent in Brooklyn are momentarily forgotten; it is 'as though/he had never left'. Instead, the focus remains firmly on Garvaghey's natural beauty as stanza four runs into **stanza five**, describing 'a bend on the road/which still sheltered/primroses'. Unfortunately, father and son were unable to maintain their close family bond; they 'did not smile in/the shared complicity/of a dream'. **Montague's personal disappointment is obvious.** The gulf between himself and his estranged father was simply too wide. In retrospect, he compares it to the uneasy relationship between Odysseus and Telemachus from classical mythology.

The **final stanza** reverts to the present and the poet's continuing fascination with his father's memory. In his mind's eye, he keeps seeing the old man 'as I descend/into subway or underground'. There seems to be no escape from the sad, defining image of a wasted life 'behind/the bars of the small booth'. The alliterative 'b' emphasises his father's confinement. Montague is also haunted by the mark of an old injury on his father's 'ghostly forehead'. **The stark images and slow rhythm are in keeping with the overwhelmingly remorseful mood.** In presenting this vivid character sketch of his father's vulnerable existence, Montague is characteristically compassionate. Just as in 'The Locket', written about his mother, he uses the poem to re-evaluate perceptions about his father, clarifying in the process his own personal and historical identity.

ANALYSIS

'One explores an inheritance to free oneself and others.' (Montague) Discuss this statement with close reference to 'The Cage'.

Sample Paragraph

I felt the poem, 'The Cage' was a very honest exploration by John Montague of his personal inheritance. He must have felt a tremendous hurt at being separated from his parents, and this is clearly seen in his poems, 'The Locket' and 'The Cage'. Yet, Montague never shows anger, but explains the situation as it was. In 'The Cage' he does not shy away from his father's alcoholism. He recounts how he drank 'neat whiskey' until he reached 'brute oblivion'. The poet does not judge. He records. Indeed, he is generous enough to respect his father's spirit as he 'picks himself/up, most mornings' to 'march down the street/extending his smile'. Montague remembers their reunion many years later and openly admits that although they spent time together in the beautiful countryside 'to see hawthorn on the summer/hedges', they did not feel at ease as father and son. Too much had passed unshared between them and so that special secret shared connection will forever be denied them. Montague avoids gushing, dishonest sentimentality, preferring to speak plainly. His father remains with him to the present day, but as a shadowy, sad figure, still cut off by 'the bars of the small booth'. The precise description, 'his ghostly forehead' rings true. Although Montague does not have the usual memories of his father, he has freed himself from bitterness by facing the past with candour and honesty. This has enabled him survive it. We also can now look at painful hurts in our own past, and if we look at them with detachment and honesty, we can free ourselves from crippling resentment.

Examiner's Comment

Close reading of the poem is evident throughout. This excellent top grade response explores how Montague comes to terms with the past: 'he has freed himself from bitterness by facing the past with candour and honesty'. Quotations are integrated effectively into the discussion and the expression is impressively managed throughout. The brief cross-reference to 'The Locket' also adds interest, as does the final personal comment.

CLASS/HOMEWORK EXERCISES

1. 'Never sentimental, yet full of sentiment, his is a talent that can recreate a memory or an emotion with almost preternatural precision.' Discuss this statement with reference to the poems by Montague on your course.

2. 'Montague's most heart-rending poems often highlight the failure of relationships.' Discuss this statement, with particular reference to 'The Cage'.

SUMMARY POINTS

- Disappointment, failed relationships, exile, love and regret are key themes.
- 'Cage' symbol represents both the father's isolation and the son's sense of loss.
- Effective use of onomatopoeia, alliteration and sibilance.
- Varying tones – reflective, conversational, ironic, sympathetic.

WINDHARP

for Patrick Collins

The sounds of Ireland,
that restless whispering
you never get away
from, seeping out of
low bushes and grass,
heatherbells and fern,
wrinkling bog pools,
scraping tree branches,
light hunting cloud,
sound hounding sight,
a hand ceaselessly
combing and stroking
the landscape, till
the valley gleams
like the pile upon
a mountain pony's coat.

'wrinkling bog pools'

Glossary

Windharp: an allusion to Greek mythology. The windharp has existed for over 3,000 years. Aeolus was appointed keeper of the winds and this Aeolian harp is named after him. It is a stringed instrument played not by hand but by the movement of the wind over its strings which are of different thicknesses but all tuned to the one note.

Dedication: Patrick Collins is an 'atmospheric' landscape artist who 'worked like a poet condensing, abstracting and interpreting fragments from memory'.

4   *seeping*: leaking, discharging.

15   *pile*: soft projected surface.

INITIAL RESPONSE

1. Why, in your opinion, has the poet dedicated this poem to a painter of the Irish landscape?
2. Does Montague convey a disturbing or a pleasant picture of Ireland? Refer particularly to the poet's choice of verbs in your response.
3. In what ways do you think the last image (the final five lines) contrasts with what went before in the poem? Comment on the poet's choice of image to conclude the poem.

STUDY NOTES

'Windharp', written in 1975, presents a word picture of the Irish landscape. John Montague, in one intricate sentence, evokes the unique sights and sounds of Ireland. The Romantic poets regarded the windharp as a symbol of poetic inspiration and Montague uses the windharp as a metaphor for the Irish landscape as it changes tonally, both visually and aurally, with the breath of the passing wind.

    The **opening line** suggests that what is to follow is special to one place, 'The sounds of Ireland'. The rushing movement of the single fifteen-line sentence mimics the wind sweeping through the landscape unhampered by barriers or borders. The opening sounds are very particular to Ireland as the wind sighs over the bushes and grasses which act as strings and so produce **Ireland's delicate rustling sound** which is beautifully captured in the sibilant phrase, 'restless whispering'. It is evocative of the soft babble of many voices and it hints at the folklore of the 'little people' said to populate the countryside of Ireland. This sound is always present, as is illustrated by the run-on line 'you never get away/from'. It is like a breath which oozes from the landscape. The verb 'seeping' with its long 'ee' vowel sound effectively conveys the exuding moan which comes 'out of/low bushes and grass'. It then rises as it tinkles melodiously through the higher flora, 'heatherbells and fern'.

In **line 6**, the poet switches his focus from the sounds the wind produces from the Irish landscape. Now the **centre of interest becomes the visual effects which the wind produces** on the countryside as it rearranges features, 'wrinkling bog pools'. The rippling effect of wind on water is described, the smooth plane now furrowed, ridged and fluted. The cacophony of 'scraping tree branches' is heard as its unpleasant grating friction is noted. Although this is a poem where there is no human present, it is very much a personal poem as Montague records his own impressions and invites the reader to partake too. He does not shirk from recording perturbing details, he is not an idealist. The mood now darkens further. The marauding aspect of the wind is shown in a phrase of internal rhyme, 'sound hounding sight'. The quickly changing light effects as shadow is followed by blindingly bright sunlight, is conjured up. The huge clouds scud across the sky in a never-ending relentless pursuit. Is there a suggestion of the loud clap of thunder before the flash of lightning?

In the final **five lines**, the **tone changes to one of quiet intimacy** as if the calm has arrived after the storm. The wind is personified – 'a hand' stroking an animal. Just as a pony's coat is groomed by 'combing and stroking' until the hair shines, so nature takes care of the landscape with the energising force of the wind: 'the valley gleams'. Nature has made the countryside beautiful with the luminous surface of the wind-animated land and water.

A wind knows no impediment. It moves freely where it will in its mysterious enigmatic timeless dance. Is Montague suggesting that the deep division of the North's Troubles can be healed by the remedy of inclusivity, that different voices and views can blend just as the different facets of the countryside's sounds and sights do under the **harmonising force** of the prevailing wind?

ANALYSIS

'John Montague's poetry creates a definite sense of place through a clear and precise use of language.' Discuss this statement in relation to the poems by Montague prescribed on your course. Refer to both style and content in your response.

Sample Paragraph

I found the poem 'Windharp' beautifully evocative of the unique qualities of the landscape of Ireland. Its sounds are unsettling as there is rarely a day without a light breeze. The soft sibilant 's' in the phrase, 'restless whispering' caught this ceaseless music of the wind's rustling. I thought the clear light ringing sound of the wind whistling over the great bogs sounds in the assonant line 'heatherbells and fern'. The adjective 'wrinkling' suggested to me the corrugated appearance of the water disturbed and agitated by the wind's passing. It is almost as if the pool frowned at the interruption. The great play of light which is so much a feature of the Irish landscape and beloved of so many artists is uniquely described as shadow and light chase each other in hot pursuit, 'light hunting cloud'. Montague's language is deceptively simple because it is so carefully chosen and seems able to convey effortlessly the exact impression to the reader of the reforming appearance and sounds of the land. This deeply personal poem affects the reader's sensibilities in a profound way, particularly the final tender image which personifies the wind as a caressing hand which leaves a valley gleaming like the burnished coat of a well-loved pony, brushed to perfection. The beautiful clear luminous quality of the landscape of Ireland with its whispering sounds has been seared indelibly into my mind.

Examiner's Comment

An assured paragraph, focusing successfully on the poet's use of sound effects: 'The soft sibilant "s" in the phrase "restless whispering" caught this ceaseless music of the wind's rustling'. There is a sustained emphasis on analysing language: 'The adjective "wrinkling" suggested to me the corrugated appearance of the water'. Accurate and apt quotations are effectively integrated into the discussion and the varied expression is well controlled throughout. An excellent top grade response.

CLASS/HOMEWORK EXERCISES

1. 'John Montague is a realist not an idealist.' Discuss this view of the poet referring closely to the poems prescribed on your course.

2. 'Montague makes imaginative use of evocative aural effects to convey meaning in his poems.' Discuss this statement, with particular reference to 'The Windharp'.

SUMMARY POINTS

- Key theme – Ireland's natural beauty.
- Impact of rich musical effects – repetition, internal rhyme, sibilance and assonance.
- Effective use of powerful verbs, memorable comparisons.
- Sensuous visual and tactile imagery evoke a sense of the windswept landscape.

6 ALL LEGENDARY OBSTACLES

All legendary obstacles lay between
Us, the long imaginary plain,
The monstrous ruck of mountains
And, swinging across the night,
Flooding the Sacramento, San Joaquin,   5
The hissing drift of winter rain.

All day I waited, shifting
Nervously from station to bar
As I saw another train sail
By, the San Francisco Chief or   10
Golden Gate, water dripping
From great flanged wheels.

At midnight you came, pale
Above the negro porter's lamp.
I was too blind with rain   15
And doubt to speak, but
Reached from the platform
Until our chilled hands met.

You had been travelling for days
With an old lady who marked   20
A neat circle on the glass
With her glove, to watch us
Move into the wet darkness
Kissing, still unable to speak.

'As I saw another train sail/By'

Glossary

1. *legendary*: famous, fabled.
2. *imaginary*: imagined by the waiting poet.
2. *plain*: extensive expanse of open country.
3. *ruck*: stack, heap.
5. *Sacramento, San Joaquin*: Californian rivers.
10. *San Francisco Chief*: well-known North American train.
11. *Golden Gate*: another famous American train.
12. *flanged*: protected, rimmed.

INITIAL RESPONSE

1. How does the poet convey the nervousness of the waiting lover at the train station? Support your answer with suitable reference or quotation.

2. Montague makes effective use of sound in the poem. Select one aural image that you consider particularly effective. Briefly explain your choice.

3. Write your own short personal response to the poem.

STUDY NOTES

John Montague is a romantic poet whose material comes from lived experience and direct observations. 'All Legendary Obstacles' explores both the delights and difficulties of love. This short lyric resonates with the uncertainty of love's early stages. Set against the dramatic landscape of the western plains of America, the poem refers to an incident which occurred in 1956 when Montague's future wife, Madeleine de Brauer, was visiting him in California, 'but her train got delayed in the Mojave Desert when the rains came'. Shortly after she arrived, the poet proposed to her.

Stanza one opens with a sweeping introduction, 'All legendary obstacles lay between/Us', as the poet lists the impediments the trains carrying his loved one faces. The adjective 'legendary' suggests that these obstructions are majestic. They also refer to the barriers the early pioneers had to overcome in their great trek west. The physical deterrents are the American flatlands, the mountains and the pouring rain. **Montague's precise eloquence is seen in his descriptions.** Broad vowels stretch the line, 'long imaginary plain'. The grandeur of Mid-West America's prairies is laid before the reader. It is 'imaginary' because the poet is picturing this place in his mind as he constructs the journey his lover is making. The harshly onomatopoeic 'ruck' is used to describe the jagged mountain ranges. Montague suggests the flux and movement of the enormous sheets of 'hissing' rain 'swinging across the night' when the swollen rivers, 'Sacramento, San Joaquin' burst their banks. The enormous physical space between the lovers is marked by placing the pronoun 'Us' at the beginning of line 2. It also references the emotional gap which has to be overcome by any couple in a long-distance relationship. Do the mountains and rainstorm symbolise doubts and fears? Just as the train has to overcome physical barriers to arrive safely at its destination, lovers must often negotiate emotional hurdles before they can find happiness.

The panoramic scene gives way to a more personal, intimate setting at the rail station in **stanza two**. The poet anxiously scans each train in anticipation. This place of countless arrivals and departures emphasises transience. Montague's restless mood is illustrated by his edgy movements, 'shifting/Nervously from station to bar'. He describes his growing disappointment, 'As I saw another train sail/By'. The line break stresses the powerful locomotive's flashing movement as it passed. **John Montague is a poet of place**, and he firmly locates his narrative using familiar names of the great trains which travel vast distances over the American plains, 'San Francisco Chief, or/Golden Gate'. The visual detail and technical terms ('water dripping/From great flanged wheels') brings us onto the platform to wait alongside the apprehensive poet and to marvel at the grace and majesty of these impressive machines. For a moment, we share the poet's apprehension. Will she really come? What will the reunion be like?

Stanza three describes the **delicate moment of that crucial meeting** through a series of short detailed descriptions. The anxious wait is over. Dark and light are contrasted as his loved one is 'pale/Above the negro porter's lamp'. She arrives, rather like Eurydice in the Orpheus legend, from a threatening place. This, however, is no clichéd lovers' meeting. Little awkwardnesses are described, 'I was too blind with rain/And doubt to speak'. Their hands meet, but are 'chilled', from the cold or the long separation.

In the **fourth stanza**, we see the lovers from the viewpoint of the old lady 'who marked/A neat circle on the glass/With her glove'. Had her young travelling companion been regaling her with the purpose of her journey? Is she blessing their reunion or is she a little envious? Meanwhile, the lovers on the platform 'Move into the wet darkness/Kissing'. Has Orpheus managed to rescue his Eurydice from the unknown? Two circles ring-fence the couple, the porter's lamp and the old lady's drawing, as love triumphs despite all the problems encountered. Montague concludes with a **haunting, cinematic image** worthy of any Hollywood romance. But is there an underlying tinge of darkness? They are 'still unable to speak'. A cool sense of unease lingers in the air.

The poet's use of verbal music, assonance, onomatopoeia, cacophony (harsh sounds) and sibilance conjure up an authentic picture of the waiting lover at the rain-swept station. The **controlled structure** of four six-line stanzas juxtaposes the various scenes clearly as each stanza concludes with a full stop. This tense little drama culminates in a heartening final scene of the lovers' departure from uncertainty, old age and transience.

ANALYSIS

'Montague does not offer an overly idealistic view of love and relationships.' Discuss this assessment of the poet's work with reference to 'All Legendary Obstacles'. Refer closely to the poem in your response.

Sample Paragraph

I agree that Montague does not offer a utopian view of romantic love and relationships. In 'All Legendary Obstacles', the poet explores the expectation, the intimacy and difficulties of early love. The list of 'legendary obstacles' with which the poem opens, 'the long imaginary plain', the 'monstrous ruck of mountains' and 'hissing drift of winter rain' not only refer to the physical barriers between the lovers, but also to the emotional barriers they will have to overcome. The lover on the platform is anxious, unsure of his loved one, 'shifting/Nervously' as he waits. The difficulty of easy, natural communication is revealed, the poet 'too blind with rain/And doubt to speak'. Their hands are 'chilled'. This image economically conveys their predicament. Even the conclusion of the poem has a slight hint of doubt. Yes, they kiss and seem to be given a blessing as the old lady on the train draws a 'neat circle' on the carriage window. But their inability to communicate remains – they are 'still unable to speak'. Perhaps there was no need for words. I was left wondering if the couple's relationship will survive after the initial passion has passed. Montague is a poet of romance, but he is also a poet who observes reality – including the various facets of bright and dark in a relationship exactly as it occurs in the real world, not as it does in a fairy-story.

Examiner's Comment

This is a very well-focused response, with interesting discussion of the development of thought in the poem: 'The list of "legendary obstacles"', 'The lover on the platform', 'their predicament', 'the conclusion of the poem has a slight hint of doubt'. Apt and accurate quotations are effectively used to support points. There is some evidence of personal engagement: 'I was left wondering if the couple's relationship will survive'. Assured expression also raises this answer to the top grade.

CLASS/HOMEWORK EXERCISES

1. 'John Montague's poetic style can be strikingly cinematic.' To what extent is this true of 'All Legendary Obstacles'? Support the points you make with suitable reference to the poem.

2. 'A sense of restlessness can often be detected in Montague's poetry'. To what extent is this true of 'All Legendary Obstacles'? Support your answer with reference to the poem.

SUMMARY POINTS

- Aspects of romantic love explored against a Californian background.
- Underlying sense of dramatic tension throughout.
- Onomatopoeic effects – assonance, sibilance, cacophony.
- Eloquently precise language and poignant cinematic images.

7 THE SAME GESTURE

There is a secret room
of golden light where
everything – love, violence,
hatred is possible;
and, again, love.

Such intimacy of hand
and mind is achieved
under its healing light
that the shifting of
hands is a rite

like court music.
We barely know our
selves there though
it is what we always were –
most nakedly are –

and must remember
when we leave, re-
suming our habits
with our clothes:
work, phone, drive

through late traffic
changing gears with
the same gesture as
eased your snowbound
heart and flesh.

'changing gears with/the same gesture'

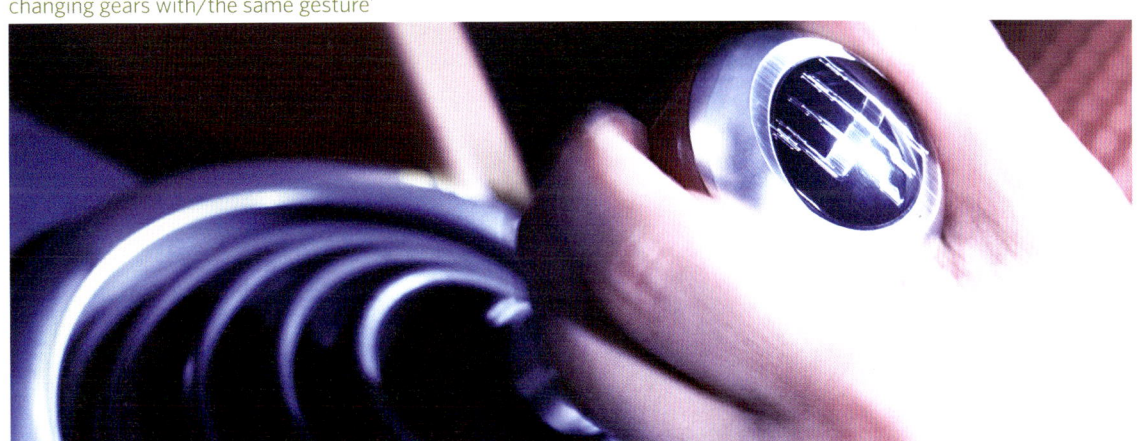

Glossary

10   *rite*: ritual, ceremony.
11   *court music*: elegant, formal music.

24   *snowbound*: encased by snow and ice.

INITIAL RESPONSE

1. What does the image, 'a secret room/of golden light' convey to you? Briefly explain your answer.

2. How would you describe the mood of the poem in the last two stanzas? Refer to the text in support of your views.

3. Briefly comment on the significance of 'The Same Gesture' as a title for the poem.

STUDY NOTES

John Montague's love poetry explores a great range of emotions, including delight, desire, pleasure, devotion, betrayal and serenity. He has said: 'I'm fascinated by the whole idea of love... its intimacy, its harshness, its tenderness'. This moving celebration of romance is part of a longer sequence called 'Anchor' from Montague's collection 'The Great Cloak'. Here he explores the realisation that the same gesture can take on a different meaning depending on the setting and circumstances.

    Stanza one begins on a confidential note: 'There is a secret room/of golden light'. This **private hideaway is depicted as being an almost heavenly place** to which the poet and his lover can escape. Montague evokes an extraordinarily dramatic atmosphere 'where/everything – love, violence,/hatred is possible'. Although the intricacies of a real relationship are acknowledged, the poet highlights the most powerful emotion of all: 'and, again, love'.

    Run-on lines catch the overwhelming nature of the lovers' passionate feelings in **stanza two**. Their closeness is conveyed sensitively, 'Such intimacy of hand/and mind is achieved'. Montague's mystical reference suggests the **spiritual bond they share** within this special room, 'under its healing light'. Even the couple's physical caresses have religious overtones, with the affectionate motion of their hands described as a 'rite'. They move as if performing a graceful dance. Montague's apt simile considers how in tune they both are, 'like court music'. For them, romance is a refined, complex experience. It is almost timeless as they seem to exist in their own exclusive world.

Stanza three focuses on the **intensity of the lovers' relationship**: 'We barely know our/selves there'. The line break emphasises how their normal individual identity is shed as their true selves emerge, 'though/it is what we always were'. Their souls had been laid bare to each other while the real world – and its usual worries – disappears. For a short time, the room they are sharing becomes their whole existence. However, **stanza four** makes it clear that they must always return to their mundane lives, 're-/suming our habits/with our clothes'. Again, Montague uses another obvious line break to convey this recommencement of routine responsibilities. The couple's psychic bond dissolves and their magical, self-enclosed sanctuary is left behind. The outside world's demands are economically shown: 'work, phone, drive/through late traffic'.

Nevertheless, through all the humdrum routine of life, the memory of romance is never forgotten. Indeed, Montague even finds echoes of their precious time in such banal acts as 'changing gears'. This everyday gesture immediately loses its functionality when he recalls how a similar movement 'eased your snowbound/heart and flesh'. The gentle sibilant 's' sounds here reflect the poet's depth of emotion. In an earlier moment of intimacy, the same action had meant excitement and pleasure for the couple. **Montague's poem is cleverly structured** within a compact five-line stanza form. The Italian word for room is stanza and 'The Same Gesture' is organised like a suite of familiar rooms which suggest this fleeting love story. In keeping with the confident mood throughout, **stanza five** is carefully rounded off with a beautifully positive image celebrating the genuine warmth of the lovers' relationship.

ANALYSIS

'John Montague's poetry, though rich in imagery and description, deals with ordinary events in economical, everyday language.' Discuss this statement in relation to 'The Same Gesture', supporting your opinions with accurate quotation.

Sample Paragraph

John Montague's poetry is filled with vibrant imagery, whether the 'mysterious blessing' of his mother's locket or the cage-like booth of his father's job. In 'The Same Gesture' the poet invites us to share a discreet love-nest, 'There is a secret room/of golden light'. This image of a private heavenly space is economically conveyed. Religious imagery is used to show the sacred bond between the couple. I particularly liked the idea of love's 'healing light' which transformed the couple into a harmonious unit. The simile, 'like court music', is equally striking as it suggested the elegance of the couple's movements. Real life's interruptions are also present, 'work, phone, drive/through late traffic' and soon bring Montague down to earth. The dual interpretation of the routine action of 'changing gear' was most impressive. Any action has different meanings depending on the context. In this case, the poet is more interested in remembering how he caressed his lover when they were alone together rather than concentrating on the functional action of changing gear. The adjective, 'snowbound', to describe the 'heart and flesh' of his loved one created for me a picture of how an individual is isolated on his own and how we all need the loving touch of another to bring us to life. For me, Montague's concise use of language and rich imagery were the basis of this powerful love poem.

Examiner's Comment

This top grade paragraph succeeded in analysing the text of the poem by addressing the effectiveness of key images: 'private heavenly space', 'sacred bond', 'court music'. There was clear evidence of close personal engagement and the focused points were explored with clarity and confidence. Early cross-references to other poems by Montague added weight to the discussion resulting in a high standard of answering.

CLASS/HOMEWORK EXERCISES

1. 'John Montague explores his personal and historical identity through lively character sketches and clever stylistic devices.' Discuss this statement in relation to the poems on your course by John Montague. Quote in support of your opinions.

2. 'Montague addresses universal themes in an honest and convincing manner.' Discuss this statement, with particular reference to 'The Same Gesture'.

SUMMARY POINTS

- Central themes – romance, intimacy and the beauty of a loving relationship.
- Acute sense of confidentiality, drama and secrecy.
- Varying tones/moods – celebration, confidence, timeless delight.
- Effective use of compact structure, run-on lines and sibilance.

8 LIKE DOLMENS ROUND MY CHILDHOOD

Like dolmens round my childhood, the old people.

Jamie MacCrystal sang to himself,
A broken song without tune, without words;
He tipped me a penny every pension day,
Fed kindly crusts to winter birds.   5
When he died, his cottage was robbed,
Mattress and money-box torn and searched.
Only the corpse they didn't disturb.

Maggie Owens was surrounded by animals,
A mongrel bitch and shivering pups,   10
Even in her bedroom a she-goat cried.
She was a well of gossip defiled,
Fanged chronicler of a whole countryside;
Reputed a witch, all I could find
Was her lonely need to deride.   15

The Nialls lived along a mountain lane
Where heather bells bloomed, clumps of foxglove.
All were blind, with Blind Pension and Wireless,
Dead eyes serpent-flicked as one entered
To shelter from a downpour of mountain rain.   20
Crickets chirped under the rocking hearthstone
Until the muddy sun shone out again.

Mary Moore lived in a crumbling gatehouse,
Famous as Pisa for its leaning gable.
Bag-apron and boots, she tramped the fields   25
Driving lean cattle from a miry stable.
A by-word for fierceness, she fell asleep
Over love stories, *Red Star* and *Red Circle*,
Dreamed of gypsy love-rites, by firelight sealed.

Wild Billy Eagleson married a Catholic servant girl   30
When all his Loyal family passed on:
We danced round him shouting 'To Hell with King Billy',
And dodged from the arc of his flailing blackthorn.
Forsaken by both creeds, he showed little concern
Until the Orange drums banged past in the summer   35
And bowler and sash aggressively shone.

Curate and doctor trudged to attend them,
Through knee-deep snow, through summer heat,
From main road to lane to broken path,
Gulping the mountain air with painful breath.   40
Sometimes they were found by neighbours,
Silent keepers of a smokeless hearth,
Suddenly cast in the mould of death.

Ancient Ireland, indeed! I was reared by her bedside,
The rune and the chant, evil eye and averted head,   45
Fomorian fierceness of family and local feud.
Gaunt figures of fear and of friendliness,
For years they trespassed on my dreams,
Until once, in a standing circle of stones,
I felt their shadows pass   50

Into that dark permanence of ancient forms.

'their shadows pass'

Glossary

   dolmens: pre-historic tombs with a large flat stone laid on top of upright stones, like an altar.
12 *defiled*: contaminated, infected, polluted.
13 *Fanged*: sharp-toothed.
13 *chronicler*: recorder of events.
14 *Reputed*: gossiped about.
15 *deride*: ridicule, sneer at.
17 *foxglove*: tall plant with purple or white flowers.
24 *Pisa*: well-known Italian town with a famous leaning tower.
26 *miry*: muddy, boggy.
27 *by-word*: sign.
32 *King Billy*: King William of Orange who defeated the Irish Catholic forces at the Battle of the Boyne in 1690. He remains a popular hero for Ulster Loyalists.
33 *blackthorn*: walking stick.
37 *Curate*: assistant to parish priest.
45 *rune*: magical symbol.
46 *Fomorian*: war-like (Fomorians in Irish mythology were a fiendish race).
47 *Gaunt*: lean, bony.
48 *trespassed*: intruded.

INITIAL RESPONSE

1. Why, in your opinion, does John Montague compare the old people to dolmens? Refer closely to the poem in your answer.

2. Which one of the old people described in the poem made the greatest impact on you? Explain your choice.

3. Identify and comment on Montague's tone in the last stanza.

STUDY NOTES

According to John Montague himself, 'Like Dolmens Round My Childhood' is 'riddled with human pain'. A series of cinematic long-shots and close-ups vividly portray some of the eccentric individuals who inhabited the poet's childhood in his adopted County Tyrone. This eerie poem shows how the resonance of other people's distant voices forge his identity. Montague writes sensitively about communities which belong to an older lifestyle.

The poem begins with two contrasting pictures, one of inert matter (the dolmens) and another of pulsing life (the elderly neighbours he remembers from his youth). **Line 1** presents a dramatic simile of dolmens and people. The stones are from ancient pre-historic time, protecting and imprisoning old burial places. **These boulders loom large, forming a frightening circle around Montague's vulnerable childhood**. Similarly, the old people he knew also confine the boy. Lively character sketches list these memorable individuals and their distinctive households. For the poet, people and places merge as he recalls their scarred lives in this harsh environment.

In **line 2**, we are given the first vibrant pen picture – of Jamie MacCrystal who 'sang to himself'. Montague recalls the old man's 'broken song', with neither tune nor words. Readers are left wondering if Jamie sang to break the silence of his isolated existence. His generosity is noted, 'He tipped me a penny every pension day', the repetition of 'p' suggesting his natural kindness. The poet has fond memories of a simple man who fed 'crusts to winter birds'. However, **the pitiless reality of Montague's childhood world is soon revealed** when we learn that MacCrystal's home was ransacked shortly after his death: 'Mattress and money-box' are 'torn and searched'. Montague is not directly judgemental. But the facts themselves are enough to show us how undeserved this shameful incident is: 'Only the corpse they didn't disturb.'

Line 9 introduces the lonely figure of Maggie Owens 'surrounded by animals'. Widely perceived as a vicious, poisonous gossip ('Reputed a witch'), she even keeps a she-goat in her bedroom. The striking phrase, 'Fanged chronicler' reveals the old woman's corrupting reputation as if the bitter saliva of gossip flowed from her very teeth. Her spiteful stories are endless as 'a well'. But characteristically, **Montague also makes us look at Maggie's hidden personality, the vulnerable underside**. He remarks that all he could find 'Was her lonely need to deride'. Her gossip is merely a response to the cold isolation of her own unhappy life.

The poet turns his attention to an entire family in **line 16**. Ironically, the Nialls live in a beautiful setting that they themselves cannot see: 'All were blind'. Alliteration memorably captures the sight of the exuberant flowers, 'heather bells bloomed'. Again, Montague portrays the family sympathetically. They existed in a dark world, dependent on the 'Blind Pension and the Wireless'. The **effect on the boy is registered dramatically in grotesque imagery**: 'Dead eyes serpent-flicked'. The colourless darting eyes of a snake are contrasted with the traditional warm Irish hospitality of the open door ready to receive anyone who needed 'shelter from a downpour of mountain rain'. The 'muddy sun' image further emphasises the tragic irony of this unusual family.

The curious figure of Mary Moore ('A by-word for fierceness') appears in **line 23**. Her 'crumbling gatehouse' seems to be poised on the edge of a disappearing way of life associated with the fading Anglo-Irish influence. Montague's dry humour is evident in the comparison of the 'leaning gable' to the world famous Leaning Tower of Pisa. Poverty is Mary's true reality as she struggles to survive on subsistence farming, 'Driving lean cattle from a miry stable'. But there are other sides to her character. We are told 'she fell asleep/Over love stories' and devoured popular romance magazines, '*Red Star*', '*Red Circle*'. She even dreamt of romantic trysts, 'gypsy love-rites, by firelight sealed'. **From the poet's nostalgic perspective, all these individuals tried to survive by whatever means they could.** In Mary's case, she coped by dreaming of finding love.

Montague's final character, Wild Billy Eagleson, is named in **line 30**. This Protestant man marries a 'Catholic servant girl/When all his Loyal family passed on'. **The poet highlights the blatant sectarianism on both sides of the Northern Ireland divide.** Isolated as a suitable target for ridicule, Billy Eagleson is taunted by local children. The use of alliteration in 'danced' and 'dodged' stresses the persistent nature of this routine abuse: 'To Hell with King Billy'. Although Eagleson ineffectually retaliates with his 'flailing blackthorn', he is in a no-win situation, forsaken by both communities in a deeply divided society. In the bitter mid-summer marching season, however, he realised what an obvious outcast he had become. Montague's dramatic imagery suggests the tense atmosphere of such occasions through stirring onomatopoeia and ominous assonance: 'Orange drums banged past'.

In **line 37**, the common humanity of all these marginalised individuals is underlined by the inescapable fact that they inevitably get sick and die. The difficult environment in which they attempted to exist is shown by the verb 'trudged' to describe the laborious visits of priest and doctor. The disconnection of these scattered people is evident in the description of the 'main road' turning into a 'lane' and finally to a 'broken path'. Sadly, they lived and died alone: 'Sometimes they were found by neighbours' who recognised them as 'Silent keepers of a smokeless hearth'. **For Montague, their corpses are like megalithic tombs, marking a place of death.** Their individuality has passed on as all are 'Suddenly cast in the mould of death'. The lively country characters of old are now mere shadows.

The poet considers the impact of these eccentric people on his own life. **Line 44** signals an abrupt change of tone as he pours scorn on the idea of 'Ancient Ireland, indeed!'. Montague is dismissive of any idealised version of Ireland's past. From bitter experience ('I was reared by her bedside'), he is well aware of Irish poverty, loneliness, and pagan superstition, 'The rune and the chant'. The alliterative line, 'Fomorian fierceness of family and local feud' shows his deep-seated resentment of such disputes. The poet's **final lines** focus again on the unusual individuals who dominated his early years. These 'Gaunt figures' – uninvited and unwelcome – have haunted the young boy: 'For years they trespassed on my dreams'. But Montague also knows that he is liberated from the fearful grip of superstition and hate-fuelled feuds. He now stands as a young man in a circle of stones. **These 'shadows' have passed into memory and myth.** The poem's last line – like the first – stands apart. People merge into place, into 'that dark permanence of ancient forms'. The young man has acquired a clearer perspective. Montague has undergone a rite of passage as he asserts his own unique personal identity.

ANALYSIS

'Montague's cinematic imagination and anecdotal skill conjure up a lost way of life.' Write your response to this statement, supporting the points you make with suitable reference to 'Like Dolmens Round My Childhood'.

Sample Paragraph

I fully agree that John Montague uses the techniques of cinema to establish the lost lonely figures scattered through the harsh rural terrain in his poem, 'Like Dolmens Round My Childhood'. The poem is book-ended with two dark long shots of shadowy shapes crowding in on the young boy's days. These people and places are presented in stand-alone lines, 'Like dolmens round my childhood, the old people' and 'Into that dark permanence of ancient forms' – and define the poem like the ancient monuments. In between there is a bright series of close-ups of unique characters doing their best to survive a harsh world. Jamie MacCrystal who 'Fed kindly crusts to winter birds' is followed by Maggie Owens 'surrounded by animals'. Then come the Nialls with their 'Dead eyes serpent-flicked' and Mary Moore at her 'crumbling gatehouse'. Wild Billy Eagleson and his 'flailing blackthorn' is another dramatic figure. Sad poignant images of all these solitary people create a tragic image of 'Ancient Ireland, indeed!' The country's dark side is glimpsed through Jamie's ransacked cottage, 'mattress and moneybox torn and searched', the image of Mary who 'tramped the fields' falling asleep dreaming of 'gypsy love-rites, by firelight sealed', followed by the bravado of the Orange March when 'bowler and sash aggressively shone' and from which Wild Billy is excluded forever. They are all forsaken. Montague's ability for story-telling is shown in vigorous images, 'Crickets chirped… until the muddy sun shone out again', 'Fanged chronicler of a whole countryside', 'the miry stable'. These dramatically realised characters come alive for me through visual images and the poet's capacity for reminiscence.

Examiner's Comment

This paragraph is filled with interesting and penetrating analysis: 'The poem is book-ended with two dark long shots of shadowy shapes crowding in on the young boy's days'. Quotations are used very effectively to support several perceptive points about Montague's visual and narrative techniques: 'Montague's ability for story-telling is shown in vigorous images'. Varied expression and some good personal engagement contribute to this highly successful top grade answer.

CLASS/HOMEWORK EXERCISES

1. It has been said that John Montague writes 'contemporary but formal poems about ancestors, lost rural ways, neighbours, place and language'. Discuss this statement with reference to 'Like Dolmens Round My Childhood'.

2. 'John Montague's most sensitive poems can offer revealing insights into disturbing themes.' Discuss this statement, with particular reference to 'Like Dolmens Round My Childhood'.

SUMMARY POINTS

- Key themes – poverty, isolation, sectarianism and the harsh reality of Irish life.
- Series of striking characters from the poet's youth portrayed with some sympathy.
- Memorable onomatopoeic effects - alliteration, sibilance.
- Language combines narration, description and cryptic commentary.

THE WILD DOG ROSE

In memoriam of Minnie Kearney

1

I go to say goodbye to the *cailleach*,
that terrible figure who haunted my childhood
but no longer harsh, a human being
merely, hurt by event.
              The cottage,
circled by trees, weathered to admonitory
shapes of desolation by the mountain winds,
straggles into view. The rank thistles
and leathery bracken of untilled fields
stretch behind with – a final outcrop –
the hooped figure by the roadside,
its retinue of dogs
              which give tongue
as I approach, with savage, whingeing cries
so that she slowly turns, a moving nest
of shawls and rags, to view, to stare
the stranger down.
              And I feel again
that ancient awe, the terror of a child
before the great hooked nose, the cheeks
dewlapped with dirt, the staring blue
of the sunken eyes, the mottled claws
clutching a stick
              but now hold
and return her gaze, to greet her,
as she greets me, in friendliness.
Memories have wrought reconciliation
between us, we talk in ease at last,
like old friends, lovers almost,
sharing secrets
              of neighbours
she quarrelled with, who now lie
in Garvaghey graveyard, beyond all hatred;
of my family and hers, how she never married,

though a man came asking in her youth.
'You would be loath to leave your own,'
she sighs, 'and go among strangers' –
his parish ten miles off.
                For sixty years
since, she has lived alone, in one place.
Obscurely honoured by such confidences,
I idle by the summer roadside, listening,
while the monologue falters, continues,
rehearsing the small events of her life.
The only true madness is loneliness,
the monotonous voice in the skull
that never stops
                because never heard.

  2

And there
where the dog rose shines in the hedge
she tells me a story so terrible
that I try to push it away,
my bones melting.
                Late at night
a drunk came beating at her door
to break it in, the bolt snapping
from the soft wood, the thin mongrels
rushing to cut, but yelping as
he whirls with his farm boots
to crush their skulls.
                In the darkness
they wrestle, two creatures crazed
with loneliness, the smell of the
decaying cottage in his nostrils
like a drug, his body heavy on hers,
the tasteless trunk of a seventy-year-
old virgin, which he rummages while
she battles for life
                bony fingers
reaching desperately to push
against his bull neck. 'I prayed
to the Blessed Virgin herself

for help and after a time
I broke his grip.'
                  He rolls
to the floor, snores asleep,
while she cowers until dawn
and the dogs' whimpering starts
him awake, to lurch back across
the wet bog.

    3

And still
the dog rose shines in the hedge.
Petals beaten wide by rain, it
sways slightly, at the tip of a
slender, tangled, arching branch
which, with her stick, she gathers
into us.
              'The wild rose
is the only rose without thorns,'
she says, holding a wet blossom
for a second, in a hand knotted
as the knob of her stick.
'Whenever I see it, I remember
the Holy Mother of God and
all she suffered.'
           Briefly
the air is strong with the smell
of that weak flower, offering
its crumbling yellow cup
and pale bleeding lips
fading to white
                at the rim
of each bruised and heart-
shaped petal.

'the dog rose shines'

Glossary

Wild Dog Rose: thornless rose with pink or white flowers, widespread in Ireland.

1 *cailleach*: a hag; offensive Gaelic term for elderly woman.
6 *admonitory*: hostile, uninviting.
7 *desolation*: barrenness, despair.
8 *straggles*: drifts, rambles.
8 *rank*: foul, rancid.
9 *untilled*: uncultivated.
10 *outcrop*: rock formation.
12 *retinue*: pack.
21 *dewlapped*: loose skin.
22 *mottled*: blotchy, freckled.
27 *wrought reconciliation*: found agreement.
36 *loath*: hate.
41 *Obscurely*: faintly.
43 *monologue*: long speech.
57 *mongrels*: dogs of unknown or mixed breeds.
71 *bull*: thick.
77 *cowers*: crouches, trembles.

INITIAL RESPONSE

1. Why does Montague no longer see the old woman as 'that terrible figure who haunted my childhood'? Refer closely to the poem in your response.

2. Select two interesting metaphors from the poem and comment on the effectiveness of each.

3. Write your own personal response to the poem, supporting the points you make with reference to the text.

STUDY NOTES

'The Wild Dog Rose' first appeared in John Montague's collection 'Tides' (1970) and vividly portrayed the brutal experience of a lonely seventy-year-old spinster ('the cailleach'). Set in the barren Irish landscape of his youth, the writing is haunting and uncomfortable throughout. The poem includes various contrasts, between past and present, ugliness and beauty, violence and prayer, and between the child and adult viewpoint. It is also a good example of Montague's skilful use of carefully-chosen language.

At the start of **section 1**, Montague describes how he visits an elderly neighbour 'to say goodbye to the cailleach'. The Gaelic word brings us into the darkness of Irish folklore, with its images of banshees and evil spirits. The poet recalls his earliest impression of the old woman: 'that terrible figure who haunted my childhood'. **His lingering sense of terror is graphically captured** in a subsequent description of her appearance as an archetypical witch – 'great hooked nose, the cheeks/dewlapped with dirt… the sunken eyes, the mottled claws/clutching a stick'. As always, there are notable aural effects. The deadening alliteration of the letter 'd' emphasises the dirty folds of the old woman's excess skin while the harsh 'c' sound suggests the sinister impact she had on the child.

From an adult perspective, however, Montague recognises the woman's vulnerability: 'a human being/merely, hurt by event'. No longer a great embodiment of dread, she now appears as just another ordinary person who has simply been wounded by circumstances. The poet's **sympathetic tone is evident from the outset**. He describes the woman's remote cottage and the surrounding land, 'weathered to admonitory/shapes of desolation' as an extension of herself. Like the unwelcoming landscape itself, she has also been exposed to trauma. In personifying her small dwelling (which 'straggles into view') Montague suggests the old woman's shambling walk: 'the hooped figure by the roadside' accompanied by her yelping dogs. She herself is unkempt and uncared for, 'a moving nest/of shawls and rags'. This vivid metaphor is typical of his detailed description and highlights the isolated cocoon into which the woman has retreated. Yet she is not completely reclusive and comes to 'view, to stare/the stranger down'. Under such intense scrutiny, the poet reverts to his youthful feelings of 'ancient awe' towards the woman. The line break at **line 24** – 'but now hold/and return her gaze' – shows the sudden change of attitude. Montague seems intrigued by her presence and they greet each other 'in friendliness'.

For a while, they share memories 'of my family and hers', now dead. There is an atmosphere of 'reconciliation' between the two. They even exchange secrets as the neighbour explains how she chose not to leave her family for marriage. We hear her voice in direct speech. Montague frequently uses **dialogue to reveal characters in their cultural and religious context**. The conversation recalls old times and forgotten disputes between local families who are now 'beyond all hatred'. The insular nature of this countrywoman is shown in her explanation that she did not want to 'go among strangers' even though her would-be husband only lived 'ten miles off'. Her decision has meant living alone for 'sixty years' in 'one place'. It is clear that the poet feels secretly 'honoured by such confidences'. As the woman remembers some of the 'small events of her life', the poet's sympathetic understanding of her isolated existence is conveyed in his reflective comment: 'The only true madness is loneliness'. He realises that because she has no-one to converse with, her voice is 'never heard'. It exists only 'in the skull'.

Section 2 leads to the climax of the poem. Although it starts brightly ('And there/where the dog rose shines in the hedge'), the mood darkens unexpectedly as the woman recounts a 'story so terrible' that the poet can hardly listen: 'I try to push it away'. In fact, Montague's reaction is shown even before the story is told: 'my bones melting'. The disturbing account of a violent attack on the woman reveals the stark reality of Irish rural life at its worst. The frenzied assault is conveyed in the relentless pounding alliteration: 'a drunk came beating at her door/to break it in, the bolt snapping'. Forceful verbs illustrate the increasing aggression ('whirls', 'crush') as the drunken man attacks her dogs. **The horror is devastatingly relayed**, 'In the darkness/they wrestle'. Yet even in the midst of all this hideous activity, Montague can find it in himself to attempt to understand the motives, 'crazed/with loneliness'. Throughout the ordeal, the woman fiercely resists: 'bony fingers/reaching desperately to push/against his bull neck'. Again, the poet allows the reader to hear the victim's desperate voice praying to 'the Blessed Virgin herself' until she manages to break 'his grip'. The broad rolling 'o' assonance echoes the involuntary action of the drunken intruder, 'He rolls/to the floor' and sleeps. Verbs economically and dramatically convey the terrible scene as the woman 'cowers', the dogs are 'whimpering' and the man wakes to 'lurch back across/the wet bog'.

In **section 3**, Montague focuses on the beautiful **image of the shimmering wild rose**, 'And still/the dog rose shines in the hedge'. Is this nature's indifference to the sufferings of man? Or is it showing that life goes on despite the occurrence of terrible events? The rose has been battered by the rain, just as the woman has been hurt by life. Her voice is heard once more, explaining that the fragile flower is the 'only rose without thorns', without the ability to hurt. She admits that it is her enduring religious faith which sustains her: 'I remember/the Holy Mother of God and/all she suffered'. Montague also shows his regard for the natural world where the 'air is strong' because of the sweet-smelling aroma of 'that weak flower'. Momentarily, the old woman and wild rose become personified as one: 'offering/its crumbling yellow cup/and pale bleeding lips'. The poet's compassionate description of human loneliness concludes with the evocative image of 'each bruised and heart-/shaped petal'. Significantly, both nature and human nature continue to endure. Readers are left to consider all that has been damaged by violence… the old woman, the rose, and perhaps Ireland itself.

> ### ANALYSIS
>
> 'Montague can bring characters before our eyes through the precision of his language and his descriptive flair.' Discuss this statement with particular reference to 'The Wild Dog Rose'.
>
> #### Sample Paragraph
> In 'The Wild Dog Rose', John Montague presents an unforgettable image of an old woman and her unwavering religious belief and resilience in the midst of life's darkness. We see her through two pairs of eyes, a young boy's terrified stare and the compassionate, empathetic gaze of the adult poet. At first she seems like a stereotypical witch figure, 'cailleach', 'hooped figure', 'great hooked nose', 'mottled claws'. Each precise, descriptive detail conveys the 'ancient awe' in which the young boy held the woman. But then the poet allows us to hear her. We hear the lilt of the woman's voice in internal rhyme and alliteration as she explains why she never married, 'You would be loath to leave your own'. Her simple faith is conveyed in the colloquial, 'I prayed/to the Blessed Virgin

herself for help'. Like generations of Irish Catholics, she holds onto her religion, 'I remember the Holy Mother of God and/all she suffered'. There is no trace of self-pity. The care with which Montague captures everyday speech rhythms vividly brings this woman to life. His detailed description of the dog rose battered by weather, 'each bruised and heart-/shaped petal', is both sweet and sad. It conveys the beauty and ugliness of life. Montague's portrayal of Minnie Kearney teaches us that we must look beyond the surface of a person before we judge, and we must see their unique beauty. This 'moving nest/of shawls and rags' stands revealed in all its beauty and it 'shines' thanks to the careful skill of Montague's language and his ability to describe what we don't always see.

Examiner's Comment

This response shows a sensitive reading of the poem and focuses clearly on the task set in the question. Developed discussion on the visual description of the 'cailleach' is well supported with accurate quotation: 'a stereotypical witch figure…great hooked nose…mottled claws'. Expression is very impressive, varied and well-managed, particularly the final sentence. A strong top grade answer.

CLASS/HOMEWORK EXERCISES

1. 'John Montague is a deeply compassionate poet who reserves judgement on people and issues.' Discuss this statement with reference to the poems prescribed on your course.

2. 'Montague writes haunting poetry set in the bleak landscape of loneliness and isolation.' Discuss this statement, with particular reference to 'The Wild Dog Rose'.

SUMMARY POINTS

- Key theme - rural Ireland at its darkest.
- Precise, graphic details convey a sense of terror.
- Poet's sympathetic tone evident throughout.
- Effective use of evocative imagery, metaphor, onomatopoeia and alliteration.

A WELCOMING PARTY

Wie war das möglich?

That final newsreel of the war:
A welcoming party of almost shades
Met us at the cinema door
Clicking what remained of their heels.

From nests of bodies like hatching eggs
Flickered insectlike hands and legs
And rose an ululation, terrible, shy;
Children conjugating the verb 'to die'.

One clamoured mutely of love
From a mouth like a burnt glove;
Others upheld hands bleak as begging bowls
Claiming the small change of our souls.

Some smiled at us as protectors.
Can these bones live?
Our parochial brand of innocence
Was all we had to give.

To be always at the periphery of incident
Gave my childhood its Irish dimension; drama of unevent:
Yet doves of mercy, as doves of air,
Can falter here as anywhere.

That long dead Sunday in Armagh
I learnt one meaning of total war
And went home to my Christian school
To belt a football through the air.

'almost shades'

Glossary

German epigraph: How was it possible?
7 *ululation*: howling, wailing.
8 *conjugating*: listing.
9 *clamoured*: cried out.
9 *mutely*: noiselessly.
14 *Can these bones live?* (a biblical reference): 'Son of man, can these bones live?'
15 *parochial*: localised, small-minded.
17 *periphery*: the edge; in the Second World War, Ireland was neutral.
20 *falter*: fall away.

INITIAL RESPONSE

1. Comment on the significance of the poem's title, 'A Welcoming Party'.

2. Choose one image or phrase from the poem that you find particularly effective, and say why you found it so.

3. In your opinion, what lesson did Montague learn about 'total war'? Explain your response.

STUDY NOTES

As a sixteen-year-old student in St Patrick's College, Co. Armagh, Montague and his classmates were brought to the local cinema to see the 'final' newsreel films of the Second World War. This was the ultimate result of the conflict, the liberation of the concentration camps and the horrifying conditions found there. 'A Welcoming Party' is the adult poet's response to the deep impact these images made on him on that 'dead Sunday in Armagh'. The poem's title is an ironic one, suggesting a happy event with people lining up to greet important guests. Yet the German epigraph sounds a jarring note ('Wie war das möglich?'). Who is asking the question: 'How was it possible?'

From the outset, Montague establishes an atmosphere of uncertainty, shock and disbelief. **Stanza one** opens with the poet's memory of the **crucial moment when he watched 'That final newsreel of the war' and understood the significance of the Nazi death camps**. The detainees who greeted the liberating armies are described as 'almost shades', emaciated, skeletal figures who are so insubstantial that they seem to scarcely exist. These images are so shocking to the young Montague that the distinction between appearance and reality is blurred. The experience suddenly becomes surreal and he imagines that he is actually meeting these incarcerated victims 'at the cinema door'.

The horrendous realism of the newsreel is continued into **stanza two** with graphic effect. Montague's description of the prisoners' wasted bodies conveys **a shocking sense of war's**

dehumanising consequences: 'From nests of bodies like hatching eggs/Flickered insectlike heads and legs'. The 'hatching eggs' simile should suggest new life. Instead, it evokes a truly gruesome sight. Assonance captures the piercing wail ('ululation') of these degraded people. Children who ought to be in school conjugating verbs are making lists of different ways to die.

Stanza three begins with an oxymoron (apparent contradiction) which focuses on one helpless child who 'clamoured mutely' in a desperate search for 'love'. The grotesque simile, 'From a mouth like a burnt glove', attempts to describe the indescribable. Is it a reference to the incineration which occurred routinely in these prison camps? The mood of despair is heightened by alliteration of the blunt 'b' and long vowel sounds: 'Others upheld hands bleak as begging bowls'. These distraught inmates beg not for coins ('small change') but for simple compassion, which is the basic currency of all human 'souls'.

Vividly recalling the haunting experience in **stanza four**, Montague felt that he and his schoolmates were being directly drawn into the horrific scene: 'Some smiled at us as protectors'. His response is incredulous: 'Can these bones live?' He can hardly understand how these starving figures are able to breathe. **Faced with such inhumanity, he becomes acutely conscious of his own powerlessness.** All he has to offer is 'Our parochial brand of innocence'. His youthful inexperience is no match for such terror. The poet develops this idea through **stanza five**, commenting on Ireland's remote geographical location, 'always at the periphery of incident'. For many Irish citizens, World War Two was a 'drama of unevent' as they were not actively involved. Montague recounts that 'doves of air' can tire and rest 'here as anywhere'. Is he suggesting that pacifists like himself ('doves of mercy') failed to respond adequately to the conflict?

The poet's critical tone becomes increasingly frustrated in the **final stanza** as he reflects on 'That long dead Sunday in Armagh'. However, this seemingly colloquial expression marks **a life-changing moment for Montague, a coming-of-age experience when he 'learnt one meaning of total war'**. The young man's enduring outrage at his helplessness is caught in the aggressive image of him returning to his comfortable boarding-school to 'belt a football through the air'. It is characteristic of Montague that his compelling imagery can seem impenetrable at times as he struggles to fully realise the incomprehensible events of war. Nonetheless, the harrowing lessons of the on-screen images remain etched indelibly on his young mind. 'A Welcoming Party' succeeds in combining the actual and metaphorical to explore the poet's reaction to the genocide of six million Jewish people. Typically, the poem reflects Montague's emotional honesty in addressing important themes which have a resonant universal significance.

ANALYSIS

'Montague's poetry is often concerned with victims.' Discuss this statement referring to both the content and style of the poems prescribed on your course. Support the points you make with suitable reference or quotation.

Sample Paragraph

In many of Montague's poems, childhood experiences are stored and distilled in the poet's memory until he is ready to confront them in adulthood. The event which inspired 'A Welcoming Party' occurred when the poet was brought from his school to the local cinema in Armagh to watch a newsreel film about the liberation of Nazi concentration camps. I wondered if Auschwitz was a suitable subject for poetry. But Montague has created a moving poem from the horrific sights, 'almost shades', 'nests of bodies'. Their terrible cries are heard in the assonance of 'ululation'. The gruesome reality of the incinerator is conveyed in the dramatic simile, 'mouth like a burnt glove'. I can now see that the language of poetry is exactly right for expressing the tragedy and the feelings of these nameless victims. All of us should be affected. We should ask, like Montague, 'Can those bones live?' We must ask, 'Wie war das möglich?' The heart-rending impact of these sights on the young poet is shown by the blurring of boundaries between fact and fiction as he imagines himself in the company of the victims, 'Some smiled at us as protectors'. The distasteful truth is confronted by Montague, the young student who is unable to help these desperate people. Is he himself also a victim of this war, feeling frustration as he goes home to 'belt a football through the air'? There are no winners in this poem, no comfortable solutions for anyone, even the reader. All are victims.

Examiner's Comment

This is a successful personal response to the question and engages directly with the young boy in the poem. Points are focused effectively on Montague's use of language and supported by apt quotation: 'Their terrible cries are heard in the assonance of "ululation"'. The final discussion about war's wider diminishing effects is particularly interesting: 'There are no winners'. Expression is excellent throughout – a top grade answer.

CLASS/HOMEWORK EXERCISES

1. 'John Montague's poetry is personal and anecdotal.' Discuss this statement, referring to the poems by Montague on your prescribed course. Refer closely to the texts in your answer.

2. 'Montague's poems often make a profound impact in exploring themes of national and international shame.' Discuss this statement, with particular reference to 'A Welcoming Party'.

SUMMARY POINTS

- Themes include the evil of Nazi death camps and the loss of innocence.
- Startling, unusual and aggressive imagery.
- Contrasting tones – shock, rage, criticism, guilt, despair, frustration.
- Effective use of assonance, oxymoron and figurative language.

LEAVING CERT SAMPLE ESSAY

'John Montague addresses questions of personal identity and belonging in a compassionate manner.' Discuss this view, support the points you make with suitable reference to the poems on your course.

Marking Scheme Guidelines
Candidates are free to agree and/or disagree with the statement. Expect discussion on how Montague uses language to explore themes of identity. Evidence of genuine engagement with the poems should be rewarded.

Indicative Material:
- Insightful reflections on childhood settings.
- Contrasting attitudes to nature, family and community.
- Various views on relationships, romantic love.
- Poems explore pain, brutality, harshness of life.
- Questions relate to the past and Irish identity.
- Varying tones – sympathetic, nostalgic, critical.
- Revealing stylistic devices – imagery, mood and atmosphere, etc.

Sample Essay
(Montague's compassionate approach in addressing themes of personal identity)

1. In studying John Montague's poems, I was very aware of how so many were autobiographical. He seemed to be someone who is constantly searching to understand his own self in terms of his origins and early influences in N. Ireland. To a great extent, he explores his childhood experiences and early relationships, perhaps to explain the adult he has become. What I found interesting was the honesty of the self-analysis, his sensitive treatment of other people and the subtle use of language throughout his poems.

2. Montague's awareness of place is a recurring feature of his work. Rural Tyrone – and particularly Garvaghey – provides a familiar setting for interesting glimpses of his early life. From my reading of 'The Trout' and 'Killing the Pig', I get the impression that he has been deeply affected by the realities of life during the 1930s onwards. His earliest years have clearly been marked by the unusual characters and everyday poverty around him. His terror of the 'screeching' pig being slaughtered was an incident of farmyard violence that has never been forgotten. The excitement of handling a terrified fish has created in him a lifelong respect for nature. What Montague seems to be saying is that he has been shaped by places and people from his past. In addition to his parents, the eccentric local characters he remembers have taught him to empathise with individuals. It's evident that particular locations define his coming of age – whether as a young boy beside a river-bank, a small farmyard or a 'bend of the road' in Co. Tyrone. He associates places with turning-points in his life. In 'A Welcoming Party', for example, he discovered the atrocities of Nazi death camps while watching a film one 'long dead summer in Armagh'.

3. Family life – especially the poet's awkward relationships with his parents – are taken up in 'The Locket' and 'The Cage'. He faces up to the truth of being rejected by his mother – 'you never nursed me', but uses the poem to accept his mother for what she was – a disappointed person afraid of showing emotion – 'a forlorn woman'. The poet's tone seems gentle throughout, even when he describes how he was abandoned, 'So you never nursed me', as though he can imagine her loss as well as his own. He is overjoyed at the 'mysterious blessing' of his late mother's 'oval locket/with an old picture in it/of a child in Brooklyn'. I found this to be a very sincere poem, revealing Montague's generosity. He is never bitter, seemingly more concerned for his mother than himself. Instead of feeling anger, he puts himself in her place, 'Naturally, she longed for a girl'. His account of 'lovely Molly' who ended up 'mournful and chill' is typical of his considerate attitude.

4. Similarly, the dramatic opening lines of 'The Cage' reflect Montague's heartfelt sympathy for his father – 'the least happy/man I have known'. Background details give a harrowing picture of this desperate Irish exile – working in the New York underground and relying on 'neat whiskey' to survive. As in 'The Locket',

Montague never judges, but merely outlines his father's troubled ritual, drinking himself into 'brute oblivion'. The symbol of the small ticket kiosk with its window grille is a simple metaphor for a life of captivity. Once again, the poet's tone is sensitive, fully aware that he never really knew his father and had little opportunity to have a normal relationship with him. Despite this, the poet still honours the failed life of this unfortunate emigrant. For me, this tribute is characteristic of Montague. His own sense of self has been shaped by the obvious sympathy he has for both his parents.

5. It seems clear that John Montague has mellowed in later life and uses his poems to express a more tolerant understanding of people. 'Like Dolmens Round My Childhood' recalls some of the elderly rural people who once terrified him. But he now sees them as tragic individuals, a product of a distinctively superstitious Irish community. Jamie MacCrystal and his 'broken song' was peculiar but kind-hearted. Montague realises that the old man was a victim of local crime – 'his cottage was robbed'. Ironically, the adult poet can now see the darker side and he has no sympathy for the local thugs who took advantage of the old bachelor. Other characters in the poem, such as Maggie Owens and Mary Moore are also remembered with fondness. The poet's dual perspective – as child and adult – helps him to understand his own divided life. Montague almost seems to be apologising for not understanding Mary Moore's frustrated existence in her 'crumbling gatehouse'. He still imagines her sad night-time routine, reading romantic stories and dreaming of 'gypsy love-rites'. Montague presents a series of images of such solitary people. For him, they are like the ancient dolmens, in that they maintain a mysterious hold over him. These 'Gaunt figures of fear' are ingrained in his own personality and clearly reflect his sense of being Irish.

6. I believe that Montague's poems allow him to come to terms with his own identity. His compassion is based on a realistic vision of the past. His poems will have meaning for anyone who tries to understand the influence of childhood on forming adult character. In his case, he becomes resigned to seeing himself as the child of distant parents and the product of a sometimes harsh 1930s rural Ireland.

(approx. 900 words)

Examiner's Comment

This is a well prepared and focused personal response to a challenging question and shows genuine engagement with Montague's poems. There is some very good discussion on the poet's compassionate tone: 'deeply affected', 'never bitter', 'obvious sympathy'. The expression is generally clear and controlled throughout. 'The poet's dual perspective – as child and adult – helps him to understand his own divided life'. An excellent top grade answer.

MARKING SCHEME
P = 15/15
C = 13/15
L = 13/15
M = 5/5
Total = 46/50

SAMPLE LEAVING CERT QUESTIONS ON MONTAGUE'S POETRY

1. 'John Montague's distinctive poetic world is primarily concerned with trying to make sense of the past.' Write a response to this statement, supporting the points you make with suitable reference to the poetry on your course.

2. 'Personal memories and a unique writing style are the defining hallmarks of John Montague's poetry.' Discuss this view, supporting your points with reference to the poems by Montague on your course.

3. 'While Montague's poetic voice is essentially located within Ireland, his work has a universal significance.' To what extent would you agree with this statement? In your response, refer to the poems you have studied.

Sample Essay Plan (Q2)

'Personal memories and a unique writing style are the defining hallmarks of John Montague's poetry.' Discuss this view, supporting your points with reference to the poems by Montague on your course.

- Intro: Montague – the sympathetic image-maker. Poems of people and places – family, childhood, the natural world. A unique poetic voice – varying tones, moods, dramatic moments, vivid images and sound effects.

- Point 1: 'The Trout' – dramatic reconstruction – the boy's developing appreciation of nature. Montague's controlled onomatopoeic effects.

- Point 2: 'Windharp' – recalls the beauty of Ireland's remote landscape – sibilant sounds, visual and tactile imagery.

- Point 3: 'The Cage' and 'The Locket' – acute and revealing memories of the poet's parents. Underlying mood of sadness and sympathy.

- Point 4: The reality of 1930s rural Ireland seen in 'Like Dolmens Round My Childhood' and 'The Wild Dog Rose' – poverty, loneliness, sectarianism, brutality. Characteristic language use – memorable imagery, descriptive details, compassionate tone, etc.
- Conclusion: Poetry defined by two elements. Montague's intensely personal poems – significant moments based around specific characters and settings. Unique style dominated by a sense of empathy.

Sample Essay Plan (Q2)
Develop one of the above points into a paragraph.

Sample Paragraph: Point 2
Montague's regard for the Irish landscape is typical of his sense of being Irish. I thought that his poem 'Windharp' sums up his memories of the remote countryside – and symbolizes his love for windswept rural places – especially the 'sounds of Ireland'. But the poem is much more than a description. The 'restless whispering' seems to represent the country's unsettled history which in turn makes Irish people distinct. It is not unusual for Montague to use such a haunting metaphor to represent the subtle aspects of what it means to be Irish. The sound of the wind on the hillsides is suggested by the run-through line 'you never get away/ from'. The poet uses effective personification to bring the countryside to life. The verb 'seeping' with its elongated vowel sound conveys the poignant noise which comes 'out of low bushes and grass'. But as always, there is a realistic recognition of a darker Ireland, echoed in the tactile image of the sharp wind 'scraping tree branches'. Montague's vision of the country is never a sentimental or idyllic one. However, there is no denying his underlying love for its rugged beauty. The short poem ends on a note of intense intimacy, with the low wind compared to 'a hand' stroking an animal. Ingrained in Montague's memory is an appreciation of the Irish landscape as somewhere mysterious and luminous.

Examiner's Comment
This engaging personal response focuses effectively on the poetic techniques used to recall Ireland's remote landscape: sound effects, use of metaphor, personification, vivid verbs and tactile imagery. There is a sense of close engagement with the poem throughout. Expressive language, such as the concluding sentence, raises this paragraph to the top grade.

LAST WORDS

'John Montague is a poet of enormous lyrical gifts, but he has as well an acute and dramatic sense of history.'

C. K. Williams

'Ulster past, present and future is in the marrow of his bones.'

Hugh MacDiarmid

'He is a world-class poet, one of that extraordinary group – perhaps a dozen? – who illuminate our lives, not just for now, but for as long as words have meaning.'

Carolyn Kizer

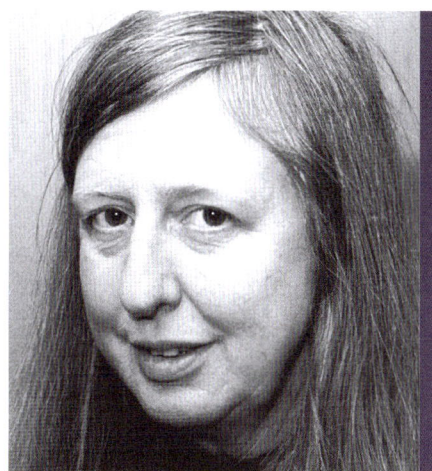

EILÉAN NÍ CHUILLEANÁIN

1942-

'I chose poetry because it was different.'

Eiléan Ní Chuilleanáin is regarded by many as one of the most important contemporary Irish women poets. Her subject matter ranges from social commentary and considerations of religious issues to quiet, introspective poems about human nature. She has also translated poetry from a number of languages. Ní Chuilleanáin is noted for being mysterious and complex; her poems usually have subtle messages that unfold only through multiple readings. She is well read in history and a strong sense of connection between past and present characterises her work, in which she often draws interesting parallels between historical events and modern situations. Many of her poems highlight the contrast between fluidity and stillness, life and death, and of the undeniable passing of time and humanity's attempts to stop change. They are usually intricately layered, often subtle half-revelations, but always both carefully controlled and even startling. She herself has frequently referred to the importance of secrecy in her poetry. Most critics agree that Ní Chuilleanáin's poems resist easy explanations and variously show her interest in explorations of transition, the sacred, women's experience and history.

INVESTIGATE FURTHER

To find out more about Eiléan Ní Chuilleanáin or to hear readings of her poems, you could do a search of some of the useful websites available such as YouTube, bbc.co.uk and poetryarchive.org or access additional material on this page of your eBook.

Prescribed Poems HIGHER LEVEL

1 'Lucina Schynning in Silence of the Nicht'
While this strangely compelling poem touches on fascinating aspects of Irish history, it is much more than a meditation on past events. The poet achieves immediacy by means of a dramatic monologue that recreates the desolation following Cromwell's devastating march through Ireland.   **419**

2 'The Second Voyage'
Transitions are central to Ní Chuilleanáin's poems. Here, she explores the relationship between past and present through the story of Odysseus, who is frustrated by his ocean journeys and decides that his next voyage will be on land. In the end, he is forced to accept that he cannot ignore his urge to control the sea.   **424**

3 'Deaths and Engines'
The poet contextualises her experience of death within the setting of another 'burnt-out' ruin, the abandoned wreckage of an aircraft engine. Characteristically, Ní Chuilleanáin's metaphorical sense dominates the poem, constantly inviting readers to tease out meaningful connections within the language.   **430**

4 'Street'*
From the outset, Ní Chuilleanáin's story of a man falling in love with a woman, 'the butcher's daughter', is unnerving. This typically elusive drama includes various references to Mary Magdalene and the experience of women throughout history.   **434**

5 'Fireman's Lift'
Following her mother's death, the poet used the scene depicted in the painter Correggio's masterpiece, *Assumption of the Virgin,* as the setting for this extraordinary poem, which is infused with an astounding sense of enduring love, loss and triumph as the ascending figure disappears into the clouds.   **438**

6 'All for You'
This multi-layered narrative offers glimpses of salvation and hope. Resonating with detailed references to the Bible story of the birth of Jesus, the poem focuses on the experience of Christian faith as imagined through the imposing challenge and triumph of religious vocations. **443**

7 'Following'
A vividly realised journey by a young girl through a busy Irish fair day invites readers into this mysterious story. The power of memory is central to the poem, which suggests that the past is not dead. Ní Chuilleanáin's final lines offer readers a sense of comfort and hope. **448**

8 'Kilcash'
This version of the old Irish elegy, *Caoine Cill Chais*, mourns the death of Margaret Butler, Viscountess Iveagh. However, the traditional lament for the lost Catholic aristocracy suggests unanswered questions about Ireland's troubled and complex history. **453**

9 'Translation'
Ní Chuilleanáin's poem was read at the reburial ceremony to commemorate Magdalene laundry women from all over Ireland. 'Translation' links the poet's work with the belated acknowledgement of the stolen lives of generations of Irishwomen in some Magdalene convents. **459**

10 'The Bend in the Road'
The poet recalls a journey when a child was suffering from car sickness. For her, the roadside location marks the realisation of time passing. This recollection is not static, but becomes interwoven with other memories of absence and loss that have deep personal significance. **464**

⑪ 'On Lacking the Killer Instinct'
The poem intrigues and unsettles from its vivid opening description of a stationary hare – engrossed and 'absorbed'. Ní Chuilleanáin's interconnecting narratives recall her response to her dying father and her imagined account of an episode in his life during the Irish Civil War. **469**

⑫ 'To Niall Woods and Xenya Ostrovskia, Married in Dublin on 9 September 2009'*
This epithalamium (celebrating the wedding of Eiléan Ní Chuilleanáin's son Niall and his bride, Xenya) is the introductory dedication in her poetry collection *The Sun-fish*. Using references to folktales and a Bible story, the poet offers timely advice and good wishes to the newlyweds. **474**

LUCINA SCHYNNING IN SILENCE OF THE NICHT

Moon shining in silence of the night
The heaven being all full of stars
I was reading my book in a ruin
By a sour candle, without roast meat or music
Strong drink or a shield from the air   5
Blowing in the crazed window, and I felt
Moonlight on my head, clear after three days' rain.

I washed in cold water; it was orange, channelled down bogs
Dipped between cresses.
The bats flew through my room where I slept safely.   10
Sheep stared at me when I woke.

Behind me the waves of darkness lay, the plague
Of mice, plague of beetles
Crawling out of the spines of books,
Plague shadowing pale faces with clay   15
The disease of the moon gone astray.

In the desert I relaxed, amazed
As the mosaic beasts on the chapel floor
When Cromwell had departed and they saw
The sky growing through the hole in the roof.   20

Sheepdogs embraced me; the grasshopper
Returned with a lark and bee.
I looked down between hedges of high thorn and saw
The hare, absorbed, sitting still
In the middle of the track; I heard   25
Again the chirp of the stream running.

'shining in silence of the night'

Glossary

Title: Lucina is another name for Diana, the moon goddess. In Roman mythology, Lucina was the goddess of childbirth. Ní Chuilleanáin's title comes from the opening line of 'The Antichrist', a satirical poem by the Scottish poet William Dunbar (c. 1460-1517).

9 *cresses*: small strongly flavoured leaves.
12 *plague*: curse, diseased group.
14 *spines*: inner parts, backs.
16 *astray*: off course.
18 *mosaic*: mixed, assorted.
19 *Cromwell*: Oliver Cromwell (1599-1658), controversial English military and political leader who led an army of invasion in 1649-50, which conquered most of Ireland. Cromwell is still regarded largely as a figure of hatred in the Irish Republic, his name being associated with massacre, religious persecution and mass dispossession of the Catholic community.
26 *chirp*: lively sound, twitter.

INITIAL RESPONSE

1. How would you describe the atmosphere in the poem's opening stanza? Refer to the text in your answer.

2. Choose one image taken from the natural world that you found particularly interesting. Comment briefly on its effectiveness.

3. Based on your reading of this poem, do you think Ní Chuilleanáin presents a realistic view of Irish history? Give reasons for your response.

STUDY NOTES

Eiléan Ní Chuilleanáin takes her title from a Middle Scots poem by William Dunbar. 'Lucina Schynning in Silence of the Nicht' is set in a ruin somewhere in Ireland, after Oliver Cromwell had devastated the country in 1649. However, Ní Chuilleanáin's beautiful and haunting poem is much more than a meditation on an historical event. The poet achieves immediacy by means of a dramatic monologue that recreates the whisperings of desolation in the aftermath of Cromwell's march through Ireland.

As in so many of her poems, Ní Chuilleanáin invites readers into a **strangely compelling setting**. The poet personifies the moon, creating an uneasy atmosphere. Silence enhances the dramatic effect: 'The heaven being all full of stars'. This eerie scene is described in a series of random details. The language – with its archaic Scottish dialect – is note-like and seemingly timeless. There is a notable absence of punctuation and a stilted rhythm as the unknown speaker's voice is introduced: 'I was reading my book in a ruin' (**line 3**). The series of fragmentary images – 'a sour candle', 'the crazed window' – are immediately unsettling, drawing us back to a darker age in Ireland's troubled history.

Characteristically, Ní Chuilleanáin leaves readers to unravel the poem's veiled meanings and the identity of the dispossessed narrator is never made known. Instead, this forlorn figure 'without roast meat or music' is associated with material and cultural deprivation – **a likely symbol of an oppressed Ireland**? Does the absence of 'Strong drink or a shield' add to the notion of a defeated people? Despite the obvious indications of almost incomprehensible suffering, some respite can still be found: 'I felt/ Moonlight on my head, clear after three days' rain' (**line 7**). This simple image of nature – illuminating and refreshing – suggests comforting signs of recovery.

Ní Chuilleanáin's startling drama moves into the wild Irish landscape: 'I washed in cold water; it was orange'. The sense of native Irish resistance against foreign invasion is clearly evident in the reference to Dutch-born Protestant William of Orange, who defeated the army of Catholic James II at the Battle of the Boyne in 1690. But the poet focuses on the speaker's experience of displacement, illustrating the **alienation which existed within nationalist Ireland**. The narrator, surrounded by animal life and the open sky, becomes an extension of animate and inanimate nature: 'The bats flew through my room … Sheep stared at me' (**line 10**).

In an increasingly surreal atmosphere, the mood becomes much more disturbed. The poet's apocalyptic dream-vision highlights the 'waves of darkness' in an uninterrupted nightmarish sequence of repulsive images: 'plague/Of mice, plague of beetles/Crawling'. The **emphatic repetition of 'plague' resonates with images of widespread misery, disease and famine**. Nor does the poet ignore the distorted history of Ireland that has resulted from prejudice, propaganda and vested interest 'Crawling out of the spines of books' (**line 14**). What stands out, however, is Ní Chuilleanáin's ability to suggest distressing glimpses of our island's dark past, poignantly depicted in her heart-rending language describing innocent death: 'Plague shadowing pale faces with clay/The disease of the moon gone astray'.

There is a distinctive change of mood in **lines 17–20** as the speaker reflects on the aching aftermath in the period after 'Cromwell had departed'. References to Christian retreat and renewal indicate the **consolation provided by religious faith**: 'In the desert I relaxed, amazed/As the mosaic beasts on the chapel floor'. This sense of wonder through the possibility of spiritual fulfilment is developed in the metaphorical image of 'The sky growing through the hole in the roof'. As always, landscape and nature are features of Ní Chuilleanáin's poem, allowing readers access to her subtle thinking.

In sharp contrast to the earlier trauma, the final tone is remarkably composed and harmonious. The language – which has been somewhat archaic throughout much of the poem – is noticeably biblical: 'Sheepdogs embraced me; the grasshopper/Returned with a lark and bee'. **There is an unmistakable sense of survival and newfound confidence** in **line 23**: 'I looked down between hedges of high thorn'. Ní Chuilleanáin's recognition of 'The hare, absorbed, sitting still' (a cross-reference to her poem 'On Lacking the Killer Instinct') reinforces the feeling of quiet resignation. Is she alluding to the maturity and relative peace of the present Irish state? At any rate, the poem ends on a hopeful note of vigorous resilience, with one of nature's liveliest sounds, 'the chirp of the stream running'.

Throughout this elusive poem, Ní Chuilleanáin has explored fascinating aspects of Irish history – a story that has been often lost in the 'silence of the night'. So much of Ireland's past is marked by exploitation and resistance. The poem has deep undercurrents of countless conflicts springing from both without and within. The moon has long been associated with love, beauty, loneliness, lunacy and death. Some critics have suggested that Ní Chuilleanáin's poem uses the moon to symbolise the struggle of women through the centuries. As usual, readers are free to judge for themselves. However, there is little doubt that 'Lucina Schynning in Silence of the Nicht' presents us with **an intense, self-enclosed world** – but one where the tensions and aspirations of Ireland's complex story are imaginatively encapsulated.

ANALYSIS

'Eiléan Ní Chuilleanáin's poems offer rich rewards to the perceptive reader.' Discuss this view, with particular reference to 'Lucina Schynning in Silence of the Nicht'.

Sample Paragraph

While I first found Ní Chuilleanáin's poetry obscure and quite difficult, I really enjoyed reading 'Lucina Schynning'. The strange title and eerie atmosphere under the moonlight is typical of a poet who makes us, the reader, imagine the 'world' of the poem. I found it all very dramatic. The narrative voice seemed very traumatised and was convincing as it represented Ireland's troubled history – 'I washed myself in cold water', 'Behind me, waves of darkness'. What I really liked about the poet was that she suggested, rather than explained. The description of Irish people starving and dying was very moving – especially because of the word 'plague'. Ní Chuilleanáin's images of suffering were balanced by the positive ending. The character in the poem was at one with nature – 'sheep embraced me'. The poem asked many questions about how people today look at the past. I thought the final lines were really encouraging. The poet used many simple nature images of the hare 'sitting still' and the 'chirp of the stream' to show a present-day Ireland where there is peace and contentment – unlike the war-torn past of the history books. Overall, I did enjoy 'Lucina Schynning' as it reminded me that there is still meaning in the beauty of nature.

Examiner's Comment

This sensitive reaction to Ní Chuilleanáin's poem reflected on both the subject matter and style of the text using accurate quotations to support the discussion points. The poem's narrative was disclosed by drawing together its significant details. Very impressive vocabulary throughout: 'the pattern on the floor of the church curled into serenity while Ireland regained some of its equilibrium'. A solid high-grade response.

CLASS/HOMEWORK EXERCISES

1. 'Ní Chuilleanáin's distinctive poetry is filled with subtle messages.' Discuss this statement, with particular reference to 'Lucina Schynning in Silence of the Nicht'.

2. 'Eiléan Ní Chuilleanáin's "Lucina Schynning in Silence of the Nicht" is a highly atmospheric poem that has an elusive dream-like quality.' To what extent do you agree or disagree with this statement? Support your answer with reference to the poem.

SUMMARY POINTS

- Evocative mid-seventeenth century Irish setting.
- Dramatic monologue form recreates Irish alienation after Cromwell's invasion.
- Themes include suffering, loss, human resilience and the celebration of nature.
- Effective use of startling imagery, repetition, sibilance and alliteration.

2 THE SECOND VOYAGE

Odysseus rested on his oar and saw
The ruffled foreheads of the waves
Crocodiling and mincing past: he rammed
The oar between their jaws and looked down
In the simmering sea where scribbles of weed defined   5
Uncertain depth, and the slim fishes progressed
In fatal formation, and thought
                If there was a single
Streak of decency in these waves now, they'd be ridged
Pocked and dented with the battering they've had,   10
And we could name them as Adam named the beasts,
Saluting a new one with dismay, or a notorious one
With admiration; they'd notice us passing
And rejoice at our shipwreck, but these
Have less character than sheep and need more patience.   15

I know what I'll do he said;
I'll park my ship in the crook of a long pier
(And I'll take you with me he said to the oar)
I'll face the rising ground and walk away
From tidal waters, up riverbeds   20
Where herons parcel out the miles of stream,
Over gaps in the hills, through warm
Silent valleys, and when I meet a farmer
Bold enough to look me in the eye
With 'where are you off to with that long   25
Winnowing fan over your shoulder?'
There I will stand still
And I'll plant you for a gatepost or a hitching-post
And leave you as a tidemark. I can go back
And organise my house then.   30
                But the profound
Unfenced valleys of the ocean still held him;
He had only the oar to make them keep their distance;
The sea was still frying under the ship's side.

He considered the water-lilies, and thought about fountains   35
Spraying as wide as willows in empty squares,

The sugarstick of water clattering into the kettle,
The flat lakes bisecting the rushes. He remembered spiders and frogs
Housekeeping at the roadside in brown trickles floored with mud,
Horsetroughs, the black canal, pale swans at dark;   40
His face grew damp with tears that tasted
Like his own sweat or the insults of the sea.

'the simmering sea'

Glossary
1 *Odysseus*: Greek mythic king and warrior. He is also the literary hero of Homer's epic tale, *The Odyssey*, which tells of Odysseus's 10-year struggle to return home from the Trojan War.
2 *ruffled:* wrinkled, tangled.
3 *Crocodiling*: gliding.
3 *mincing*: moving daintily.
10 *Pocked*: disfigured.
12 *notorious*: infamous.
21 *herons*: long-necked wading birds.
21 *parcel*: mark, measure.
26 *Winnowing*: probing.
38 *bisecting*: cutting through.

INITIAL RESPONSE

1. From your reading of the first stanza (lines 1–15), describe Odysseus's relationship with the sea. Refer to the text in your response.

2. Select two interesting images from the poem and comment on the effectiveness of each.

3. Write your own personal response to 'The Second Voyage', supporting the points you make with reference to the text.

STUDY NOTES

The relationship between past and present is one of Eiléan Ní Chuilleanáin's recurring themes. In addressing the present within the context of history, she often explores contrasts, such as life and death, motion and stillness, and the inevitable tension between time passing and people's desire to resist change. 'The Second Voyage' refers to the Greek hero Odysseus, whose first epic journey was a relentless battle with the treacherous ocean. But growing frustrated by the endless struggle against nature, he decides that his next voyage will be on land and therefore less demanding.

From the outset, Odysseus is presented as a slightly bemused and ridiculous figure. There is a cartoon-like quality to the exaggerated ocean setting as Ní Chuilleanáin immediately portrays this legendary hero resting on his oar and watching the 'ruffled foreheads of the waves/Crocodiling and mincing past' (**line 3**). The poet expands this metaphor, describing the waves as great beasts to be challenged: 'he rammed/The oar between their jaws'. **Ní Chuilleanáin's derisive humour mocks the great wanderer's inflated sense of his own masculinity.** But there is no denying that Odysseus is still excited by the 'Uncertain depth' beneath him. For him, anything is possible at sea, where he is truly in his element. The personification is childlike, suggesting his peevish annoyance at being unable to conquer the ocean waves, which don't possess 'a single/Streak of decency' (**line 9**).

Ní Chuilleanáin's tone is playfully critical. As always, the poet's skill lies in her vigorous images, such as the 'slim fishes' beneath 'scribbles of weeds'. Odysseus's powerful physicality is contrasted with the seemingly pretty waves, which somehow resist the 'battering they've had'. Lording over this surreal scene and filled with disappointment, the egotistical Greek warrior thinks about the Garden of Eden. He is soon envying Adam, who was given God-given control over all living things and had 'named the beasts' of the earth. Completely unaware of the irony of his excessive pride, Odysseus is overwhelmed by self-pity and resorts to ridiculing these foolish waves, which fail to 'rejoice at our shipwreck' (**line 14**).

Ní Chuilleanáin develops the whimsical drama by letting us hear Odysseus's petulant voice as he prepares to seek recognition onshore. Armed with renewed confidence and his trusty oar – ('I'll take you with me he said to the oar') – he sets out to 'face the rising ground' and seek affirmation far away 'From tidal waters'. But despite the purposeful rhythm and self-assured tone, there is a strong underlying sense that he is deluding himself. The landscape might be serenely beautiful, but it is confined. Unlike the boundless sea, birds define it: 'herons parcel out the miles of stream' (**line 21**). Yet the brave warrior is eager to boast of his exploits in the outside world and hopes to tell his story to the first farmer he meets who is 'Bold enough to look me in the eye'. **Odysseus even tries to convince himself that it is time to put down roots**, to plant his oar as 'a gatepost or a hitching-post'. Then he will be ready to return home and 'organise my house'. However, the laboured rhythm and imposing multi-syllabic language convey his half-heartedness about settling down.

Indeed, there are already signs that Odysseus will never surrender the freedom and adventure of dangerous ocean voyages. The powerful oar, which once signified dynamism and exhilaration, is now seen as a decorative symbol of stillness, a 'Winnowing fan'. Unable to deny his true destiny any longer, **he accepts that he cannot ignore his urge to control the sea**: the 'Unfenced valleys of the ocean still held him' (**line 32**). But his ironic situation remains; while the freedom he yearns for is unattainable on land, he is still unable to conquer the seemingly infinite sea.

The poem's final section is sympathetic to Odysseus's dilemma. Ní Chuilleanáin replaces the pompous first-person pronouns with her own measured narrative account: 'He considered the water-lilies, and thought about fountains' (**line 35**). The poet makes extensive use of **contrasting water images to highlight land and sea**. Unlike the water 'frying under the ship's side', settled life appears controlled, but unattractive ('Horsetroughs, the black canal'). His uneasy memories of home ('water clattering', 'pale swans at dark') are ominous. For Odysseus, his second excursion into landlocked civilisation offers so little fulfillment that 'His face grew damp with tears'. The hero is forever drawn to that first epic voyage and the wonderful experience of ocean living, with which he is inextricably bound: 'Like his own sweat or the insults of the sea'.

The fluctuating water images – another familiar feature of Eiléan Ní Chuilleanáin's writing – reflect the complex narrative threads throughout the poem. Transitions of various kinds are central to her work. The poet has also been very involved in translating texts, and believes that because of the limits imposed by the translator, the process can never be completely true to the original language. Some literary critics see 'The Second Voyage' as an **extended metaphor exploring how language and culture resist translation**, but like so many of Ní Chuilleanáin's enigmatic poems, the ultimate interpretation is left to individual readers themselves.

ANALYSIS

'Ní Chuilleanáin's poetry makes effective use of contrasts to illuminate her themes.' Discuss this view, with particular reference to 'The Second Voyage'.

Sample Paragraph

Contrasting themes, such as life and death, permanence and transience, and motion and stillness are all prominent within Eiléan Ní Chuilleanáin's 'The Second Voyage'. Such contrasts make it easier to understand her poetic world. The opening description of arrogant Odysseus who 'rammed' his oar against the waves shows a macho larger-than-life character whose extrovert behaviour could not be more unlike the silent sea with its 'Uncertain depth' which he will never tame. Momentarily, the irritated hero makes up his mind to undertake a new 'voyage' by seeking glory on land. But the reality of settled life disappoints him. Revealing images of fixed landmarks – 'a gatepost', 'hitching-post', 'tidemark' – all convey the sense of motionless disinterest. Odysseus is immediately aware of the contrasting dynamic qualities of the sea's 'Unfenced valleys'. Throughout the last stanza, Odysseus debates the relative attractions of land and sea. I found it interesting that the man-made images were all water-based – 'fountains', 'brown trickles', 'the black canal' – and all lacking the mystery and danger of the open sea which Odysseus longs for. The ending of the poem rounds off the choices facing Odysseus. Once again, Ní Chuilleanáin succeeds in juxtaposing his love-hate obsession with the mysterious ocean as his tears taste 'Like his own sweat or the insults of the sea'.

Examiner's Comment

The introductory overview established a very good basis for exploring interesting contrasts within the poem. There is some well-focused personal engagement with the text: 'I found it interesting that the man-made images were all water-based'. Suitable quotations provide valuable support. Diction and expression – in the final sentence, for example – are also excellent. This confident response fully merits the top grade.

CLASS/HOMEWORK EXERCISES

1. 'Eiléan Ní Chuilleanáin presents readers with unsettling scenes, both real and otherworldly.' Discuss this statement, with particular reference to 'The Second Voyage'. Refer to the text in your answer.

2. 'In "The Second Voyage", Ní Chuilleanáin addresses the idea of transition and the difficulties associated with change.' Discuss this view, supporting your answer with reference to the poem.

SUMMARY POINTS

- Evocative mid-seventeenth century Irish setting.
- Dramatic monologue form recreates Irish alienation after Cromwell's invasion.
- Themes include suffering, loss, human resilience and the celebration of nature.
- Effective use of startling imagery, repetition, sibilance and alliteration.

3 DEATHS AND ENGINES

We came down above the houses
In a stiff curve, and
At the edge of Paris airport
Saw an empty tunnel
– The back half of a plane, black   5
On the snow, nobody near it,
Tubular, burnt-out and frozen.

When we faced again
The snow-white runways in the dark
No sound came over   10
The loudspeakers, except the sighs
Of the lonely pilot.

The cold of metal wings is contagious:
Soon you will need wings of your own,
Cornered in the angle where   15
Time and life like a knife and fork
Cross, and the lifeline in your palm
Breaks, and the curve of an aeroplane's track
Meets the straight skyline.

The images of relief: 20
Hospital pyjamas, screens round a bed
A man with a bloody face
Sitting up in bed, conversing cheerfully
Through cut lips:
These will fail you some time.   25

You will find yourself alone
Accelerating down a blind
Alley, too late to stop
And know how light your death is;

You will be scattered like wreckage,   30
The pieces every one a different shape
Will spin and lodge in the hearts
Of all who love you.

'snow-white runways'

Glossary

7 *Tubular*: cylindrical, tube shaped.
13 *contagious*: catching.
23 *conversing*: chatting.

27 *Accelerating*: speeding.
32 *lodge*: settle.

INITIAL RESPONSE

1. Describe the atmosphere at the airport in the first two stanzas. Refer to the text in your response.

2. Based on your reading of lines 13–25, choose one image that you found particularly memorable and comment on its effectiveness.

3. Write your personal response to 'Deaths and Engines', referring closely to the poem in your answer.

STUDY NOTES

'Deaths and Engines' contextualises Eiléan Ní Chuilleanáin's experience of death – and particularly her father's death – within the setting of another 'burnt-out' ruin: the abandoned wreckage of an aircraft engine. Characteristically, the poet's metaphorical sense is so complete that at times it dominates the poem, constantly inviting readers to tease out meaningful connections within the language.

As with so many of her poems, Ní Chuilleanáin begins mid-narrative – as dreams often do – with an aeroplane coming in to land in Paris. The sense of danger as the plane descends in 'a stiff curve' is typical of the edgy imagery found in **stanza one**. **The memory immediately suggests a moment of insight – of coming down to earth**: 'We came down above the houses/In a stiff curve'. Details are stark – particularly the absorbing description of the 'empty tunnel' and the peculiar sight of the 'back half of a plane' that has been 'burnt-out and frozen' against the wintry landscape. The contrast of the deserted 'black' wreckage 'On the snow' accentuates the visual effect, adding drama to the memory.

Stanza two emphasises the surreal nature of the hushed 'snow-white runways in the dark'. The poet continues to construct a dreamlike sense of uneasy silence and chilling alienation. The only sounds coming over the loudspeakers are the unsettling 'sighs/Of the lonely pilot'. There is an underlying suggestion of a weary individual – perhaps facing death. This is given a wider relevance by the unnerving opening of **stanza three**: 'The cold of metal wings is contagious'. For the poet, this insightful moment marks a changing perspective: 'Soon you will need wings of your own'. The 'you' might refer to Ní Chuilleanáin's dying father or the poet herself or possibly the reader. From this point onwards, the metaphor of the wrecked aircraft is central to the fragmentary memories of her father's illness and death. **The poet interweaves two narratives**: the trajectory of the plane as it 'Meets the straight skyline' and the mark of her father's natural life span ('the lifeline in your palm'). Ní Chuilleanáin uses the memorable image of the crossed knife and fork to suggest the inescapable destiny that confronts the dying.

The poet's familiar preoccupations of tension and mystery are even more obvious in **stanza four**. Disjointed scenes of 'Hospital pyjamas, screens round a bed' are introduced as 'images of relief'– at least temporarily. **But the prevailing mood is of inevitable death** – 'These will fail you some time'. The poet expresses the final reality of every human being in **stanza five**: 'You will find yourself alone'. Ní Chuilleanáin conveys the nightmarish realisation of irreversible death through recognisable images of losing control: 'Accelerating down a blind/Alley, too late to stop'. Run-on lines and a persistent rhythm add to the sense of powerlessness. Once again, there are echoes of the 'empty tunnel' and the 'burnt-out' plane. Nevertheless, in imagining her father's final moments, the poet can relate to his experience of dying as a release, so that they both understood 'how light your death is'.

The resigned tone of **stanza six** reflects Ní Chuilleanáin's deeper understanding of mortality. In celebrating her father's life within a context of enduring love, the poet is able to simultaneously dismantle and preserve the relationship she has had with her father. She returns to the image of the wrecked aeroplane, accepting that in death, 'You will be scattered like wreckage'. However, far from feeling sadness for her father's loss, **Ní Chuilleanáin takes comfort in knowing that he will live 'in the hearts/Of all who love you'**. The sentiment is subdued and poignant, and all the more powerful since it comes from a poet who rarely expresses her feelings directly.

To a great extent, the poem is about families and how they process their personal tragedies. As always, Ní Chuilleanáin's oblique approach is open to many interpretations. But she seems to be suggesting that it takes the sudden shock of death to acknowledge the closeness of relationships in our lives. Typically, in dealing with such emotional subjects as separation, grief and the death of a loved one, **the poet never lapses into sentimentality**. 'Deaths and Engines' was written during the escalation of violence in Northern Ireland, and some critics have understood the poem as a commentary on the human cost of conflict. In the end, readers are left to make up their own minds.

ANALYSIS

'Ní Chuilleanáin's poems of separation and estrangement transcend the limits of personal experience.' Discuss this view, with particular reference to 'Deaths and Engines'.

Sample Paragraph

One of the most interesting aspects of Eiléan Ní Chuilleanáin's poetry is her focus on the natural life cycle. Even though she deals with the distressing subject of her father's death in 'Deaths and Engines', I found the poem to be more uplifting than depressing. In closely comparing his death to the wrecked plane she saw in Paris, 'Tubular, burnt-out and frozen', she eventually realises that all the 'pieces' of the wreckage 'Will spin and lodge in the hearts/Of all who love you'. Just because death has separated her from her father physically does not mean the end of their love. The poem also shows Ní Chuilleanáin empathising with her father and stressing the individual experience of death for every human being: 'You will find yourself alone/Accelerating down a blind/Alley, too late to stop'. Her message is simple – every individual must face death unaccompanied. In her poems, Ní Chuilleanáin can really accept the natural cycle – and this has meaning for every reader. In 'Fireman's Lift', for example, she also came to terms with a close family death – that of her mother – by comparing her passing to the glorious Assumption of the Virgin Mary. I believe that such poems transcend the individual and emphasise the naturalness of separation and loss.

Examiner's Comment

This is a well-focused response to the question and shows a close understanding of the poem, particularly in the cross-reference to 'Fireman's Lift'. Accurate quotations are used effectively to support key points. Expression is fluent, varied and clear, with some good personal engagement, such as in the final sentence. A very assured performance securing the highest grade.

CLASS/HOMEWORK EXERCISES

1. 'What defines Eiléan Ní Chuilleanáin's poetry is its imaginative power and precision of language.' Discuss this statement, with particular reference to 'Deaths and Engines'.

2. 'In "Deaths and Engines", Ní Chuilleanáin explores aspects of suffering and death by effectively using the metaphor of an aeroplane coming in to land.' Discuss this view, with reference to the poem.

SUMMARY POINTS

- Key themes – memory, family bonds and coming to terms with death.
- An underlying sense of tension pervades the poem.
- Effective use of metaphor, contrast and repetition throughout.
- Positive conclusion: love can transcend death.

4 STREET

He fell in love with the butcher's daughter
When he saw her passing by in her white trousers
Dangling a knife on a ring at her belt.
He stared at the dark shining drops on the paving-stones.

One day he followed her   5
Down the slanting lane at the back of the shambles.
A door stood half-open
And the stairs were brushed and clean,
Her shoes paired on the bottom step,
Each tread marked with the red crescent   10
Her bare heels left, fading to faintest at the top.

'And the stairs were brushed and clean'

Glossary

3 *Dangling*: hanging freely, displaying.
6 *shambles*: untidy market scene; place of slaughter.
10 *tread*: undersole of a shoe; top surface of a step in a staircase.
10 *crescent*: half-moon; sickle shape.
11 *fading*: dwindling, perishing.
11 *faintest*: weakest, exhausted.

Eiléan Ní Chuilleanáin

INITIAL RESPONSE

1. Why do you think Ní Chuilleanáin chose to name her poem 'Street' and yet gives the street no name? Give reasons for your response.

2. Which image did you find most intriguing in the poem? Refer closely to the text in your answer.

3. Were you satisfied by the poem's conclusion? Briefly explain your response.

STUDY NOTES

'Street' is a short lyric poem from Ní Chuilleanáin's collection The Magdalene Sermon *(1989). Mary Magdalene was the first person to witness the Resurrection of Christ and these poems reflect on women's religious experiences. The poems also depict edges, borders and crossings between different kinds of worlds as though passing through thresholds and intersections from one realm of experience to another, just as Christ rose from the dead. Characteristically, the poet reveals and conceals women and their strange responsibilities in a graceful, luminous voice.*

Ní Chuilleanáin believed in the importance of the ordinary and the domestic as new metaphors for human experience. In the **first section** of the poem, she quietly tells a somewhat unusual tale, giving readers a memorable glimpse into another reality. It is the story of a man falling in love with a woman, 'the butcher's daughter'. Flowing run-on lines depict the rising emotions of the man as he catches sight of her 'in her white trousers'. This colour is often associated with purity and innocence, but it is also the traditional colour butchers wear in their work. **A close-up shot captures a disturbing detail.** 'Dangling' describes the careless movement of the knife as it sways from the 'ring at her belt'. The verb is carefully positioned at the beginning of the line, as it tantalises and entices like a piece of shining jewellery; yet this knife has a deadly purpose. The man is captivated: 'He stared at the dark shining drops on the paving-stones'. Has this knife recently been used? Has blood just been spilled? Is he, as if in a fairytale, suddenly enthralled by the glittering yet lethal trade of the slaughterer?

In the **second section**, the narrative continues, becoming increasingly menacing: 'One day he followed her'. The assonant 'ow' sound disquietly enhances his journey. Ní Chuilleanáin specialises in the 'poetic of descriptive places'. The man's journey takes him 'Down the slanting lane at the back of the shambles'. **Varying line lengths add to the growing tension.** The adjective 'slanting' suggests a sinister backstreet where everything is oblique, tilted, half-concealed. The 'shambles' is a rough market where meat is carved and animals are slaughtered. To the outside world, it is a place of violence and mayhem. Is Ní Chuilleanáin making a hidden reference to the slaughter of Christ on the cross? 'A door stood half-open'. Does the door admit or shut out? Is this a symbol of the threshold between life and death which Christ breached? As always, the poet invites the reader to make sense of the clues. A secret is being half-revealed, a mystery is being highlighted. Where does the door lead?

Eiléan Ní Chuilleanáin often peoples her poems with women who studiously attend to their chores. (Mary Magdalene attended to Jesus, washing his feet with her tears and drying them with her hair.) Here 'the stairs were brushed and clean'. Are they awaiting a visit or is this the attention to hygiene which is normal in the butchering trade? This poet's population of silent figures disclose little information. The 'butcher's daughter' had left 'shoes paired on the bottom step'. Yet even this tangible detail reveals only mystery. The full narrative is missing. Is there a suggestion that the man and woman will soon be a pair as well? An inviting flight of stairs leads to all sorts of possibilities. **Ní Chuilleanáin has created a typically ambivalent scenario** filled with underlying danger and excitement. This dreamlike encounter is imbued with an unforgettable atmosphere of edgy anticipation as profound silence echoes.

The poem concludes with a defined image. The girl's 'bare heels' have left traces which become more indistinct as they ascend the stairs. This is emphasised by the alliterative phrase 'fading to faintest'. These are 'marked with the red crescent', like a secret sign beckoning through the enjambed lines. **The mystery resonates.** What really is marked with the bow shapes? The stairs? Her shoes? The heels? Readers are kept wondering. What does the future hold for this couple? Detailed close-ups have been presented, yet there are tantalising gaps in the narrative as we are left like the man who was enticed by the 'Dangling' knife, lured into this ominous atmosphere. As in so many of her elusive dramas, disrupting patterns of communication allows the poet to draw attention to the problem of communication itself. Is this the rounded insight to be glimpsed in the poem?

ANALYSIS

'Poems of waiting, dramatic and incident rich, are told quietly by Ní Chuilleanáin.' Discuss this statement in relation to the poem 'Street'.

Sample Paragraph

I felt that the poem 'Street' inveigled me into its dreamlike, surreal yet tangible world rather like the man is lured by the 'butcher's daughter'. I was caught as if in a dream, that state of consciousness which shimmers between sleep and wakefulness, where details are clearly recognisable, 'the dark shining drops', 'the red crescent/her bare heels left', yet their meaning is shrouded in mystery. Just as the 'half-open' door both invites and repels, this poem reveals and conceals as the reader wonders what is about to happen. Will the encounter take place between the man and the woman?

Will he disappear at the top of the steps? Is she waiting for him there or has she disappeared? What has she been doing? What will she do? The reader has been brought like the man on a 'slanting' journey. The full view of the lane was obscured from him, the full story is hidden from the reader by the obliqueness of the poem. Yet just like a dream the atmosphere is unforgettable, the waiting is palpably ominous. The poem disappears at its conclusion as the 'red crescent' marks flow 'fading to faintest at the top'. Suspense and tension reverberate. As in life nobody knows what will happen next. This tale is told calmly as the poet carefully positions the instrument of allure at the edge of the line 'Dangling' to highlight its swaying inviting movement. The reader is led like the man, by well-realised signs, 'drops', a 'lane', a 'door', 'stairs' and footprints as if following a trail in a fairytale. Yet the poet does not release the dramatic tensions at the poem's conclusion leaving it to resonate in the reader's consciousness.

Examiner's Comment

This response shows a remarkably close reading of the poem, using suitable reference and quotation to address the task in the question throughout. Discussion is coherent and the analysis incisive, especially the point about the dreamlike atmosphere. Expression is also impressive – fluent, varied and well controlled: 'the full story is hidden from the reader by the obliqueness of the poem'. Fully deserves the top grade.

CLASS/HOMEWORK EXERCISES

1. 'Ní Chuilleanáin's poetry is oblique, yet concrete.' Discuss this statement in relation to 'Street'.

2. 'Ní Chuilleanáin creates an unnerving nightmarish atmosphere in her poem, "Street".' To what extent do you agree with this view? Support your answer with reference to the text.

SUMMARY POINTS

- Highly dramatic poem filled with suspense and intrigue.
- Close-up details create interest.
- Run-through lines add a sense of urgency.
- Sense of mystery resonates at the end.

5 FIREMAN'S LIFT

I was standing beside you looking up
Through the big tree of the cupola
Where the church splits wide open to admit
Celestial choirs, the fall-out of brightness.

The Virgin was spiralling to heaven,　　　　　　　　　5
Hauled up in stages. Past mist and shining,
Teams of angelic arms were heaving,
Supporting, crowding her, and we stepped

Back, as the painter longed to
While his arm swept in the large strokes.　　　　　　10
We saw the work entire, and how light

Melted and faded bodies so that
Loose feet and elbows and staring eyes
Floated in the wide stone petticoat
Clear and free as weeds.　　　　　　　　　　　　　15

This is what love sees, that angle:
The crick in the branch loaded with fruit,
A jaw defining itself, a shoulder yoked,

The back making itself a roof
The legs a bridge, the hands　　　　　　　　　　　20
A crane and a cradle.

Their heads bowed over to reflect on her
Fair face and hair so like their own
As she passed through their hands. We saw them
Lifting her, the pillars of their arms　　　　　　　　25

(Her face a capital leaning into an arch)
As the muscles clung and shifted
For a final purchase together
Under her weight as she came to the edge of the cloud.

Parma 1963 – Dublin 1994

'spiralling to heaven'

Glossary

Fireman's Lift: The term refers to a technique commonly used by emergency service workers to carry someone to safety by placing the carried person across the shoulders of the carrier.

The Assumption of the Virgin: Roman Catholic Church teaching states that the Virgin Mary, having completed the course of her earthly life, was assumed (or elevated) body and soul into heavenly glory.

Antonio Allegri da Correggio (1489–1534), usually known as Correggio, was the foremost painter of the Parma school of the Italian Renaissance. One of his best-known works, *The Assumption of the Virgin*, is a fresco which decorates the dome of the Duomo (Cathedral) of Parma, in northern Italy.

2 *cupola*: dome-shaped roof.
4 *Celestial*: heavenly, divine.
5 *spiralling*: whirling, twisting.
17 *crick*: arch, strain.
18 *yoked*: forced, strained.
26 *capital*: upper section of a column supporting a ceiling or arch.

INITIAL RESPONSE

1. Based on your reading of the poem, comment on the appropriateness of the title, 'Fireman's Lift'.

2. Choose one visual image from the poem which you consider particularly effective. Briefly explain your choice.

3. Write your own short personal response to the poem.

STUDY NOTES

This extraordinary poem describes the scene depicted in the painter Correggio's masterpiece, Assumption of the Virgin. *In 1963 Eiléan Ní Chuilleanáin and her mother had visited Parma Cathedral. Following her mother's death in 1994, the poet used the visit as the setting for 'Fireman's Lift', describing it as a 'cheering-up poem, when my mother was dying because I absolutely knew that she would want me to write a poem about her dying…'*

The poem begins with Ní Chuilleanáin's vivid memory of the moment when she and her mother were looking up at Correggio's celebrated ceiling mural. In the **opening stanza**, she invites readers into the Italian setting: 'I was standing beside you looking up/Through the big tree of the cupola'. There is an **immediate dreamlike sense of intimacy and closeness between mother and daughter**, as though they were both aware that something significant was happening. From the outset, the focus is on the majestic painting's mystery and symbolism, reaching heavenwards to imagined 'Celestial choirs'.

Stanza two emphasises the struggle of the angels to lift Mary into the heavens, and the awkwardness and wonder of being pushed in such a similar manner to birth. We are encouraged to become part of the dynamic scene within the reality of this great spectacle. The dynamic verbs 'spiralling' and 'heaving' suggest **the physical effort involved in raising the Virgin from her earthly life**. Line breaks and frequent commas are used to create a sluggish pace. Ní Chuilleanáin is drawn to the collective energy which becomes a fireman's lift of 'Teams of angelic arms', and the effort to raise Mary 'Past mist and shining' is relentless.

Ní Chuilleanáin then considers the overwhelming effect of Correggio's 'work entire', designed to give the illusion of real and simulated architecture within the painted fresco. This awe-inspiring achievement is reflected in the pulsating run-through rhythms and hushed tones of **stanzas three** and **four**. **Dramatic images of the angelic figures and saints assisting Mary's Assumption give expression to the artist's powerful vision**: 'Melted and faded bodies' are intermingled with 'elbows and staring eyes'. Within the dome/petticoat image, Ní Chuilleanáin describes Correggio's Virgin passing into another glorious life. All the time, this vortex of bodies and faces around her are fully engaged in assisting Mary to reach the waiting Christ.

Stanza five defines an important turning point for the poet, who can now make sense of her mother's death through a fresh understanding of Correggio's perspective: 'This is what love sees, that angle'. **The assured tone marks a coming-to-terms with deep personal loss.** Ní Chuilleanáin's renewed appreciation of the painting enables her to accept the burden of letting the dead go. Her resignation is evident in the poignant image of a 'branch loaded with fruit', an obvious symbol of the natural cycle.

Stanzas six and **seven** return to **Correggio's mesmerising skill in his interaction of art and architecture** within the cathedral dome. This intricate collusion is seen in sharper focus, providing a context for Ní Chuilleanáin to reassert her changing relationship with her mother. The restless limbs of the painted angels are in perfect harmony with the great Duomo ceiling: 'The back making itself a roof/ The legs a bridge'. This intriguingly harmonious composition merging paint and plaster adds to the urgency of ensuring that the dying soul achieves its ultimate ascension to heaven.

The **final stanzas** observe the figures attending on Mary, 'heads bowed over to reflect on her/ Fair face'. Their tenderness is evident in both sound and tone. The poet has said that, on one level, 'Fireman's Lift' is about the nurses who looked after her mother when she was dying. Typically, the poet broadens our understanding of suffering, showing people caring and concerned. The concluding lines, however, acknowledge **the strength of spirit which Ní Chuilleanáin singles out as the hallmark of her mother's life and death**. This is reflected in the purposeful expression on the Virgin's face: 'As the muscles clung and shifted/For a final purchase'. Tactile 'u' sounds ('usc', 'ung', 'urch', etc.) and the drawn-out rhythms emphasise that body goes with soul in the movement across this threshold: 'to the edge of the cloud'.

Death and rebirth are recurring themes in Ní Chuilleanáin's work. But in honouring her mother's life and associating her passing with the Assumption of the Virgin, the poet has brought together Italian art, religion and a deep sense of sorrow. Essentially, however, **'Fireman's Lift' is a moving expression of the poet's enduring love** for her mother. It is not unusual for readers of Ní Chuilleanáin's poetry to encounter beautiful images which leave them searching. Nevertheless, this poem has a universal significance. It is infused with an astounding sense of love, loss and triumph as the ascending figure disappears into the clouds. Poised on the edge of this unknowable boundary, the rest is mystery.

ANALYSIS

'For Eiléan Ní Chuilleanáin, boundaries and transitions are central concerns.' Discuss this view with particular reference to 'Fireman's Lift'.

Sample Paragraph

I found 'Fireman's Lift' both puzzling and interesting. Ní Chuilleanáin managed to link her mother's death with the famous painting by Antonio Correggio, *The Assumption of the Virgin*. In describing her memory of a holiday visit to Parma Cathedral, the poet seemed to enter the reality of the mural and see her own relationship with her mother in a new way – almost like one of the angels who desperately tries to raise Mary to heaven, 'Teams of angelic arms were heaving'. The transition is shown in terms of brute strength – the Virgin is 'Hauled up in stages'. But the poet also reflects the transition between this life and the next in the optical illusions painted on the dome's structure. Everything appears to be integrated – for example, the hands of angels act as a 'crane and a cradle' supporting Mary. She leans on the 'pillars of their arms'. This metaphor blurs the distinction between stonework and painted figures. The poet sees no difference between her own prayers for her mother's soul and the work of the saints who raise the Virgin. To me, Ní Chuilleanáin is absorbed in the art work. I found this typical of her poetry in that she wanders beyond borders and margins, just as Correggio did within his celebrated painting.

Examiner's Comment

A very well-written response which addresses this challenging question directly. There is good personal interaction: 'To me, Ní Chuilleanáin is absorbed in the artwork', and effective use of supportive references. Clearly made points explore the poet's emphasis on the blurred lines within the Correggio painting, and between it and Ní Chuilleanáin's own involvement. Such in-depth analysis merits the top grade.

CLASS/HOMEWORK EXERCISES

1. 'Eiléan Ní Chuilleanáin's poems explore the persistence of memory in a highly distinctive style.' Discuss this statement with particular reference to 'Fireman's Lift'.

2. '"Fireman's Lift" is typical of Ní Chuilleanáin's poems in that it is layered with hidden meaning.' To what extent do you agree with this view? Support your answer with reference to the text.

SUMMARY POINTS

- Characteristic narrative opening recalling a significant memory.
- Effective use of run-on lines, symbolism, dramatic images of art and architecture.
- Vivid details and powerful verbs suggest physical effort.
- Key themes – death, rebirth, family relationships and enduring love.

ALL FOR YOU

Once beyond the gate of the strange stableyard, we dismount.
The donkey walks on, straight in at a wide door
And sticks his head in a manger.

The great staircase of the hall slouches back,
Sprawling between warm wings. It is for you. 5
As the steps wind and warp
Among the vaults, their thick ribs part; the doors
Of guardroom, chapel, storeroom
Swing wide and the breath of ovens
Flows out, the rage of brushwood, 10
The roots torn and butchered.

It is for you, the dry fragrance of tea-chests
The tins shining in ranks, the ten-pound jars
Rich with shrivelled fruit. Where better to lie down
And sleep, along the labelled shelves, 15
With the key still in your pocket?

'steps wind and warp/Among the vaults'

Glossary

6 **wind**: curve, meander.
6 **warp**: bend, buckle.
7 **vaults**: large rooms often used for storage; chambers beneath a church.
7 **ribs**: curved structures that support a vault.
10 **brushwood**: undergrowth, small twigs and branches.

INITIAL RESPONSE

1. Based on your reading of the poem, comment on the appropriateness of the title, 'All for You'.

2. Choose one memorable image from the poem and briefly explain its effectiveness.

3. Write your own individual response to the poem, referring closely to the text in your answer.

STUDY NOTES

'All for You' comes from Eiléan Ní Chuilleanáin's The Brazen Serpent *(1994). The book's title refers to the biblical story of Moses and the Israelites in the desert. God had become angry with his people, as they had spoken against their leader, Moses, and He let fierce snakes crawl among them and bite them. Moses prayed for the people and God instructed Moses to make a bronze serpent and place it upon a pole in public view. Anyone who was bitten could then look on the brazen snake and they would be cured. This foreshadows the raising onto the cross of Jesus Christ, who died to save sinners. Therefore, God made this sacrifice 'All for You'. Ní Chuilleanáin's collection of poems brings the possibility of hope, of getting through bad times, of being redeemed.*

Ní Chuilleanáin **collapses time and distinctions betweeen places** in 'All for You'. Line by line, the reader is drawn into deeper water until the bottom can no longer be touched, a recurring feature of this poet's complex work. The **first three lines** describe a scene that resonates with detail from the Bible story of the birth of Jesus: 'the strange stableyard', 'The donkey', the 'manger'. Why is the stableyard 'strange'? In the biblical account, Joseph and Mary had to leave their home town and travel to Bethlehem to be listed for a tax census. As is often the case with Ní Chuilleanáin's dramatic presentations, the reader must piece together a bare minimum of narrative sense. However, there is a sense of inevitability about the journey being described.

In **lines 4–11**, a noticeably different time and space is realised. What follows is **a series of evocative images and metaphors relating to a transitional experience.** Personification brings a staircase vividly to life as it 'slouches back', lolling and slumping – 'Sprawling' almost like a reclining animal as it sits between the 'warm wings' of the hall. Is it ominous or welcoming? It is waiting, as the bronze serpent awaited the Israelites, like a gift 'for you'. Ní Chuilleanáin does not determine the identity of 'you', instead leaving it open to speculation so that 'you' could have a universal application and refer to anyone. Is this gift for all? The poet's descriptive talent engages the reader as the grand staircase is depicted with great clarity, yet its full significance is never defined. Alliteration ('wind and warp') conveys the stairs' sinuous movement, curling like an uncoiling animal through the 'thick ribs' of the intimidating vaults.

The architectural metaphor is a strong element in Ní Chuilleanáin's poetry, which is full of mysterious crannies and alcoves. Could this imposing building be a convent waiting to welcome a young woman as its doors open, revealing the imposing interior of 'guardroom, chapel' and 'storeroom'? The poet's three aunts were nuns and she has commented, 'One is constantly made aware of the fact that the past does not go away, that it is walking around the place causing trouble at every moment.' Is this reference therefore autobiographical or does it encompass a wider significance? Could the staircase lead to salvation and heaven?

A rush of heat from the nearby ovens is suddenly palpable – again conveyed through the poet's effective working of personification: 'the breath of ovens/Flows out'. Ní Chuilleanáin uses a violent image to describe the fierce temperature: 'the rage of brushwood'. This is continued in the savagery with which the kindling has been collected: 'roots torn out and butchered'. Is there an echo of the biblical tale of the burning bush from the **Book of Exodus**, where God directed Moses to the Promised Land? This story teaches that we should be able to obey God whenever he calls us. Is the poet also referencing the story of Christ, 'butchered' on the cross for the sins of the world? The forceful rhythm of these dramatic lines creates an intensity, a climax of dread, almost like an ecstatic spiritual experience.

There is a marked **change of tone** in the **last five lines**. All the tension eases within the ordered space of the building's provisions store. Readers are now immersed in the moment, smelling the 'dry fragrance of tea-chests', observing 'tins shining in ranks, the ten-pound jars'. Repetition of the rich 'r' sound suggests the store's abundance of goods. Yet there is also an unease secreted in this image of confined order. The fruit is 'shrivelled', the fragrance is 'dry'. Is there a life withering, unable to reproduce? Is this another central dimension of religious life? The poem concludes with a rhetorical question intimating that there is nowhere better to take rest, just as Joseph and Mary did long ago in that 'strange stable yard', than here 'along the labelled shelves'. The body's surrender and submission to God's will enables it to act.

Another biblical reference is suggested in the final detail of the 'key still in your pocket'. In Isaiah 33:6, faith is the key to salvation: 'He will be the sure foundation of your times, a rich store of salvation and wisdom and knowledge; the fear of the Lord is the key to this treasure.' Ní Chuilleanáin's poem focuses on the experience of Christian faith as imagined through the imposing challenge and triumph of religious vocations. The 'key' image is typically contradictory – symbolising both confinement and freedom. Is the poet presenting the central paradox of Christian belief? Can the soul's redemption only be achieved through submission to God's will? Characteristically, Ní Chuilleanáin's multi-layered narrative has been subtly woven, offering a glimpse, perhaps, of salvation and hope.

ANALYSIS

'Eiléan Ní Chuilleanáin's poetry is an unshaped fire demanding to be organised into a sequence of words and images.' Discuss this statement in relation to 'All for You'.

Sample Paragraph

'All for You' is an unsettling poem which seems to emerge from the subconscious like an unformed fire. This poet's work resists containment as she wanders beyond borders. The poem springs from the idea of a gift which is 'All for You'. This can be the reward of spiritual salvation as the continuous references to the Bible – the story of Christ's birth is interwoven with references to Old Testament scenes, such as 'the rage of brushwood'. Like an 'unshaped fire', the poem's religious theme 'Flows out' like the heat from the ovens. Yet it is carefully layered. Fragmentary narratives are overlaid and remain long after the poem is read. I thought the image of the writhing staircase which 'slouches back' was very effective as it suggested the brazen serpent which Moses erected to gain salvation for his own people. The image also symbolised the harsh ladder of life which Christians must climb to reach salvation. Ní Chuilleanáin's use of alliteration, 'wind and warp', emphasised the twisting turns life takes and also called to mind the uncoiling serpent – the devil, perhaps. The poet has often written about nuns and she includes several interesting images relating to the enclosed life of a convent. I got the sense of being in a strange building with old-fashioned rooms and vaults. The storeroom imagery reflected the enclosed religious world, with 'the dry fragrance of tea-chests' and 'shrivelled fruit'. The sense of routine and order was also present: 'The tins shining in ranks'. Ironically, this strict religious life of submission represented the 'key' to salvation. The repetition of 'It is for you' suggests a generous God wishing to give a precious gift and what gift could be more important than the gift of hope? All the poet's ideas are expressed in patterns of visionary and spiritual language which can be seen as a powerful 'unshaped fire'.

Examiner's Comment

A clear personal response to a challenging question. Key discussion points are very well developed and effectively illustrated. This shows a good understanding of this complex poem – and particularly the poet's use of dense symbols and overlapping images. Expression throughout is confident, fluent and well controlled. An excellent response that merits the highest grade.

CLASS/HOMEWORK EXERCISES

1. 'Ní Chuilleanáin's language is supple and acute enough to undertake its most difficult subject: how we perceive and understand the world.' Discuss this statement in relation to the prescribed work of the poet on your course.

2. '"All for You" illustrates Ní Chuilleanáin's deep interest in the mysteries of Christianity.' To what extent do you agree with this view? Support your answer with reference to the poem.

SUMMARY POINTS

- The poem explores various aspects of choosing the Christian life.
- Personification and architectural imagery create a sense of mystery.
- Effective use of Biblical and religious references.
- Descriptive details and provocative images add drama.

7 FOLLOWING

So she follows the trail of her father's coat through the fair
Shouldering past beasts packed solid as books,
And the dealing men nearly as slow to give way –
A block of a belly, a back like a mountain,
A shifting elbow like a plumber's bend –   5
When she catches a glimpse of a shirt-cuff, a handkerchief,
Then the hard brim of his hat, skimming along,

Until she is tracing light footsteps
Across the shivering bog by starlight,
The dead corpse risen from the wakehouse   10
Gliding before her in a white habit.
The ground is forested with gesturing trunks,
Hands of women dragging needles,
Half-choked heads in the water of cuttings,
Mouths that roar like the noise of the fair day.   15

She comes to where he is seated
With whiskey poured in two glasses
In a library where the light is clean,
His clothes all finely laundered,
Ironed facings and linings.   20
The smooth foxed leaf has been hidden
In a forest of fine shufflings,
The square of white linen
That held three drops
Of her heart's blood is shelved   25
Between the gatherings
That go to make a book –
The crushed flowers among the pages crack
The spine open, push the bindings apart.

'And the dealing men nearly as slow to give way'

Glossary

Following: coming after in time or sequence, people about to be mentioned or listed; those who admire or support somebody.
2 *beasts*: animals at an Irish mart.
3 *dealing men*: dealers, men who bargain as they buy and sell animals at an Irish fair.
5 *plumber's bend*: length of 18 inches from the bend of the elbow to the tip of the middle finger.
7 *brim*: edge.
10 *wakehouse*: house, particularly in Ireland, where a dead person is laid out; people come to console the grieving relatives and to pay their respects to the deceased.
14 *cuttings*: small pieces of plants.
20 *facings*: strengthening linings; collar, cuffs and trimmings on a uniform coat.
20 *linings*: layers of material used to cover and protect.
21 *foxed*: soiled; marked with fox-like reddish spots and stains, often found on old books and documents.
21 *leaf*: single sheet of paper.
22 *shufflings*: walking slowly and awkwardly.
29 *spine*: vertical back of book to which pages are attached.
29 *bindings*: material which holds pages together.

INITIAL RESPONSE

1. Based on your reading of the poem, show how Eiléan Ní Chuilleanáin conjures up the atmosphere of an Irish fair day. Refer closely to the text in your response.

2. In your opinion, how many settings are there in this poem? Which one did you prefer? Give reasons for your choice, quoting to support your answer.

3. Choose one vivid image from the third stanza of the poem and briefly explain its effectiveness.

STUDY NOTES

Eiléan Ní Chuilleanáin often assumes a storytelling role in her poems as she relates memories from the past. She readjusts the perspective of readers by taking us into the lives of ordinary people who literally and physically made history. In her collection The Brazen Serpent, *Ní Chuilleanáin highlights family and women as makers of history. She hints at the untold through her use of characters, silences and secrets. These confidential witnesses, like the poet herself, reconstruct subtle revelations of family unease and discontentment. Female imagery expresses what is silenced. The poet frequently explores religious themes as well as death and rebirth. Quietly and precisely, she offers us the comfort that the past does not go away.*

In the **opening section**, the poet begins her story in her usual oblique, non-confessional style, yet deeply engages the reader despite her seeming detachment. A vividly realised journey by a girl through the hurly-burly of an Irish fair day catapults the reader into the story. She is trying to follow her father through the dense crowds: 'the trail of her father's coat through the fair'. Long run-on lines and broad vowels convey the difficulty of negotiating the route as she attempts to push past 'beasts packed as solid as books'. This unusual simile illustrates the tightly packed rows of animals. Nor could she easily make her way through the dealers, men caught up in the very serious business of buying and selling, making a deal. Their thick-set bodies, bulky like their animals, are described through a tumbling list of similes and metaphors to highlight their immobile weight: 'A block of a belly, a back like a mountain'. A 'shifting elbow' is like the measure used in plumbing. All these images reinforce the **tough, masculine world of the fair**. Ní Chuilleanáin has pushed the reader, through her unwavering gaze, into the poem's self-enclosed world.

Suddenly, in **line 6**, the girl catches a glimpse of her father. This is shown by a list of his clothing: 'a shirt-cuff, a handkerchief,/Then the hard brim of his hat'. His progress is swift and effortless. He moves as swiftly as the punctuation (a series of fast-moving commas) accelerates the motion of the line. Sharp contrast in the verbs used to describe the progress of the girl and her father **highlight their different rates of success in moving through the fair**. The girl is struggling, 'Shouldering past', while the father moves with ease, 'skimming along'. Is Ní Chuilleanáin suggesting that a woman finds it difficult to negotiate a man's world? The poet has hypnotically caught the excitement as well as the danger of the fair day.

Distance and time blur in the **second section**. Ní Chuilleanáin shifts the scene and time frame from the noise and physical bulk of the fair to the **'shivering bog'**. Personification and slender vowels effectively convey the cold 'starlight' scene as she is revisiting, 'tracing light footsteps', mapping faint prints. **A surreal, nightmarish world is presented**, as 'The dead corpse risen from the wakehouse' appears 'before her in a white habit'. Whose corpse is this? The effortless sense of 'Gliding' suggests the agile movement of the father. Momentarily, the packed animals of the fair have given way to the ground 'forested with gesturing trunks'. Now the heavy trees are highlighting her way, as she will ultimately follow her father into death. Thin waving rushes are evocatively described as 'Hands of women dragging needles'. Their slow cumbersome movement is presented in visionary terms. Is this a reference to the story from the Bible when the Pharaoh of Egypt decreed that because of the increasing numbers of Israelites, all first-born boys were to be drowned in the River Nile? Are these the half-choked heads? Is this the wail of Israelite women and children as they cry and 'roar' like the beasts in the fair, aware of their fate? Or is it a reference to the subordination of women as they work?

In the poem's **concluding section**, the girl meets her father in a much more hospitable setting with 'whiskey poured in two glasses', 'His clothes all finely laundered'. Within these domestic interiors of the poet's imagination lies the remote **possibility of utopia**. The 'square of white linen', redolent of the survivor's suffering, shrunk and stained by the body's signifiers of hurt, becomes a relic of love and loss. Ní Chuilleanáin has commented, 'A relic is something you enclose, and then you enclose the reliquary in something else. In the *The Book of Kells* exhibition, the book satchel is in leather, which is meant to protect, and there is a shrine which in turn is meant to protect the book'. A relic is associated with people seeking comfort in difficult times. The past is beautifully evoked in the phrase 'The smooth foxed leaf has been hidden', with its haunting image of time-stained pages. Inside the book are 'crushed flowers', reminders that love was violated, yet something of it remains. These memories have tremendous power; they 'crack' and push apart as if being reborn. Living and dead touch each other through such memories. The dust and noise of the cattle market, the cold starry bog have all evaporated to be replaced by this interior where the 'light is clean', making it easy to see. Comfort and hope are being offered as the poem suggests that the past is not dead.

ANALYSIS

'Ní Chuilleanáin's poems explore how the most basic legends – family stories – fragment and alter in each individual's memory.' Discuss this statement with particular reference to the poem 'Following'.

Sample Paragraph

I think we tell ourselves stories about the past and I wonder do we need to revisit them in order to see the past differently, to assimilate it and move on in hope? Ní Chuilleanáin's poem, 'Following', dredges up fragments of uniquely Irish family stories (the fair day, a wake, women sewing) and rearranges them, as cards are moved in 'shufflings'. This reconstructs and transforms the past so that we can see and understand from a new perspective. We are brought as followers, just like the girl in the fair, on a journey to discover that the past is not dead, but resonates through the present by means of relics, 'The square of white linen', and so gives hope and comfort to those left behind. The title suggests to me that we are all following one another on the same journey through life, but at different paces, as the girl and the father in the fair. In the masculine world of the fair, 'beasts packed solid as books' the girl found it hard to negotiate her way. The poet has identified the difficult role women have in life, 'dragging needles', employed in repetitive domestic drudgery. These women are unable to express their opinions and concerns, 'Half-choked'. The legends become 'crushed flowers' yet the poet suggests that they are so potent that they can 'crack' open and push apart the book in which they are enclosed. I felt that she was communicating the message of hope that the past does not stay in the past but reverberates and pulses through the present. Our memories do not remain 'shelved' but live again in the present through the power of relics.

Examiner's Comment

This is a very impressive response which fully merits the highest grade. The focus throughout is firmly placed on addressing the various parts of the question. Quotations are integrated effectively and the answer ranges widely from the title to the individual stories and the imagery used in conveying the narratives. Language is carefully controlled to express points clearly, e.g. 'This reconstructs and transforms the past so that we can see and understand from a new perspective'.

CLASS/HOMEWORK EXERCISES

1. 'The mysterious writing style of Ní Chuilleanáin allows the reader to explore the poems on many levels, each tracking a different aspect of the cycle of life.' Discuss this statement in relation to the prescribed poems of this poet on your course.

2. 'Ní Chuilleanáin's poetry can often seem deceptively simple.' Discuss this statement with particular reference to the poem 'Following'. Support your answer with reference to the text.

SUMMARY POINTS

- The poet assumes a familiar story-telling role in this mystery tale.
- Themes include Irish identity and the power of memory.
- Effective use of commas, dashes and run-on lines.
- Prominent sound effects (alliteration and assonance) add emphasis.

8 KILCASH

From the Irish, c.1800

What will we do now for timber,
With the last of the woods laid low –
No word of Kilcash nor its household,
Their bell is silenced now,
Where the lady lived with such honour,   5
No woman so heaped with praise,
Earls came across oceans to see her
And heard the sweet words of Mass.

It's the cause of my long affliction
To see your neat gates knocked down,   10
The long walks affording no shade now
And the avenue overgrown,
The fine house that kept out the weather,
Its people depressed and tamed;
And their names with the faithful departed,   15
The Bishop and Lady Iveagh!

The geese and the ducks' commotion,
The eagle's shout, are no more,
The roar of the bees gone silent,
Their wax and their honey store   20
Deserted. Now at evening
The musical birds are stilled
And the cuckoo is dumb in the treetops
That sang lullaby to the world.

Even the deer and the hunters   25
That follow the mountain way
Look down upon us with pity,
The house that was famed in its day;
The smooth wide lawn is all broken,
No shelter from wind and rain;   30
The paddock has turned to a dairy
Where the fine creatures grazed.

Mist hangs low on the branches
No sunlight can sweep aside,
Darkness falls among daylight   35
And the streams are all run dry;
No hazel, no holly, no berry,
Bare naked rocks and cold;
The forest park is leafless
And all the game gone wild.   40

And now the worst of our troubles:
She has followed the prince of the Gaels –
He has borne off the gentle maiden,
Summoned to France and to Spain.
Her company laments her   45
That she fed with silver and gold:
One who never preyed on the people
But was the poor souls' friend.

My prayer to Mary and Jesus
She may come safe home to us here   50
To dancing and rejoicing
To fiddling and bonfire
That our ancestors' house will rise up,
Kilcash built up anew
And from now to the end of the story   55
May it never again be laid low.

'long walks affording no shade now'

Glossary

Title: Eiléan Ní Chuilleanáin's translation of the early 19th-century ballad *Caoine Cill Chais* (The Lament for Kilcash), an anonymous lament that the castle of Cill Chais stood empty, its woods cut down and all its old grandeur disappeared. Kilcash was one of the great houses of a branch of the Butler family near Clonmel, Co. Tipperary, until well into the 18th century. Ní Chuilleanáin's poem encompasses several generations of the Butler family, but the presiding spirit is that of Margaret Butler, Viscountess Iveagh (who died in 1744).

2 **the last of the woods**: a reference to the mass clearance of native Irish forests by plantation settlers to create agricultural land and to fuel the colonial economy. The woodland belonging to the Butlers of Kilcash were sold in 1797 and 1801.

5 **the lady**: Margaret Butler, Viscountess Iveagh, a staunch Catholic (d.1744).

16 **The Bishop**: Catholic clergy – including Lady Iveagh's brother-in-law – were often given shelter in Kilcash.

17 **commotion**: noise, clamour.

24 **lullaby**: soothing song.

31 **paddock**: enclosure.

42 **prince of the Gaels**: probably a reference to the 18th Earl of Ormonde.

43 **the gentle maiden**: Countess, wife of the 18th Earl.

47 **preyed**: harmed, took advantage of.

INITIAL RESPONSE

1. From your reading of the poem, what is your impression of Lady Iveagh? Refer to the text in your answer.

2. Choose one interesting image from 'Kilcash' that you consider particularly effective. Give reasons to explain why this image appealed to you.

3. Write your own individual response to the poem, referring closely to the text in your answer.

STUDY NOTES

'Kilcash' comes from Eiléan Ní Chuilleanáin's *The Girl Who Married the Reindeer* (2001). Many of the poems in this collection deal with outsiders and the dispossessed. Kilcash was the great house of one of the branches of the Butler family near Clonmel, Co. Tipperary, until the 18th century. The Butlers were Catholic landed gentry who had come to Ireland as part of an Anglo-Norman invasion during the 12th century and had taken over vast amounts of land. Over time, the family became absorbed into Irish ways. Ní Chuilleanáin's version of the traditional Irish elegy, *Caoine Cill Chais*, mourns the death of Margaret Butler, Viscountess Iveagh.

Stanza one opens with a plaintive voice lamenting 'What will we do now for timber'. The ballad was originally composed in the early 1800s following the demise of the Butlers of Kilcash and the eventual clearing of the family's extensive woodlands, which had supplied timber for local people. **The early tone typifies the entire poem's sense of hopelessness now that the woods are 'laid low'.** The systematic felling of trees is symbolic of the decline of this aristocratic Catholic family. Following colonisation, the Irish were consigned to Nature as a symbol of their barbarity. In some British circles, they were referred to as the 'natural wild Irish' because the country's remote boglands and forests offered shelter to Irish rebels. The poem emphasises the uneasy silence around Kilcash and the speaker pays extravagant tribute to 'the lady' of the house, who is immediately associated with Ireland's Catholic resistance: 'Earls came across oceans to see her'.

As always, Ní Chuilleanáin's approach is layered, recognising the genuine feelings of loss while suggesting a misplaced dependence on all those who exploited the native population. For the most part, however, the poem's anonymous narrator appears to express the desolation ('long affliction') felt by the impoverished and leaderless Irish of the time. There is no shortage of evidence to illustrate what has happened to the 'fine house'. Throughout **stanzas two** and **three**, broad assonant sounds add to the maudlin sentiments. **The 'neat gates knocked down' and the 'avenue overgrown' reflect the dramatic turnaround in fortunes.** But is Ní Chuilleanáin's translation of the old song also unearthing an underlying sense of delight in the sudden fall of the mighty? There is 'no shade now' for the once powerful gentry as well as the impoverished community. Many of the references to the 'stilled' birds and animals can also be seen as both a loss and a possible release from an unhappy phase of oppression and dependence.

Images of hardship taken from nature dominate **stanzas four** and **five**. The abandoned peasants are depicted as pitiable. The atmosphere becomes increasingly disturbing as the natural world order is transformed: 'Darkness falls among daylight/And the streams are all run dry'. **As in so many other Irish legends, the landscape reflects the terms of the Butlers' exile**: 'The forest park is leafless'. Negative language patterns – 'No sunlight', 'No hazel, no holly' – highlight the sense of mordant despondency resulting from abandonment. Relentlessly, the regular lines and ponderous rhythm work together to create a monotonous trance-like effect. The extravagant praise for 'the gentle maiden' (a likely reference to the wife of the 18th Earl) dominates **stanza six**. As a representative of the Butler dynasty, her absence is seen as 'the worst of our troubles' and she is glorified as someone 'who never preyed on the people' despite her privileged lifestyle.

The prayer-like tone of the **final stanza** is in keeping with the deep yearning for a return to the old ways in Kilcash. The Catholic allusion also reinforces the central importance of religion in expressing political and cultural identity. In wishing to restore the former Gaelic order, the speaker imagines lively scenes of communal celebration: 'fiddling and bonfire'. **The aspiration that the castle will be 'built up anew' offers a clear symbol of recovery.** This rallying call is in keeping with traditional laments and is characteristic of the poet's sympathies for the oppressed. Ní Chuilleanáin has retained the rhetorical style of Gaelic poetry throughout, revealing the experience of isolated communities through numerous images of restless desolation and uncomfortable silences.

'Kilcash' marks a significant transition in Irish history. As the old native aristocracy suffered military and political defeat and, in many cases, exile, the world order that had supported the bardic poets disappeared. In these circumstances, it is hardly surprising that much Irish poetry of this period laments these changes and the poet's plight. However, **Ní Chuilleanáin's translation of the old ballad differs from other versions in being more ambivalent towards Viscountess Iveagh and what she represented**. Is the poem a poignant expression of loss and a genuine tribute to those landlords who were seen as humane? Does the poet satirise the subservient native Irish who had been conditioned to accept some convenient generosity from the Catholic gentry? To what extent did the original lament present a romantic distortion of Ireland's history? Readers are left to decide for themselves.

ANALYSIS

'Eiléan Ní Chuilleanáin's poems retain the power to connect past and present in ways that never cease to fascinate.' Discuss this statement, with particular reference to 'Kilcash'.

Sample Paragraph

On a first reading, I thought that 'Kilcash' was a simple adaptation of the old Gaelic ballad, 'Caoine Cill Chais'. After studying the poem, however, I feel that Eiléan Ní Chuilleanáin has raised many interesting questions about Irish history. For a start, the poem is a translation and the original bard's view of the 18th century Butler line is buried beneath Ní Chuilleanáin's. The opening lament of the deprived peasants seems self-pitying – 'What will we do now for timber'. The compliments paid to Lady Iveagh (Margaret Butler) are lavish and focus on her Catholic faith and support for the old Gaelic culture – 'Earls came across oceans to see her'. As a young person looking back on this period of upheaval, I could appreciate the way dispossessed Irish people had become dependent on the Catholic gentry as symbols of freedom. The poem repeatedly places 'the lady' as the epitome of hope – 'the poor souls' friend'. It was interesting to see how the flight of the Butlers reduced people to complete dependence, so that all they could do was pray for a miraculous reversal of history 'that our ancestors' house will rise up'. The main insight I gained from the poem was that colonisation – whether by Catholic or Protestant landlords – had broken the Irish spirit. Ní Chuilleanáin manages to link past and present very subtly, broadening our view of the complex relationships between powerful interests and a conquered population.

Examiner's Comment
An assured personal response, focused throughout and very well illustrated with suitable quotations. The paragraph carefully highlights Ní Chuilleanáin's exploration of the plight of the native Irish community in various ways: 'the original bard's view of the eighteenth century Butler line is buried beneath Ní Chuilleanáin's'. Points are clearly expressed throughout in this excellent, top grade answer.

CLASS/HOMEWORK EXERCISES

1. 'Ní Chuilleanáin's distinctive poetic world provides an accessible platform for voices from the margin.' Discuss this view, with particular reference to 'Kilcash'.

2. 'In her poem, "Kilcash", Ní Chuilleanáin explores themes of loss and dispossession.' To what extent do you agree with this statement? Support your answer with reference to the text.

SUMMARY POINTS

- Traditional lament for Catholic aristocracy raises questions about Ireland's past.
- Desolate landscape and negative language reflect the mood of hopelessness.
- Regular rhythm, the prayer-like tone and stark images emphasise the atmosphere.
- Ambivalent ending intrigues readers about the poet's own viewpoint.

9 TRANSLATION

for the reburial of the Magdalenes

The soil frayed and sifted evens the score —
There are women here from every county,
Just as there were in the laundry.

White light blinded and bleached out
The high relief of a glance, where steam danced 5
Around stone drains and giggled and slipped across water.

Assist them now, ridges under the veil, shifting,
Searching for their parents, their names,
The edges of words grinding against nature,

As if, when water sank between the rotten teeth 10
Of soap, and every grasp seemed melted, one voice
Had begun, rising above the shuffle and hum

Until every pocket in her skull blared with the note —
Allow us now to hear it, sharp as an infant's cry
While the grass takes root, while the steam rises: 15

Washed clean of idiom · the baked crust
Of words that made my temporary name ·
A parasite that grew in me · that spell
Lifted · I lie in earth sifted to dust ·
Let the bunched keys I bore slacken and fall · 20
I rise and forget · a cloud over my time.

'Washed clean of idiom'

460 POETRY FOCUS

Glossary

Subtitle: The Magdalenes refers to Irish women, particularly unmarried mothers, who were separated from their children and forced to work in convent laundries. Inmates were required to undertake hard physical labour, including washing and needlework. They also endured a daily regime that included long periods of prayer and enforced silence. In Ireland, such institutions were known as Magdalene laundries. It has been estimated that up to 30,000 women passed through such laundries in Ireland, the last one of which (in Waterford) closed on 25 September 1996.

- 1 *frayed*: ragged.
- 1 *sifted*: sorted, examined.
- 3 *the laundry*: clothes washing area.
- 13 *blared*: rang out, resounded.
- 16 *idiom*: language, misinterpretation.
- 18 *parasite*: bloodsucker.

INITIAL RESPONSE

1. Comment on the effectiveness of the poem's title, 'Translation', in relation to the themes that Ní Chuilleanáin addresses in the poem.

2. Choose one image from the poem that you found particularly interesting. Briefly explain your choice.

3. How does the poem make you feel? Give reasons for your response, supporting the points you make with reference to the text.

STUDY NOTES

During the early 1990s, the remains of more than 150 women were discovered at several Dublin religious institutions as the properties were being excavated. The bones, from women buried over a very long period, were cremated and reburied in Glasnevin Cemetery. Eiléan Ní Chuilleanáin's poem was read at the reburial ceremony to commemorate Magdalene laundry women from all over Ireland. 'Translation' links the writer's work with the belated acknowledgement, in the late 20th century, of the stolen lives and hidden deaths of generations of Irishwomen incarcerated in Magdalene convents.

The poem begins with a macabre description of the Glasnevin grave where the reburial is taking place: 'The soil frayed and sifted evens the score'. Ní Chuilleanáin expresses the feelings of the mourners ('here from every county') who are **united by a shared sense of injustice**. This dramatic ceremony represents a formal acknowledgement of a dark period in Ireland's social history. **Line 4** takes readers back in time behind convent walls and imagines the grim laundry rooms in which the

Magdelene women worked: 'White light blinded and bleached out/The high relief of a glance'.

The poet's delicate and precise language contrasts the grinding oppression of routine manual labour with the young women's natural playfulness. **Their stolen youth and lost gaiety are poignantly conveyed through familiar images of the laundry,** 'where steam danced/Around stone drains and giggled and slipped across water' (**line 6**). Vigorous verbs and a jaunty rhythm add emphasis to the sad irony of their broken lives. The relentless scrubbing was intended to wash away the women's sins. However, no matter how much the women washed, they were considered dirty and sinful throughout their lives.

All through the poem, Ní Chuilleanáin focuses on the importance of words and naming as though she herself is aiming to make sense of the shocking Magdalene story. But how is she to respond to the women who have come to the graveyard, 'Searching for their parents, their names'? Typically, the language is dense and multi-layered. In death, these former laundry workers are mere 'ridges under the veil' of the anonymous earth. The metaphor in **line 7** also evokes images of the stern Magdalene nuns. **Ní Chuilleanáin sees all these women as victims of less enlightened times**, ironically recalled in the prayer-like note of invocation: 'Assist them now'.

The poem's title becomes clear as we recognise **Ní Chuilleanáin's intention to communicate ('translate') decades of silence into meaningful expression on behalf of the Magdalene laundry inmates.** Their relentless efforts to eventually become a 'voice' is compared to the almost impossible challenge of 'rising above the shuffle and hum' within the noisy laundry itself. In **line 9**, Ní Chuilleanáin visualises the women setting 'The edges of words grinding against nature' until their misrepresentation is overcome as it is turned to dust along with their bodies.

From **line 13**, much of the **focus is placed on exploring the experience of one of the nuns who managed the laundries**. As the true history emerges, she is also being cleansed of 'the baked crust/ Of words that made my temporary name'. The 'temporary name' is her name in religion, that is, the saint's name she chose upon entering strict convent life, which, as Ní Chuilleanáin notes, involved relinquishing her previous identity as an individual. She too has been exploited and the poet's generous tone reflects an understanding of this woman, who is caught between conflicting influences of duty, care, indoctrination and doubt, 'Until every pocket in her skull blared'. The evocative reference to the 'infant's cry' echoes the enduring sense of loss felt by young mothers who were forced to give up their babies shortly after birth.

In the poem's **final lines**, we hear the voice of a convent reverend mother, whose role is defined by 'the bunched keys I bore'. The reburial ceremony has also cleansed her from 'that spell' which maintained the cruel system she once served. Almost overwhelmed, she now recognises the 'parasite' power 'that grew in me' and only now can the keys she carries, an obvious symbol of her role as gaoler, 'slacken and fall'. **Bleak, disturbing images and broken rhythms have an unnerving, timeless effect.** This woman's punitive authority over others has haunted her beyond the grave.

In the end, Ní Chuilleanáin's measured and balanced approach shows genuine compassion for all institutionalised victims, drawing together the countless young women and those in charge in their common confinement. In addition to their time spent in convents, they are now reunited, sifting the earth that they have all become. **The tragic legacy of these institutions involves women at many levels.** Nevertheless, the poem itself is a faithful translation, as these victims have been raised from their graves by the poet's response to their collective dead voice. Ní Chuilleanáin relates their compelling story to 'Allow us now to hear it'. She also tenderly acknowledges the complete silencing of the Irish Magdalenes as they did their enforced and, in some cases, lifelong penance.

Although Eiléan Ní Chuilleanáin's mournful 'translation' reveals glimpses of their true history, **none of these Magdalene women can ever be given back the lives they had before they entered the laundries**. The poem stops short of pretending to even the score in terms of power between those in authority and the totally subservient and permanently disgraced women under their control. At best, their small voices rise up together like 'steam' and form a 'cloud over my time' (**line 21**). This metaphor of the cloud can be construed as a shadow of shame over Irish society, but it can also be seen as a warning that the cycle of abuse is likely to be repeated.

ANALYSIS

'Ní Chuilleanáin's poems often address important aspects of women's experiences in an insightful fashion.' Discuss this view, with particular reference to 'Translations'.

Sample Paragraph

I would completely agree that 'Translations' deals with an issue which is important to Irish women. The scandal of what happened to the unfortunate girls who were locked up in Magdalene convents deserves to be publicised. Eiléan Ní Chuilleanáin's poem certainly gave me a deeper understanding of their disturbing story. The dramatic opening description of the reburial service was attended by relatives 'from every county', suggesting the scale of the mistreatment. The details of the cold laundries – where 'White light blinded' seemed a subtle way of symbolising the misguided actions of those religious orders who punished young girls. I admired the poet's fair treatment of those nuns who are also presented as being imprisoned, even replacing their own natural identities with 'temporary' saints' names. The poem's last stanza was revealing as it envisaged one of the severe nuns who was still confused by her part in the cruelty. She only recognises the 'parasite' of heartless authority within her when it is too late. The poet makes it clear that she was a product of an oppressive Catholic Ireland and under the 'spell' of misguided power. In my opinion, 'Translation' succeeds in explaining the true story of the Magdalene women. It is all the more powerful because

Ní Chuilleanáin avoids being over-emotional. Her quiet tone conveys sensitivity and sadness for this dreadful period in Irish history which still lingers like 'a cloud over my time'.

Examiner's Comment

This top grade response shows a clear understanding of Ní Chuilleanáin's considered approach to her theme, empathising with both those imprisoned and those in charge. Short quotations are well integrated while discussion points are clear and coherent, ranging over much of the poem. There is also some very good personal interaction, including the final sentence. An excellent standard.

CLASS/HOMEWORK EXERCISES

1. 'Eiléan Ní Chuilleanáin's poetry offers a variety of interesting perspectives that vividly convey themes of universal relevance.' Discuss this statement with particular reference to 'Translation'.

2. 'In her poem, "Translation", Ní Chuilleanáin's poetic voice is both critical and compassionate.' Discuss this statement with particular reference to the text.

SUMMARY POINTS

- The poet addresses aspects of the Magdalene laundries scandal.
- Several changes and translations are explored in the poem.
- Sensuous imagery evokes the harsh atmosphere in the laundry.
- Effective use of sound, contrast, mood, and viewpoint throughout.

THE BEND IN THE ROAD

This is the place where the child
Felt sick in the car and they pulled over
And waited in the shadow of a house.
A tall tree like a cat's tail waited too.
They opened the windows and breathed   5
Easily, while nothing moved. Then he was better.

Over twelve years it has become the place
Where you were sick one day on the way to the lake.
You are taller now than us.
The tree is taller, the house is quite covered in   10
With green creeper, and the bend
In the road is as silent as ever it was on that day.

Piled high, wrapped lightly, like the one cumulus cloud
In a perfect sky, softly packed like the air,
Is all that went on in those years, the absences,   15
The faces never long absent from thought,
The bodies alive then and the airy space they took up
When we saw them wrapped and sealed by sickness
Guessing the piled weight of sleep
We knew they could not carry for long;   20
This is the place of their presence: in the tree, in the air.

'This is the place'

Glossary

11 *creeper*: climbing plant.

13 *cumulus*: rounded, fluffy.

INITIAL RESPONSE

1. Based on your reading of the poem, comment on the appropriateness of the title, 'The Bend in the Road'.

2. Choose one image from 'The Bend in the Road' that you consider effective. Give reasons why this image appealed to you.

3. How would you describe the poem's conclusion? Is it mysterious? Hopeful? Comforting? Bitter? Briefly explain your response.

STUDY NOTES

'The Bend in the Road' is part of Eiléan Ní Chuilleanáin's poetry collection The Girl Who Married the Reindeer. *In many of these poems, the autobiographical becomes transformed as Ní Chuilleanáin takes a moment in time and fills it with arresting images, exact description, stillness and secrecy, linking together selected memories from various times and places. This poem's title suggests that the road will go on even though it is not visible at the moment.*

Stanza one opens with Ní Chuilleanáin pointing to the exact place where 'the child/Felt sick in the car and they pulled over'. The memory of such a familiar occurrence is given significance by the use of the demonstrative pronoun, 'This'. Run-on lines catch the flurry of activity as concerned adults attend to the sick child. Everything is still as they 'waited' for the sickness to pass. This suspended moment resonates as they linger 'in the shadow of a house'. **For a split second, an ominous – almost surreal – atmosphere begins to develop.** The poet introduces a slightly sinister simile, 'A tall tree like a cat's tail', peeking in from the world of fairytale. Then the tree is personified: it 'waited too' as people and landscape merge in the moment of hush. Suddenly, a simple action ('They opened the windows') relieves the tension and everyone 'breathed/Easily'. The position of the adverb at the beginning of the line captures the relief at the recovery of the child. Yet the stationary atmosphere remained: 'while nothing moved'. However, the routine narrative of everyday life quickly resumes: 'Then he was better'.

In the **second stanza**, this roadside location takes on the shared resonance of memory: 'Over twelve years'. Readers are left imagining how the adults and child, when passing 'the place', would point it out as 'Where you were sick one day on the way to the lake'. The length of the line mirrors the long car journey. There is a sense of time being concentrated. Ní Chuilleanáin marvels at how the child has grown to adulthood: 'You are taller now than us'. The place has also changed – and even the tree is 'taller'. Assonance pinpoints how the nearby house is becoming yet more mysterious, 'quite covered in/With green creeper'. The insidious 'ee' sound mimics the silent takeover of the house by nature, as it recedes more and more into the shadows. Nature is alive. Creepings and rustlings stir, dispersing solidity and sureness. The poet cleverly places the line as if on a bend at the turn of a line: 'the bend/In the road is as silent as ever it was on that day'. Everything seems focused on the serenity of the place. **A bend in a road prevents seeing what is coming next. Is this an obvious symbol of the human experience?** No one knows what lies ahead. The tone of this reflective stanza is introspective as Ní Chuilleanáin considers the undeniable passing of time and the human condition.

In the **final stanza**, memory and place interplay with other recollections. The poet's attention turns towards the sky, which she imagines 'Piled high' with past experiences. A lifetime's memories now tower 'like the one cumulus cloud/In a perfect sky'. The alliteration of the hard 'c' successfully captures the billowing cloud as it sails through the sky. **Similarly, the recollections of 'all that went on in those years' heave and surge as they drift through the poet's consciousness.** Naturally, they flow from the exact description of 'the bend/In the road'. They are now visible as feelings of loss expand into the present: 'The faces never long absent from thought'. Ní Chuilleanáin had lost not only her father and mother, but also her sister. But she remembers them **similarly** as they were, 'bodies alive then and the airy space they took up', just as the cloud in the sky. Poignantly, the poet also recalls them in their final sickness, 'wrapped and sealed by sickness', as if they had been parcelled for dispatch away from the ordinary routine of life by the ordeal of suffering.

However, the harsh reality of sickness and old age is also recognised: 'We knew they could not carry for long'. Just as the cloud grows bigger as it absorbs moisture, finally dissolving into rain, so did the poet's loved ones buckle beneath the weight of their illness, under the 'piled weight of sleep'. **Ní Chuilleanáin finds constant reminders of her family's past in the natural world.** She uses a simple image of cloud-like shapes of pillows and bed-covers as they surrender to sickness. Characteristically, the thinking within the poem has progressed considerably. The poet has widened its scope, its spatial dimension, to include those external experiences to which she so eloquently pays witness. Indeed, the poem now stands as a monument to silence and time, absence and presence, past and present. The moment of stillness is evoked. This roadside location takes on a special importance. It marks the place where lost family members now reside. Ní Chuilleanáin's alliterative language is emphatic: 'This is the place of their presence'. They belong 'in the tree, in the air'. As in so many of her poems, Ní Chuilleanáin honours the invisible, unseen presence of other thoughts and feelings that – just like the bend in the road – lie waiting in silence to be discovered and brought to life again.

ANALYSIS

'Eiléan Ní Chuilleanáin's poetry illuminates ephemeral moments of perception in exact description.' Discuss this view in relation to 'The Bend in the Road'. Use suitable reference and quotation to support the points you make.

Sample Paragraph

I agree that Ní Chuilleanáin's poem 'The Bend in the Road' is filled with meticulously accurate description. The opening lines pinpoint the exact place where 'the child/Felt sick in the car' and they 'pulled over'. The ordinary conversational language, 'They opened the windows', 'Then he was better', brings me into this precise moment in time and place. I can see the dark, cool shadow of the house. I experience the tree, as if a child, through the almost cartoon-like simile, 'A tall tree like a cat's tail'. Yet, an otherworldly experience hovers as personification transforms the tree into a living being; it 'waited too'. The poet reveals that 'nothing moved' as if all was in suspense awaiting some dramatic revelation. And then it is displayed. The place has become a metaphor for the reality of being human. Everything in life changes. The poet suddenly realises that the child has now grown into a man, 'You are taller than us now'. Nothing has remained the same, 'The tree is taller'. Assonance subtly illustrates the changed house now overgrown with 'green creeper'. Another layer is added with the perception that the place has become suffused with the 'presence' of those 'faces never long absent from thought'. This still, silent moment has allowed boundaries to be crossed as memories float 'Piled high, wrapped lightly, like the one cumulus cloud/In a perfect sky'. I now began to understand that in a static moment, the conventional distinctions between life and death, being and memory, all recede and become blurred. The past now lives again, 'in the tree, in the air'. Through carefully observed, precise description of material things, this poet transports readers into a different place to an understanding that many experiences, 'all that went on in those years', can be savoured in various forms, 'softly packed like the air'.

Examiner's Comment

This is a top grade personal response that addresses the poet's interest in transience and memory. Apt, accurate quotes provide good support for developed discussion points which range effectively through the poem. There is some highly impressive focus on aspects of the poet's distinctive style. Expression is also excellent throughout, e.g. 'The place has become a metaphor for the reality of being human'.

CLASS/HOMEWORK EXERCISES

1. 'Space in Ní Chuilleanáin's poetry is used as an expression of one's experience of the world and is a metaphor for the linking together of self and the world, within and without.' Discuss this statement, with particular reference to 'The Bend in the Road'.

2. 'The evocative power of a specific location is central to Ní Chuilleanáin's "The Bend in the Road".' Discuss this view, supporting your answer with reference to the poem.

SUMMARY POINTS

- Key themes include memory, family, transience, loss and grief.
- Symbolism used throughout the poem to suggest meaning.
- Effective use of assonance and alliteration to create atmosphere.
- Recurring references to sickness add unity to the poem.

11 ON LACKING THE KILLER INSTINCT

One hare, absorbed, sitting still,
Right in the grassy middle of the track,
I met when I fled up into the hills, that time
My father was dying in a hospital –
I see her suddenly again, borne back   5
By the morning paper's prize photograph:
Two greyhounds tumbling over, absurdly gross,
While the hare shoots off to the left, her bright eye
Full not only of speed and fear
But surely in the moment a glad power,   10

Like my father's, running from a lorry-load of soldiers
In nineteen twenty-one, nineteen years old, never
Such gladness, he said, cornering in the narrow road
Between high hedges, in summer dusk.
                                 The hare   15

Like him should never have been coursed,
But, clever, she gets off; another day
She'll fool the stupid dogs, double back
On her own scent, downhill, and choose her time
To spring away out of the frame, all while   20
The pack is labouring up.
                        The lorry was growling
And he was clever, he saw a house
And risked an open kitchen door. The soldiers
Found six people in a country kitchen, one   25
Drying his face, dazed-looking, the towel
Half covering his face. The lorry left,
The people let him sleep there, he came out
Into a blissful dawn. Should he have chanced that door?
If the sheltering house had been burned down, what good 30
Could all his bright running have done
For those that harboured him?
                          And I should not
Have run away, but I went back to the city
Next morning, washed in brown bog water,   35
And I thought about the hare, in her hour of ease.

'While the hare shoots off to the left'

Glossary

1 *hare*: mammal resembling a large rabbit.
1 *absorbed*: engrossed, immersed, preoccupied.
7 *absurdly*: ridiculously, nonsensically.
7 *gross*: disgusting, outrageous.
16 *coursed*: hunted with greyhounds.
20 *frame*: picture, enclosure.
21 *labouring*: moving with difficulty.

INITIAL RESPONSE

1. Who, in your opinion, lacked the killer instinct in this poem? Was it the hare, the soldiers, the greyhounds, the father, the poet? Refer closely to the text in your response.

2. The poet alters time and place frequently in this poem. With the aid of quotations, trace these changes as the poem develops.

3. Did you find the poem's conclusion satisfying or mystifying? Give reasons for your response, referring closely to the text.

STUDY NOTES

'On Lacking the Killer Instinct' is part of Eiléan Ní Chuilleanáin's *The Sun-fish* collection. A sunfish is so-called due to its habit of basking on the water's surface. Ní Chuilleanáin often presents daily life with a sense of mystery and otherworldliness as the poems move between various realms of experience. Each scene lies open to another version of the narrative. She blurs the distance between past and present in this three-part poem. History, which is something of an Irish obsession, always informs the present. This poet discovers and remembers. As she herself has said, 'In order for the poem to get written, something has to happen.'

The title of the poem immediately intrigues and unsettles. The **opening lines** focus on a stationary hare, silent, engrossed, 'absorbed', at rest. It is a vivid picture. Why is this hare preoccupied? The sibilant alliterative phrase, 'sitting still', captures the motionless animal in 'the middle of the track'. This **naturalistic setting** and image is brought into high resolution as the poet recounts that her own journey 'up into the hills' caused her to meet this creature. Ní Chuilleanáin juxtaposes the stillness of the wild hare with her own headlong flight from the awful reality, 'that time/My father was dying in a hospital'. In describing this terrible experience, her tone is remarkably controlled – detached, yet compassionate.

Another narrative thread is introduced in **line 6** when the poet recalls the 'morning paper's prize photograph'. Here the predators are presented as ungainly, almost comical characters incapable of purposeful action: 'Two greyhounds tumbling over, absurdly gross'. The broad vowels and repetition of 'r' highlight the hounds' unattractively large appearance. Irish coursing is a competitive sport where dogs are tested on their ability to run and overtake the hare, turning it without capturing it. It is often regarded as a cruel activity that causes pain and suffering to the pursued creature. From the start of the poem, **readers are left wondering who exactly lacks the killer instinct**. Do the dogs not have the urge to pounce and kill? Has the hare got the killer instinct, running for its life, showing the strong will to survive against all odds? The rapid run-on lines mimic the speed and agility of the hare exulting in 'glad power'.

In **line 11**, the **reader is taken into another realm** – a common feature of Ní Chuilleanáin's interconnected narratives. In this case, she recalls another pursuit. Her father was a combatant in the Irish Civil War in 1922 and was on the run. Like the hare, he fled, 'cornering in the narrow road/ Between high hedges, in summer dusk'. Both are linked through 'gladness' as they exult in their capacity to outrun their pursuers. For her father, this was a 'lorry-load of soldiers' – the compound word emphasising the unequal odds against which the poet's father struggled. This is similar to the hare's predicament against the 'Two greyhounds'. The precise placing of 'The hare' tucked away at the end of **line 15** suggests the animal's escape. Ní Chuilleanáin comments that neither the hare nor her father should ever have 'been coursed'. She is happy to think that on some other occasion, the hare is likely to outwit the 'stupid dogs' and will 'spring away out of the frame', nimbly escaping her pursuers. In Irish coursing, the hare is not run on open land but in a secure enclosure over a set distance. The heavy, panting exertions of the pursuing dogs is illustrated in the run-through line, 'all while/ The pack is labouring up'.

Ní Chuilleanáin returns to her father's story in **line 22**, imagining a moment of danger from his time as a fugitive. The scene is dominated by the threatening sound of a lorry, 'growling' like a pursuing hound. The repetition of the adjective 'clever' links her father and the hare as he too made his escape. Intent on surviving, 'he saw a house/And risked an open kitchen door'. The **enemy soldiers go through the motions of pursuit cursorily, seemingly lacking the killer instinct** when they 'Found six people in a country kitchen'. Ní Chuilleanáin is characteristically ambivalent about why the rebels were not challenged, reminding us of the contradictory attitudes among the various combatants of the Civil War. For whatever reason, the fugitives ('one/Drying his face, dazed-looking') were not arrested and their deception worked. The poet's father is allowed refuge: 'The people let him sleep there'. Throughout Ireland's troubled history, 'safe houses' existed that sheltered those on the run. In her mind's eye, the poet pictures her father emerging in triumph the next day 'Into a blissful dawn' (**line 29**). In a series of questions, she considers his crucial decision to stand his ground and feign innocence. In retrospect, anything might have happened to affect the outcome at 'the sheltering house'. Ní Chuilleanáin emphasises how chance has played such a significant role – not just in her father's life, but in Ireland's history.

The poet concludes by returning to the opening scene. Having observed the hare and remembered her father's encounter during the Civil War, she now realises that she should never have run away from her dying father. Her decision to return is seen as a mature one – almost like a religious ritual in which the poet cleanses herself, 'washed in brown bog water'. Is this a form of absolution to remove her guilt for running away? Typically, she uses this unifying symbol to gently draw the poem's three narratives together. After the common experience of the turbulence of the run, all three (the hare, the father and the poet herself) have entered a new state of being – calm composure. Ní Chuilleanáin reflects on 'the hare, in her hour of ease', the soft monosyllabic final word gently conveying a sense of peace and reconciliation. The poem closes as it began, with the **beautiful silent image of the hare**, self-possessed and serene after all the turmoil of the chase.

ANALYSIS

'Eiléan Ní Chuilleanáin is a quiet, introspective, enigmatic poet.' Discuss this statement with particular reference to 'On Lacking the Killer Instinct'.

Sample Paragraph

I thought the poem, 'On Lacking the Killer Instinct', moved effortlessly, mysteriously weaving three different narratives: the intently observed story of the hare and greyhounds, the quietly detached family history of her father's escape in 1921 and her own headlong flight from the city. Ní Chuilleanáin creates small clear windows into the narratives and the reader can then glimpse multi-views of human experience and discord, 'One hare ... I met ... that time/My father was dying in a hospital'. She celebrates resilience, the hare's 'bright eye' is full of 'a glad power'. Similarly, her father exulted in his cleverness, 'never/Such gladness' as he out-manoeuvred the 'lorry-load of soldiers'. The poet also faced up to the unpalatable fact of death and 'went back to the city/Next morning'. Her impressionistic style is similar to watching a photograph as it slowly develops before our eyes. At first there are vague unconnected shapes, but as the order establishes itself, the meaning becomes clear. Ní Chuilleanáin gazes intently on a familiar sight, the still hare, which becomes more strange under her spellbound observation and she links it to the flight and survival contest which underpins all of life. The reader is effortlessly guided through different times and places as the focus of the poet's gaze shifts from the hunt of the hare in coursing to the hunt of her father in his role in the Civil War, 'In nineteen twenty-one, nineteen years old'. She then quietly reflects on her own flight and concludes that running does not solve problems, 'what good/Could all his bright running have done/For those that harboured him?' In the end, this poet poses questions that resonate. Does she too lack the killer instinct, the capacity to seize and capture rather than suggest? The long monosyllabic word 'ease' suggests that staying calm and still is more effective than running. Yet who lacked the killer instinct, the hare, the greyhounds, the father, the soldiers, the poet? Is the killer instinct worth having? This enigmatic, introspective poet leaves us with an image of quiet stillness to ponder.

Examiner's Comment

This lengthy paragraph offers a very clear and focused response to a testing question. Interesting critical discussion – aptly illustrated by accurate quotations – ranges widely, tracing the subtle development of the poem's various narrative threads. Impressive use of language throughout adds clarity to the key points. The questions posed towards the end round off the discussion effectively in this excellent top grade answer.

CLASS/HOMEWORK EXERCISES

1. 'Eiléan Ní Chuilleanáin's poems elude categories and invite and challenge the reader in equal measure.' Discuss this statement with particular reference to 'On Lacking the Killer Instinct'.

2. 'Ní Chuilleanáin is capable of blending multiple narratives with great skill in her poetry.' To what extent is this the case in 'On Lacking the Killer Instinct'? Support your answer with reference to the poem.

SUMMARY POINTS

- Interwoven stories: hunting the hare, her father's death and Ireland's Civil War.
- Effective use of rhythm and contrast – movement and stillness.
- Subtle blending of past and present, time and place.
- Alliterative and sibilant sound effects echo related ideas throughout.

TO NIALL WOODS AND XENYA OSTROVSKIA, MARRIED IN DUBLIN ON 9 SEPTEMBER 2009

When you look out across the fields
And you both see the same star
Pitching its tent on the point of the steeple –
That is the time to set out on your journey,
With half a loaf and your mother's blessing. 5

Leave behind the places that you knew:
All that you leave behind you will find once more,
You will find it in the stories;
The sleeping beauty in her high tower
With her talking cat asleep 10
Solid beside her feet – you will see her again.

When the cat wakes up he will speak in Irish and Russian
And every night he will tell you a different tale
About the firebird that stole the golden apples,
Gone every morning out of the emperor's garden, 15
And about the King of Ireland's Son and the Enchanter's Daughter.

The story the cat does not know is the Book of Ruth
And I have no time to tell you how she fared
When she went out at night and she was afraid,
In the beginning of the barley harvest, 20
Or how she trusted to strangers, and stood by her word:

You will have to trust me, she lived happily ever after.

'the firebird that stole the golden apples'

Glossary

Title: An epithalamium is a poem (or song) in celebration of a wedding. Eiléan Ní Chuilleanáin has included this poem (to her son Niall and his bride, Xenya) as the introductory dedication in her poetry collection *The Sun-fish*.

9 **sleeping beauty**: European fairytale from 'La Belle au bois dormant' (Beauty of the sleeping wood) by Charles Perrault and 'Dornroschen' (Little Briar Rose) by the Brothers Grimm.

14 **the firebird**: Russian fairytale; 'Tsarevitch Ivan, the Fire Bird and the Gray Wolf' by Alexander Afanasyev.

16 **the King of Ireland's Son**: Irish fairytale; 'The King of Ireland's Son' by Padraic Colum.

17 **Book of Ruth**: religious story from the Old Testament.

21 **Or how she trusted to strangers**: In the Bible story, Boaz owned the field Ruth harvested. He was a relative of the family and by law could 'redeem' her if he married her now that she was a widow. He wished to do so because he admired how she had stood by her mother-in-law, 'For wherever you go, I will go'.

INITIAL RESPONSE

1. Do you think the references to fairytales are appropriate on the occasion of Eiléan Ní Chuilleanáin's son's marriage? Give one reason for your answer.

2. In your opinion, what is the dominant tone of voice in the poem? Is it one of warning, reassurance, hope, consolation? Briefly explain your response with reference to the poem.

3. Why do you think the poet placed the last line apart from the rest of the poem? Give one reason for your opinion.

STUDY NOTES

'I write poems that mean a lot to me.' (Eiléan Ní Chuilleanáin) This particular poem is dedicated to her son, Niall, and his new bride, Xenya, on the happy occasion of their marriage. Folklore is central to this poet's work. Her mother, Eilís Dillon, was a famous writer of children's stories. Fairytales allow Ní Chuilleanáin the opportunity to approach a subject from an oblique, non-confessional perspective. It gives distance. Story-tellers rarely comment on or explain what happens. They simply tell the tale. In this poem, Ní Chuilleanáin refers to folklore and a well-known Bible story as she addresses the young couple.

The **first stanza** opens with **warm advice** from a loving mother as she gives the young man leave to set out on his own journey through life with his new partner. Run-on lines contain a beautiful, romantic image of a harmonious vision: 'you both see the same star'. Personification and alliteration bring this natural image to radiant life, 'Pitching its tent on the point of the steeple', suggesting the new home which the young couple are about to set up for themselves. **Ní Chuilleanáin's gaze is one of relentless clarity and attentiveness. She illuminates details.** She also counsels that it is the right time to go, 'to set out on your journey' when you are prepared ('With half a loaf') and with good wishes ('and your mother's blessing'). She combines colloquial and fairytale language. The tone is warm, but also pragmatic – offering practical advice to the newlyweds to make the most of whatever they have to start with: 'half a loaf is better than none'.

Stanza two begins with the imperative warning: 'Leave behind'. The mother is advising the couple to forget 'the places that you knew'. Is 'places' a metaphor for their actual homes or their cultural environments? Or does it refer to values the young people hold sacred? She consoles them that past experiences can still be found 'in the stories'. Ní Chuilleanáin now weaves an intricate web of such stories from many different sources. The first tale is that of 'sleeping beauty in her high tower'. This classic folk story involves a beautiful princess, enchantment, and a handsome prince who has to brave the obstacles of tall trees that surround the castle and its sleeping princess. **Is Ní Chuilleanáin illustrating that the path to true love is filled with difficulties and that only the brave will be successful?** The extended run-on lines suggest the hundred years' sleep of the spellbound princess, who can only be awakened by a kiss. The poet also makes use of another familiar element of fairytales – talking animals. In this case, the 'talking cat' probably refers to Irish folklore, and the King of Cats, a renowned teller of tales. Ní Chuilleanáin is able to link the basic characteristics of the animal with human behaviour. The cat slumbers with the princess, 'Solid', stable and dependable, beside her feet. Despite the poet's realism, however, this fairytale allusion is primarily optimistic.

In **stanza three**, Ní Chuilleanáin imagines the cat awakening and telling stories in both 'Irish and Russian', a likely reference to the young couple's **two cultural backgrounds**. The poet has said that in her work she is trying 'to suggest, to phrase, to find a way to make it possible for somebody to pick up certain suggestions … They might not be seeing what I am seeing'. The poet continues to set her personal wishes for Niall and Xenya within the context of folktales, turning to the Russian tradition: 'Tsarevitch, the Fire Bird and the Gray Wolf'. Again, the hero of this story is on a challenging mission, as he attempts to catch the 'firebird that stole the golden apples … out of the emperor's garden'. The assonance of the broad vowel 'o' emphasises the exasperation of the repeated theft. As always in folklore, courage and determination are required before the hero can overcome many ordeals and find true happiness.

Ní Chuilleanáin introduces the Irish tradition with the story of the King of Ireland's son, who must pluck three hairs from the Enchanter's beard in order to save his own life. On his quest, he gains the hand of Fedelma, the Enchanter's youngest daughter. But he falls asleep and loses her to the King of the Land of Mist. **Is the poet simply advising her son and daughter-in-law that love must be cherished and never taken for granted?** Throughout the poem, she draws heavily on stories where heroes have to fight for what they believe in. All of these tales convey the same central meaning – that lasting love has to be won through daring, determination and sacrifice.

In the playful link into **stanza four**, Ní Chuilleanáin remarks that 'the story the cat does not know is the Book of Ruth'. This final story is not from the world of folklore, but from the Bible, (although the poet has commented that 'a lot of religious narrative is very folkloric'). The Book of Ruth teaches that **genuine love can require uncompromising sacrifice**, and that such unselfish love will be well rewarded. This particular tale of inclusivity shows two different cultures coming together. The Israelites (sons of Naomi) marry women from the Moab tribe, one of whom is Ruth. She embraces Naomi's people, land, culture and God. This is very pertinent to the newly married couple, as they are also from different lands and cultures. Not surprisingly, the biblical tale is one of loving kindness – but it also includes a realistic message. After her husband's death, Ruth chooses to stay with her mother-in-law and undertakes the backbreaking farm work of gleaning to support the family. This involves lifting the grain and stalks left behind after the harvesting of barley. The metaphor of the harvest is another reminder that married couples will reap what they sow, depending on the effort and commitment made to their relationship.

The poem's last line is placed apart to emphasise its significance. Ní Chuilleanáin tells the newlyweds that they 'will have to trust me' – presumably just as Ruth trusted her mother-in-law, Naomi. For doing this, she was rewarded with living 'happily ever after', as in the best tales. The poet's quietly light-hearted approach, however, does not lessen her own deeply felt hopes for Niall and Xenya. **All the stories she has used are concerned with the essential qualities of a loving relationship** – and share a common thread of courage, faithfulness and honesty as the couple journey to a happy future. Tales and dreams are the shadow-truths that will endure. Ní Chuilleanáin's final tone is clearly sincere, upbeat and forward looking.

ANALYSIS

'The imagination is not the refuge but the true site of authority.' Comment on this statement in relation to the poem 'To Niall Woods and Xenya Ostrovskia, Married in Dublin on 9 September 2009'.

Sample Paragraph

I feel that Ní Chuilleanáin's poem has subtle messages which only become clear after several readings. I think the poet is counselling her son and his new bride, Xenya, that stories, 'the imagination' are where truth, 'the true site of authority' lies. Stories are not escapism, although we may scoff in this modern age at 'Once upon a time'. The stories she chooses, 'sleeping beauty in her high tower', 'the firebird that stole the golden apples' and the 'King of Ireland's Son and the Enchanter's Daughter' all suggest that perseverance and sincerity win the day. I believe that this is a good message to give to the couple as they 'set out' on their journey. Nothing worthwhile is won easily. This is not escapism, but reality. While the language, 'half a loaf and your mother's blessing', and imagery (even the beautiful lines which describe the 'star/Pitching its tent on the point of the steeple') seem to be from the land of children's fiction, they resound with good sense. I thought the inclusion of the story of Ruth was very apt as it involved two cultures which is relevant to the couple's Irish and Russian origins, but also to many other situations in this time of immigration. People in this new era will have to 'trust to strangers'. But if integrity and loving kindness is shown, as Ruth's story demonstrated long ago, the prize of a happy future can be won. 'You will have to trust me, she lived happily ever after.' I understood that Ní Chuilleanáin is showing that no matter where these imaginative tales come from, Europe, Russia, Ireland or the Bible, obstacles have to be overcome in life through resolution and perseverance. This is a tough message, there is no hiding here. I thought the poet was clever because by putting this insight into the realm of a fairy story, it does not sound like preaching which the young couple might resent, yet the message rings true throughout time from this 'site of authority' the kingdom of story-telling.

Examiner's Comment

A well-supported and sustained personal response showing genuine engagement with the poem. The focused opening tackles the discussion question directly. This is followed by several clear points, e.g. 'perseverance and sincerity win the day', 'Nothing worthwhile is won easily', 'obstacles have to be overcome', tracing the development of thought throughout the poem. Accurate quotations and clear expression ensure the highest grade.

CLASS/HOMEWORK EXERCISES

1. What impression of Ní Chuilleanáin do you get from reading 'To Niall Woods and Xenya Ostrovskia, Married in Dublin on 9 September 2009'? Write at least one paragraph in response, illustrating your views with reference to the text of the poem.

2. 'Ní Chuilleanáin's poems are often seen as challenging, but ultimately rewarding.' To what extent is this true of 'To Niall Woods and Xenia Ostrovskia, married in Dublin on 9 September 2009'? Support your answer with reference to the poem.

Eiléan Ní Chuilleanáin

SUMMARY POINTS

- The advice to the young couple is couched in the language of a fairy-tale.
- Recurring references to Bible stories and legends.
- Effective use of personification, alliteration and sibilance.
- Ending is sincere, sympathetic and optimistic.

LEAVING CERT SAMPLE ESSAY

'Eiléan Ní Chuilleanáin's extraordinary poetic world reveals compelling narratives which never cease to captivate readers.' Discuss this view, supporting your answer with suitable reference to the poems on your course.

Marking Scheme Guidelines

Candidates are free to agree and/or disagree with the given statement. The poet's treatment of themes and subject matter should be addressed, as well as her individual approach, distinctive writing style, etc. Reward responses that show clear evidence of genuine engagement with the poems. Expect discussion on how Ní Chuilleanáin's poetry appeals/does not appeal to readers.

Indicative material:

- Poet's views on life/relationships.
- Recurring optimistic themes on life and rebirth; the continuous past
- Fragmented narrative; innovative narrative blending
- Collapse of time and place
- Atmospheric detail; artistic and architectural references
- Dispassionate, detached tone of storyteller
- Focus on uniquely Irish phenomena
- Biblical, historical and mythical references
- Mystical/spiritual experience
- Layered and interwoven nuances challenge the reader, etc.

Sample Essay
(Ní Chuilleanáin's extraordinary poetic world reveals compelling narratives which captivate readers)

1. To me, Eiléan Ní Chuilleanáin's lyrical world thrives on the creeping rustlings and barely noticed stirrings of life. Enthralling stories are quietly let slip to bewitch and enchant her readers in a wide range of variety,

from hopeful poems such as 'All for You' to the family stories of 'Fireman's Lift' and 'To Niall Woods and Xenya.'

2. 'The Bend in the Road' takes a normal event, a child becoming car-sick, and transforms it with arresting images from the surreal, ominous world of the fairytale, 'A tall tree like a cat's tail'. The poet links together selected memories from various times and places and so mesmerises the reader with the resonance from this 'bend/In the road'. The family all point, on subsequent journeys, to 'Where you were sick on the way to the lake'. Ní Chuilleanáin's intent gaze reminds us that a bend in the road, which is cleverly emphasised by its line placement, prevents seeing what is around the corner. Now the poet interjects another memory into the story, the death of loved ones 'Piled high, wrapped lightly, like the one cumulus cloud/In a perfect sky'. This place now becomes 'the place of their presence'. They live now 'in the tree, in the air' because this is where they are remembered. Ní Chuilleanáin fuses parallel narratives, the ill child, the revisited bend in the road, the sick and dying relatives to uncover the mystical truth, the past shines through the present.

3. The driving narrative of the young girl in 'Following' as she attempts to keep up with her father on a hectic fair day holds the readers who are pulled into this world by the unusual description of 'beasts packed solid as books'. The explosive 'b' links 'beasts' and 'books' and I can really picture the crammed animals standing in lines as they await sale. Other stories are woven into the poem, as the image of the dead father appears, not 'skimming' as before but 'Gliding' as the girl crosses the 'shivering bog'. He is now sitting in 'the library where the light is clear'. The poet is tantalising readers, challenging us to engage and 'push ... open' the poem, just as the 'crushed flowers', an evocative image for past shared memories, force the book open. Once more the reader is comforted by the message that the past is not dead. The girl's suffering is represented by 'The square of white linen'. It is not 'shelved', never to be thought of or experienced again. It will emerge, 'crack/The spine open'.

4. Ní Chuilleanáin has remarked that she has been 'captivated by history'. She recounts a story in the poem, 'On Lacking the Killer Instinct', which her father had told her about running away from the Black and Tans when he was a young man. The reader is submerged into the Ireland of 1922 as the soldiers hunt her father. He seeks refuge in a 'safe house'. The blessed relief of the escape is graphically conveyed in the detail, 'he came out/Into a blissful dawn'. In my opinion, the reader is delighted at the father's breath-taking escape. It is similar to the escape of the hare, recounted in the earlier part of the poem, 'her bright eye/Full not only of speed and fear/But surely in the moment a glad power'. Narratives are blended together seamlessly as the poet relates her own flight from the awful reality of her father's final illness, 'I fled up into the hills, that time/My father was dying a in hospital'.

5. 'Fireman's Lift' also deals with the harsh truth of her mother's death. They had both visited Parma Cathedral once and their close relationship is clearly caught. 'I was standing beside you looking up/ Through the big tree of the cupola'. The strong verbs, 'spiralling' and 'heaving' capture the huge effort of the angels as they lifted Mary in to the heavens from her earthly life. The hands of the angels act as a 'crane and support' for Mary. 'Their heads bowed to reflect on her/Fair face' reminded the poet of the nurses who tended her mother in her final illness. Readers become immersed in the poem's storyline when the poet comments, 'This is what love sees, that angle'. The poet is coming to terms with the harsh reality that life has a natural cycle, 'The crick in the branch loaded with fruit'. The reader stands with mother and daughter marvelling as 'The Virgin was spiralling to heaven'. Now it is time for the poet's mother to go too.

6. Although Ní Chuilleanáin tells a story from an oblique, non-confessional perspective, this detachment does not prevent her engaging her reader. In the epithalamium, 'To Niall Woods and Xenya' she intricately weaves Russian ('the firebird') and Irish ('the Enchanter's Daughter') stories as she celebrates the two diverse cultures of the young couple. She also uses the story to gently pass on her thoughts and advice on their new life together. I thought the phrase, 'you both see the same star', showed how she understood that the young couple had a shared vision of life. But Ruth's story from the Bible was most fascinating. She had to show courage to succeed as she trusted to strangers. The young people will also need these qualities if they are to succeed in the best tradition of the fairytale to 'live happily ever after'. This, of course, is what every reader dreams of.

7. For me, Ní Chuilleanáin has opened a poetic world in which she intertwines stories from the fabric of her own family life, 'poems that mean a lot to me', with those from many other varied sources. The reader stands fascinated and delighted by a bend in the road, a hare 'sitting still', 'The sleeping beauty in her high tower', the Virgin Mary as 'she came to the edge of the cloud', a 'key still in your pocket', all thanks to the gaze and skill of a remarkable poet.

(approx. 990 words)

Examiner's Comment

This is a well-sustained top grade personal response that shows clear engagement with Ní Chuilleanáin's poems. Effective use is made of accurate quotations and detailed reference to support perceptive critical discussion. For example, in paragraph 3: 'The explosive "b" links "beasts" and "books" and I can really picture the crammed animals standing in lines as they await sale'. This clearly-organised essay is very well written and highly impressive.

MARKING SCHEME
P = 15/15
C = 13/15
L = 13/15
M = 5/5
Total = 46/50

SAMPLE LEAVING CERT QUESTIONS ON NÍ CHUILLEANÁIN'S POETRY

1. 'Ní Chuilleanáin's beguiling poems emerge from an intense but insightful imagination.' Do you agree with this assessment of her poetry? Write a response, supporting your points with reference to the poems on your course.

2. 'Eiléan Ní Chuilleanáin is a truly original poet who leads us into altered landscapes and enhances our understanding of the world around us.' To what extent would you agree with this statement? In your response, refer to the poems on your course.

3. 'Ní Chuilleanáin's subject matter can be challenging at times, but her writing style is always highly impressive.' Write a response to this view, supporting the points you make with suitable reference to the poetry on your course.

Sample Essay Plan (Q1)

'Ní Chuilleanáin's beguiling poems emerge from an intense but insightful imagination.' Do you agree with this assessment of her poetry? Write a response, supporting your points with reference to the poems on your course.

- Intro: Ní Chuilleanáin's innovative treatment of a broad thematic range – Irish history, myth, transience, memory, relationships, loss, religious life, the dispossessed, etc.

- Point 1: 'Fireman's Lift' – compelling treatment of her mother's death. Importance of dramatic setting as a context for personal experiences/memories. Poet's sympathetic tone, atmospheric detail, artistic references.

- Point 2: 'Translation' – perceptive account of the Magdalene laundry workers. Sensitive approach to women victims. Use of effective symbols. Collapse of time. Silence and understated meanings. Imaginative and interwoven nuances affect readers.

- Point 3: Dispassionate, detached tone of storyteller – 'Deaths and Engines', 'Kilcash'. Underlying sense of the poet's compassion. Interlinked layered narrative threads entice the reader.

- Conclusion: Poetry can challenge/excite responses – Ní Chuilleanáin's mesmeric exploration of universal themes invites readers to unravel the secrets of her work.

Sample Essay Plan (Q1)

Develop one of the above points into a paragraph.

Sample Paragraph: Point 2

'Translation' offers an intriguing account of a dark period in recent Irish history. Ní Chuilleanáin's quiet dramatisation of the Magdalene laundry victims begins in Glasnevin Cemetery, with an unnerving description: 'soil frayed and sifted evens the score'. This image is typical of the poet, suggesting both the surface of the communal grave and the horrifying injustice that has happened over the years. In death, these women have become 'ridges under the veil' of the earth. The reference also conveys a sense of the strict Magdalene nuns who are also viewed as victims of an unchristian era. Time and places blend throughout the poem. The poet's concentrated vision of the laundries is associated with their exploitation – 'where steam danced/Around stone drains and giggled and slipped across water'. She contrasts the girls' youthful spirit with the cold conditions around them. I could make sense of the poem's title as Ní Chuilleanáin's aim was to reveal (or 'translate') the true Magdalene story. Without a trace of sentimentality, 'Translation' movingly recalls a whole generation of women whose lives were ruined. Generously, the ending focuses on the authoritarian figure of an unnamed nun who is envisioned in death and who finally understands the tragedy – 'Allow us now to hear it, sharp as an infant's cry'. This line suggested the communal suffering shared by the nuns and the unmarried mothers who were separated from their babies. The poet's intense depiction of the Magdalene experience is highly compelling, allowing me to relate to this truly regrettable 'cloud over my time'.

Examiner's Comment

As part of a full essay, this is a strong, top grade paragraph that shows clear engagement with the poem. The discussion relating to Ní Chuilleanáin's dense imagery is particularly impressive. Apt – and accurate – quotations are used effectively. Language use is also excellent throughout.

LAST WORDS

'There is something second-sighted about Eiléan Ní Chuilleanáin's work. Her poems see things anew, in a rinsed and dreamstruck light.'

Seamus Heaney

'Ní Chuilleanáin's eccentric poems uncover hidden dramas in many guises, and she continually holds us captive by her luminous voice.'

Molly Bendall

'Her voice and technique are so solid, so secure, and contain deep echoes of older poetry, as Irish verse tends to do.'

Robert Hudson

Glossary of Common Literary Terms

alliteration: the use of the same letter at the beginning of each word or stressed syllable in a line of verse, e.g. 'boilers bursting'.

assonance: the use of the same vowel sound in a group of words, e.g. 'bleared, smeared with toil'.

aubade: a celebratory morning song, sometimes lamenting the parting of lovers.

blank verse: unrhymed iambic pentameter, e.g. 'These waters, rolling from their mountain-springs'.

conceit: an elaborate image or far-fetched comparison, e.g. 'This flea is you and I, and this/Our marriage bed'.

couplet: two successive lines of verse, usually rhymed and of the same metre, e.g. 'So long as men can breathe or eyes can see,/So long lives this, and this gives life to thee'.

elegy: a mournful poem, usually for the dead, e.g. 'Sleep in a world your final sleep has woken'.

emotive language: language designed to arouse an emotional response in the reader, e.g. 'For this that all that blood was shed?'

epiphany: a moment of insight or understanding, e.g. 'Somebody loves us all'.

free verse: unrhymed and unmetred poetry, often used by modern poets, e.g. 'but the words are shadows and you cannot hear me./You walk away and I cannot follow'.

imagery: descriptive language or word-pictures, especially appealing to the senses, e.g. 'He was speckled with barnacles,/fine rosettes of lime'.

irony: when one thing is said and the opposite is meant, e.g. 'For men were born to pray and save'.

lyric: short musical poem expressing feeling.

metaphor: image that compares two things without using the words 'like' or 'as', e.g. 'I am gall, I am heartburn'.

onomatopoeia: the sound of the word imitates or echoes the sound being described, e.g. 'The murmurous haunt of flies on summer eves'.

paradox: a statement that on the surface appears self-contradictory, e.g. 'I shall have written him one/poem maybe as cold/And passionate as the dawn'.

persona: the speaker or voice in the poem. This is not always the poet, e.g. 'I know that I shall meet my fate/Somewhere among the clouds above'.

personification: where the characteristics of an animate or living being are given to something inanimate, e.g. 'The yellow fog that rubs its back upon the window panes'.

rhyme: identical sound of words, usually at the end of lines of verse, e.g. 'I get down on my knees and do what must be done/And kiss Achilles' hand, the killer of my son'.

rhythm: the beat or movement of words, the arrangement of stressed and unstressed, short and long syllables in a line of poetry, e.g. 'I will arise and go now, and go to Innisfree'.

sestina: a complex 39-line verse form which can be traced back to twelfth-century France. The sestina relies on end-word repetition in place of rhyme. It consists of six sestets (6-line stanzas) followed by a concluding tercet (3-line stanza). The six words at the end of each of the lines of the first stanza are repeated in a different order at the end of lines in the subsequent stanzas. These six words are also included in the closing tercet.

sibilance: the whispering, hissing 's' sound, e.g. 'Singest of summer in full-throated ease'.

sonnet: a 14-line poem. The Petrarchan or Italian sonnet is divided into eight lines (octave), which present a problem or situation. The remaining six lines (sestet) resolve the problem or present another view of the situation. The Shakespearean sonnet is divided into three quatrains and concludes with a rhyming couplet, either summing up what preceded or reversing it.

symbol: a word or phrase representing something other than itself, e.g. 'A tattered coat upon a stick'.

theme: the central idea or message in a poem.

tone: the type of voice or attitude used by the poet towards his or her subject, e.g. 'O but it is dirty'.

villanelle: a five-stanza poem of three lines each, with a concluding quatrain, using only two end rhyming words throughout, e.g. 'I am just going outside and may be some time,/At the heart of the ridiculous, the sublime'.

Acknowledgements

The authors and publisher are grateful to the following for permission to reproduce copyrighted material:

'Child of our Time', 'Love', 'Outside History', 'The Black Lace Fan My Mother Gave Me', 'The Famine Road', 'The Pomegranate', 'The Shadow Doll', 'The War Horse', 'This Moment' and 'White Hawthorn in the West of Ireland' by Eavan Boland from Collected Poems (Carcanet Press, 2005). Copyright © Eavan Boland. Reprinted by permission of the publisher, Carcanet Press Ltd;

The poems 'The Tuft of Flowers', 'Mending Wall', 'After Apple-Picking', 'The Road Not Taken', 'Birches', 'Out, Out—', 'Spring Pools', 'Acquainted with the Night', 'Design' and 'Provide, Provide' by Robert Frost are from The Poetry of Robert Frost edited by Edward Connery Lathem. Copyright 1916, 1928, 1930, 1934, 1939, 1969 by Henry Holt and Company, copyright 1936, 1944, 1951, 1956, 1958 by Robert Frost, copyright © 1964, 1967 by Lesley Frost Ballantine:

'En Famille, 1979', 'Father's Day, 21 June 1992', 'Ireland 2002', 'Madman', 'Nessa', 'Parents', 'Rosie Joyce', 'Six Nuns Die in Convent Inferno', 'Sport', 'The Arnolfini Marriage', 'The Difficulty That Is Marriage', 'The Girl with the Key's to Pearse's Cottage', 'The MacBride Dynasty', 'Wife Who Smashed Television Gets Jail' and ' "Windfall", 8 Parnell Hill, Cork', by Paul Durcan from Life is a Dream: 40 Years Reading Poems 1967-2007 (Harvill Secker, 2009). Copyright © Paul Durcan 2009. Reproduced by permission of the author c/o Rogers, Coleridge & White Ltd., 20 Powis Mews, London W11 1JN:

'Ambulances', 'An Arundel Tomb', 'At Grass', 'Church Going', 'Cut Grass', 'MCMXIV', 'The Explosion', 'The Trees', 'The Whitsun Weddings' and 'Wedding-Wind' by Philip Larkin are reproduced by kind permission of Faber and Faber Ltd;

Poems of John Montague reprinted by kind permission of the author and The Gallery Press, Loughcrew, Oldcastle, County Meath, Ireland, from New Collected Poems (2012).

Poems of Eiléan Ní Chuilleanáin reprinted by kind permission of the author and The Gallery Press, Loughcrew, Oldcastle, County Meath, Ireland, from Selected Poems (2008) and The Sun-fish (2009).

The authors and publisher have made every effort to trace all copyright holders, but if any has been inadvertently overlooked we would be pleased to make the necessary arrangement at the first opportunity.